The Role of the Lector in Ancient Egyptian Society

Roger Forshaw

To Gwynefer

Roger Forshaw

Archaeopress Egyptology 5

Archaeopress
Gordon House
276 Banbury Road
Oxford OX2 7ED

www.archaeopress.com

ISBN 978 1 78491 032 7
ISBN 978 1 78491 033 4 (e-Pdf)

Cover illustration: Lectors – from the tomb Qar (G 7101) (adapted from Simpson 1976: fig. 28)
Left Figure: Presenting offerings by the elder lector, Qar (*wdn ẖt in ẖry-ḥbt smsw ḳ3r*).
Right Figure: Reciting numerous transfigurations by the elder lector, the revered one before the great god, Qar (*šdt s3ḫw ʿš3 in ẖry-ḥbt smsw im3ḫw ḫr nṯr ʿ3 ḳ3r*).

Printed in England by CMP (UK) Ltd
This book is available direct from Archaeopress or from our website www.archaeopress.com

Contents

List of Figures

List of Tables

Abbreviations

BD	Book of the Dead
CG	Catalogue Général des Antiquités Égyptiennes du Musée du Caire, Le Caire
CT	Coffin Text
JD	Journal d'Entrée (Egyptian Museum, Cairo)
LÄ	W. Helck, E. Otto & W. Westendorf, eds., (1972-92). *Lexikon der Ägyptologie,* 7 vols. (Wiesbaden: Otto Harassowitz)
LD	Lepsius, C. R. (1849-59), *Denkmäler aus Ägypten und Äthiopien: Nach den Zeichnungen der von Seiner Majestät dem Koenige von Preussen Freidrich Wilhelm IV nach diesen Ländern gesendeten und in den Jahren 1842-1845 ausgeführten wissenshaftlichen Expedition*, 12 vols. (Berlin: Nicolaische Buchandlung)
PM	Porter, B. & Moss, L. B. & Málek, J. (1927-), *Topographical Bibliography of Ancient Egyptian Hieroglyphic Texts, Reliefs and Paintings*, (1st edn. 7 vols, 2nd edn. ongoing) (Oxford: Griffith Institute)
PT	Pyramid Text
Urk IV	Sethe, K. (1906-9) *Urkunden des Neuen Reiches, historische-biographische Urkunden,* Heft 1-16, (Leipzig: J.C. Hinrichs'sche Buchhandlung) continued by W. Helck (1955-8), heft 17-22, (Berlin: Aakademie Verlag)
Wb	A. Erman & H. Grapow, eds., (1926-63) *Wörterbuch der äegyptischen Sprache,* 7 vols (Berlin & Leipzig: J.C. Hinrichs'sche Buchhandlung)

Acknowledgements

The present publication is a revised edition of my 2013 doctoral thesis submitted to the University of Manchester. In preparation of this study I have benefited from the wisdom and experience of a number of colleagues and it is a pleasure to acknowledge their contributions.

My thanks to Professor Rosalie David who advised and encouraged me throughout. To Dr. Karen Exell who guided me during the early part of this study.

Very many thanks to Dr. Campbell Price whose enthusiasm and advice proved invaluable. I will miss the many interesting discussions we had and the insight he brought to bear on this project.

To Professor Andrew Chamberlain, Dr. Ian Burney and Angela Thomas. Also to Dr Roland Enmarch who provided a number of constructive comments on an earlier version of this work.

Finally, to my wife Gill for her patience over many years and who never quite knew whether I was working in my study in the 21st century or in ancient Egypt somewhere around 2000 BC.

Introduction

1. The 'lector priest'

The lector priest (*ḫry-ḥbt*) - "he who carries (literally 'is under') the ritual book" has been considered in previous studies to be one of the several categories of priesthood that functioned in ancient Egypt, e.g. Gardiner 1947: II, 55*. There is a perception that he was responsible for the correct performance of rites and that he recited hymns and invocations during temple and state ritual. In addition he was considered to have carried out recitations and performed ritual actions during private apotropaic magic and funerary rites (*LÄ* I: 940-3). Textual and iconographic evidence demonstrates his presence at rituals and frequently refers to the title of lector but these sources do not accurately provide an explanation of his role.

However, the role of the priesthood in ancient Egypt should not be considered in the same manner as today's religious leaders fulfil their obligations. There are significant differences between the functions of the Egyptian priesthood and the modern clergy. The term 'priest' is a modern translation of a number of religious offices that were a feature of ancient Egyptian society. The term priest is a mere label, the idea of a reference in contemporary perception. What this label would mean in a different culture or time period would necessarily change.

The Egyptian priest was not a messenger of revealed truth or a preacher seeking to convert people to a particular faith. He was not an expert in religious doctrine and had no pastoral role. Religious knowledge was not a requirement of the priesthood, and priests were either appointed, inherited their posts from their fathers or in later periods priestly offices could be purchased. The Egyptian priest was an officiant who variously rendered material and magical services to the god in the particular temple that he was based and performed a variety of ritual functions.

In most studies of the priesthood priests are divided into distinct categories often varying with different cults, regions and historical periods, and as stated, the lector is customarily listed as one of the categories of the priesthood.

2. Previous Studies Relating to the Lector

This present study aims to explore and define the role of the lector in ancient Egyptian society. Previous approaches to the treatment of the lector have rarely considered the full extent of his activities, either focusing on specific aspects of his work in the academically orientated papers or passing general comments in the more popular textbooks on Egyptology. The only publication that exclusively considers the role of the lector in ancient Egyptian society is *'Der sogenannte oberste Vorlesepriester'* by Hermann Kees (1962), however, this paper only refers to the workings of the chief lector.

The lector is conspicuous in a number of different working environments and a review of the relevant literature correlating to these separate areas needs to be considered. However, it has to be accepted that such divisions are artificial and do not necessarily represent the actual working practices of the lector but are merely indicative of the main spheres where he was active.

Magic

Ritner (1993: 220-33), in his discussions on magic, analyses the diverse practitioners who were involved in its practice, among them being the lector. He recognises the lector as a ritualist who officiates at temple, state and funerary ceremonies and he particularly associates the chief lector (*ḫry-ḥbt ḥry-tp*) with magical practices. He notes how the title became abridged to *ḥry-tb* in Late Egyptian and became the word for a magician.

Ritner extensively engages with both primary sources and secondary literature when considering the many examples of the lector in magical practices and performance. He notes the non-exclusive nature of the occupation of the lector in the Old Kingdom, and this is a feature that can also be recognised throughout Egyptian history (1993: 228, n. 1058). The officials of the Middle Kingdom through to the Late Period routinely listed lector among their many titles, and the accumulation of numerous titles by an individual was a typical feature of the ancient Egyptian elite.

Pinch (2006) in her general overview of Egyptian magic considers the various roles of the lector and suggests that when he officiates at private funeral services he forms an important link between the temple priesthood and society in general. She considers that lectors probably did not officiate in the daily service in the sanctuary (Pinch 2006: 51). However, the 'Ritual of Amenhotep I' includes many episodes of the Daily Temple Ritual and specifically mentions that lectors recited various spells (see pages 53-5 of this publication for the Daily Temple Ritual). Additionally, reliefs from the temples of Karnak and Abydos list the lector as being one of the officiants present during the Daily Ritual.

Pinch briefly discusses the remuneration of the lector in relation to the rites he performed at funeral services, debating whether the fee for the service would go to the temple or to the individual lector. As the lector was paid a fixed share of the temple offerings, it was in their own interests to increase temple revenues (Pinch 2006: 52). In another departure from the more popular representation of the lector she considers abuse of the role of the lector, using examples of the Setna Cycle where princes attempted to steal and misuse spells, and Papyrus Vandier where royal magicians are represented as incompetent, vicious and greedy. In an unreferenced statement she states that protective inscriptions on tombs indicate that the lector was considered to have knowledge of fatal curses. This may refer to Ebers 855u:

> 'As to vanishing of the heart and forgetfulness: it is the breath of the (harmful) doing of the lector that does it' (see page 115 of this publication).

Priesthood

Many popular and academic publications discuss the priesthood in ancient Egypt and within these descriptions a brief account of the lector is routinely included. Such a description usually entails comments about origin, dress, function and the development of the role of the lector throughout Pharaonic history. One of the more concise accounts is that of Doxey (2001), although because of the nature of this type of article, specific references are not included. There is a tendency among these popular publications to separate the various categories of priest and then briefly define their various roles, whereas in reality there may have been an overlapping of functions.

Gardiner (1947: II, 56*) in his *Ancient Egyptian Onomastica* suggests that although lectors were often priests it is by no means certain that they always were, as their magical powers were often exerted for non-religious means such as providing medical treatment (as in P. Berlin 3038, see chapter 9 of this publication) and the 'tales of wonder' in Papyrus Westcar (P. Berlin 3033, see pages 135-6 of this publication). Gardiner reviews the development of the office of lector from the Old Kingdom through into the Ptolemaic and Roman Periods noting how they could be distinguished in these later reliefs by feathers worn on their heads.

Sauneron's (1957) publication *The Priests of Ancient Egypt* provides a useful compendium of the functions and activities of Egyptian priests. The lector is included amongst these officiants and unlike some other publications in this category there are many references to original sources and to the activities of individual priests. Sauneron, similar to Gardiner, suggests that lectors were not always priests as they are frequently mentioned in a purely secular context. He cites funeral ceremonies where they functioned as private ritualists and prescriptions in the medical papyri which are attributed to their science, and he also considers that they were the model of the popular magician found in Egyptian literature. His conclusion, similar to that of Gardiner, appears to be that there were two categories of lector, one attached to the priesthood and another working in the secular field.

The evidence surveyed in this present study will suggest that this apparent division into two categories of lector is unnecessary as lectors were specialists in ritual practices and operated in a wide variety of spheres. No apparent division of duties is noticeable throughout any of the time periods of ancient Egypt and to avoid possible confusion this publication will use the title 'lector' and not lector priest.

There are a number of encyclopaedic publications that refer to the lector within their subject matter. The *Lexikon der Ägyptologie* (1984: 1097, s.v. *'Priester'*) includes the lector amongst its comprehensive summary of the major categories of priest and the organisation of the priestly system. Also in the *Lexikon* (11975: 940-3, s.v. 'Cheriheb') in the usual format of this publication is a summary of the activities of the lector.

Grajetzki (2009) discusses in some detail court officials of the Middle Kingdom, differentiating between titles relating to function and those bestowed in an honorary capacity. He considers the lector as a lower ranking title and describes how local governors of the Middle Kingdom were also high priests of their local temples and carried the title of lector or chief lector.

Quirke (1992: 103) considers the lector together with the *sem*-priest and the *imy-ḫnt,* as the principal officiants at ritual practices. Unlike most of the works on this subject he understands the ranking as 'ordinary lector' and 'master lector' rather than 'lector' and 'chief lector' which is the more popular recognised classification. He suggests that the House of Life was an institution for transmitting knowledge and maintaining the Pharaonic world view and comments: 'The lector priest, the person who spent his life preserving and producing the hieroglyphic core of that tradition.' He recognises that the terms 'physician', lector' and 'embalmer' became interchangeable in the late first-millennium BC texts (Quirke 1992: 152).

A different approach in researching the role of the priesthood in the Graeco-Roman Period is that taken by Dieleman, in which he considers the prestige attached to the different priestly titles and explores the image that the priests tried to portray to the outer world. Dieleman understands the lector as playing a major role in the transfer and translation of temple knowledge. He identifies him as a 'scribe of the divine book' and distinguishes lectors from 'scribes of the House of Life', although Gardiner (1938a: 157-79) tends to see some connection between these titles. Dieleman considers how the priests in general presented themselves in the documentary sources of the time, such as inscriptions on private monuments as well as in the 'official' temple ideology with its requirements for priestly purity and social morality (Dieleman 2005: 211-21).

In a discussion of Egyptian literary texts, Dieleman (2005: 222-38) suggests that lectors were prominent characters in these types of scripts either as sages or as miracle workers. He selects the *Tale of King Khufu's Court* together with *Setna I* and *II* as examples, noting how the lector utilised magical practices and how his engagement with books and ritual texts was repeatedly emphasised.

Unlike Dieleman who predominately refers to Greek texts to study the priesthood, Johnson's (1986) short study of the economic and social role of the Egyptian priesthood in Ptolemaic Egypt is based largely on Demotic materials. Her study involved the examination of marriage contracts, sale documents, loans and other economic agreements, from which she was able to identify different sources of priestly income. She recognised remuneration of the lector as derived from regular temple income, from performing private burial rites and from servicing communal funerary chapels as well as in buying and selling 'days of endowment'.

Shafer (1997: 1-30) in his review of the priesthood considers the position of the lector throughout ancient Egyptian history recognising that the priesthood was not an unchanging institution. He states that the earliest lectors were members of the royal family or from the highest nobility with the position later being held by nomarchs, overseers of priests and great *wab*-priests, information that is also available in the *Lexikon* (Brovarski, *LÄ* VI: 389). Shafer (1997: 15) also refers to the existence of the categories of Second, Third and Fourth lectors and how lectors presided at oracles and divinations, but these comments are unreferenced.

Lloyd (1983: 306-9) examines the priesthood and temple staff in his study of the Late Period and considers that there were no significant changes in their organisation during that time. He bases this view on a series of inscriptions ranging from the biographical texts of Montuemhet at the beginning of the period to those of Petosiris at the end.

Funerary Ceremonies

One of the prime roles of the lector was his carrying out of 'transfiguration rites' during funeral ceremonies. Early studies of ancient Egyptian funerals by Kees (1926, 1956) and Junker (1940) suggested a protocol for funerary ceremonies, but these included few details concerning the role of the lector. Wilson (1944) in his study of funeral ceremonies in the Old Kingdom analysed these rites as separate episodes commencing with the period of embalmment and ending with the service at the tomb. He comprehensively reviewed a large number of tomb scenes in which the actions and words spoken by the various officiants were studied, among whom was the lector. This detailed analysis has been referred to in many later publications (Brovarski 1977, Assmann 2005 and Snape 2011).

Wilson concluded that in the earlier burial ceremonies the major officiant was the embalmer or *wt*. Using the 4th Dynasty tomb of Debehni as an example he noted that it was the embalmer who carried out some of the ritual functions which were later performed by the lector. He makes reference to a scene from the tomb of Mereruka which depicted a selection of boxes, baskets, jars, sandals and amulets and which was labelled 'the requirements of the craft of the lector'. This particular relief provides some insight into the equipment a lector might have used in a funeral ceremony, but the equipment that a lector used in the pursuit of his professional duties is a topic infrequently examined in the literature.

Badawy (1981) studied the transfiguration rites (*s3ḫw*) portrayed in the 6th Dynasty tomb of Kagemni. This is an informative study, for this research, as the funeral of Kagemni is rather elaborately rendered with the depiction of sixteen officiants, eight of whom are lectors. Badawy (1981: 93) compared the Kagemni inscriptions with a number of similar funeral scenes of different periods such as those of Userhat, Pepyankh and Akhethotep, in order to consider variations in funeral ceremonies. A more recent study of the tomb of Kagemni is that of Harpur and Scremin (2006), a publication in which the much improved black and white photographs assist further with the analysis of funerary ceremonies.

Other important studies of ancient Egyptian funerals include Settgast (1963) who provided a detailed analysis of funeral scenes from the Old, Middle and New Kingdoms, and Bolshakov's studies (1991, 1997) of Old Kingdom representations of funeral processions. However, the emphasis of these investigations was on the development and representation of tombs and funerary scenes rather than an examination of the roles of the officiants.

Comprehensive discussions of funerary rituals also include those of Assmann *et al.* (2002-10) and Assmann (2005) which incorporate perceptive studies of the concepts of transfiguration and transfiguring speeches. Assmann notes how the lector directed the oral aspect of the proceedings - 'a recitation that, in the mouth of the lector and at the moment of cultic action, became divine speech'. In a complex and philosophical discourse, Assmann analyses the semantics of the transfigurative speech delivered by the lector. Using the Ramesseum Dramatic Papyrus as an example, the mortuary cult is acknowledged as where there is a distinction between this world and the next, the 'cultic realm' and the 'divine realm'. Transformation of the deceased is achieved through the establishment of a relationship between these two realms, using the medium of the transfigurative speech delivered by the lector (Assmann 2005: 349-55).

Assmann (1990: 1-45) makes a clear distinction between mortuary literature and mortuary liturgies, with the former being recognised as texts placed in the tomb in order to be of use to the deceased in the afterlife, and mortuary liturgies as texts intended to be recited for the mortuary cult. Following the embalmment rituals the various mortuary liturgies are considered as rituals of transition, commencing at the home of the deceased and ending with the final interment in the tomb. It is from these mortuary liturgies that the lector would recite the various funerary rites. The depiction of the lector with his papyrus roll, upon which were written the ritual texts, is portrayed in many tomb scenes and symbolically ensures the exactitude of the recitation. Assmann examines the type of ritual action that might have been carried out by the lector when carrying out recitations using examples such as the *hnw* rite and the handling of the leg of the bull by the chief lector during the Opening of the Mouth ritual.

A more recent study by Hays (2010) provides an overview of funerary rituals which includes a brief mention of the role of the lector. Snape (2011) examined ancient Egyptian tombs throughout the Pharaonic Period and within the work included a standard reference to the role of the lector. He suggests that in the early Old Kingdom the function of the *wt* may have been to organise a broad range of activities connected with the funeral ceremonies, a role which would later fall to the *sem*-priest and the lector (Snape 2011: 73). Interestingly, as late as the 6th Dynasty, a text from the tomb of Idu indicates that the *wt* was still performing the same transfiguration roles along with the lector (G 7102, *PM* 111²: 185-6):

> 'and that he might be greatly transfigured by the lector and the *wt*'(translation after Strudwick 2005: 278).

The Opening of the Mouth ceremony, an important element during the funerary rituals and a rite in which the lector actively participated, has been addressed by many of the above authors. Otto's synoptic edition (1960) is still one of the definitive studies, whilst Schulman (1984) provides a study of this rite based on an in-depth analysis of 'commemorative' New Kingdom stelae. Schulman commented that this genre of stela provides a useful source of historical documents, illustrating as they do specific real events. Altenmüller (2010) is a more recent treatment of this ritual.

Healing

There is some evidence to indicate that the lector was involved with healing practices, and publications addressing medicine in ancient Egypt have long recognised this association. Jonckheere (1958) was the first to publish a catalogue of physicians which listed a number who were also lectors. This catalogue was supplemented by the work of van der Walle and de Meulenaere (1973), and revised by Ghalioungui (1983) and again by Nunn (1996). Ghalioungui (1983), additionally, cited a number of examples from the medical papyri of the lector's connection with healing practices.

Other major accounts of ancient Egyptian medicine such as that of Worth Estes (1993) and Nunn's *Ancient Egyptian Medicine* (1996), a comprehensive review of disease and healing in ancient Egypt, contain only brief references to the lector. Halioua & Ziskind (2005) wrote a similar general text on medicine, and commented on the Middle Kingdom stela of Nemtyemhat from Abydos, a physician and *kherep* priest of Serkhet (CG 20088; Lange & Schäfer 1902: 105-7). Among the inscriptions on the stela is a reference to the brother of Nemtyemhat, a *sem*-priest and a *wt*, and also to his son, a lector. Halioua & Ziskind (2005: 44) suggest that the existence of these titles within a single family was not accidental but infers that they enjoyed a common technical training. Although, an interesting assumption, little evidence is provided to support this statement, but nevertheless this is a comment that perhaps warrants further research.

Temple and Royal Ritual

One of the key roles of the lector was his involvement in temple and festival rituals and to be able to comprehensively research this, an understanding of the nature and function of ritual is necessary. Shafer (1997: 18-22) provides an overview of the theories of ritual and Bell (2009), in a perceptive study, examines the linkages between ritual and social processes.

An early investigation into temple and festival ritual was that of Fairman (1954-1955) who based his study on the Temple of Horus at Edfu. This study included many references to the detailed recordings of the temple inscriptions carried out by Chassinat. From these Fairman was able to analyse the varied religious activities that took place within the temple throughout the year, including comments on the role of the lector. Another important study is that of David (1973, 1981) who provides a detailed examination of the temple of Sety I at Abydos again presenting a useful insight into the rituals performed in an Egyptian temple.

Černý (1952: 97-123) briefly addresses the role of the lector in his analysis of Egyptian religion. He states that the chief lector 'stretches the cord' in the absence of the king, although there is only one recorded example of this occurring. Gillam (2009), in a departure from the earlier standard themed accounts relating to ancient Egypt, considers the relationship of archaeology to performance, using textual and inscriptional sources. She analyses a number of the standard roles of the lector and affirms that he was also a co-ordinator of ritual activities (Gillam 2009: 151).

There is a wealth of material discussing festivals and festival ritual and a useful starting point in such an investigation is the study of Egyptian processions and processional routes. Stadelmann (1982) provides a concise overview and Stadler (2008) a more recent account of this topic. Evidence for the involvement of the lector in Egyptian festivals is limited and it is perhaps only the scenes relating to the Festival of Sokar, inscribed on the walls of the mortuary temple of Ramesses III at Medinet Habu, which provide some meaningful information (Epigraphic Survey 1940: pls. 196, 218-26; Gaballa & Kitchen 1969: 1-76).

The lector is seldom absent from scenes depicting the *Sed*-festival, and a rich source of information, therefore, concerning his ritual activities. Bleeker (1967) studied the relationship of the *Sed*-festival to other festivals and questioned whether previous studies had properly reconstructed the correct sequence of events. Lange (2009:

218) in a more recent analysis considered that the emphasis of the festival was not on the physical powers of the king but rather was a renewal of the special abilities and rights ascribed to the king by virtue of being legitimate successor of the ruling monarch.

Miscellaneous

Other than these principal areas of ritual activity, the lector is also to be found active in other sectors of ancient Egyptian life. Lectors are known to have accompanied state organised expeditions that travelled outside Egypt and recorded their presence by inscriptions on rock faces and stelae. Many authors such as Simpson (1959), Rothe *et al.* (1996), Shaw (1998, 2010) and Enmarch (2011) have analysed these inscriptions left behind by such expeditions, but the lack of evidence for the lector has resulted in few meaningful discussions for his role on these missions.

There is some evidence that the lector was involved in the legal processes of ancient Egypt, but again support for this is not strong. The presence of the lector sitting on local and temple councils (*ḳnbwt*) has been noted by a number of authors such as Helck (1963) in his study of Papyrus Berlin 3047, and both Reisner (1918) and Spalinger (1985) recognise him in the inscriptions in the tomb of Hapidjefa at Asyut. However, no studies concerning the significance of the lector in these situations have been undertaken.

Finally, the lector was a prominent actor in a number of the literary works from ancient Egypt: such as Papyrus Westcar (tales of wonder at the court of King Khufu); Papyrus St. Petersburg (the prophecies of Neferty); Papyrus Vandier (the tale of Meryre); Papyrus Cairo 30646 and Papyrus British Museum 604 (the Setna Khaemwase Cycle). These texts are useful in providing information about the workings of the lector as well as the esteem in which this individual was held by society in general.

3. Methodology

As commented previously, other than Kees's paper on the chief lector, no single study has as yet exclusively examined the role of the lector but rather has included elements of his various activities in the material being reviewed. The present study aims to challenge this selective approach and explore his diverse functions in a wide ranging review of the pertinent evidence.

The principal source materials used in this study are the relevant textual and iconographic sources inscribed in temples, tombs, on artefacts and extant papyri. A broad range of these materials has been analysed as the portrayal of the lector differs from context to context. Temple inscriptions and reliefs depict the lector engaged in ceremonies that occurred within the temple precinct; tomb scenes demonstrate his role in funerary activities, and medical papyri highlight his interest in healing practices. The translations of the ancient inscriptions and texts in this work have been translated by the author except in those cases where reference is made at the end of a text to a translation from another source.

This evidence has to be evaluated in the context of decorum, a principle of representation which is relevant to some of the questions being addressed in this research. Decorum can be specified as 'a set of rules or practices defining what may be presented pictorially with captions, displayed, and possibly written down, in which context and in what form' (Baines 1990: 20). Decorum has much to do with enacting and representing the proper order of the world, although the conventions of decorum tended to weaken through the course of Egyptian history (Baines 2007: 21).

The value of the information obtained from the source materials can be limited by factors such as deliberate distortions that have been imposed by the social importance of the subject matter. In addition the aims of the work, symbolic considerations and current attitudes all have to be taken into account in any analysis. The extent of the preserved record has to be considered as well as the manner in which it has been interpreted. A writer's interpretation of the significance can be dependant on whether he or she subscribes to the beliefs in question. Additionally, analysing the past in terms of modern concepts can be misleading and interpretations need to be based as much as possible on understandings likely to be prevalent in an ancient society at that time.

The study of the source materials referred to above has permitted the identification of a number of different roles for the lector. This publication is divided into sections examining these separate functions aiming to determine what his function was in particular situations. Although these divisions are of necessity artificial and the working practices of the lector may encompass several of these separate activities at any one time, nevertheless such a separation helps to analyse in depth and better appreciate each of these interests.

Before the evidence for these individual functions is presented and analysed, the question of how the lector is recognised in the various scenes needs to be addressed. Chapter 1, therefore, examines the varying representations of the lector, considering iconography and gestures together with an analysis of the hieroglyphic titles associated with the lector. 'Recent scholarship has consolidated that magic was integral to Egyptian thought, in which it was a basic cosmic thought, not a marginal or disruptive phenomenon' (Baines 2006: 1). The lector has been closely associated with magical practices and chapter 2 examines the concept of magic, the spoken word and the performative aspect of this activity. Execration rituals and the involvement of the lector are highlighted to further explore the ancient Egyptian perception of magic.

The implements or equipment that a priest or ritualist might utilise in the course of his professional duties may be informative as to the working practices of such an individual. This is a topic infrequently addressed in the literature and chapter 3 examines tomb scenes and burial assemblages for evidence of any such ritualised apparatus, and attempts to surmise a function for these artefacts. This section also includes an in-depth study of the burial assemblage found in Tomb 5 located underneath the Ramesseum, which is suggested by a number of researchers as being the accoutrements of a magician, possibly a lector.

Chapter 4 briefly reviews the evidence for the sources of remuneration of the lector. It is established that the lector was a frequent officiant in temple and festival practices and chapter 5 explores this role commencing with discussions of ritual and purity. The Daily Temple Ritual, the main service that was celebrated in every functioning Egyptian temple, and the great festivals which typically involved a procession of the image of the god in a sacred barque, are also central to this part of the study.

The major royal event in which the lector was known to participate was the *Sed*-festival, a celebration which is attested throughout all periods of Egyptian history. However, only four detailed representations of this festival exist, these being accompanied by short labelling texts. Chapter 6 examines the association of the lector with this festival and also explores the direct involvement of the lector with the monarchy.

In academic and popular literature the lector is perceived as an important officiant at funeral ceremonies in ancient Egypt. Following death it was believed that only by elevating the deceased individual to becoming a 'transfigured being', an *akh*, could the immortality of the departed be assured. This process of transfiguration (*s3ḫ*) involved various magical rituals and recitations, a ceremony in which the lector was the main actor. Chapter 7 analyses the textual and iconographic evidence available in the many funerary representations. Related to the funeral ceremony is the rite of Opening the Mouth and chapter 8 examines the extent of the participation of the lector in this ritual.

There is evidence to suggest that the lector was one of the categories of healers involved in treating illness. The medical papyri, which are a rich source of information on medicine in ancient Egypt, together with extant historical and literary records are among the materials that are evaluated in chapter 9 in order to critically examine this association.

The lector is known to have accompanied some of the state organised expeditions that travelled outside the Nile Valley. Chapter 10 reviews the archaeological and inscriptional evidence left behind by these expeditions and attempts to determine his function on such missions. This source material is not normally taken into account in discussions involving the lector.

Chapter 11 looks at the association of the lector with the legal processes of ancient Egypt and the evidence for him sitting on local and temple councils (*ḳnbwt*). Within this topic is reviewed the extent of the lector's involvement in major criminal investigations such as the 'Harem Conspiracy' and the 'Great Tomb Robberies of the 20th Dynasty'.

Finally, chapter 12 examines the extant literary corpus, as a number of these texts cite the lector as one of the principal actors. These works emphasise the lector's use of magical practices, his engagement with ritual texts and as previously mentioned the esteem with which society regarded him.

Chapter 1

Recognition, Origin and Hieroglyphic Representation

1. Recognition

Attire

The lector is identifiable in tomb and temple scenes by his characteristic attire. However, as with other occupations, the artisans who painted the images of the lector in ancient Egypt 'coded' representations of the image, so that status and function were obvious (Green 2001: 274). The main distinguishing item of the clothing of the lector is a broad fabric sash worn diagonally across the chest. The sash is infrequently depicted in the repertory of extant statues, particularly so for the Old Kingdom (see Staehelin 1966: 80-4, no. 116 for a rare example). Possibly, the sash was painted onto a carved figure as it was not deemed important enough to be rendered in relief, and then subsequently the paint has been lost with the passage of time (Baines 2006: 6). The sash became a less common feature of the lector's attire in the New Kingdom as attested by funerary scenes in the tombs of Rekhmire and Amenemhat (see pages 80-5 for funerary ritual in the New Kingdom). In addition, the lector is usually depicted with a papyrus scroll in his hands which is typically unrolled when he is delivering a recitation.

Similar to Egyptian men of all classes throughout the Pharaonic period the lector wore a kilt, the wrap-around garment covering the lower part of the body. The kilt is depicted as varying considerably in size and form, usually short in the Old Kingdom, becoming longer and more voluminous in the Middle Kingdom and then more ornate in the New Kingdom and Late Period. During all periods artistic convention would normally depict a more elaborate costume on a higher status individual (Vogelsang-Eastwood 1993: 53-71).

FIG. 1: WILKINSON'S ILLUSTRATION OF A PROCESSION OF PRIESTS WITH THE LECTOR OR CHIEF LECTOR DEPICTED WITH TWO FEATHERS ON HIS HEAD (WILKINSON 1878: II, FIG. 436)

In a scene from the festival of Min at Medinet Habu, celebrated during the reign of Ramesses III, the lector is depicted wearing two feathers on his head (Epigraphic Survey 1940: pl. 60). Gardiner (1947: I, 57) cautions that as the majority of the individuals present at the festival wore similar feathers, then this cannot be cited as evidence of the lector's dress. Wilkinson (1878: II, fig. 436; fig. 1) depicts part of this same scene in his *Manners and Customs*.

In a later temple text from Edfu there is evidence of an elaborately dressed lector wearing a feather (Chassinat 1930: 284, l.11-12):

> 'The chief lector wears a panther skin with red and green strips, a menat necklace of gold and faience, a headband with an ostrich plume, a cape on his shoulder, a sceptre(?) and papyrus roll in his hand' (translated Sauneron 1962: 134).

The Ptolemaic coffin of Mutirdies similarly depicts an individual having two feathers on his head with an unrolled scroll in his hand. Although there is no caption the individual is in the typical pose of a lector reading from the scroll and standing before an offering table with other funerary officiants (Wieczorek & Rosendahl 2013: fig. 11).

Iconography and Gestures

a) The lector represented as summoning/invocation

b) The lector holding an unrolled papyrus and reciting from it

FIG. 2: REPRESENTATIONS OF LECTORS

A study of the iconography and gestures of the lector is important in any attempt to understand his role in society. The gestures used by the lector are widely employed to accompany verbal communication and denote a specific contextual meaning. The most frequently depicted gesture shows the lector holding a rolled up papyrus in one hand with the other hand raised up in a gesture of summoning or invocation (fig. 2a). The arm can be bent or more stretched out (fig. 2b). The lector can be summoning up the spirit of

Fig. 3: Scene from the Middle Kingdom tomb-chapel of Ukh-hotep (son of Ukh-hotep and Heny-hery-ib, Tomb C, no. 1) depicting lectors and a chief lector before the tomb-owner (adapted from Blackman & Apted 1953: pl. 17)

the deceased, making an offering or performing a ritual. This gesture is shown in Gardiner's sign list as A 26.

The lector is also depicted in a number of tomb scenes as one of the officiants bringing offerings to the deceased. In the Middle Kingdom tomb-chapel of Ukh-hotep (tomb C, no. 1) at Meir, on the north wall of the statue recess, there are represented two lectors carrying forelegs of beef. They wear the usual sash but their backs are partly draped with what may be a continuation of the cloth forming the kilt. In the second register a lector presents Ukh-hotep with a goose and he is followed by a *wt* who is performing the same function as the lector (Blackman & Apted 1953: pl. 17; fig. 3). However, similar scenes indicate that offering bearers were not always lectors, and that this role could be performed by other officiants.

hnw-gesture

The lector is often portrayed in tomb scenes accompanied by a further group of lectors who 'recite glorifications or recitations' (*šdt s3ḫw*), and when doing so adopt the so-called 'jubilee posture' or *hnw*-gesture (Gardiner sign no. A8; Dominicus 1994: 61-5; see pages 71-7 for the offering ritual). This is the same posture originally demonstrated by the sacred 'souls' when greeting the solar god each dawn, such as the souls of Pe and Nekhen which are first attested in the Pyramid Texts (Ogdon 1979: 71; fig. 4).

Fig. 4: Falcon-headed bronze statue, a 'Soul of Pe' from the Late Period
Cairo Museum CG 38594, JE 65. H. 28cm
(Daressy 1906: pl. 23)

Fig. 5: A group of three lectors depicted in the characteristic *hnw*-gesture.
A scene from the Middle Kingdom tomb chapel of Ukh-hotep's son Senbi (Tomb B, no. 1) at Meir (Blackman 1914: pl. 10)

The *hnw*-gesture, consisting of a clenched hand held above shoulder level while the other touches or beats the chest, is one of a series of sequential gestures.[1] This typical depiction, portrayed in numerous scenes is 'frozen' at its most characteristic point in representations but actually consists of a complex series of actions and gestures performed in various stances (Wilkinson 1994: 205). Representations of the *hnw*-gesture are more common in the Old and Middle Kingdoms. The lectors depicted performing the *hnw*-gesture are characteristically represented in a group of three, the typical ancient Egyptian method of indicating plurality (fig. 5).

Chief Lector

As mentioned previously the more elaborate the clothing worn in ancient Egypt then the higher would be the rank and social status of the wearer. Thus the chief lector is often depicted wearing a more elaborate tunic than the lector (fig. 6). A text from Edfu temple mentions a lector wearing accessories or insignia of office, an indication of rank and perhaps a suggestion of the lavishness of his outfit (Chassinat 1930: 1-4):

> 'The chief lector outfitted with his insignia recites the spells of appearance (going outside)' (*ẖry-ḥb tp ḏb3 m ẖkrw.f ḥr šd r3w n pr r-ḥ3*) (translated Ritner 1993: 44).

2. Origin and Evolution of the Role of the Lector

Early Evidence

Helck (1984: 103-8) suggests that the title of lector originated from a division of the activities of the *sem*-priest into two distinct occupations. Further that the *sem*-priest evolved from the shaman, an individual whose origin he considers was set in prehistoric times. However, Morenz (2003: 225) considers the evidence for 'shamanism' in Egypt is thinly scattered but phenomena close to shamanism may have played a certain role in early cultural development.

The activities of a shaman revolved around entering a trance-like state to communicate with the spirit world, and then to pass on this newly-obtained insight to the world of the living. With *sem* being the ancient Egyptian word for sleep, there is a tentative link with the title of *sem*-priest and the trance–like state achieved by the shaman. This condition is depicted in the early scenes of the Opening of the Mouth Ritual when the *sem*-priest is shown covered by a rush cloak and meditating on a couch, as attested in scenes 9 and 10 from the tomb of Rekhmire (fig. 7). Altenmüller (2010: 3) considers that the *sem*-priest was experiencing a vision in which he lived through the various phases of the manufacture of the statue of Rekhmire.

A characteristic of shamanism is identification with an animal totem, and shamans often wear costumes derived from animal skins. The leopard skin worn by the *sem*-priest could be a relic of shamanistic rites (Pinch 2006: 51). The *sem*-priest adopted this dress so that he could symbolically utilise the physical power of the animal in order to enhance his consciousness and performance in the spirit world (Lorton 1999: 159). Leopard skins feature early in Egyptian iconography with an example depicted on the Narmer Palette and king 'Scorpion' is shown wearing a leopard skin during a 'sowing ceremony' on the Scorpion macehead.[2]

Fig. 6: Middle Kingdom tomb of Amenemhat (Tomb no. 2) at Beni Hasan.
In the second register the chief lector wears a longer kilt (Newberry 1893: pl. 20)

The development of the Egyptian state in the Early Dynastic Period saw broadening bureaucracy and literacy which resulted in additional tasks for the *sem*-priest. The ritual practices and incantations were now being recorded and a standard established, so the spontaneity that the shaman and the early *sem*-priest exhibited in previous times was now lost. This writing down of the texts both on stone and on papyrus rolls had the function of making these magical incantations physically permanent and reciting them aloud conferred authority.

[1] See Ogden (1979: 71-3) for a reconstruction of this rite.

[2] Otto (1960: II, 72-3) lists numerous examples of a panther skin being worn in ritual contexts.

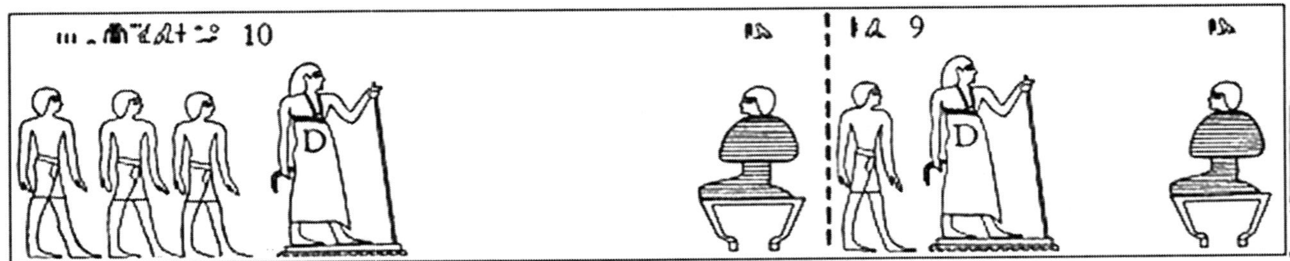

Fig. 7: A depiction of the *sem*-priest meditating on a couch (adapted from Otto 1960: I, pl. 1)

At this time a new role was attested, the lector, an individual who would recite these ritual texts. Translation of the term lector (*ḫry-ḥbt*) fundamentally implies association with papyrus rolls and writing, and so defines the main function of this individual. This role developed over time to include more participation in the ritual nature of the various ceremonies and an involvement in the composition of new incantations.

Fig. 8: Fragment of a 2nd Dynasty vase showing the earliest attested inscription of a lector (Lacau and Lauer 1959: pl. 14, no. 70)

The earliest known record for a lector is an inscription of a *ḫry-ḥbt* on a fragment of a 2nd Dynasty vase, dated to the reign of king Nynetjer (Lacau et Lauer 1959: 14, pl. 14 and 1961: 34-5; fig. 8). This unknown individual seems to have been associated with institutions termed the '*smr*-Chapel and the Red Domain'

Old Kingdom

Before the 5th Dynasty evidence for the activities of the lector is lacking, but during this dynasty he is increasingly being recognised as a regular officiant at funeral ceremonies, carrying out a role previously performed by the embalmer or *wt*. The lector is also being attested at other ritual procedures as indicated by his presence in Old Kingdom temple scenes such as those at the 'sun-temples' of Sahure and Niuserre at Abusir. In the temple of Sahure he is depicted as an officiant during the *Sed*-festival (Borchardt 1910-1913: II: pl. 19; fig. 9; see pages 65-81 of this publication).

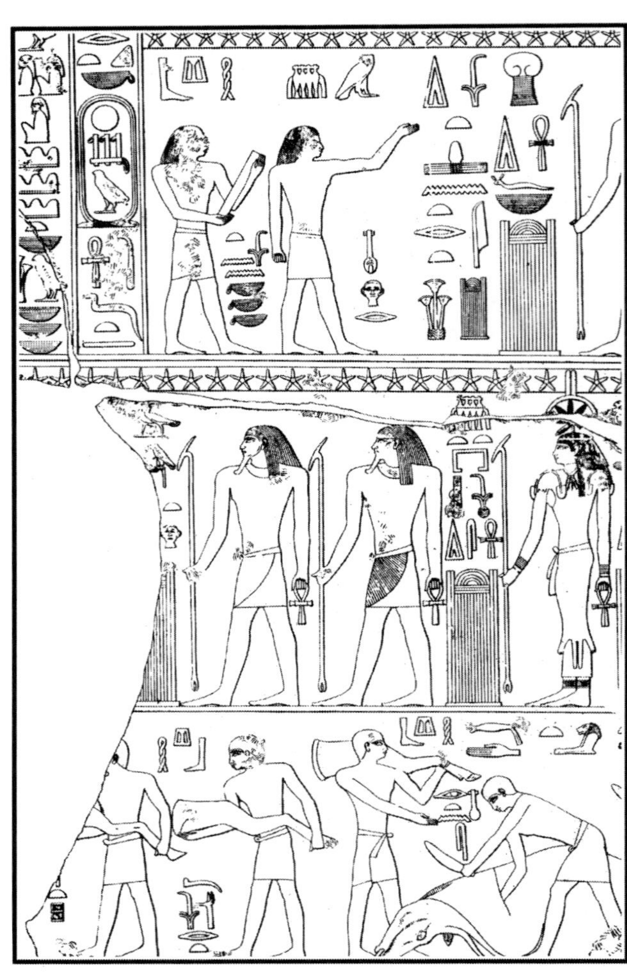

Fig. 9: Scene from the Temple of Sahure at Abusir depicting several lectors (Borchardt 1913: pl. 19)

Fig. 10: Sarenput I, a chief lector inspecting the cattle count (Müller 1940: fig. 4d)

Inscriptions from the temple of Niuserre indicate that he was not part of the temple phyle system, suggestive of him being a full-time functionary. However, a series of titles such as: 'lector priest who is in his year' (*ḫry-ḥbt imy-rnpt*), from Abusir; a similar title found in the 6th Dynasty joint tomb of Mekhu I and Sabni and the later Middle Kingdom title of 'ordinary lector in his month' (*ḫry-ḥbt ꜥšꜣ imy-r ꜣbd.f*) from the temple of Lahun, suggest that an alternative system of rotation was in operation (Kees 1962: 124; Fischer 1963: 38).

The title of lector is also seen asserted by the 6th Dynasty high priests of Heliopolis, such as Meru, Khunher and Sebeki known as Bi, as well as Sebeki who was a chief lector (Daressy 1916: 195-212). By the end of the 6th Dynasty individuals of more modest background were beginning to aspire to the title such as the expedition leaders Kheruef and Pepyankh, 'scribes of the ship's watch', as well as craftsmen and workmen (Helck 1954: 115-16; Griffith 1898: 14, 52).

At all periods the ancient Egyptians held multiple titles, perhaps better described as appellations of officialdom and administrative authority (Baer 1960: 1-11). There was a tendency to combine different titles and heighten them by gradation. Thus the title *ḫry-ḥbt* was often combined with the closely related title 'scribe of the god's book' also known as 'scribe of the divine scroll' (*sš mḏꜣt-nṯr*). In addition a role of a chief lector was created (Kees 1962: 122). The titles of the earliest known chief lector, who had a name not listed in Ranke PN, was Herhersesh (*ḥrḥrsš*) a 'hereditary nobleman, greatest of seers, chief lector' (*iry-pꜥt wr mꜣ ḫry-ḥbt ḥry-tp*). He is attested from an inscription on a diorite bowl dated to the 2nd Dynasty (JE 88355, James & Apted 1953: 50).

In the Old Kingdom the overwhelming majority of chief lectors were viziers and later nomarchs began to append 'chief lector' to their existing titles.[3] Inspectors of Priests, such as Qar, of the 6th Dynasty, whose tomb is located at Akhmim (tomb no. 1), also carried the title (Newberry 1912: 101; CG 1669, Borchardt 1937: 126-7). Similarly, *wab*-priests held the title, as exemplified by Hesesy, a 6th Dynasty great *wab*-priest of Min (CG 1407, Borchardt 1937: 69-70; *LÄ* VI: 397).

Many of the chief lectors in addition carried a number of other titles, such as 'hereditary noble' (*iry-pꜥt*), the highest court title. There was the occasional exception to recording these multiple titles such as Ka-Aper whose unfinished 5th Dynasty tomb is at Saqqara (Mastaba C8), and whose sole title was that of chief lector (Mariette 1889: 128).

Middle Kingdom

During the Middle Kingdom the lector appears as a regular member of the staff of the cult temples (Griffith 1898: 26, pl. 7; Borchardt 1902-1903: 114-15). Additionally, he is one of the officiants acting in the mortuary temples such as in the temple of Nebhepetre Mentuhotep (stela CG 20088, Lange & Schäfer 1902: 105-7). Following the First Intermediate Period and the subsequent restructuring of the country, nomarchs and high priests who were the heads of the local priesthood claimed the title of chief lector, with examples attested at Meir (Blackman 1924: pls. 4, 6, 8 and 1953: pls. 4, 6, 8, 19, 20, 21), Deir el-Bersheh (Newberry 1893: pl. 7) and Beni Hasan (Newberry 1895: pl. 16). Sarenput I of Elephantine, a 'nomarch', 'chief lector' and 'master of secrets of the god's book' (*ḥry sštꜣ n mḏꜣt nṯr*) is depicted in a wall scene from his tomb examining the cattle count (Müller 1940: fig. 4d; fig. 10):

> 'He undertakes to in order to direct the festival of the gods of Elephantine' (*irr.f r sšm ḥb n nb nṯrw ꜣbw*).

As in the Old Kingdom many officials carried large numbers of titles with a certain Ihy, whose tomb at Saqqara identifies him as a supervisor of priests and chief lector at Lisht, possessing some forty different titles (Firth & Gunn 1926: 280-3). Among the offering bearers in this tomb,

[3] Based on compilation of Jones 2000: II, 781-6.

two have the title of chief lector and a number of others are attested as 'elder lector in their year' in addition to the other titles they bore. The Middle Kingdom stela of Ibi at Abydos lists his titles as 'lector and draughtsman' (*ḫry-ḥbt sš-ḳdwt*) (CG 20243, Lange and Shafer 1902: I, 266). Thus the title of lector at this period would appear to be open to individuals from all walks of life with Kees (1962: 126) suggesting that it was an unauthorised assumption of authority. After the Middle Kingdom the title elder lector ceased to exist as did the appendage *imy-rnpt*.

New Kingdom

Although lectors are attested during the reigns of Tuthmosis I and Amenhotep II, there are conspicuously fewer examples of lectors in the New Kingdom, compared to the Old and Middle Kingdoms (*Urk* IV: 136; *LD* III: 63). Now the title of royal scribe is frequently attested, perhaps relating to the progressive bureaucratisation of the period, although being an indication of literacy, it may be a favoured title. Unlike the Old Kingdom the highest officials and high priests now assert the title of *sem*-priest rather than that of lector (Helck 1958: 496). There are exceptions, as amongst the titles that Senenmut possessed is that of chief lector, whilst Amenhotep, son of Hapu, rose via the position of a royal scribe and lector to become scribe of recruits (*Urk* IV: 136, 515).

Lectors are now regularly part of the phyle system. In the temple of Amenhotep III at Soleb there is a reference to the lector of the phyles and second prophet of Amun, Simut (*ḫry-ḥbt sȝw ḥm 2-nw imn*) (see page 15). Inscriptions in the Theban tomb of the vizier, Paser (TT 106), indicate that he originally was a lector of Amun in the first phyle (*ḫry-ḥbt n imn ḥr sȝ tpy*) (Kitchen 1975: 285).

Late Period

In the Late Period men who call themselves by their main or sole title, chief lector, emerge as confidants and learned councillors of the king. One notable official from that period is Pedamenopet, who was chief lector and chief royal scribe, and whose inscriptions especially emphasise his position as chief lector (*PM* I,1[1]: 12, 50-6; Kees 1962: 136). Pedamenopet was a wealthy individual, a patron of the arts and he may well have taken the title of chief lector because of his archaising interest and respect for the past. Similarly, on the statue of Ibi, a senior official of the God's wife Nitokris, his first title listed is that of chief lector (Daressy 1905: 95). (See Kees 1962: 136-8 for further examples of such notables). The chief lector is now being emphasised as a leading figure in a manner unseen in earlier times.

Ptolemaic Period

During the Ptolemaic Period there is considerably more documentary information relating to the activities of the lector as opposed to earlier monumental evidence.[4] There is evidence of lectors now being more practically involved with the provision of the materials and equipment for mummification (Shore and Smith 1960: 291). In the Demotic Papyrus BM Reich 10077 a family member engages a lector to complete mummification (Reich 1914: 39). Vleeming considers that now the lector probably undertook responsibility for all aspects of the mummification process, not just restricting himself to ritual activity. In the Ptolemaic Period lectors became known as 'feather bearers' due to the distinctive feathers that they wore on their heads as symbols of their profession (Dieleman 2005: 207; refer back to page 7).

Evolution of the Title of 'Chief Lector'

Quaegebeur (1985: 167-8) provides a number of examples in which the second element of the title of chief lector, *ḥry-tp*, the hieroglyph *tp* (Gardiner sign D1, a head in side view) is replaced by the triangular stretch of land (Gardiner sign N 21).

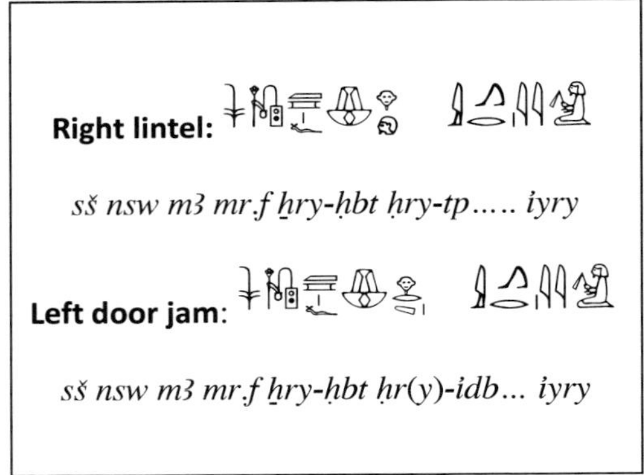

TABLE 1: TRANSLITERATION OF THE HIEROGLYPHS ON THE DOORWAY OF THE TOMB OF IYROY

One example is that of Iyroy, an official who conspired against Ramesses III (see pages 131-3 for the Harem Conspiracy). The inscription on the lintel of his tomb at Qantir was originally translated as 'the royal scribe, his truly beloved, the chief lector priest, the chief *wab*-priest of Sekhmet, Iyroy'. The parallel titles on the left door-jam are translated as 'the royal scribe, his truly beloved, the lector priest, master of largess, the chief *wab*-priest of Sekhmet Iyroy' (Habachi & Ghalioungui 1971: 59-71; table 1). Quaegebeur considers that after *ḫry-ḥbt* there needs to be read *ḥry-idb* which is considered as a sportive writing of *ḥry-tp* and not 'Master of Largess'.

Similarly, three Serapeum stelae in the Louvre from the time of Ramesses II (Malinine *et al.* 1968: 4-7) and an inscription on the 19th Dynasty statue of the vizier Paser (Kitchen 1980: 17,2) make it evident that *ḥry-idb* is a non-etymological or phonetic spelling for *ḥry-tp* (Quagebeur 1985: 167-8; Ritner 1993: 221).

[4] See list of papyri and ostraca for the Theban area in Vleeming 1995: 242.

In Late Egyptian[5] the title of chief lector became abridged to *ḥry-tp* with Quaegbeur (1985: 165) noting it as 'magician'. In Demotic the word was spelled *ḥry-tb* with *b* instead of *p* at the end of the word. This then became the basic Demotic word for magician (Quaegebeur 1985: 162-72; Ritner 1993: 220-1; Johnson 2001). The title *ḥry-tb* later became transcribed in an Assyrian list of priests, doctors and magicians as *hartibi.* It became translated in Akkadian as *asipu* (magician-priest) in the diplomatic correspondence between Egypt and the Hittites in the New Kingdom whilst in Hebrew as *hartumin* to designate a magician (Gardiner 1938a: 164-5, n. 24; Quagebeur 1985: 162-72; Ritner 1993: 220-1). By the Graeco-Roman Period it is well attested that the lector's and particularly the chief lector's association with magical practices is explicit.

Conclusion

Other than these primary roles as discussed above, the lector fulfilled various other duties which are summarised in pages 5-6 in the methodology section. The evidence for these various duties is presented and discussed in the remining chapters of this volume. The title lector is not attested for women at any period (*LÄ* IV: 1101).

3. Hieroglyphs

The titles of 'Lector' and 'Chief Lector' are recognised during all periods of ancient Egyptian history and are found inscribed in many temple and tomb scenes as well as on many artefacts (*Wb* III: 395). Lector (*ḥry-ḥb(t)*) is rendered as (Gardiner 1947: I, 55*) with variations being (Helck 1970: 9), (Davies 1926: 35) and (*Urk* IV: 123, 9). These variations appear as early as the Middle Kingdom (Steindorff 1901: 118). Chief lector is rendered as (*ḥry-ḥb(t) ḥry-tp*) (CG. 20088, Lange and Shafer 1902: 214-15). Indexes of these titles have been complied by: Jones (2000: 641, 781-6) for the Old Kingdom; Ward (1982: 126-7, 140-2) supplemented by Fischer (1997: 20, 23, 24, 64, 70) for the Middle Kingdom; and Al-Ayedi for the New Kingdom (2006: 459-64). In addition to the basic titles as listed above a number of more specific ones are attested:

Greatest of Chief Lectors

An infrequent title, found only in the Old Kingdom, is 'Greatest of Chief Lectors' (*wr ḥry-ḥbt ḥry-tp*) (Duell 1938: pls. 201, 203-6; Firth & Gunn 1926: 145). Usually, when *wr* precedes a title, the title is translated as chief or head such as 'chief of physicians' (*wr swnw*) rather than 'greatest of physicians' (*Urk* I: 38, 7).[6] Similarly, 'chief of dentists' (*wr ir ibḥ*) (Quibell 1907: 22, pl. 14 (*ḫwy*)),[7] rather than 'greatest of dentists'. Fischer (1966a: 63-5) suggests that the use of *wr* could be a flattering epithet rather than a title, as many of these examples have a simpler equivalent, without the prefix *wr*.

Senior/Elder Lector

The title 'Senior Lector' or 'Elder Lector' (*ḥry-ḥbt smsw*) is not attested before the reign of Pepy II (*Urk* I: 98.15). The sign *smsw* after *ḥry-ḥbt* has been the subject of different interpretations. The Wörterbuch (III, 395) considers it merely as a determinative whilst Firth & Gunn (1926: 283, n. 2) read it as *smsw* and translate it as 'Eldest Ritualist'. Grdseloff (1949: 7) translates the sign as 'älteste Vorlespriester'. If the sign was a determinative of the lector as suggested by the Wörterbuch then it would be expected to be used regularly in all occurrences of *ḥry-ḥbt*. However, this is not the case, as in the example of Djedy-teti from the mastaba of Khentika the sign is used regularly for a single person, whilst other lectors in the tomb do not have written after the title (James & Apted 1953: 56, nos. 153, 160 and 60, no. 190). Similarly, in the funerary temple of Pepy II there are lectors, chief lectors and senior lectors side by side (Jéquier 1938: pls. 48, 54, 57, 75). In these examples, as in the case of the tomb of Nefer-Seshemra where it is possible to study the status of a person bearing the latter title, he is depicted as having a relatively junior rank (Capart 1907: pl. 15).

In the pyramid temple of Pepy II, a senior lector wears a full shoulder-length wig whilst the lectors are close-cropped and wear no wigs. Fischer (1963: 38) suggests that this is unlikely to be due to superior status of the former as he brings up the rear in the procession (fig. 11). Again the title of senior lector would not supersede that of chief lector, since in Tomb 2 at Beni Hasan the chief lector is depicted in front of the senior lector (Newberry 1893: pl. 17; fig. 12). However, prominent persons can be at the rear of a procession and the suggestion of a less important official does clash with the idea of seniority implicit in *smsw*. Possibly the term could be honorary with the senior lector exercising duties occasionally (James & Apted 1953: 43). Fischer (1963: 38) considers that this title may relate to length and extent of experience rather than degree of command, and may indicate little more than 'qualified'.

Senior Lector of the Robing-Room

The title 'Senior Lector of the Robing-Room' (*ḥry-ḥbt smsw n ḏbꜣt*) is attested for both the Old and Middle Kingdoms. Examples from the Old Kingdom include the 6th Dynasty tombs of Khuenwakh and another Khuenwakh both being from the necropolis of Quseir el-Amarna near Asyut (Kamal 1913: 138, 142; Quibell 1902; 258). This latter Khuenwakh also carries the titles of lector and inspector of priests at Cusae (*ḥry-ḥbt sḥḏ ḥm nṯr m Qis*). Again from the 6th Dynasty is the tomb of Khuy at Saqqara (Driotin 1943: 502).

There are few Middle Kingdom examples of this title, but a limestone stela from the northern cemetery at Abydos of the chief lector Tetiemsafwer, lists one of his sons, Teti, as

[5] Junge (2001:17) defines 'Late Egyptian' as the term used for language of the Late New Kingdom.

[6] Other examples see Murray Index pl. 37 in Jones 2000: I, 396.

[7] Other examples see Jones 2000: I, 382.

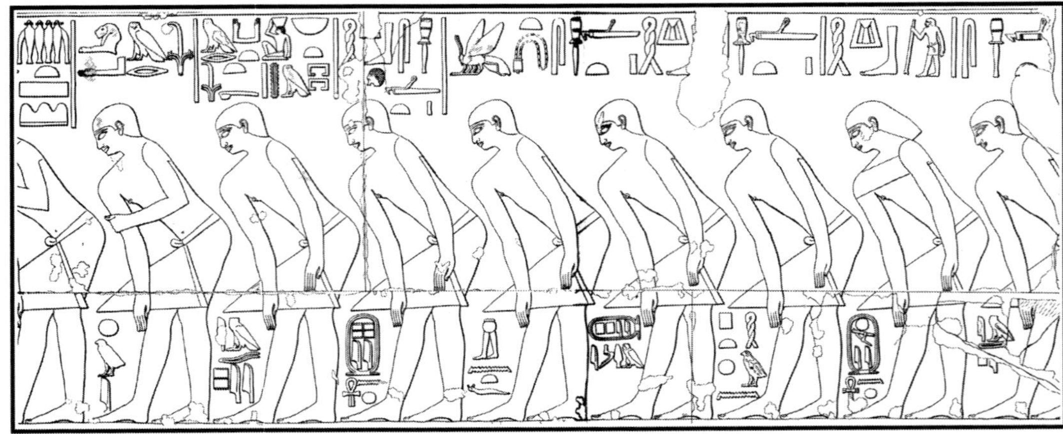

Fig. 11: Wall-scene from the pyramid temple of Pepy II
(Jéquier 1938: pl. 48)

Fig. 12: Tomb No. 2, Beni Hasan.
2nd register, a chief lector is in front of a senior lector (Newberry 1893: pl. 17)

senior lector of the robing-room (CG 20185, Lange and Schäfer 1902: 214-15).

This role may have existed in other periods but the lector who performed these tasks may have merely been known as a lector. The 'Robing-Room' (*ḏb3t*) and the 'House of the Morning' (*pr-dw3t*) may have had overlapping functions or indeed have been one and the same. The title, overseer of the *pr-dw3t*, is often combined with the care of the king's diadem, wigs, ornaments and apparel. The same courtiers who assisted the king in the *pr-dw3t* also assisted at his purifying and robing (Blackman 1918a: 148-65). The reference to the 'House of the Morning' in the Painkh stela describes how the *sdb*-vestment was placed on Piankh. Also how a chief lector 'praised the god', but here no further titles are known for lectors.

Lector of the Funerary Workshop (House of Embalming)

'Lector of the Funerary Workshop' (*ẖry-ḥbt ꜥ3 pr-nfr*) [hieroglyphs], a title indicating responsibility for the materials and equipment needed for the burial as well as for ritual procedures during the embalming process. A 12th Dynasty stela in the Louvre (C. 40) depicts a certain Seneb as lector of the funerary workshop (Gayet 1889: pl. 23). In the New Kingdom the royal scribe, Djehutynefer, has the title 'Chief Lector of the Funerary Workshop' (*ẖry-ḥbt ḥry-tp m pr-nfr*) [hieroglyphs] (Helck 1958: 510 n. 5). A Ramesside inscription at Saqqara lists Horankh as royal scribe and lector in the funerary workshop (Kitchen 1980: 493.12). Here the lector would be responsible for the materials and equipment needed for the burial as well as for ritual procedures during the embalming process.

Lector of the Funerary Estate

'Lector of the Funerary Estate' (*ẖry-ḥbt pr-ḏt*) [8] and .[9] Funerary estates were 'pious foundations' that formed a major source of the deceased's provision of funerary offerings for his cult. Frequently, these estates were granted from a royal foundation as a reward or payment to an official (Strudwick 2005: 504-5). The lector would have been employed by the estate to recite formulae and incantations for the deceased as part of the cult. This title is only attested during the Old Kingdom (Jones 2000: II, 782).

Lector of his Father/Chief Lector of his Father

There are a number of examples of 'Lector of his Father' (*ẖry-ḥbt n it.f*) ,[10] and 'Chief Lector of his Father' (*ẖry-ḥbt ḥry-tp n it.f*) ,[11] a title only attested during the Old Kingdom (Jones 2000: II, 784-5). The title would presumably refer to the lector officiating for his father. Interestingly, the two examples mentioned above both relate to the sons of the ruling king, who possibly assisted their father in his ritual duties or performed ritual after his death.

Lector of a King

There are Old Kingdom examples of the title 'Lector of a King' (*ẖry-ḥbt n KN)* such as: Lector of Shepseskare (Junker 1952: 233-7, pls. 96a, 96b, 97); Lector of Sahure (*PM* III^2: W348); and Lector of Neferirkare (Junker 1932: 135). Nebhepetre, an 11th Dynasty officiant, carries the title 'Grand lector in the king's house, in charge of the mysteries in the august chamber, priest assigned to making offerings, the lector Nebhepetre'[12] (see page 65 for the lector in the royal palace). In the New Kingdom there is the lector Ramesse Meryamun, who was lector in the royal house or mansion (*ẖry-ḥbt m ḥwt nsw*) (Bergmann 1887: 50-1).

Ordinary Lector

There are examples of the title 'Ordinary Lector' (*ẖry-ḥbt ꜥšꜣ*) in the Middle Kingdom.[13] A stela of Sobekdedu indicates that he was ordinary lector at the Semna Fortress and at Lahun as well as being a priest of Anubis (Petrie 1925: 10, pl. 12 image 7). In the tomb of Hapidjefa there is an inscription of an ordinary lector 'reciting the glorifications' (*šdt sꜣḫw in ẖry-ḥbt ꜥšꜣ*) (Montet 1928: 61, no. 128). The distinction between an ordinary lector and a lector is not made clear from any of these examples, but as with the case of the senior/elder lector it may relate to length of service, ranking or specific duties.

Lector of Amun

During the New Kingdom there is evidence of lectors being divided into hierarchical categories, perhaps relating to their importance or seniority. At Karnak there is a 'First Lector of Amun' (*ẖry-ḥbt tp n imn*) [14] and a 'Third Lector of Amun' (*ẖry-ḥbt 3 n imn*) [15] (Lefebvre 1929: 17). Presumably there would also have been a second lector of Amun.

Lector who is in his Year

Inscriptions from the 5th Dynasty sun-temple of Niuserre demonstrate the title 'Lector who is in his Year' (*ẖry-ḥbt imy-rnpt*) , suggesting a system of rotation in the duties of the lectors (see page 11). This title is most frequently seen in Saqqara monuments of the 10th Dynasty[16] and early Middle Kingdom. The title 'Senior Lector who is in his Year' is also attested from the Middle Kingdom,[17] as is 'Senior Lector who is in his Month' (Erman & Steindorff 1902-1903: 114). Suggestions proposed by Kees (1962: 124) as to an explanation of the title are either a lector who served all year round or more likely an honorary title for the senior lector of each year.

Lectors associated with Deities

Lectors were often associated with a specific god(s), particularly from the Middle Kingdom onwards (also see lector of Amun above). As the temples of ancient Egypt were typically dedicated to a specific deity, the lectors attached to a particular cult would be more likely to be found in that temple (examples listed in table 2).

Lectors associated with Temples

The high priests of Heliopolis in the Old Kingdom appended lector to their other titles (see page 11). Additionally, lectors sometimes appended the specific temple as well as possibly the deity to their title (examples listed in table 3).

Lectors associated with Localities

The name of a particular locality can be seen appended to the title of lector as illustrated in table 4.

Miscellaneous

1. 'Lector of the *mit*-Bark of Horus' and of the *ḏꜣt*-Bark of Horus' (*ẖry-ḥbt mit ḥr ḏꜣt ḥr*) (Chabân 1903: 251; Kamal 1912: 137). This is a

[8] The stela of Niuserre from Saqqara (CG 1400; Borchardt 1937: 61).
[9] The lector Kar in the mastaba of Pepy-Nefer (Daressy 1917a: 135).
[10] Nykaure possible son of Khafre (Strudwick 1985: 106, 78; Hassan 1953: 17, fig. 10; Baud 1999: I, 266, tb. 16(6)).
[11] Iunre son of Khafre (Strudwick 1985: 60, 8); Nyuserra (Hassan 1943: 185(2), fig. 132; Baud 1999: 266, tb. 16(7), 294).
[12] A polished hematite statue in the Oriental Institute, University of Chicago, 10.239 (Allen 1923: 51).
[13] Clay seal impressions of Nebiu discovered at Lahun (Martin 1971: 54, no. 650; Borchardt 1902-1903: 114).
[14] Theban tomb of Re, TT 72 (*Urk* IV: 1458, 2); Theban tomb of Ahmose, TT 121 (Gardiner & Weigall 1913: no. 121).
[15] Theban tomb of Hapu (*Urk* IV: 488, 9).
[16] Stela of Iti from Saqqara (Fischer 1963: 38).
[17] Middle Kingdom coffins of Ipiemsaf and Khennu from their Tomb (289) at Saqqara (Quibell 1908: 15-17).

common title in the Old Kingdom (for further examples see Jones 2000: II, 783).

2. 'Lector of the God's Book' (*ẖry-ḥbt mḏꜣt nṯr*). This Middle Kingdom example is inscribed on the 12th Dynasty stela of Intef (Gayet: 1889: pl. 29).
3. 'Lector who knows the Affairs of Heaven' (*ẖry-ḥbt rḫ sšm n pt*) (Maspero 1882: 126). This title taken by Anen, brother of Queen Tiy, places emphasis on knowledge and being learned rather than appearing to denote a specific function.
4. There is a Middle Kingdom example of a 'Lector of the Court' (*ẖry-ḥbt n ḫft-ḥr*). This inscription of the lector Djedu is found inscribed on a boulder in the Wadi Hammamat (see page 125 for expedition inscriptions; Goyon 1957: 94, no. 74). Goyon (1957: 21) considers that the role of Djedu and similar officials present on the mining expedition was to demonstrate authority and announce that the ruling monarch had authorised such an expedition.

			Hieroglyphs
1	**'Lector of Anubis'**	*ẖry-ḥbt n inpw*	[18]
2	**'Great Lector of Bastet'**	*ẖry-ḥbt ꜥꜣ n bꜣst*	[19]
3	**'Lector of the Great Ennead'**	*ẖry-ḥbt psḏt ꜥꜣt*	[20]
4	**'Lector of Khonsu'**	*ẖry-ḥbt n ḫnsw*	[21]
5	**'Lector of Min'**	*ẖry-ḥbt n mnw*	[22]
6	**'Lector of Montu'**	*ẖry-ḥbt n mnṯw*	[23]
7	**'Lector of Nekhbet'**	*ẖry-ḥbt n nḫbt*	[24]
8	**'Lector of Ptah'**	*ẖry-ḥbt n ptḥ*	**This title is attested for the Middle and the New Kingdom**[25]
9	**'Lector of Ptah and Mut'**	*ẖry-ḥbt n ptḥ mwt*	[26]
10	**'Lector of Osiris'**	*ẖry-ḥbt n wsir*	[27]
11	**'Lector of Wadjet'**	*ẖry-ḥbt n wꜣḏyt*	[28]

TABLE 2: LECTORS ASSOCIATED WITH DEITIES

[18] The stela of Nehi, senior warden of Nekhen, commemorates four other individuals, one of whom is Di-Sobek, the lector of Anubis (Stewart 1979: 27, no. 113). The stela is dated to the late Middle Kingdom/Second Intermediate Period.
[19] Papyrus Petersberg 1116B (Helck 1970: 10, IIb) (the Prophecy of Neferty from the Middle Kingdom).
[20] Tomb chapel of Ukh-hotep (Blackman 1915: pl. 9).
[21] New Kingdom Theban tomb (TT 54) of the sculptor of Amun, Huy (Polz: 1990: 44).
[22] Middle Kingdom (CG 1161; Borchardt 1934: 85).
[23] Bergmann 1887: 36.
[24] The Middle Kingdom seal of Sobekhotep (Martin 1971: 111, no. 1426).
[25] Tomb of the high-priest Khonsu, TT 31 (Kitchen 1980: 399. 10-15).
[26] The Middle Kingdom seal of Wehemnefer (Martin 1971: 38, no. 424).
[27] The Middle Kingdom stela of Djehutyemhat, Lector of Osiris (CG 20387, Lange and Schäfer 1902: 383-4).
[28] Montet 1931: 213, pl. 15.

1	**'Lector in the Temple of Sokar'**	*ḫry-ḥbt m ḥwt skr*	[29]
2	**'Lector of Amun in the Ramesseum'**	*ḫry-ḥbt n imn m ḥwt- wsr-mꜣꜥt-rꜥ stp-n-rꜥ*	[30]
3	**'Great (chief) Lector at Thebes'**	*ḫry-ḥbt ꜥꜣ n wꜣst*	[31]
4	**'Lector of Horus at Edfu'**	*ḫry-ḥbt n ḥr bḥdt*	**and** [32]
5	**'Chief Lector of Horus the Behdetite'**	*ḫry-ḥbt tpy n ḥr bḥdty*	[33]

Table 3: Lectors associated with temples

1	**'Lector of Dendera'**	*ḫry-ḥbt iwnt*	[34]
2	**'Lector of (the city) Amenemhat-given-life for ever, Uniter-of-the-Two-Lands'**	*ḫry-ḥbt imn-m-ḥꜣt ꜥnḫ ḏt iṯ tꜣwy*	[35]
3	**'Chief Lector in Nebhepetre's Pyramid, Most Glorious of Places'**	*ḥry-tp ḫry-ḥbt m ꜣḫ swt*	[36]
4	**'Ordinary Lector of** *sḫm sn-wsrt'*	*ḫry-ḥbt ꜥšꜣ n sḫm sn-wrst*	[37]
5	**'Chief Lector in Sneferu's Pyramid "Which Rises in Splendour"**	*ḥry-tp ḫry-ḥbt*	[38]

Table 4: Lectors associated with localities

[29] 19th Dynasty limestone pyramidion of the lector Ramesse Meryamun. Ramesse is also attested as being a lector in the Ramesseum (Kitchen 1980: 358. 6-15)

[30] New Kingdom, tomb of Amenemope (TT 177) (Kitchen 1980: 357. 5-10).

[31] Amenenmat (Gardiner 1937: 89.1).

[32] Daressy 1917b: 240, 243.

[33] Daressy 1917b: 238.

[34] The Middle Kingdom seal of Nenebbi (Martin: 1971: 62, no. 746). For *Iwnt* as Dendera temple see Gardiner 1947: II, 30.

[35] The Middle Kingdom stela of Intef excavated at Abydos, depicts Hetep who holds this title 'Lector of the City' (CG 20516, Lange & Shäfer 1902: 109). P. Kahun (Griffith 1898: pl.10,1).

[36] CG 20088, Lange and Shäfer 1902: 105-107. As attested by an ebony statue of the lector Sneferu-hotep (Fakhry 1961: 15).

[37] P. Kahun (Griffith 1898: pl.10,1).

[38] As attested by an ebony statue of the lector Sneferu-hotep (Fakhry 1961: 15).

Chapter 2

Magic and Performance

1. Magic

Definition

The lector is recognised as being closely associated with 'magic' (Ritner 1993; David 2002; Pinch 2006). In the discipline of Egyptology the category of 'magic' has long been a descriptive tool although no shared criteria have existed for defining the concept. A great deal of attention has been devoted to discussions of how magic can best be defined and the attempted distinctions between 'magical', 'medical' and 'religious' texts (Kyffin 2011: 225). However, the uncertainty of the exact lines of demarcation, if they exist at all, between religion, magic and medicine has rendered the theoretical distinctions between them untenable (Ritner 1993: 5).

Recent scholarship has emphasised that magic was integral to Egyptian thought, in which it was a basic cosmic force and not a marginal or disruptive phenomenon (Baines 2006: 1). In ancient Egypt magic can be regarded as a functional activity in which both the exact purpose of the rite and the expected result were stated. Ritner (1993: 1) suggests that any activity that aims to obtain its objective by methods outside the natural laws of cause and effect can be considered magical. Magic was a belief 'that by acting out a particular situation a result will be triggered off by symbolic means in this world or the hereafter due to an impersonal, morally neutral, mystical force which serves man as well as gods, demons and dead persons' (*LÄ* III: 1137). Three components are involved in magical practices: the word that is spoken or 'spell', the activity or rite that is performed (the performance), and often an object or material whose power is magically endorsed (see chapter 3 for discussion on the equipment and materials that might have been used by a lector).

Heka

The terms most closely related to magic is *heka (ḥkꜣ)* perhaps best understood as relating to the cosmic force of 'magic' or being a 'self-sufficient creative power' (Borghouts 1987: 29-46). The ancient Egyptians believed that *heka* resided in the body of the magician, but its use required the conscious manipulation of spell and rite (*LÄ* III: 1140). In the text *The Instruction for Merikare,* dated to the First Intermediate Period, *heka* is described as a gift from the gods to humanity to help ward off evil, a power which even the gods would use (P. St-Petersburg 1116A; Golénischeff 1913: l.137):

> 'He[1] has ordained for them magic *(ḥkꜣ)* as weapons to fend off the impact of what may come to pass' (translated Tobin 2003a: 165).

[1] 'He' refers to the creator deity (Tobin 2003a: 153).

One particular function of *heka* can be illustrated by the epithet 'great of magic' as relating to the uraeus, indicating its defensive and punitive power (*LÄ* III: 1139).

2. Word, 'Spell'

There is an intimate association of magic and words, as illustrated by Papyrus Ebers §356 (Wreszinski 1913: 101): 'You say as magic' (*ḏd ḥr.k m ḥkꜣw*). The spell draws together the written and the vocalised into one multivalent concept 'the word of power' as attested by an inscription from Edfu temple where the female equivalent of the *ka* of *Heka* is described as (Chassinat 1928: 99, l.7-9):

> 'Possessor of spells, bearing her writings in her mouth' (*nb ꜣḫw ḥr sš.s imyw rꜣ*) (translated Frankfurter: 1994: 193).

Frankfurter (1995: 457) considers that when a spell is uttered, the words draw power into the world and towards (or against) an object.

Egyptian ritual speech was not intended so much for communication as for verbal efficacy, and this accords with what have been described as 'speech acts' (Tambiah 1968: 175-208; see also page 86 of this publication for the nature of texts used by the lector). Thus the word that leaves the mouth of the speaker can be considered as a creative act indicating that the spoken word has power (Zandee 1964: 33-66). Ritual speech traditionally involved the recitation of elements of mythic narratives or *historiolae* incorporated into the spell. The central act in the *historiola* was the utterance by a deity of a name or spell which would give the narrative a strong 'presence' (Frankfurter 1995: 457-8). This inherent power in the words could be reinforced by asserting that Thoth himself was pronouncing it as attested in a healing incantation from the Ebers Papyrus (§I, 1-11):

> 'Thoth who causes the books to speak, he composed compilations of writing'

Thoth as god of writing is frequently given titles that support this image: 'great of magic' *(wr ḥkꜣ),* 'excellent of magic' *(mnḫ ḥkꜣ)*, and 'Lord of magic' *(nb ḥkꜣ)* (translation after Boylan 1922: 124-35). The Late Period *Setna I* story revolves around the search for a book of magic claimed to be written by the god Thoth.

The lector with his literacy and knowledge of texts is strongly associated with the god Thoth. (See overleaf for the lector in the temple sphere and page 85 for funerary information). In the later 'Opening of the Mouth for Breathing' ritual, the lector identifies himself with Thoth at a number of different points in the ceremony (P. BM 10209 and P. Berlin 8351, Smith 1993: 15).

The formula *ḏd-mdw* (words spoken) is used extensively in written texts and marks the words as speech acts (Meyer-Dietrich 2010: 3). Terms indicating magic by speech are numerous, with general words such as 'word' *(mdw),* 'speech' *(r3)* and 'statement' *(ḏd)* often being placed in close proximity to words such as *(ḥk3w)* and so then assuming a magical connotation. These words can be related to the ritual actions of any officiant and an example associated with a lector can be found in the autobiography of Harkhuf (*Urk* I: 122. 13):

> 'I am an excellent equipped blessed spirit, a lector who knows his spell' *(ink 3ḫ iḳr ʿpr ḫry-ḥbt rḫ r3.f).*

In a temple text from Edfu the word recite *(šd)* is used in a similar situation (Chassinat 1930: 30, 1-4):

> 'The chief lector outfitted with his adornments recites the spells of appearance (going outside)' *(ḫry-ḥb ḥry-tp ḏb3 m ḫkrw.f ḥr šd r3w n pr r-ḫ3).* (translated Ritner 1993: 44)

Importantly, these two texts are separated by some 2000 years but the same terminology is being used.

There is a lack of evidence for the way words were to be spoken during a recitation, the manner in which words were to be performed in texts. There is little in the way of information concerning the delivery of recitations or indeed evidence for training manuals, but one source of information for the Ptolemaic and Roman Periods is the *Book of the Temple.* This text discusses the training of the children of priests in the musical performance of hymns and the recitation of traditional texts (Quack 2002: 159-71; Meyer-Dietrich 2010: 2).

The ability to compose, copy or recite incantations or spells would have been limited to priests, scribes and the elite, the literate members of society, a group suggested to consist of only one per cent of the population of ancient Egypt. This figure is considered to have risen during the Graeco-Roman Period based upon the vast quantity of preserved papyrus that exists (Baines & Eyre 1983: 65-72). The lector would have been a prominent member of this group. The composition of magical incantations, hymns and rituals is known to have occurred in the House of Life, the 'scriptorium' attached to the temples. Here the lector would have been a principal official, an expert in such work, as attested by an incantation that was directed against crocodiles (Harris Magical Papyrus: col. 6/10, §K, 1-4, in Lange 1927: 53-4):

> 'First spell of enchanting all that is in the water, concerning which the chief lectors say: "Do not reveal it to others." A veritable secret of the House of Life' (translated Kyffin 2011: 233).

In this passage the suggestion that access to such spells was restricted is an indication of how powerful the spell was deemed to be, and also an attempt to reduce the threat of its misuse. Nevertheless, it could also relate to vested interests and an attempt to preserve the privilege of the priests in such matters (Ritner 1993: 204). However, the conspicuous display of the secrecy of magic is obvious, restricted knowledge was both concealed and displayed. Addresses to the living make play of their owners' knowledge of magic, calling the deceased a 'lector who knows his spell *(r3)*' (*Urk* I: 122, 13; Baines 2006: 19). One formula states 'no efficacious magical spell *(ḥk3)* was ever concealed from me' (Baines 1990: 11 -12).

There is additional evidence to suggest that magical spells were composed in the House of Life. The *Sed*-festival reliefs at Bubastis depict a procession of identical long-skirted priests which include 'magician/protectors' of the King of Lower Egypt *(s3w bity);* a lector *(ḫry-ḥbt);* and a royal scribe *(sš nsw)* (see pages 75-80). There is also a caption over a single officiant which can be translated 'company of the House of Life' *(ṯst n pr-ʿnḫ).* Gardiner (1938a: 165) considers that a plurality was meant in this situation and links all the officiants to the House of Life and the connection of magic to this institution (for further comments on the House of Life see pages 57 and 116-19).

3. Performance

Introduction

In temple and state ritual the lector would have been an agent during the performance of rites, and would have 'done' *(ir)* and 'said' *(ḏd)* things, although he would be a secondary performer to the king. The king's name is on the papyri and temple walls as the performer of the ritual, but in practice it was a priest or lector who carried out the rite. However, on a number of occasions the rank of the priest was specified in the paratext accompanying the ritual's recitation, as attested in the Ritual of Amenhotep I where the spells are stated as being recited by the lector (3, 7 and 4, 7). At the end of the Ritual (37, *Vs* 3, 3-4):

> 'It has come to an end happily. Made by the draughtsman of Amun in the Place of Truth, the lector of Amun in all his festivals' (translated Gardiner 1935: 101).

Hays (2009a: 18) suggests that on temple wall scenes, in particular, due to the public nature of this medium, the dynamics of self-presentation would have been a factor. Such contexts circumscribe what it was appropriate to depict.

The actions of the ritual are not in themselves efficacious; it requires that the officiant who performs the rite has been given the authority or authorisation. It is not sufficient that the ritual be performed; it must be performed by persons with certain stated qualifications (Tambiah 2002: 340). Additionally, a quality of purity would be required of the officiant for the speech to be effective, for it to be 'performative'.

The deed of the agent, empowered by the monarch, was the fundamental basis for the correct performance of ritual action. However, although the king may have delegated an agent to perform a rite, once the ritual was being performed deities such as Anubis, Re (as in CT 45 I, 199-200), Geb (as in PT 477 §967) and Thoth (CT 590 VI, 210) could be said to command the action. There is a reference to a lector being directed by Thoth (CT 590 VI, 210):

> 'O lector of mine, it is Thoth who has brought the lectors, those who recite it during the deeds' (translated Faulkner 1977: 191).

In the performance of rites for the dead there is a reciprocal benefit for the person performing the ritual, just as the king receives direct benefits from the gods, as demonstrated in the mastaba of Khentika (James & Apted 1953: pl. 5. B13, B15):

> 'But as for any lector or any Ka-servant who will act ... and speak for me at this tomb of mine of the necropolis, I will be their protector' (translated Hays 2009a: 22).

This 'appeal to the living' formula is inscribed on many stelae, particularly those dating to the Middle Kingdom such as those of Amenemhat (CG 20040; Simpson 1974: pl. 23) and the vizier Ameni (UC 14326; Stewart 1979: 18) (see Lichtheim 1988 for a detailed study).

Similarly, in the *Instructions for Merikare* (P. St Petersburg No. 1116A; Helck 1988):

> 'Enter into sanctuary, eat bread in the temple. Proffer libations, multiply the sacrificial loves increase the daily service, for it is what is beneficial for the one who does it' (translated Tobin 2003a: 158).

So the benefits of participation in cult activity, whether a spoken word or an involvement in ritual action, would seemingly accrue advantage for the ritualist in the afterlife (Hays 2009a: 23).

Ritual Performances

Ritual performances are evident in ancient Egypt both at public ceremonies, such as the many festivals that occurred throughout the year, and in 'private' rites as attested by the names of individuals inscribed on execration deposits. However, an attempt to separate private ritual performances from state religious ceremonies may be an artificial distinction. There is a parallel and equal development of the Apep ritual (see page 25) in both state and private magical performance without any differentiation regarding the formulaic expressions and actions. During the Ramesside era, healing statues carried a fusion of both royal and private incantations (Kousoulis 2003: 362-5). The identity of the actor or magician who performed the magical practices at private ceremonies is often the same ritualist who performed at temple services. This suggestion is reinforced by the similarity of ritual texts and magical spells, as they were all composed, compiled and performed by the same individuals (Ritner 1993: 2).

The lector is one of the key officiants in the performance of ritual action, being evident in many of the rites attested from ancient Egypt. In the temple sphere the lector is specified as one of the officiants who recited during the performance of the Daily Temple Ritual and his presence is attested at many of the festivals (see pages 58-64 for festival rituals). At royal rituals such as the celebration of the *Sed*-Festival he is depicted as one of the principal attendants and a 'master of ceremonies' or 'ritual director' (see chapter 6 for royal involvement). In private rituals, particularly the funerary rites, he was an essential officiant reciting the important transfiguration incantations allowing the deceased to become an *akh* (see chapter 7 for funerary ritual). The lector is attested as being involved in ritual performances associated with healing practices (see chapter 9). The lector displayed ritual mastery or the ability 'to take and remake schemes from the shared culture that can strategically nuance, privilege or transform' (Bell 2009: 116). One category of performative rituals with which the lector was associated and which is not explored in the main evidence sections referred to above is execration rituals.

4. Execration Rituals

Definition and History

The execration rituals can be defined as stylised magical procedures aimed at impeding or eradicating foes. The earliest known representations, which involve aspects of this rite, are motifs of bound prisoners and actions associated with trampling captives underfoot (Posener 1987; Muhlestein 2008: 1). Later they were to involve either simple lists of forces or people against whom the rite was enacted, or they could comprise complex formulae directed at an antagonist. The texts were inscribed on clay pots or figurines created from materials such as clay, wood or wax. The use of a clay figurine as a human substitute image is relevant to the Egyptian belief that the god Khnum fashioned mankind on a potter's wheel, explicitly formulated in the Great Hymn to Khnum at the Ptolemaic temple of Esna (Lichtheim 1980: 111-15).

Execration rituals are attested throughout the Pharaonic Period and over 1,000 deposits representing this rite have been excavated from various cemeteries throughout Egypt. These range from inscribed individual figures to elaborate assemblages (Posener 1975, 1987; Ritner 1993: 137, n. 611). The execration texts are quite specific in their intended victim, for by the identification through a name, the pot or figurine becomes a substitute image for those victims.

There is evidence of the lector being involved in the execration ceremonies as attested in a scene from the temple of Edfu. On the east wall of the temple library a chief lector is depicted skewering nine figurines on a spear before the king (Chassinat 1928: 349/3, pl. 83; figs. 13, 14). The title of the ritual reads:

> 'Overthrowing the enemies of the king daily as *nṯstyw* (and) as the nine bows'

nṯstyw has been translated as 'foes', but by far the commonest usage of the word is in passages relating to enemies who have been trampled upon (Blackman & Fairman 1941: 415, n. 58). Ritner (1993: 186) notes that most of the instances in which *nṯstyw* appears relate to cultic practices involving prisoner figurines, and therefore he suggests 'execration figures' as a translation for *nṯstyw*.

In this 'skewering scene' at Edfu, the officiant is depicted wearing an animal skin, a garment normally associated with a *sem*-priest. However, he is holding a papyrus roll and the inscription above him reads:

> 'The chief lector of Horus of Behdet, great god, lord of the sky' (*ḫry-ḥbt ḥry-tp n ḥr Bḥdt nṯr ꜥ3 nb pt*).

This is a similar example of the mixing of the roles as seen in three scenes from the tomb of Rekhmire and may be copyists' errors (see pages 110-14 for the Opening of the Mouth ceremony in the tomb of Rekhmire). On the west wall of Edfu temple a similar scene depicts four enemy figures being stabbed whilst being burnt before Horus (Chassinat 1928: 346-7, pl. 82). Here the actor is the king but an officiant would have deputised for him, possibly a lector.

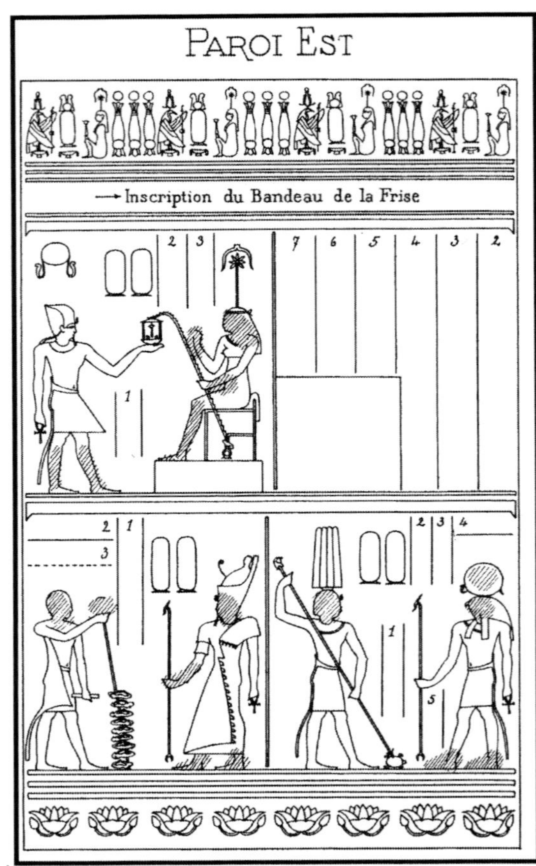

Fig. 13: A chief lector skewering figures before the king (Chassinat 1928: pl. 83)

Fig. 14: Detail of the 'skewering' in figure 13

Breaking the Red Pots

The earliest identified texts associated with the execration rituals are found on a group of artefacts known as the Berlin bowls, these consisting of a number of inscribed and shattered red clay vessels (Sethe 1926: Berlin P. 14501-14606; Quack 2006a: 72-4). Sethe (1926: 20) and Altenmüller (2010: 5) associate these fragments with a passage in the earlier Pyramid Texts (§244, §249):

> 'O [Osiris the King] here is the eye of Horus; [take] it, that you may be strong and that he may be terrified of you – break the red vases' (translated Faulkner 1969: 58).

This early reference to this ritual demonstrates that the function of the rite was to strike terror upon perceived enemies by means of the act of breaking, an action which by its very nature would imply hostility. The ritual of the red vases is recognised in burial practices and is attested in reliefs from early tombs such as those of Mereruka at Saqqara and Pepiankh at Meir (Duell 1938: pl. 67; Blackman 1924: 50-1, pl. 18.1; fig. 15).

The sequence of events leading up to the final closure of a tomb has been reconstructed by Blackman (1924: 50). After the completion of the funeral meal, there would be libations, the burning of incense, the *s3ḫw* would be recited by the lector and then the lector would be involved again in 'removing the footprints' (*int-rd*) (see page 54 for the ceremony being performed in the temple and pages 91-2 at private tombs). Following this would be 'the breaking of the red pots' (*sḏ dšrw*) in which red pottery vessels, possibly those used in the meal and during the ritual lustrations, were broken and left, perhaps, at the entrance to the tomb. Meanwhile incantations were said and, finally, the tomb would be closed and sealed. The breaking of the pots and the distribution of the pieces could either have been a continuation of the ritual of 'removing the footprints' or would closely follow it. It is not stated explicitly that the lector was responsible for this final action, but this may have been the case.

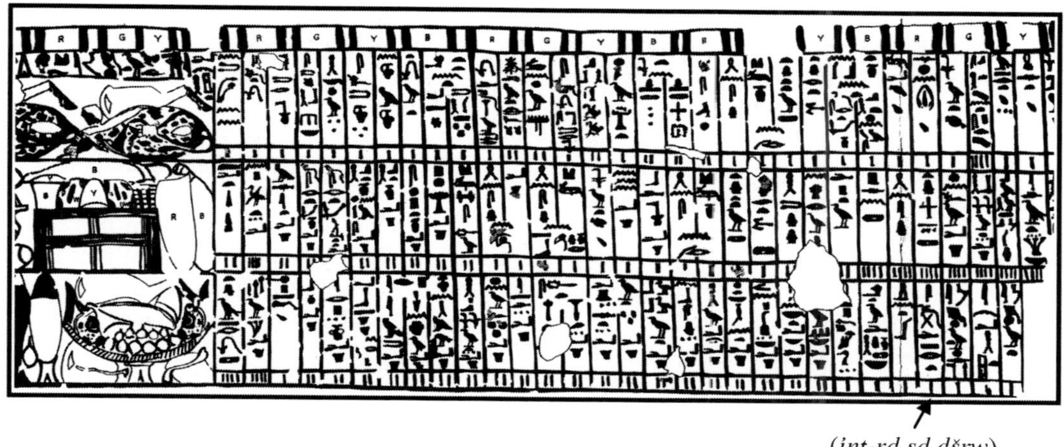

FIG. 15: WALL INSCRIPTION IN THE SOUTH BURIAL CHAMBER OF THE 6TH DYNASTY TOMB OF PEPIANKH AT MEIR DEPICTING THE LIST OF FUNERARY OFFERINGS (BLACKMAN 1924: PL. 18)

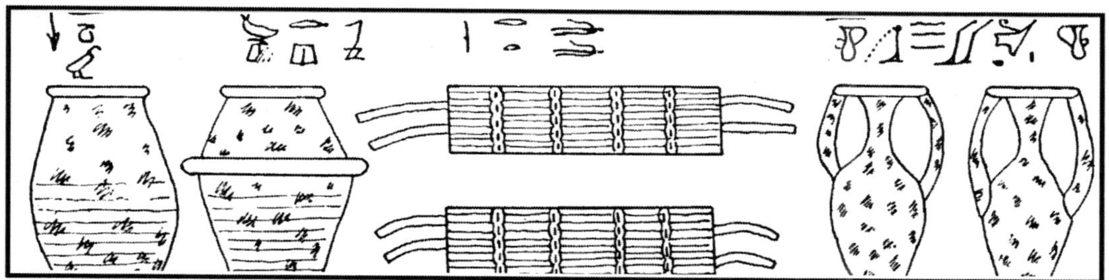

FIG. 16: FRIEZE FROM THE MIDDLE KINGDOM COFFIN OF NETJERUHOTEP DISPLAYING RED VESSELS (ADAPTED FROM GRDSELOFF 1941: PL. 6)

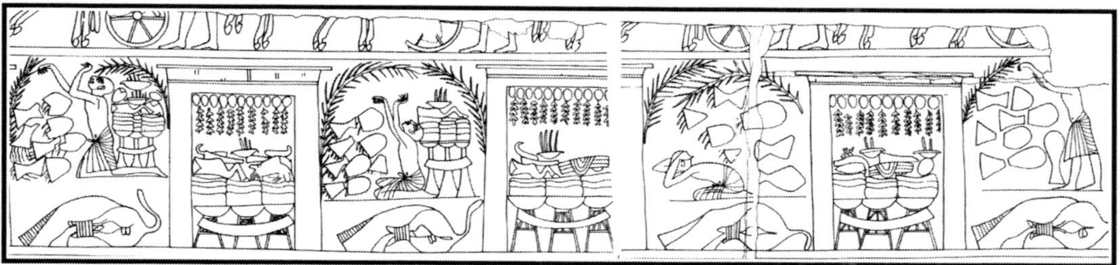

FIG. 17: BREAKING THE RED POTS AS DEPICTED IN THE TOMB OF HOREMHEB AT SAQQARA (ADAPTED FROM MARTIN 1989A: PL. 123)

This ritual is later attested in the Middle Kingdom as images of red vessels appear in friezes of purification utensils depicted on coffins of that period (Grdseloff 1941: 26, 30; fig. 16). In the New Kingdom a similar ritual was performed beside funerary offering booths and is depicted in the tomb of Horemheb at Saqqara (Davies 1948: pl. 25; Martin 1989: 101, pl. 123; fig. 17).

In the Ptolemaic Period a scene inscribed on the walls of the temple of Edfu depicts vessels being carried over a site about to be purified (Chassinat 1928: 338, 10):

> 'Go about four times with four jugs of water' (translated Ritner 1993: 146).

Whilst red pots were the earliest objects utilised in execration rituals and continued as a common article in this rite, by the late Old Kingdom hairballs, figurines, statues made out of clay, sand, stone, wax or wood were also being used (Muhlestein 2008: 2). Giza deposits from the reign of Pepi II include a clay figurine inscribed with a 'rebellion formula'. Examples from the Middle Kingdom include Cairo alabaster figurines from the reign of Senwosret I and limestone prisoner figurines in the Mirgissa deposit (Ritner 1993: 140, 153). Among late examples at the Festival of Behdet at Edfu, execration rites were performed which involved a hippopotamus of red wax, a hippopotamus of sand and some clay balls[2] (Fairman 1954-1955: 198; Ritner 1993: 210).

There are a large number of execration rituals entailing the destruction of figurines, often constructed from wax,

[2] Locks of hair have been found within these balls (Crompton 1916: 128, pl. 16)

with which the lector, by implication from the evidence presented so far, may have been associated. Wax played an important part in Egyptian symbolism and magic and was considered to be a primeval substance of great power (Raven 1983: 7). The earliest mention of wax figurines is in the Coffin Texts where the aim is to give the deceased power over his enemies. The rubric at the end of the spell specifies exactly how to conduct the ritual (CT Spell 37, 157):

> 'To be spoken over a figure of the foe made of wax and inscribed with the name of that foe on his breast, with the bone of a synodontis fish: to be put in the ground in the abode of Osiris'[3] (translated Faulkner 1973: 27-9).

There are also a number of execration rituals involving wax figurines documented in the Harem Conspiracy and the Westcar Papyrus.

Purification Rites

These rites are discussed on pages 51-3 including this example of the Victory Stela of Piye (*Urk* III: 103):

> '...the chief lector praising god that rebels might be repelled from the king...' *(ḫry-ḥbt ḥry-tp nṯr dw3 ḫsf sḫdy r nsw)*

In this rite a chief lector is specifically named and is aiming to eradicate the enemies of the king by means of a purification ceremony.

Rites of Encircling (pḫrt)

The verb *pḫr* has the basic meaning of 'to go around, surround or circumambulate', and similarly the verb *dbn* has a comparable translation (*Wb* I: 44-9 and V: 46-8). There is a magical connotation to these words as attested in many funerary and temple ceremonies from the early Dynastic Period until the Graeco-Roman Period. There are a number of rituals of circumambulation comprising both public and private ceremonies. These include: coronation rites such as a procession about the desert *(dbn ḫ3st);* a circumambulation of the walls to delimit the sacred space of the kingdom *(pḫr ḥ3);* and the ritual of encirclement which occurs during the *Sed*-festival (Wilkinson 1985: 46-51; Ritner 1993; 58-9). Ritual circumambulations are described in the Pyramid Texts (PT Spell 649, §1866; Sethe: 1910: 454-5):

> 'Take these white teeth of yours in a bowl, go round about them with an arrow in this their name of an arrow' (translated Faulkner 1969: 271).

Again in PT 509, §1122 (Sethe 1910: 128):

> 'My entrails have been washed by Anubis, and the encircling *(pḫrwt)* of Horus and the embalming of Osiris have been carried out in Abydos' (translated Faulkner 1969: 184).

Faulkner (1969: 185) suggests that the 'encircling' of Horus may refer to his walking around and around his father's body affixing the funeral wrappings.

The lector has an association with this rite of encircling as attested by an example from Papyrus Chester Beatty 8 (verso 7/7) where after the title 'Book for Banishing the Male enemy, Female Enemy, Dead Man ...' the rubric states:

> 'Spell for ignoring his staff and ... his limbs. Take care of this book ... Let no one else encompass it. To be recited by the chief lector in front of ...' (translated Gardiner 1935: 74-5).

The function of the rubric in the performance of these spells can be considered as stage directions for the lector rather than part of the spoken/performed recitation. In addition, rubrics highlight the beginnings of spells thus providing an index to the papyrus and label the function of the spell (Kyffin 2011: 245).

The magical implications of these ritual actions and the power or control implied by encircling was known to have been utilised in a hostile manner as well as in a protective form as attested in a passage in the Dramatic Ramesseum Papyrus (P. BM Ram. B, EA 10610). This text re-enacts the murder of Osiris by Seth, by ritually encircling a representation of the god with goats (Sethe 1928: 223, 225). Again in Papyrus Louvre 3129 (Schott 1929: 57/20):

> 'I shall cause a curse to circulate against the one who did it' (translated Ritner 1993: 65).

Circumambulation is mentioned in a funerary context in the fragmentary Ramesseum funerary papyrus (P. Ram. E[4] [P. BM EA 10753] col. 74):

> 'Circulating around the mastaba four times' (translated Gardiner 1955a: 9-17).

Within the papyrus there are a number of references to the lector and to another funerary officiant, the *imy-khent* priest. Both these officiants, as well as a long list of other actors, appear to be in an elaborate funeral procession. The extremely fragmentary nature of the papyrus prevents too many conclusions being drawn but Gardiner (1955: 11) speculated that the text could refer to a royal burial. Although the papyrus forms part of the Ramesseum cache and thus can be dated to the 13th Dynasty, Černý speculated that the substance of the text could go back as far as the 3rd Dynasty (Gardiner 1955a: 17). However, a similar rite dated to the reign of Ptolemy IX is inscribed

[3] Presumably meaning that the figure is to be laid in the dust to be trodden under foot (Faulkner 1973: 28).

[4] An analysis of Papyrus Rammesseum E by Herrnández (2014) was published just before this volume went to press and so was unable to be discussed here. But see discussion on the burial assemblage of Tomb No. 5 at the Ramesseum on pages 30-46 of this publication.

in the 'purgatorium' at Edfu (Chassinat 1928: 336-8): 'Circulating around four times' (translated Ritner 1993: 58).

A protective rite attested in Papyrus Salt 825, composed for the House of Life at Abydos, also includes circumambulation. The rite utilises a number of different execration methods such as the burning of bound wax figures of enemies, attacking and cutting with a flint knife, and enclosing within a jar. The text is accompanied by vignettes which depict this destruction. The conclusion of the rite involves a hostile encirclement *(pḫr)* (see below) which reinforces the constrictive nature of the binding and the enclosure within the jar (Derchain 1965: 1, 139-44, and vol. II: pls. 7*, 22*; Ritner 1993: 176; figs. 18, 19).

FIG. 18 VIGNETTE SHOWING DESTRUCTION OF POLITICAL AND DIVINE ENEMIES 'IN VILE JUG' (ADAPTED FROM DERCHAIN 1965: II, PL. 10, 22*)

FIG. 19: SCHEMATIC DRAWING OF THE 'VILE JUG'. LABELLED AS 'MAY YOU HAVE POWER OVER REBELS' AND THE INSCRIPTION WITHIN THE JUG ENDS 'GO ROUND ABOUT IT' (ADAPTED FROM DERCHAIN 1965: II, PL. 9, 21*)

The text specifies that the words are to be recited by a scribe of the House of Life who, as Gardiner (1938a: 164) notes, is an officiant who in addition carries the rank of priest. Although a lector is not specifically mentioned, he is recognised as having a strong association with the House of Life.

Rites of Protection (sꜥšꜣ)

An example of this type of ritual is to be found in the *Songs of Isis and Nephthys,* one of the works comprising the Ptolemaic Papyrus Bremner Rhind. The text commences with the instructions for the preparation of the temple and the adornment of two priestesses. The priestesses and the lector open the proceedings with preliminary invocations to Osiris before the priestesses sing, purporting to be the mournings of Isis and Nephthys, for the departed Osiris.

The text continues until line 3, 23 when a rubric indicates that the performance is interrupted by an unspecified rite of protection: 'A protective rite. Recitation by the long-haired ones', (referring to the priestesses who are impersonating Isis and Nephthys). The priestesses then resume their singing until again being interrupted, this time by the officiating lector who executes another protective magical rite before proceeding to deliver a hymn to Osiris (9, 13-11, 5):

> 'The great rite of protection *(sꜥšꜣ)* unseen, unheard. Words spoken by the lector' (translated Faulkner 1936: 127-8).

The protective nature of the rite is indicated in several of the lines:

> (4, 5) '...they ward off Seth for thee when he comes...'
> (5, 17) '...and he who rebelled against thee shall not be...'
> (6, 2) '...O! Thou art protected...'

Faulkner (1936: 134, n. 3, 23) has translated *sꜥšꜣ* as a 'protective rite'. *sꜥšꜣ* is also to be found in the Demotic Papyrus Vienna 6319 (cols. 4/31, 3/22) which Reymond (1977: 88) suggests has a meaning of 'magnify' with the implication of 'giving magical protection'. As this term is followed by *ḏd-mdw,* words spoken or recitation, the implication is that the ritual is vocal in nature.

Miscellaneous Rites

A number of other execration rituals are known where the actors performing the rituals are not always specified either in the captions or the textual sources, but as they are in similar contexts to those described previously the lector may have been the officiant at these ceremonies (Pinch 2006: 87).

The Apep ritual was aimed at providing magical protection for Re in his daily journey through the underworld from the serpent demon Apep, but in addition the ritual was secondarily directed for the protection of the king. The most detailed copy of this ritual is to be found in the Ptolemaic text the 'Book of Overthrowing Apep', which comprises the largest section of Papyrus Bremner Rhind (Pap. BM 10188; Faulkner 1937b: 166-85 and 1938: 41-53). As well as being demonstrated in temple rites the Apep ritual is also attested from texts that were in 'private use'. In a 'privately' owned Ramesside papyrus discovered at Deir el-Medina is the spell (Papyrus Chester Beatty 8, vo.7/4):

> 'I have fought for you against Apep' (translated Gardiner 1935: 74).

In funerary rites, spell 7 from the Book of the Dead addresses Apep as a wax execration figure:

> 'O you waxen one who takes by robbery...' (translated Allen 1974: 9).

In the temple of Hibis, Spell 146 from the Book of the Dead is inscribed on a stairway leading to the Osiris chapel in which an address is spoken by Horus. On the south wall Thoth is depicted reciting from the ritual for the 'Feast of Hacking the Earth'. With Horus representing the loving son (a priest), and Thoth representing the lector, then it could be imagined that a priest and a lector could have recited these spells (Lievan: 2012: 259).

Other attested execration rites are the rite against Seth, an example of which is to be found in Papyrus Salt 825 (Derchain 1965: I, 138, col 5. 3-4 and II, pls. 5*, V); the rite of Sokar-Osiris, as attested by an Edfu temple scene (Chassinat 1930: 293 and 1960: pl. 134; Goyon 1978: 415-38); and the ritual for the protection of the divine bark as attested in Papyrus Louvre E 3219 and Papyrus BM 10252 (Schott 1929:1).

So-called 'Letters to the Dead' are appeals to a deceased individual requesting assistance in matters of health, fertility and general day-to-day matters. The letters all appear to be composed by relatives of a recently deceased person and were inscribed on bowls filled with offerings as well as on linen and papyrus (Wente 1990: 210-19). Relatives of the deceased may have sought assistance from the lector in composing or 'activating' these letters because of his known literary abilities and his knowledge of spells that might be invoked in these practices. However, the lector is not directly mentioned in any of the surviving texts.

Spitting, Licking and Swallowing

The ritualised use of spitting, licking and swallowing are practices which are prominent within many cultures, being used to transfer powers whether beneficial or harmful (Ritner 1993: 74-110). In ancient Egypt there are many instances of these ritual acts being utilised as in the Heliopolitan creation myth (Coffin Text 76) where spittle from the sun god Atum produced new life in the form of the gods Shu and Tefnut (Faulkner 1973: 77).

Both the Pyramid and the Coffin Texts describe the licking of written spells and drawn images in order to ingest their efficacy. In texts of purification rituals, saliva serves as a medium to convey invigorating power, and its curative nature is emphasised in funerary literature (Ritner 1993: 78-9). Coffin Spell 1113:

> 'I am one whom Apep detests, since I know how to spit on your (assumed Re's) wounds; I see, for I am one who spits on wounds which will heal' (translated Faulkner 1978: 162).

In the Book of the Heavenly Cow the speaker's justification is assured by tracing an image of the goddess Maat on his tongue. Words that are then spoken pass over the tongue and become infused with truth (Hornung 1982: 25, 46; Ritner 1993: 88). Although there appears to be no direct evidence of the involvement of the lector in these ritual actions, nevertheless with his prominent role in funerary, purification and healing practices it is possible that such actions may have formed part of the professional repertoire of the lector and were utilised when he was reciting ritualised texts.

Chapter 3

Equipment of the Lector

1. Old Kingdom Inscriptional Evidence

As has been previously commented upon, the lector is commonly depicted in tomb and temple scenes carrying a papyrus roll from which he would recite the appropriate utterances. It would seem likely that the lector would also use a range of equipment during the course of his daily work. The lector was well versed in incantations both of a protective and of a healing nature, and he may have reinforced the recitation of these by the use of a ritual device such as a wand. A discussion of wands and other individual items of equipment such as magic rods, ivory clappers, amulets and fertility figurines is included in the second part of this chapter. In chapter 9 evidence will be supplied to demonstrate that the lector had some knowledge of particular remedies used in a healing capacity. It is possible, therefore, that he may also have carried a selection of medicaments with him, particularly if he was visiting the sick.

Some indications of ritual equipment used by the lector are provided by inscriptions from certain Old Kingdom tombs where there is reference to 'the skilled craft of the lector' *(ḥmwt)* and to 'the requirements of the craft of the lector' *(dbḥw n ḥmt ḫry-ḥbt)*. In this latter case *dbḥw* is translated as needs, requirements or necessaries and could imply ritual or working equipment (*Wb* V: 440).

An example of the use of these terms is afforded in the funeral scene reliefs of the 6th Dynasty mastaba of Mereruka at Saqqara. Here on the south wall of chamber A13 the inscriptions chart the funeral cortège travelling from the deceased's house to a body of water (which is assumed to be the river Nile) before loading the coffin onto a barge (Duell 1938: II, pl. 130). The funeral procession crosses the water and then disembarks at a landing place or wharf (figs. 20, 21). On this structure are arranged quantities of baskets, pots, sandals, chests and representations of what are possibly amulets. Above the chests there is a label 'the requirements of the craft of the lector' (Wilson 1944: 210).

From this Mereruka relief and from similar funerary scenes it is possible to provide a fuller description and explanation of this wharf-like structure. In the 5th Dynasty tomb of Qar at Giza (G 7101) the structure is labelled on the left side with 'the requirements of the craft of the lector' *(dbḥw n ḥmt ḫry-ḥbt)*, but on the right the same structure is labelled 'the requirements of the *ibw*' *(dbḥw n ibw)* (fig. 22). The *ibw* refers to the 'the tent of purification' *(ibw n wꜥb)* and it was here that the body of the deceased was ritually purified and washed, before being transferred to the *wꜥbt nt wt* for mummification (Duell 1938: II, pl. 130; Grdseloff 1951: 130-3; Brovarski 1977: 108). It is possible that these two structures were similar or closely related but Grdseloff (1951: 134) considers that in the mastabas of the Old Kingdom the *ibw n wꜥb* and the *wꜥbt nt wt* stood independent of each other. However, Brovarski (1977: 109-11) suggests that the valley temples of the pyramids were the royal *ibw* but that there is no evidence in the Old Kingdom that there was an *ibw* associated with private tombs.

The *ibw* is usually represented as being a rectangular booth having large poles with matting on the walls and roof. The booth shown in the tomb of Qar is suggestive of a rather substantial construction, whereas in the 6th Dynasty tomb of Pepyankh Heny-Kem at Meir, a much lighter arcade shape is shown (fig. 23). The reliefs from the 5th/6th Dynasty tomb of Idu at Giza (G 7102) depict a heavier construction devoid of matting (fig. 24). In addition to this representational evidence supporting the existence of these structures, archaeological remains of these booths have also been discovered. Hassan (1943: 85-6) found the remains of walls, rock-cut basins and drains when he excavated the area in front of the tombs of Nofer and Kai at Giza. These he later identified as embalming workshops.

The only labelling in the scene from the tomb of Mereruka associated with the *ibw* is that of 'requirements of the lector' *(dbḥw n ḥmt ḫry-ḥbt)*, possibly implying that all the objects depicted were for the use of the lector, although the inscription is immediately above the chests (fig. 21). In the tomb of Qar the label, *dbḥw n ḥmt ḫry-ḥbt,* again appears directly over the chests, but here the chests are portrayed as being in a separate section or room (fig. 22). Although the contents of these chests are not revealed it is possible that they may have been storage containers for papyrus rolls. One possible example of such a chest is described in the second part of this chapter (see pages 32 and 45).

Other than chests there are a variety of other articles arranged on top of these structures which may have been part of the working equipment of the lector. There are food offerings as well as jars and baskets, and these latter two items may have been associated with purification rituals. One particular group of objects shown in the scene from the tomb of Mereruka are representations of what appear to be *tyet* knots.

The origin of the *tyet* knot is uncertain but it is identifiable as a decorative symbol by at least the 3rd Dynasty, often appearing with both the *ankh* and the *djed* signs. It may originally have been a variant of the *ankh* sign, to which it bears a close resemblance, and the sign is often translated as 'life' or 'welfare' (Gardiner 1957: 508; Wilkinson 1992: 201; Shaw & Nicholson 1997: 298).

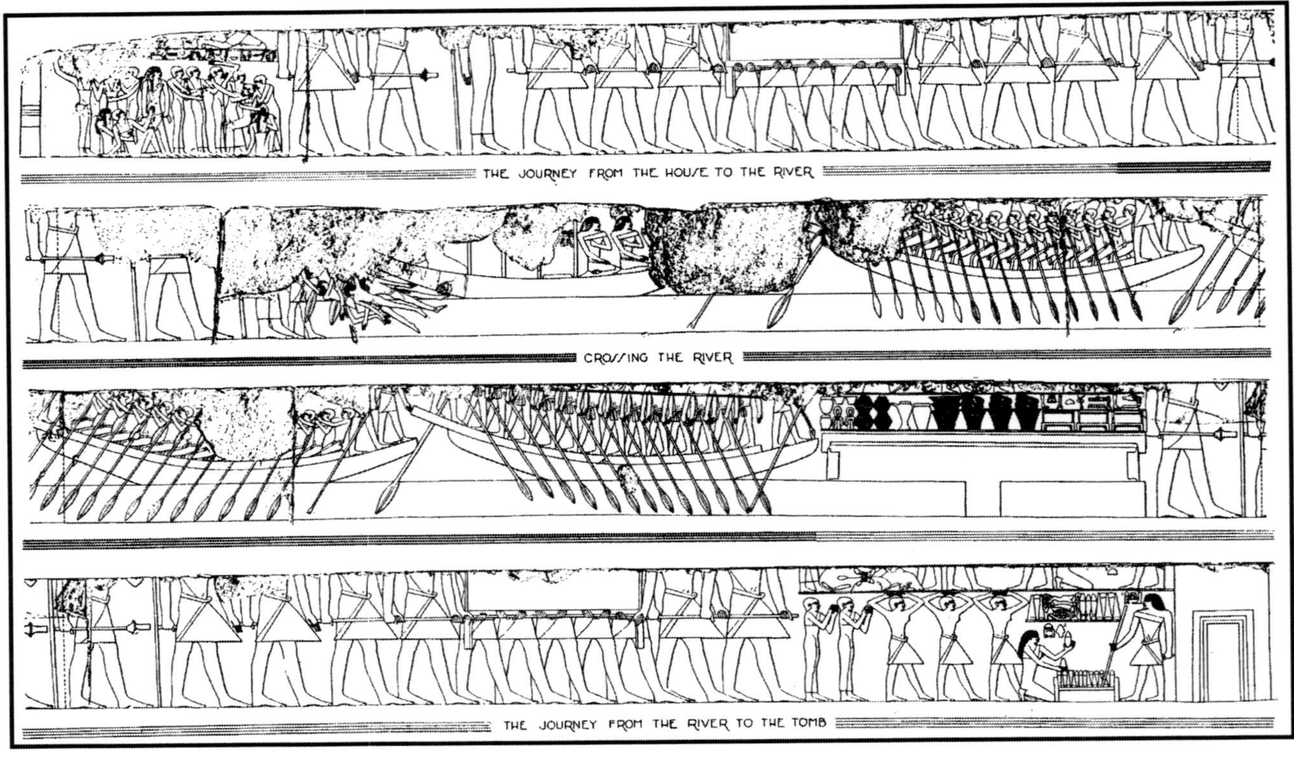

Fig. 20: Funerary procession from the 6th Dynasty Mastaba of Mereruka (Wilson 1944: pl. 15)

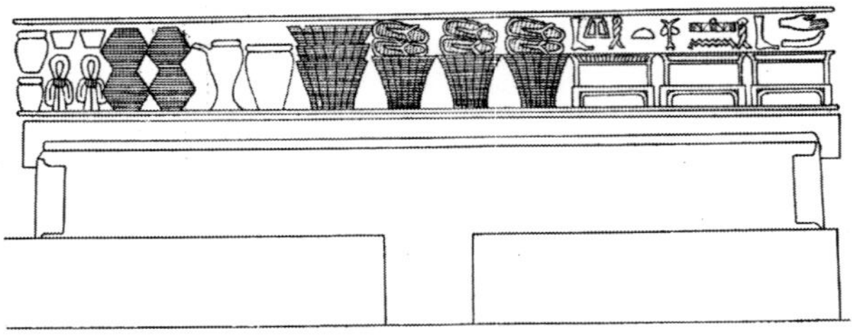

Fig. 21: Detail from fig. 20 above showing equipment and goods stacked on the 'landing stage'

The form of the *tyet* knot is suggestive of a girdle, perhaps an indication of its role in being that of encirclement and protection. The sign is associated with the Goddess Isis, and spell 156 of the later *Book of Going Forth by Day* implies a spell for a knot-amulet made from red jasper:

> 'You have your blood, O Isis; you have your power, O Isis; you have your magic, O Isis. The amulet is a protection for the great One which will drive away whoever would commit a crime against him' (translated Faulkner 1985: 155).

The knot, therefore, is important as a funerary amulet intended to assist the deceased to pass through the perils of the underworld and reach the afterlife. Although the *Book of the Dead* is dated to the New Kingdom, many amuletic types have been identified by the end of the Old Kingdom (Andrews 2001: 81). The depiction of the amulet among the objects on top of the *ibw* could refer, therefore, to its usage as a protective device intended to be placed within the wrappings of the mummy, although its use for this purpose, as mentioned above, is not recorded before the New Kingdom. Possibly the *tyet* knot was used as a ritual device, either placed on the mummy or held by the lector when reciting an incantation.

Fig. 22: Funeral scene from the tomb of Qar (G 7101) (Grdseloff 1941: fig. 2)

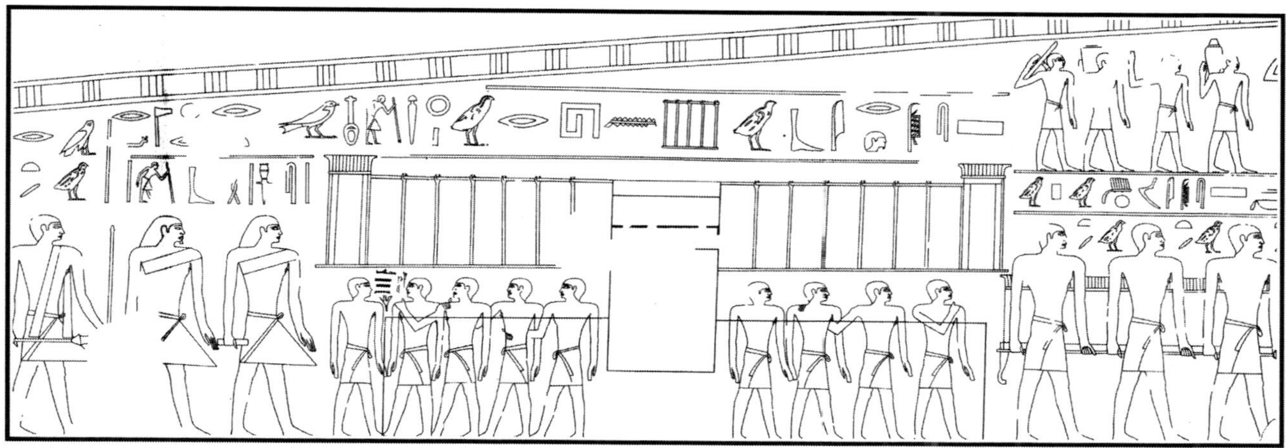

Fig. 23 Funeral scene from the tomb of Pepyankh Heny-Kem (Blackman & Apted 1953: V, pl. 43)

Another indication of the equipment that a lector may have used is identifiable in the 6th Dynasty tomb of Sneferu-Inshetef at Dahshur (Mastaba 2). Here in the upper register of one of the funerary scenes is a boat which is being towed across water, and in the centre of which is a covered booth probably containing the statue of the deceased. In the front of the boat sits a woman who is described as the 'kite', and sitting behind her are two undesignated men with their left arms in the *hnw* gesture. Before the statue booth is a seated lector and in front of him is a container which could perhaps hold his equipment (de Morgan 1903: 4-7, pl. 22; Wilson 1944: 207; fig. 25).

There is perhaps a comparable scene on a relief in the 5th Dynasty mastaba of Hetepherakhti at Saqqara, a relief which is now in the Rijksmuseum van Oudheden, Leiden. In the middle register of this relief a similar style of boat is being towed, again with a seated lector and again with a container of equipment. Due to the damage to this particular relief it is difficult to determine with accuracy all the details of the particular scene.

Both these containers appear cylindrical and if drawn to scale would suggest a height of approximately one metre. It is difficult to speculate from what the receptacle is constructed, but its rigid form may imply pottery, wood or basketry. Possibly the receptacle is a storage container for papyrus scrolls or alternatively, the shaped top to the container could represent a spout suggesting a pottery receptacle, perhaps laden with some form of liquid to be used for ritual purposes. There is an apparent 'tie closure' at the top which could possibly suggest linen. The container resembles the hieroglyphic sign *ʿpr* 'equip' in Gardiner's sign list (Gardiner 1957: 542, Aa 20). This term could therefore also relate to equipment.

Fig. 24: Funeral scene from tomb of Idu (G 7102) (Grdseloff 1941: fig. 3)

Fig. 25: The funeral procession of Sneferu-Inshetef from his 6th Dynasty tomb at Dashur (Wilson 1944: pl. 14)

2. The Burial Assemblage of Tomb No. 5 at the Ramesseum

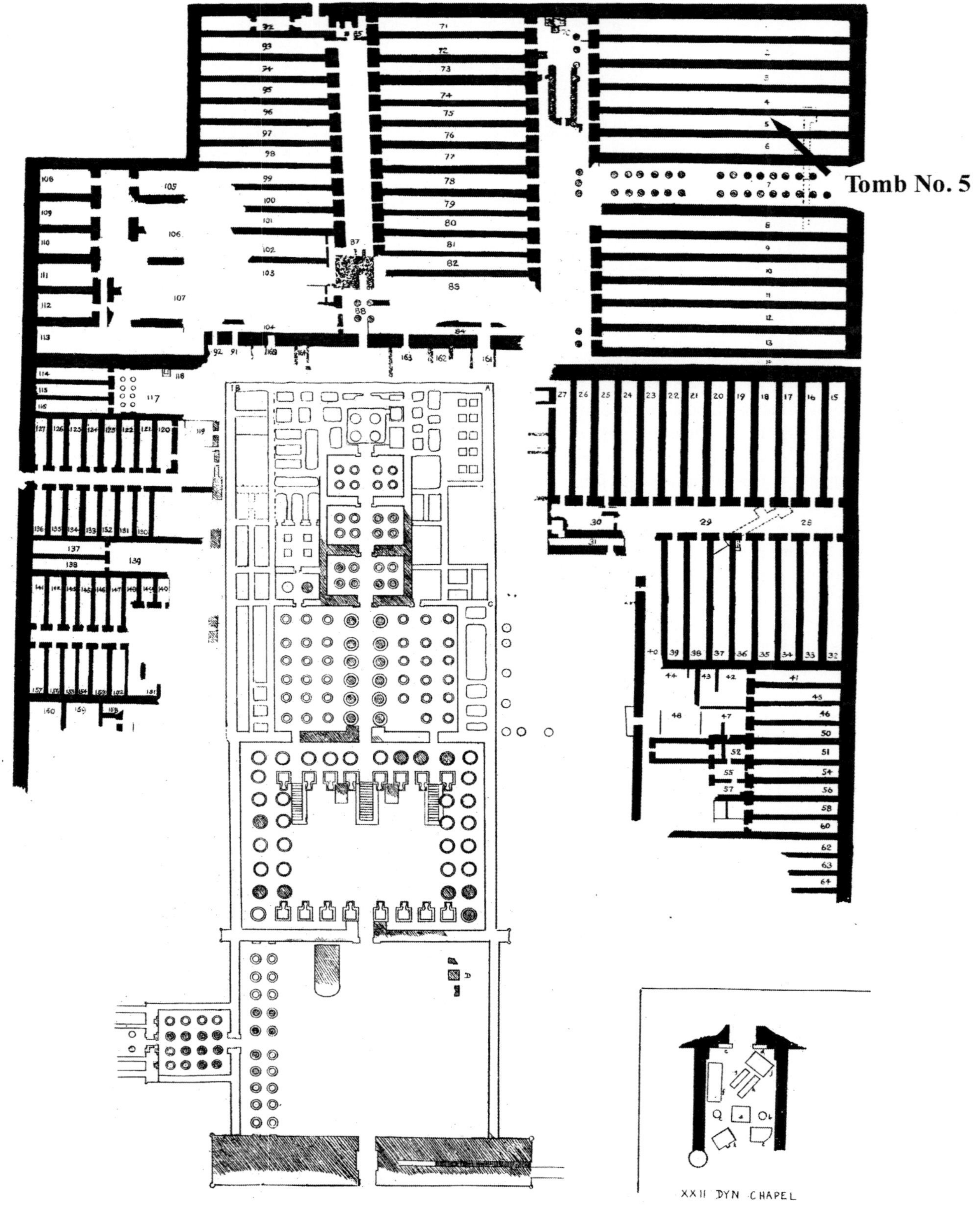

Fig. 26: Plan of the Ramesseum
(Quibell 1898: pl. 2)

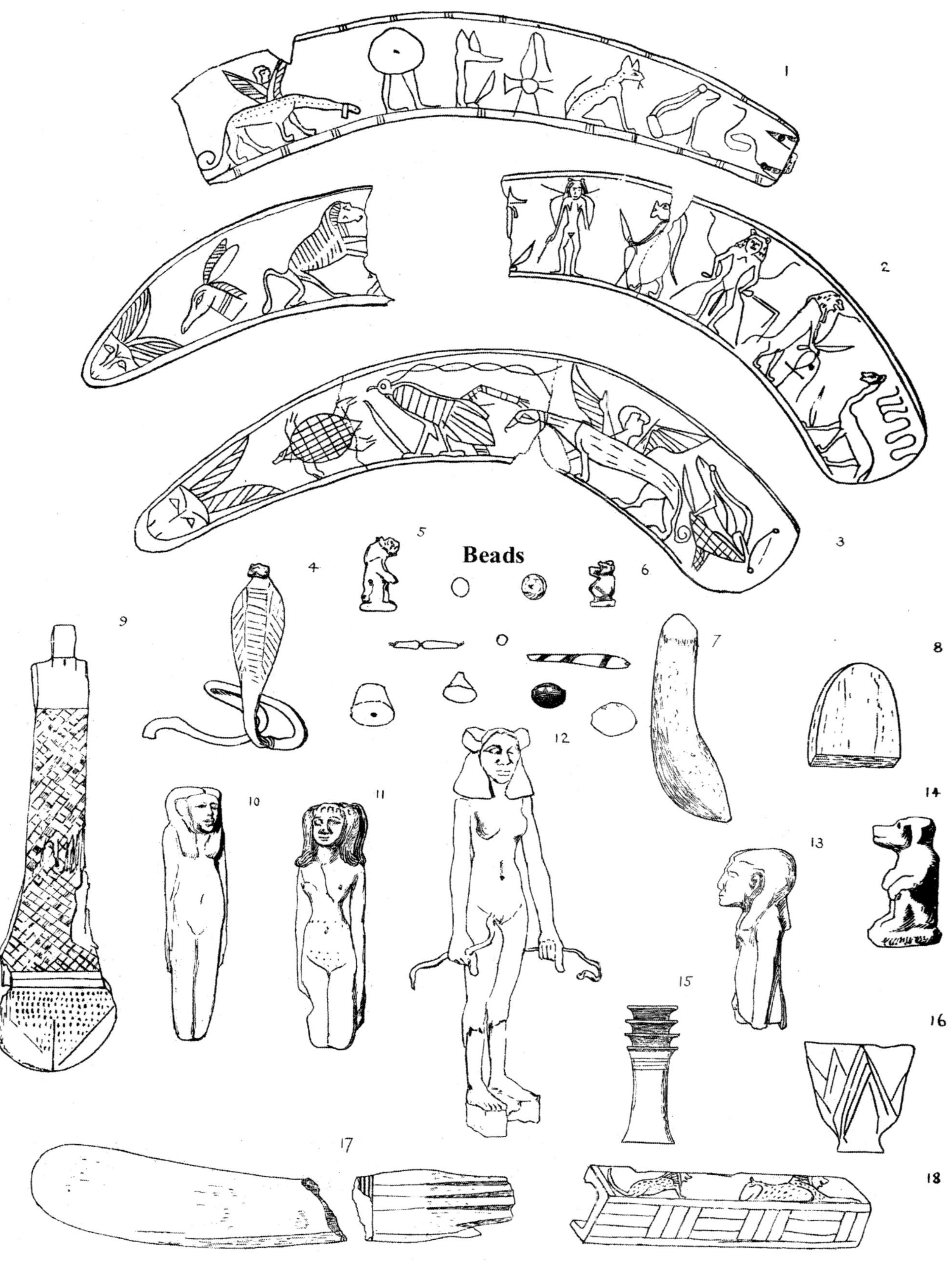

Fig. 27: Objects found in Tomb No. 5
(Quibell 1898: pl. 3)

Introduction

This next section examines a group of artefacts considered by a number of investigators to have been the ritual equipment of a magician or healer from ancient Egypt, with some of these researchers speculating that a lector could have been the owner of this apparatus (Ritner 1993: 222; Forman & Quirke 1996: 107; Pinch 2006: 131; Parkinson 2009: 157). The collection was found in Tomb 5, a Middle Kingdom shaft tomb discovered underneath the Ramesseum, the mortuary temple of Ramesses II. This is a rare assemblage, as few such groupings have been discovered in context, and which not only includes a wide range of different objects but also a sizeable number of papyri with varying textual content.

The collection was unearthed by Flinders Petrie and James Quibell in 1895-6, when they were excavating the store rooms in the northeast corner of the Ramesseum, and their findings were later published by Quibell (1898: 3-4) in *The Ramesseum*. This excavation report describes how Petrie and Quibell discovered a number of Middle Kingdom shaft-tombs under the Ramesseum's store rooms, one of which, Tomb 5, was found to contain the artefacts. Brief details of the excavation are included in the report, but the exact location of the tomb is not specified and the inventory of the collection is incomplete.

This tomb was described as a 'long oblong shaft, skew to the wall of one of the chambers and running underneath it' (fig. 26). Scattered in the shaft were discovered a few 22nd Dynasty artefacts such as shabtis, a wooden head and some wax figures. However, when the chambers at the bottom of the shaft had been cleared, there was found to be a 60 cm square space containing another group of objects (Quibell 1898: 1-3; fig. 27).

This second group of artefacts consisted of a white plastered wooden box surrounded by a mass of uninscribed burial goods. The box measuring 45 cm x 30 cm x 30 cm was one-third full of poorly preserved papyri, now known as the Ramesseum Papyri. The box also contained a bundle of 118 seemingly unused reed pens.

On the lid of the box roughly drawn in black ink was the figure of a jackal, but no photograph of the box has been published and the lid and box are now unlocated (Leach 2006: 225). Parkinson (2009: 141) suggests that despite their close proximity to each other it is not certain that all of these objects from the assemblage were from the same burial, although he considers this more than likely.

Quibell proposes that the sequence of events was that this Middle Kingdom tomb was disturbed and robbed by the later builders of the Ramesseum who probably removed some of the more valuable grave goods but discarded this collection. Kemp and Merrillees (1980: 166) concur with this suggestion that the objects may be the material left by tomb robbers. Later when the Ramesseum fell into disrepair, the ready-made shaft tomb was reused during the 22nd Dynasty. Later still these 22nd Dynasty burials were disturbed and robbed, but the debris at the bottom of the tomb was never cleared away to reveal this discarded Middle Kingdom assemblage.

Appendix 1 is a list of the grave goods from Tomb No. 5, including their present location where known. Many of these objects are now located in the Manchester Museum and have been variously listed and described by Quibell (1898: 3); Kemp and Merrillees (1980: 166); Bourriau (1988: 110-11); Ritner (1993: 220-33); Forman & Quirke (1996: 106-7); Quack (2006: 72-89); Lorand (2009: 13-22); Parkinson (2009: 142-4 and 2012 [BM online research catalogue]). This present discussion on the objects groups them into a number of categories as listed below and uses the present museum accession number as well as Quibell's original notation in pl. 3 (fig. 27).

Objects

Apotropaic Animal Statuettes/Amulets

Squatting baboon (Manchester 1835, Quibell 14); small squatting baboon (Manchester 1837, Quibell 6); upright lion (Manchester 1839, Quibell 5). (Location: The Manchester Museum).

These three bluish green faience animal statuettes are squatting or standing upright; they have disproportionately large heads, and are similar in appearance to those seen inscribed on apotropaic wands and rods such as E.426.1982 in the Fitzwilliam Museum, Cambridge, and EA 22892 at the British Museum, London (Bourriau 1988: pl. 104a, b; Pinch 2006: pl. 39; figs. 28, 29, 30). Bourriau (1988: 116) considers that they are three-dimensional versions of the protective demons which appear on these objects, and their additional presence may have been necessary for the enactment of a successful ritual.

Fig. 28: Squatting baboon Manchester 1835, Quibell 14 (Courtesy of The Manchester Museum, University of Manchester)

Fig. 29: Small squatting baboon
Manchester 1837, Quibell 6 (Courtesy of The Manchester Museum, University of Manchester)

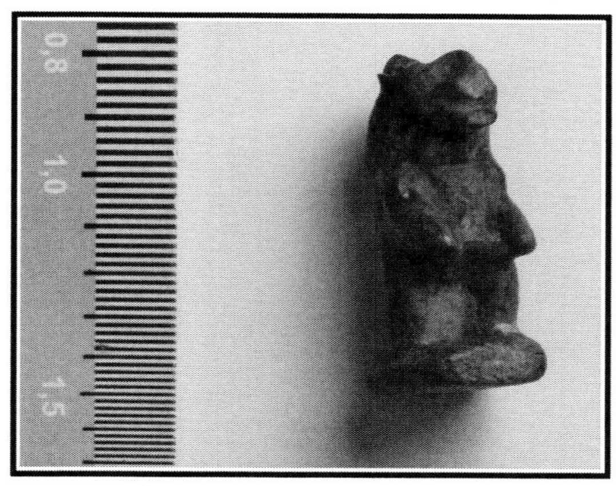

Fig. 30: Lion
Manchester 1839, Quibell 5 (Courtesy of The Manchester Museum, University of Manchester)

Although faience model animals were a feature of Middle Kingdom burials, their function may not have been solely funerary. Lion figures feature in spells for the living and are also found inscribed on apotropaic wands as protective creatures (Altenmüller 1979: 11; Bourriau 1988: 116-7; Parkinson 2009: 144). Similarly, baboon figures are protective and again found on wands, an example of this being the god Thoth, as a baboon, found in a basket of scribal equipment in Tomb 37 of the Birabi (the area adjacent to Deir el-Bahri, on the west bank at Luxor) (Carnarvon & Carter 1912: 78).

Apotropaic Wands

Fragments of ivory wands engraved with protective demons: A) a fragment (Manchester 1798, Quibell 2a); B) two fragments (Manchester 1799, Quibell 2b); C) one wand in two pieces (Manchester 1800, Quibell 3); D) two fragments (Manchester 1801, Quibell 1). (Location: The Manchester Museum).

Various terms are used to describe these objects ranging from magic knives, magic wands, apotropaic wands, and birthing tusks (figs. 31, 32, 33, 34). In this publication apotropaic wand is the term that will be employed. These wands are fashioned from hippopotamus ivory and engraved upon them are a range of creatures which include lions, cats, turtles, frogs, crocodiles and snakes. In addition symbols, hieroglyphs and an array of 'composite' animals are inscribed on the artefacts. The composite animals can be defined as creatures not found in nature, but products of human imagination (Altenmüller 1979: 7-12; 1983: 30-45; 1986: 1-27; Steindorff 1946: 41-51, 106-7).

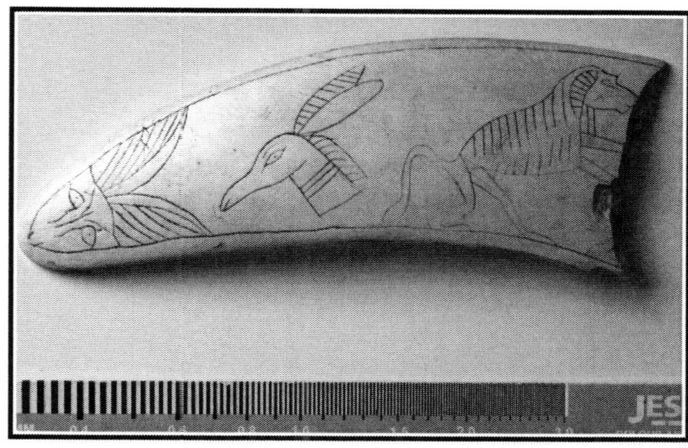

Fig. 31: Fragment of an apotropaic wand
Manchester 1798, Quibell 2 (Courtesy of The Manchester Museum, University of Manchester)

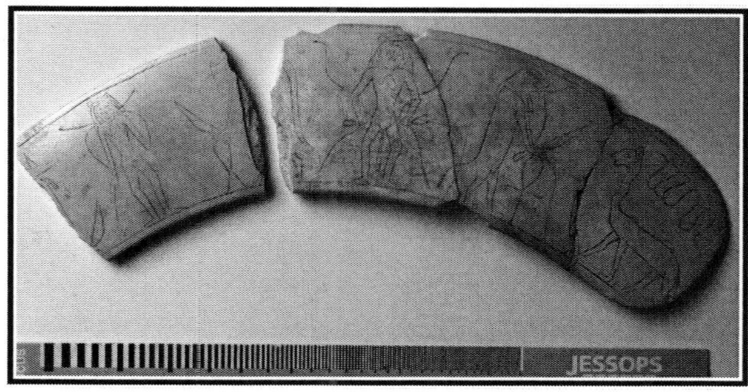

Fig. 32: Fragments of an apotropaic wand
Manchester 1799; Quibell 2 (Courtesy of The Manchester Museum, University of Manchester)

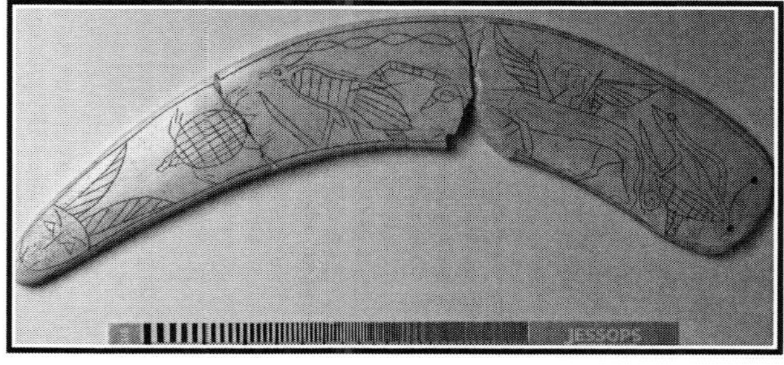

Fig. 33: Apotropaic wand
Manchester 1800, Quibell 3 (Courtesy of The Manchester Museum, University of Manchester)

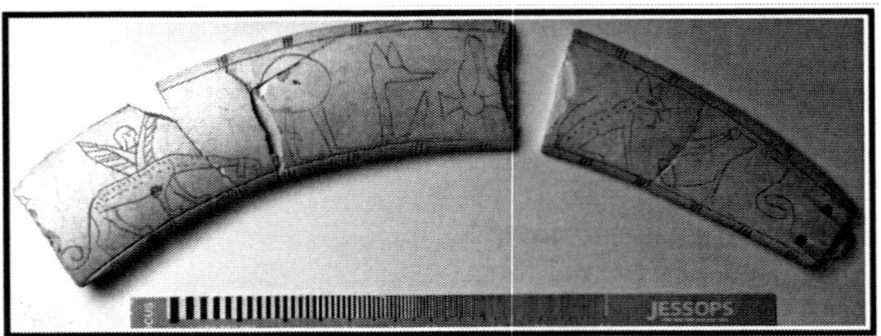

FIG. 34: APOTROPAIC WAND
MANCHESTER 1801, QUIBELL 1 (COURTESY OF THE MANCHESTER MUSEUM, UNIVERSITY OF MANCHESTER)

Generally, the parts of the animal bodies are borrowed from different species and joined together to represent demons or gods. These animals were thought to live in the wild and inhabit the desert regions and marshes surrounding the Nile (Meeks 2001: 504). The range of animals represented on the wands and rods are limited in number, but they are repeated frequently and are thought to represent powers that can be controlled by the manipulation of an image that represents them (Bourriau 1988: 111). Inscriptions on the wands describe them as gods, fighters, or protectors, and they are often shown brandishing knives or torches and are sometimes portrayed attacking snakes and other dangerous animals (Pinch 2006: 42).

The purpose of the apotropaic wands seems to have been to confer protection by warding off evil forces, and they often appear to have been directed at the most vulnerable in society such as children as well as pregnant and nursing women (Bourriau 1988: 114). It has been suggested that they may also have been laid on the stomachs of pregnant women in order to protect the unborn child (Pinch 2006: 130).

Many of the wands show evidence of wear which is considered to have been caused by the action of drawing out a defensive perimeter or magical circle around the bed of a mother or a child. They are attested in the hands of wet nurses and women entrusted with the rearing of children (Ritner 2001a: 328). An apotropaic wand in the Metropolitan Museum, New York (MMA 26.7.1288a, b) illustrates this protective nature as it is inscribed on its reverse with:

> 'Words spoken by the multitude of amuletic figures: We have come to protect the lady Meriseneb' (www.metmuseum.org).

Similarly, another wand (MMA 22.1.154a, b) is inscribed with the words 'Protecting the night, protecting the day' (www.metmuseum.org; Lorand 2009: 14).

As many of the wands have been discovered in tombs, they may have been placed there to protect the recently deceased person before he or she was reborn into the afterlife (Taylor 2001: 209). Further evidence to support this is provided in the tomb of Bebi, where women are shown holding both apotropaic and serpent wands behind epresentations of the seated tomb owners and their family (Ritner 2006: 212).

The Ramesseum wands themselves are not inscribed but wand 1800 shows evidence of scratch marks. Wands 1799-1801 have also been repaired following wear and then cut down and reshaped, indicating their use during life. Many other examples of apotropaic wands similarly show signs of wear and damage, particularly in the mid-section where they were gripped, and again a number have been repaired in ancient times (Taylor 2001: 209; Pinch 2006: 78; Parkinson 2009: 145)

Wooden Figurine

Wooden figurine of a naked woman with a mask or the face of a lion, holding two bronze serpents (Manchester 1790, Quibell 12). (Location: The Manchester Museum).

FIG. 35: WOODEN FIGURINE
MANCHESTER 1790, QUIBELL 12 (COURTESY OF THE MANCHESTER MUSEUM, UNIVERSITY OF MANCHESTER)

The nude wooden female figurine measures 20 cm in height and displays some remaining traces of yellow and black paint (fig. 35). The figurine holds a bronze serpent in each hand, and is similar to a figure holding serpents which is portrayed on one of the magic wands in the collection

(Manchester 1799, Quibell 2b). Pieces of wood under her feet suggest that she was intended to stand on a plinth.

The statuette is either wearing a lion mask (Bosse-Griffiths 1977: 103; Bourriau 1988: 110; Pinch 2006: 131) or has the face of a lion (Forman & Quirke 1996: 106). Parkinson (2009: 144) considers that the figure either represents a female Aha or Bes, a goddess often depicted as protecting women and children, or someone acting as this goddess. Pinch (2006: 56) considers that the figurine may denote a *s3w* a 'female magician' who is acting as a divine helper. She defines a *s3w* as someone who might have practised magic but primarily a person who made protective charms and utilised spoken and written magic. However, Ritner (1993: 223) considers that the figurine represents a goddess and not a female impersonator. He suggests that such a statue would be used as an intermediary for divine power, whilst a masked statuette would be unnecessarily redundant in masking an image of a deity. Lorand (2009: 18) concurs with this and comments that the appearance of the figurine is also suggestive of a leonine head and not a mask, and resembles the demon lions shown on apotropaic wands.

However, Petrie excavated a 12th Dynasty painted cartonnage mask with leonine features from a private house in the southernmost row of housing at Lahun (Rank A), which established that such masks did exist, although this appears to be a rather unique find (Petrie 1890: 30). Quirke (2005: 82) interprets this particular object as suggestive of deities that protected mother and child, and considers that the leonine face could belong to either a male or a female. Ancient repairs to the mask suggested that it had been frequently used.

David (1996: 137) notes that the Lahun mask was part of a group of objects comprising a wooden figurine representing a dancer wearing a mask and a pair of ivory clappers, a similar connection with the Ramesseum assemblage. She suggests that the group could have belonged to a dancer who wore the mask during the enactment of a ritual. Support for this suggestion is provided by Pinch's interpretation (2006: 131) of the objects from Tomb 5. She suggests that they could have been owned by a lector who worked with female assistants wearing masks who would then have borne a resemblance to the lion-masked statuette.

Quirke (2005: 83) tentatively suggests that the owner of the objects living in the house could have been a professional healer. He notes that the house was located close to the valley temple of the pyramid of Senwosret II, and so this might suggest the healer's involvement in ritual including the ritual of birth, particularly as the finds were birth-related. However, he cautions that many wealthy houses could have possessed such objects for their own protection, providing the example of Middle Kingdom apotropaic wands inscribed with the name and title of a woman or a male child, and so a connection to a healer is not certain (Quirke 2005: 84).

Bourriau (1988: 110) offers an explanation for the presence of lions in the Ramesseum assemblage which are symbolised in the lion-headed figurine; they are inscribed on the apotropaic wands, and represented as animal statuettes. She suggests that as the lion was the most powerful of the animals known to the ancient Egyptians, this was the chief character most frequently depicted battling against evil forces. She further discusses how the power of lions and indeed of the other beasts that are represented, is able to be controlled by the manipulation of their images in magical rituals, and this power could then be used for protection.

Serpent Wand

A worn and broken bronze serpent wand entangled with hair, Cambridge (E.63.1896, Quibell 4). (Location: Fitzwilliam Museum, Cambridge).

One of the most distinctive items in the collection is the bronze cobra wand which has a rearing head and a body twisted in a series of coils (fig. 36). The wand measures 16 cm in length, approximately 7 cm in height and is 0.5 cm in diameter. The piece is flattened in the middle, perhaps where it was grasped and is broken at this point. There are incised line markings on the head. The wand is thought to represent the goddess Weret Hekau, 'great of magic', who is usually shown in cobra form, but this name was originally an epithet applied to several goddesses (Wilkinson 2003: 228; Lorand 2009: 20). She later became identified as one of the goddesses acting as foster mother to the kings of Egypt. The king included the cobra among his titles and insignia, and the serpent seen on the brow of the king was believed to spit fire and represents the serpent's power immanent in the king (Pinch 2006: 11).

FIG. 36: SERPENT WAND
FITZWILLIAM E.63.1896, QUIBELL 4 (COURTESY OF FITZWILLIAM MUSEUM, CAMBRIDGE)

As a protective image the cobra or uraeus is highly significant in ancient Egypt with many attested examples. A pair of cobras guarded the gates that divided the individual hours of the underworld in the *Book of Gates*

(Shaw & Nicholson 1997: 67; Hornung 1999: 55-75). Four uraei guarded the cardinal points in temple rituals at Edfu on behalf of the king, and in the ritual of the 'House of Life' on behalf of Osiris (Derchain 1965: 84, 142; Ritner 1993: 224).

Bourriau (1988: 113) considers that the wand would have been part of the equipment of a healer or magician that was used when reciting magic spells. Ritner (2006: 206) notices the importance of the cobra in the burial assemblage as a whole, with representations of figures wielding snakes on the apotropaic wands, the naked wooden figurine grasping the cobras and the bronze wand itself. Forman and Quirke (1996: 106) suggest that the Ramesseum burial was being defended by the serpent wand and the serpent-wielding figurine. Thus the objects may well have been used by the occupant during life, but now have an important function in protecting the body of the deceased.

A link between the serpent wand and Egyptian magicians is provided in the Hebrew Bible with the description of Moses at the court of Pharaoh in Exodus (7, 8-12) which describes how the staff of Aaron was turned into a snake, and how this was quickly followed by the staffs of the Egyptian magicians (Forman & Quirke 1996: 106; Ritner 2006: 205).

A lock of hair was found entwined in the wand and this has been suggested as evidence of a technique used in sympathetic magic in which the use of part of an object or person is considered to represent the whole, and the presence therefore of this personal effect would strengthen the magic (Ritner 1993: 225). A further example of this practice is the 'Rite of the four balls' (Goyon 1979: 61-5, pl. 25) and locks of hair have been found in such balls (Crompton 1916: 128, pl.16).

This wand is one of only a few similar objects known from ancient Egypt and is thought to be the earliest datable bronze serpent wand yet discovered (Ritner 2006: 207). Among other examples are two bronze serpent wands housed in the Museum of Fine Arts, Boston (2002.31-32). These are both dated to the 13th Dynasty and are some 57 cm in length with each wand displaying two flaring cobra heads (Ritner 2006: 207-8, pl. 1). A wand with an extended hood and a long body measuring 164 cm in length is located in the British Museum (EA 52831; Taylor 2010: 40, pl. 8). It was discovered inside an early 18th Dynasty anthropoid coffin of a certain Mentuhotep and found under the shroud that covered the mummy. The inscriptions on the coffin do not give the occupation of Mentuhotep, but the presence of the wand with the mummy could possibly suggest that he was also a magician (Reeves & Taylor 1992: 97).

However, ritual instruments were often reused for mortuary purposes and buried in tombs not necessarily associated with the user of the object. The Louvre has three further serpent staffs, but two of these (E.4851 and N4190) have pegs for attachment and are thought likely to be design elements or ornaments attached to a barque or shrine. The third staff which measures 70 cm in length is dated to the Late Period, and may be the only genuine serpent staff of the three (Ritner 2006: 209). A number of wooden serpent staffs are also known, such as 21.11941 excavated from Deir el-Bersha and dated to the 12th Dynasty, and 72.4816 which is of unknown provenance. Both of these wooden staffs are now located in the Museum of Fine Arts, Boston (Ritner 2006: 210-11).

The serpent wands identified are therefore few in number, and their individual material, lengths, shapes, workmanship and dates vary considerably (Ritner 2006: 212). However, the Ramesseum example is by far the shortest in length and it appears to be designed to rest on a flat surface rather than being held in a hand (Kargacin 2010: 20). Perhaps the mere presence of the wand may have had a ritual function rather than being used in hand gesturing. Also, as mentioned previously, the 'Aha/Bes' naked figurine holds a serpent in each hand.

There are, in addition, very many depictions of serpents on objects: such as apotropaic wands (e.g. BM EA 18175 [Quirke 1992: fig. 64] and Manchester 1799); Horus cippi such as the Metternich stela in the Metropolitan Museum of Art (50.85; Allen: 2005: 49-62); scenes in the 18th Dynasty tomb of Bebi, a governor at el- Kab (*PM* 1^2: 184); as well as associated with images of Heka, the deity of 'magic' (Ritner 2006: 212). In the tomb of Bebi there are two individual scenes which show the seated tomb owner, Bebi, with his wife Sobeknakht in the company of their daughters. Behind each child stands a smaller female figure holding both a raised apotropaic wand and a serpent wand. The titles of the women holding these particular implements are given as wet nurses and housekeepers, although Gardiner (1917: 32) and Ritner (2006: 212) consider that the females could be considered as 'magicians of the nursery' (*ḥk3yw n k3p*). Altenmüller (1986: 36) suggests that in this scene Bebi, as well as the children, would participate in the protection. These scenes are significant in understanding the protective function of both magic wands and serpent staffs.

Amongst the papyri found in the Ramesseum cache are two that make reference to protection from snakes. P. Ram. 9 (EA 10762) describes rituals to protect a house from magic, ghosts and serpents, whilst P. Ram. 10 (EA 10763) includes a spell for the protection of the limbs against any male and female serpent (Gardiner 1955a: 12-13; Parkinson 2009: 152). It is possible that the serpent wand could well have been used during these particular rituals.

Female Fertility Figurines

Female fertility figurines: blue faience (Manchester 1787, Quibell 11); limestone (Manchester 1788, not illustrated by Quibell); limestone (Manchester 1789, Quibell 10); limestone (Manchester 1794, Quibell 13); a flat wooden figure (Manchester 1832, Quibell 9). (Location: The Manchester Museum).

These objects belong to the general category of fertility figurines and are best represented from the Middle Kingdom onwards. They are made out of stone, pottery, faience or wood, and as shown in figures 37, 38, 39, and 40 are usually depicted naked, often with elaborate hairstyles such as tripartite or Hathor styles (Bourriau 1988: 125; Waraksa 2008: 1-6). Although naked they are often shown with painted jewellery, amuletic tattoos and scarification or body paintings (Pinch 2006: 126). An example showing this style of decoration is Manchester 1787 which has a dotted line above the navel, possibly representing a tattoo or a stylised cowrie shell belt (fig. 38). The breasts and pubic triangle areas are emphasised, the figures are rounded off at their knees and the arms are at their sides, again the standard representation of this type of object. None of the figures carry inscriptions, again a common practice.

FIG. 38: FEMALE FERTILITY FIGURINE MANCHESTER 1787, QUIBELL 11(COURTESY OF THE MANCHESTER MUSEUM, UNIVERSITY OF MANCHESTER)

FIG. 37: FEMALE FERTILITY FIGURINE MANCHESTER 1789, QUIBELL 10 (COURTESY OF THE MANCHESTER MUSEUM, UNIVERSITY OF MANCHESTER)

The absence of lower limbs and feet in these objects has been reconciled with the practice of mutilation of hieroglyphs in that these figures could be animated by magic and so their power to leave the tomb had therefore to be curtailed. Alternatively, another suggestion is that it was thought important to include only the parts of the body needed for the conception and rearing of children (Bourriau 1988: 125; Pinch 2006: 126; Lorand 2009: 17).

Some of the female figurines that have been excavated are broken and the pattern of breakage is that of a clean horizontal break through the torso-hip region. Such breakage is indicative of deliberate destruction suggesting their function as part of a ritual procedure (Kemp & Merrillees 1980: 30; Waraksa 2008: 2). Figures 1788 and 1794 are both fractured and could therefore have been involved in such a ritual.

FIG. 39: FEMALE FERTILITY FIGURINE MANCHESTER 1794, QUIBELL 13 (COURTESY OF THE MANCHESTER MUSEUM, UNIVERSITY OF MANCHESTER)

Fig. 40: Female fertility figurine Manchester 1788 (Courtesy of The Manchester Museum, University of Manchester)

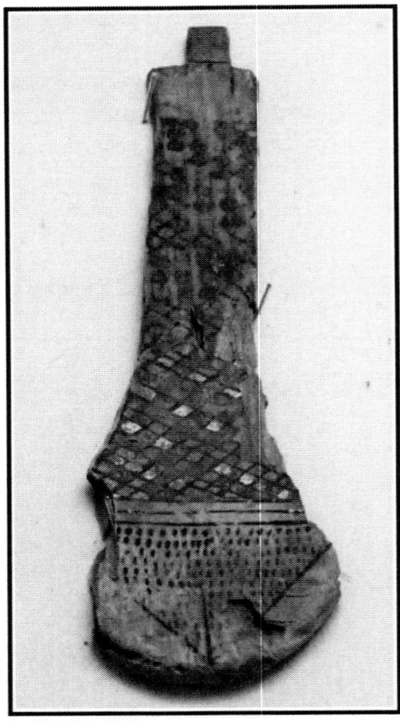

Fig. 41: Flat wooden preformal figure Manchester 1832, Quibell 9 (Courtesy of The Manchester Museum, University of Manchester)

The flat wooden painted figure (Manchester 1832) relates to a group of objects once known as 'paddle dolls', again a type of fertility figurine (fig. 41). The figure has an elongated body flaring down to the pubic region, the head is not represented and the limbs are not present. Probably at one time it would have displayed a crudely modelled face, and many of the surviving examples include elaborate hairstyles often fabricated from faience beads (e.g. Metropolitan Museum of Art, Rogers Fund 1931 (31.3.35), Hayes 1953: fig. 135; BM EA 6459, Strudwick 2006: 74-5). A double horizontal line, possibly a belt, separates a dress decorated with geometric figures and the emphasis is given to graphically portraying the pubic area (Lorand 2009: 16).

All the paddle dolls that survive are dissimilar from one another and Quirke (1992: 124) considers that they were representations of female fertility, and when placed in a grave would be a guarantee of eternal rebirth. The extreme emphasis on the pubic area is clearly to stress the female fertility.

Earlier theories tended to suggest that the function of female figurines was that of concubine figures placed in the tombs of males for the pleasure of the deceased in the afterlife, and indeed they were often called dolls or dancing girls (Hayes 1953: 219). However, research has since determined that they were not only located in male but were also found in female and child burials. Additionally, they were found in the full range of excavated sites in Egypt including houses, temples, mining sites and Nubian forts, thus indicating their use for both the living and the dead (Taylor 2001: 209; Waraksa 2008: 2; Parkinson 2009: 143-4).

Bourriau (1988: 125) suggests that their funerary function was, along with the use of other magical items, that of protecting the recent dead against the dangers of the transition between death and rebirth. She develops this argument by further suggesting that these figurines would then help the newly reborn to recover their sexual potency and their fertility. Pinch (1993: 199) considers that their function was one of reinforcing or symbolising the general concepts of fertility, sexuality and conception as well as the bearing and rearing of children. She indicates that such figures were dedicated in temples to Hathor, and therefore by placing them in the vicinity of a deity this would result in them being charged with power to act as fertility amulets (Pinch 2006: 126). They can, perhaps, be seen as ritual objects used in a range of magico-medical procedures, and so it is possible that they formed part of the working implements of a healer.

Ivory Dwarf

Ivory statuette of a naked dwarf carrying a calf. 5 cm (Location: University of Pennsylvania Museum of Archaeology and Anthropology, E13405).

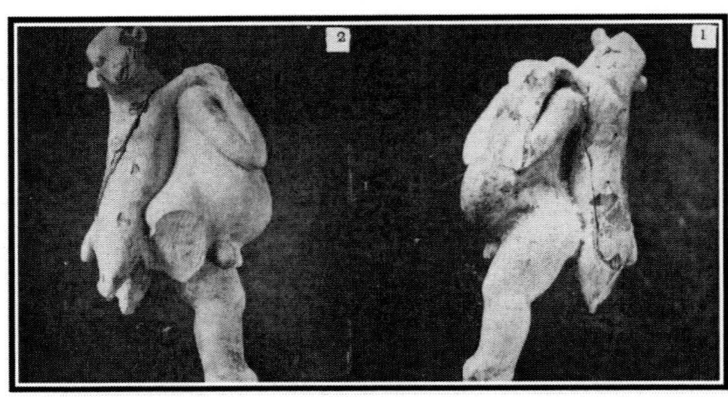

Fig. 42: Statuette of a naked dwarf (Quibell 1898: pl. 2, 1)

The ivory dwarf statuette was found associated with the assemblage and although Quibell (1898: 3) believes it to be part of the same deposit he did comment that it resembled a later Roman object (fig. 42). Bourriau (1988: 110) also considers it to be of a later date, suggesting it originated from a later intrusive burial.

The statuette, possibly representing a herdsman, is represented naked with arms bent on his chest and holding the front limbs of a calf over his shoulders. The head and right leg of the dwarf, as well as the tail of the calf, are missing. The significance of this broken ivory figurine has yet to be established with certainty. Dasen (1993: 138) notes that few comparable Middle Kingdom examples of this type of statuette exist but suggests that the calf could represent the new-born Re, with the implication that the role of the dwarf is as a defender of the sun-god and consequently of new-born children assimilated to Re. Such a suggestion is supported by the various other medico-magical items in the assemblage which are present for the protection of childbirth.

Although this particular type of figure carrying a calf is comparatively rare, examples of dwarfs in other poses found in funerary contexts are not uncommon. Bourriau (1988: 122) cites examples found at Abydos and in the Faiyum (Fitzwilliam E.60.1984, Dasen 1993: 137, 284; University of Liverpool E.7081). Their function is usually seen as protective but they can also represent servants bringing offerings or even portray companions of the tomb owner (Dasen 1993: 135; Parkinson 2009: 144). Quirke (2005: 99) also notes that a small number of late Middle Kingdom burial assemblages contained dwarf figurines alongside animal figurines and vegetables. He further comments that there appears to be no fixed selection for these objects but their presence in the funerary context indicates the power they were believed to possess.

Ritner (1993: 225-30) sees similarities between the dwarf figure and fording scenes such as those depicted in the Old Kingdom tombs of Ankhmahor, Mereruka and Kagemeni at the Saqqara necropolis. These scenes show a herdsman carrying a calf into the water to induce the escorted cattle to follow, and they are often accompanied by the recitation of a 'water spell', intended to protect the cattle during the crossing.[1] He considers that the statuette was a substitute figure over which the incantation could be recited during crossing. Close examination of some of these scenes shows the presence of another figure, who could be a priest reciting the spell whilst the herdsman is performing a magical gesture. Because the statuette was made out of ivory this may have had some significance, in that the power of the hippopotamus was available in the statuette to be used by the performer.

[1] For rituals concerned with crossing a body of water see pages 85-7 of this publication.

Model Food and Vessels

White faience cucumber (Manchester 1792, Quibell 7); blue faience bunch of grapes or possibly part of a body of an animal (Manchester 1841, not listed by Quibell); a miniature bluish green faience lotus shaped cup (Manchester 1791, Quibell 16). (Location: The Manchester Museum).

Miniaturized replicas of food offerings depicted on offering tables and on pottery were part of the range of ritual objects that began to appear in burials during the Middle Kingdom, and as such can be considered as normal grave goods (Bourriau 1991: 10). They were magical substitutes for real offerings presented to the deceased, and the faience cucumber and bunch of grapes found in the burial would be appropriate to this category (fig. 43, 44). The bluish green faience lotus-shaped vase, with petals highlighted in black paint, is probably a miniature version of tableware and similarly such items tended to appear in the same context as model food offerings (fig. 45).

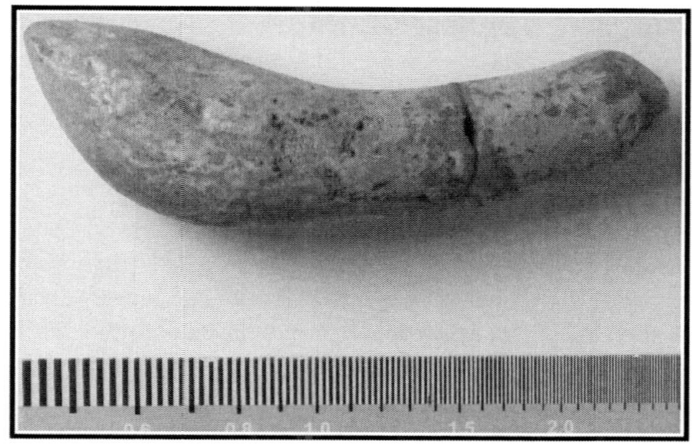

FIG. 43: WHITE FAIENCE CUCUMBER MANCHESTER 1792, QUIBELL 7 (COURTESY OF THE MANCHESTER MUSEUM, UNIVERSITY OF MANCHESTER)

FIG. 44: BUNCH OF GRAPES/BODY OF AN ANIMAL MANCHESTER 1841 (COURTESY OF THE MANCHESTER MUSEUM, UNIVERSITY OF MANCHESTER)

FIG. 45: MINIATURE BLUE FAIENCE LOTUS SHAPED CUP MANCHESTER 1791, QUIBELL 16 (COURTESY OF THE MANCHESTER MUSEUM, UNIVERSITY OF MANCHESTER)

Parkinson (2009: 143) suggests that the object resembling a bunch of grapes could alternatively be the body of a hedgehog, as there are examples of similar such figurines found in other Middle Kingdom burials (Fitzwilliam E.345.1954, Vassilika 1995: 40, fig. 140; BM E22873, Andrews 2000: 238-9). If the object is a hedgehog it could still be considered as a coherent part of the assemblage since the hedgehog has a magical protective significance, in that it has a defensive ability to roll into a ball and also has the capacity to resist venomous stings and bites (Houlihan 2001: 88).

Some doubts have been expressed that the object resembling a white cucumber is a cucumber at all. Although faience model cucumbers served as burial goods, Parkinson (2009: 143) suggests it could resemble a gourd. Other suggestions have been a squash or possibly a form of melon (Ikram 2001: 394). Alternatively Lorand (2009: 21) considers that in view of the fact that the items in the assemblage were predominately apotropaic and that many of the texts were magico-medical, then this item could possibly be a stylised phallus. Manniche (1987: 48) notes the existence of model phalloi and considers that in ancient Egypt their function was as votive gifts. However, as Pinch (1993: 235) points out, excavators have in the past tended to suppress or ignore phallic objects and many museums have been reticent about displaying such items and so it is difficult to discuss comparative material.

Ivory Clappers

Ivory clappers in the form of a hand, broken in two pieces (Manchester 1796. a-b, Quibell 17 and Manchester 1797. a-b not mentioned by Quibell). (Location: The Manchester Museum).

Clappers operate as a pair and they are similar to castanets in being capable of producing a rhythmic noise when they knock against each other. They are made from hippopotamus ivory and are regarded as ritual instruments used as an accompaniment to singing or chanting (Bourriau 1988: 112). These two curved clappers found in the assemblage are shaped like human hands, and are unmatched and so would originally have been from separate pairs (figs. 46, 47).

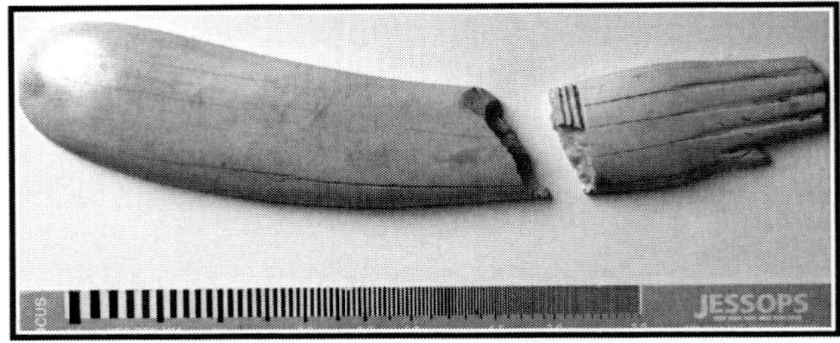

FIG. 46: IVORY CLAPPER
MANCHESTER 1796A, B, QUIBELL 17 (COURTESY OF THE MANCHESTER MUSEUM, UNIVERSITY OF MANCHESTER)

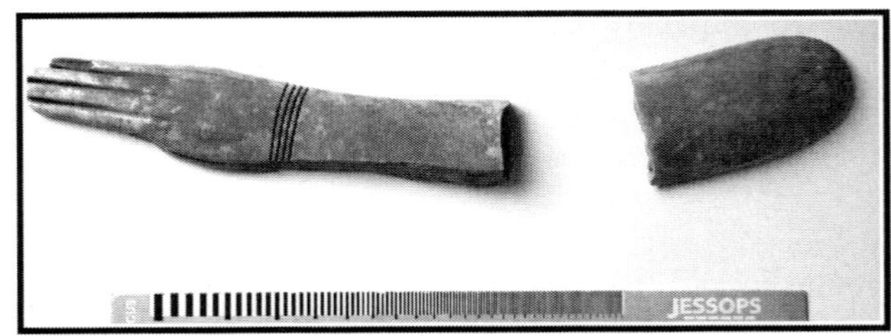

FIG. 47: IVORY CLAPPER
MANCHESTER 1797A, B (COURTESY OF THE MANCHESTER MUSEUM, UNIVERSITY OF MANCHESTER)

The noise of clappers similar to that of cymbals and rattles was thought to scare off hostile forces. Such instruments can often be seen in the hands of dancers as protective dances were often enacted in order to banish dangerous spirits (Pinch 2006: 85). Clappers are often associated with the goddess Hathor where the hand is combined with the head of Hathor (fig. 48). They have been linked with Hathor as she is associated with music and is recognised as a protectress of women, children and the dead (Bourriau 1988: 113). In a literary text, *The Contendings of Horus and Seth,* she displayed her feminine charms to banish the bad mood of the sun-god Re (Lichtheim 1976: 216). She was given the epithet 'Hand of Atum', which refers to the myth of Ra-Atum masturbating on the Primeval Mound and producing from himself the divine couple Shu and Tefnut (Pinch 2006: 24).

Unlike many other such instruments these clappers do not have a hole drilled in them, capable of inserting a binding to link them together (see Fitzwilliam E.151a-b.1939, Bourriau 1988: 113-14; BM EA 20799-80; fig. 48). Additionally, they do not show much evidence of wear, and are broken which corresponds to many similar such finds. Bourriau (1988: 114) considers that it is puzzling that such clappers are fabricated from ivory as this material would be too fragile to withstand much usage. Possibly they were merely held whilst rhythmically chanting and then broken at the end of the ritual. If this was the case, and also taking into consideration their protective nature, then this does place them in the same context as the serpent wand, apotropaic wands and magic rod.

FIG. 48: PAIR OF IVORY CLAPPERS
BM EA 20779-80 (COURTESY OF THE BRITISH MUSEUM)

Magical Rod or Wand

Section of an ivory magical rod or wand engraved with lions (Manchester 1795; Quibell 18). (Location: The Manchester Museum).

FIG. 49: SECTION OF IVORY MAGICAL ROD
MANCHESTER 1795, QUIBELL 18 (COURTESY OF THE MANCHESTER MUSEUM, UNIVERSITY OF MANCHESTER)

This ivory rod-like object is decorated with two figures of lions on one face and on another face displays several sets of vertical lines alternating with horizontal lines. Lorand (2009: 21) considers that this design could form part of a plant motif (fig. 49). This piece belongs to the category of objects known as magic rods with many of the described ones being fashioned from steatite (see Fitzwilliam E.426.1982, Bourriau 1988: 115-16; Metropolitan Museum of Art 26.7.1275, Fischer 1966b: 197, fig. 7). Many of the surviving examples are made up of separate segments joined together by dowels. Some other examples display three-dimensional versions of lions and other creatures attached to the top of the rod, although none were found connected to the Ramesseum rod (fig. 50).

The iconography displayed on the rods as well as the date range is similar to that of the apotropaic wands. On occasions these two types of items have been found together which suggests that they both may have had a similar protective function (Hayes 1953: 228; Bourriau 1988: 115-16; Szpakowska 2008: 30). These rods are only attested from the late Middle Kingdom, which Szpakowska (2008: 30) suggests may be due to the perception that they were considered less effective than the apotropaic wands and therefore fell out of use. The association with the *s3* sign for protection inscribed on some of the rods also demonstrates the apotropaic nature of this type of object (Étienne 2000: 71; Pinch 2006: 79).

Beads

Group of beads. (Location: unknown).

Very little is known about these particular artefacts. Quibell (1898: 3) describes them in his excavation report as 'spherical beads in amethyst and agate, barrel-shaped in haematite and carnelian, glaze and carnelian beads of the shape of an almond, and one covered with minute crumbs of glaze'. They are drawn in Quibell's publication but the number is not specified and their present location is unknown (fig. 27). There are instances of beads being used as amulets, and it is known that Coffin Text spell 576, which was to be recited over a bead of carnelian or amethyst, was aimed at enabling a man to copulate in the underworld (Faulkner 1977: 181; Ritner 1993: 224). Alternatively, these items could have been part of a necklace, funerary flail or even have formed part of the elaborate hairstyle that once may have been present on the 'paddle doll'.

FIG. 50: GLAZED STEATITE MAGIC ROD FROM A 12TH DYNASTY TOMB NEAR HELIOPOLIS, ADORNED WITH FIGURES OF ANIMALS. (ADAPTED FROM IMAGE 26.7.1275, COURTESY OF THE METROPOLITAN MUSEUM OF ART)

Ivory Djed column

Ivory djed column pierced vertically (Manchester 1838, Quibell 15). (Location: The Manchester Museum).

This *djed* column which is 6.0 cm tall is fashioned from ivory and displays evidence of wear (fig. 51). The column is likely to be an amulet in the form of a hieroglyphic sign meaning stability or endurance, and is intended to afford magical protection. This shape is often seen in jewellery and is the most common of all the funerary amulets, often with several being found on a single mummy, these usually being positioned across the lower torso (Andrews 1994: 83).

It is possible that this item from the assemblage was worn by the living and then after death placed with the burial apparel, either as a separate item or attached to the mummy wrappings of the owner of Tomb 5. However, Parkinson (2009: 143) noting the presence of these holes in the column suggested that it could have been attached to the ivory rod (Manchester 1795, fig. 49), and as such would have then been involved with the apotropaic nature of this implement.

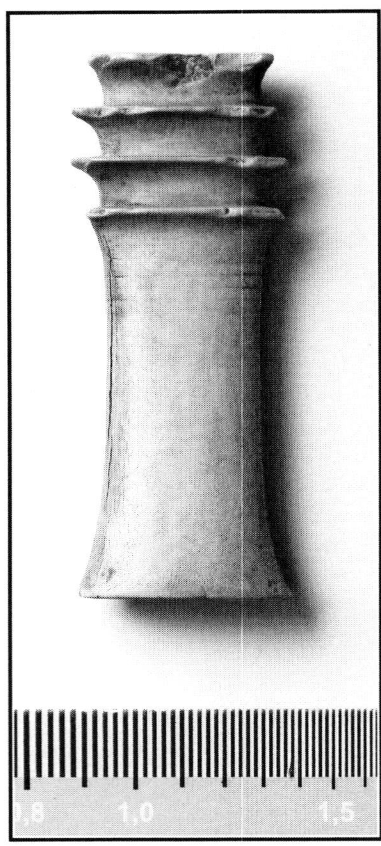

Fig. 51: Ivory djed column
Manchester 1838, Quibell 15 (Courtesy of The Manchester Museum, University of Manchester)

Burnisher

Ivory burnisher (Manchester 1834, Quibell 8). (Location: The Manchester Museum).

This object was described by Quibell (1898: 3) as an ivory piece with an unknown function, but this type of artefact has since been recognised as a burnisher or mallet (fig. 52). At one time it would have had a handle inserted into it and would have been used to smooth together papyrus strips to make sheets and papyrus rolls, possibly by prolonged pounding. Many scratch marks on the burnisher indicate frequent usage.

Similar pieces have been described by Carnarvon & Carter (1912: 76, pl. 66; fig. 53) as being found in the Middle Kingdom Theban Tomb 37, and by Hayes (1953: 292, fig. 193) also found in a Middle Kingdom burial grouping. This object is part of the scribal equipment relating perhaps to the activities of the tomb owner during life.

Fig. 52: Burnisher
Manchester 1834, Quibell 8 (Courtesy of The Manchester Museum, University of Manchester)

Seeds

Doum palm and Balanite seeds. (Location: unknown).

Quibell (1898: 3) also describes seeds of doum palm and of balanites as being present in the assemblage, which Parkinson (2009: 142) suggests could indicate that real fruit had been placed in the burial chamber as part of the food offerings. However, amongst the grave goods discovered in Theban Tomb 37 near Deir el-Bahri was an oval basket containing a scribe's outfit, and in it were two groups of seeds. One of these was found inside a case containing fifteen thin reeds used for writing (Carnarvon & Carter 1912: 76). Possibly there is some association between the seeds, the papyri, the reeds and the burnisher which comprise part of the scribal equipment.

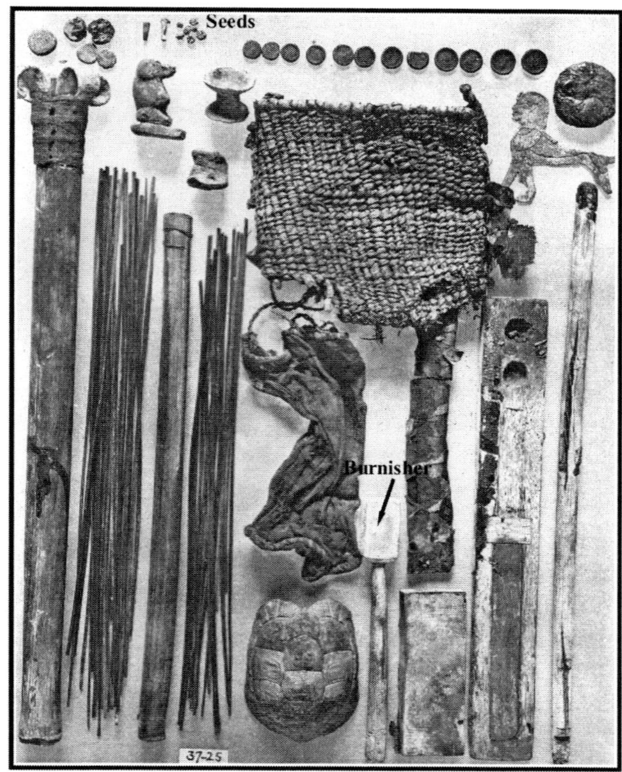

FIG. 53: SCRIBE'S OUTFIT, TOMB 37 (CARNARVON & CARTER 1912: PL. 66)

Papyri

Approximately twenty-four papyri were found inside the wooden box, and are described by Quibell as being very fragmented and in a poor state of preservation. They have been studied and categorised by various researchers including: Gardiner (1955a, b), Barns (1956), Kemp and Merrillees (1980: 166), Forman and Quirke (1996: 107-9), Quack (2006: 72-7), Lorand (2009) and Parkinson (2009: 146-69). Separating them into various groupings would indicate that there were three rolls of liturgical texts in linear hieroglyphs (P. Ram. B, E and 6); sixteen texts mostly written in hieratic concerning healing and protection (P. Ram. 3, 4, 5, 7, 8, 9, 10, 11, 12, 13, 14, 15, 16, 17, C+18 and 19), and five other texts that are mainly literary in nature (P. Ram. 1, 2, D, A, and possibly small fragments of an administrative text - Berlin P. 10131). There are also other administrative texts that appear to be later additions to the main body of the papyri (Quirke 1990: 187-95; Parkinson 2009: 150 and 2012). The subject matter of the papyri is thus wide-ranging and this in itself may be able to provide some insight into the tomb owner's social identity. (Appendix 2 is a list of the papyri based on Gardiner 1955b, Lorand 2009 and Parkinson 2009, 2012).

The consensus of the various researchers is that the collection dates to the 13th Dynasty and may well have been built up from a number of sources. Some of the texts display the remains of previous administrative usage and particularly notable among these is one roll identified as P. Ram. C + P. Ram. 18. This papyrus roll has an earlier administrative text consisting of official dispatches from the Nubian fortresses written on the recto, and then later magical texts of healing were entered on the verso. These dispatches known as the Semna Dispatches may have come from an administrative archive and are dated to year 3 of the reign of Amenemhat III (Kemp & Merrillees 1980: 166; Quirke 1990: 192-3; Parkinson 2009: 147). Dating is also aided by another text, P. Ram. 6, a text consisting of hymns to the god Sobek which was compiled in honour of an unknown king, Amenemhat. One of the literary texts, the tale of Sinuhe, has been dated based on palaeographic considerations to the early to mid 13th Dynasty (Kemp & Merrillees 1980: 166; Bourriau 1988: 110).

The verso of the Funerary Liturgy (P. Ram. E) comprises a continuous but highly fragmentary series of accounts referring to granaries from a single estate, and includes amounts of grain supplied by individuals, among whom are lectors and a *wab*-priest. In P. Ram. 3 (l. 82) there is a reference to an amount of cargo transferred from a ship 'to my estate', implying that the papyrus owner possessed a personal estate and was therefore wealthy (Quirke 1990: 189-90). However, these administrative details seem accidental additions, possibly made when no other papyrus was to hand, but may supply some evidence for the social status of the owner of the papyrus (Parkinson 2009: 150).

Parkinson (2009: 148) considers that the papyri written in linear hieroglyphs (the liturgical texts), the hymns to Sobek and two of the healing texts, show some similarities to each other both in style, quality of papyri and not being written on re-used rolls. This he suggests may indicate a temple origin obtained, perhaps, by the owner through his professional work or priestly contacts. The connection of such manuscripts to a temple is further evidenced by a late Middle Kingdom archive, discovered in the pyramid temple complex of Meryre Pepy I which was found to contain similar liturgical texts. Parkinson further describes other instances of temple papyri, both originals and copies, being placed in priestly and non-priestly tombs, such as those discovered in the tomb of Qenherkhepshef mentioned below. The Hymn to Sobek and the Dramatic Ritual concern kingship, whilst the archaic Funeral Liturgy may have originally been intended for royal use, again an indication of a possible temple library origin for these manuscripts.

The hieratic documents can be grouped by similarities in style into three separate phases. The earliest papyri were written in vertical lines which changed to horizontal lines in later texts. The second later phase includes a number of papyri such as P. Ram. A and D and by this time the collection was predominately concerned with ritual and healing. The final group again demonstrating a different style are exclusively magico-medical in nature and appear to be of slightly later composition (Parkinson 2009: 150).

It would appear that the papyri were amassed by the owner from a number of sources or maybe compiled by different generations of the same family. A parallel for the latter scenario is the example of Qenherkhepshef and his successors at Deir el-Medina where a collection of some forty different texts is considered to have passed through several generations of the same family. These texts again comprise a number of different themes consisting of literary and non-literary documents, religious texts, as well as medical and magico medical papyri (Gardiner 1955b: 1; Pestman 1982: 160; McDowell 1999: 134; Parkinson 2009: 149).

Lectors are mentioned as actors in two of the liturgical papyri, in P. Ram. B (a dramatic festival ritual) and P. Ram. E (a funerary liturgy for ceremonies at a mastaba [2], see section 3.3.3.4). However, it is uncertain whether these manuscripts were acquired in order to be performed professionally as rituals by the owner or by an individual with another profession (Parkinson 2009: 157).

Comparable Burial Assemblages

Although funerary equipment recovered in any excavation will usually have been adversely affected by tomb robbery and decay, the types of object remaining are often significant and worthy of detailed analysis. The quality, numbers and range of the grave goods would depend to some extent on the social status of the owner, but customs and fashions of funerary beliefs at a particular time in history are also important. An analysis of such funerary equipment will not only provide information about the owner of the tomb but may provide an insight into the Egyptian view of the afterlife that was prevalent at that period.

Protection against malignant forces was not only considered necessary during life but these powers were also thought to be a threat to the deceased. Consequently, grave goods not only included foodstuffs and drink, clothing and items for personal adornment and furniture, but also objects designed to protect the individual in death. Many of the goods found in Tomb 5 that surrounded the wooden papyrus box are protective in nature and are considered to be typical of a late Middle Kingdom burial. They are comparable to similar grave goods found in a number of other burials such as Tomb 416.A.07 at Abydos, the el-Matarîya (Heliopolis) tomb group and the E. L. B. Terrace group, thought to be from Lisht. These burial assemblages have been described in detail by Kemp and Merrillees (1980: 105-75) and are notable as they comprise similar groupings of models and figurines to those found in Tomb 5 beneath the Ramesseum.

Perhaps the most important of these is Tomb 416.A.07 in the 'North Cemetery' at Abydos, which was excavated by Garstang between the years 1906-1909 (Garstang 1913: 107-11). Unfortunately, records of this excavation are incomplete and the report published by Garstang in 1913 was only preliminary. Additionally, some of the many and varied finds excavated from the tomb were dispersed soon after discovery. However, Kemp and Merrillees (1980) have researched the original excavation reports and examined additional archival material, and from these sources have been able to reconstruct an account of most of the original finds.

The list of burial goods includes pottery, kohl pots and grinding palettes as well as models and figurines similar to those excavated from Tomb 5. These models included: fragments of a miniature bunch of grapes (416.A.07.84); fragments of a naked male achondroplastic dwarf figurine standing on a base (416.A.07.87); two hedgehog figurines (416.A.07.93 + 416.A.07.97); a rearing lion (416.A.07.94); a recumbent lion (416.A.07.99); two squatting baboons (416.A.07.95 + 416.A.07.96), and a hippopotamus figurine (416.A.07.106). There were also a number of bead groups and fragments of other animal figurines which were not able to be identified with certainty.

The el-Matarîya tomb group was sold by a dealer of antiquities in Cairo in the 1920's and was claimed to be the contents of a single tomb. There are no details as to the exact location of this tomb or any contextual information relating to its contents. Amongst the finds were again listed model foods, faience hippopotamus figurines, hedgehogs, an ape, a recumbent lion and a small faience doll.

Again the E. L. B. Terrace tomb group was sold by a dealer of antiquities in Cairo and is therefore similarly of uncertain provenance. The dealer claimed the finds were discovered in a tomb at el-Lisht and listed amongst them are again various faience objects. These include model foods, a naked dwarf figurine, two squatting baboons and two hippopotamus figurines.

Kemp and Merrillees (1980: 167-8) consider a further three tombs, two at el-Lisht and one at el-Kab within which were found similar faience objects. However, in all these tomb groupings there is no mention of any apotropaic wands, magic rods or papyri being unearthed, similar to those found in Tomb 5. Kemp and Merrillees comment that the purpose of the faience and limestone figurines and models being present in the tombs is not clear, noting how such objects were not manufactured exclusively for funerary use. Similar artefacts were discovered by Petrie (1927: 59) at Lahun, and these were not found in a funerary context. In an alternative viewpoint Kemp and Merrillees (1980: 168) commented that 'it is hard to escape the conclusion that they were simply made and kept to give pleasure' and further 'a relatively small number of Middle Kingdom Egyptians must have collected them'. However, they failed to discuss the supposed magical protective nature of the items.

[2] See Altenmüller (2010: 11) and 'Rites of Encircling' in this publication on pages 24-5.

Bourriau (1988: 110-27) discusses the objects found in Tomb 5 and as mentioned previously comments on further similar Middle Kingdom examples of protective demons, clappers, apotropaic wands, magic rods, apotropaic statuettes and female figurines. She proposes the lion and lion demon as a protagonist in the struggle against evil and also emphasises the restricted menagerie of beasts that were represented in the funerary equipment.

Interpretation

To fully comprehend the Ramesseum burial assemblage itself and formulate possible conclusions concerning its ownership is difficult as there are a number of problems and unanswered questions associated with the objects. Quibell's excavation report is fairly brief, very few photographs were taken and as a result the contextual evidence is incomplete. There are no inscribed items, the burial was disturbed at least twice in antiquity and it is not completely certain that all the objects came from the same burial. These factors make it difficult to assess the occupation or social status of the artefacts' owner.

Nevertheless, certain factors can be established and this is perhaps best discussed by dividing the objects into three broad categories. Firstly, the scribal equipment which consists of the missing papyrus box, the enclosed papyri, the reeds, the burnisher and possibly the seeds. Secondly, the standard Middle Kingdom grave goods consisting of the model foodstuffs, model cup and the beads. Finally, the remainder of the objects which consist of the apotropaic wands, magic rod, serpent wand and ivory clappers, together with the animal statuettes and female figurines, all of which can all be categorised as magical or magico-medical.

Some of the burial objects from Tomb 5 appear to have been used during life as is evidenced by the wear, the alterations and the repairs that are present. The serpent wand is fractured in the middle where it was presumably held, although Bourriau (1988: 113) comments that it shows no obvious signs of wear. The *djed* pillar shows signs of wear on the cross-sectional members, and the base of the naked wooden figure seems to have been altered. Similarly, the apotropaic wands are worn and they display signs of having been repaired and reshaped. These factors tend to suggest that these items had considerable use before being buried, and might therefore provide some clues as to the occupation of the tomb owner (Parkinson: 2009: 145). However, the apotropaic wands, ivory clappers and fertility figurines may have been deliberately broken before being placed in the tomb as part of a ritual procedure. Quirke (1992: 113) suggests that in the case of the apotropaic wands they may have been thought to be too powerful to be kept in one piece next to the deceased person.

Scribal training is apparent from the presence of a range of papyri texts which could be consulted and the pens with which to write charms and rituals. As mentioned the papyri can be categorised into different groupings which can then find a common theme with some of the objects. The texts associated with protection and healing find a common theme with the magico-medical objects. Bourriau (1988: 87, 110) considers that the combination of liturgical, magico-medical, and literary papyri together with the various magical and protective objects found in the cache indicate someone who was educated and was a 'sage, storyteller, priest and doctor'. She also considers that the quality of the burial goods suggests someone who had wealth and status. There is also support for the owner being wealthy from the administrative jottings on P. Ram. E and P. Ram. 3 which concern ownership of granaries and the delivery of cargo to the estate. Quirke (1990: 190) comments that the accounts jotted on the back of this latter papyrus suggest that the person making the notes would be wealthy enough to need such accounts, whilst Gardiner (1955b: 18) noted that all the papyri were of the finest quality throughout.

Ritner (1993: 231) has made a number of observations on the find, suggesting that the objects point to someone who was competent in medicine, feminine fertility and protection, whereas the presence of papyri and pens indicate someone with scribal knowledge. He further suggests that the painted jackal on the lid of the plastered wooden box when considered with the box as a whole reproduces the hieroglyphic title 𓁷, *ḥry-sšt3*, 'He who is over the secrets'. This might relate to the title 'Master of Secrets' (*ḥry-sšt3*), a title perhaps held by the tomb owner, or possibly referring to the box as containing 'written secrets'. The title 'Master of Secrets' was given to officials with access to cultic mysteries. He comments that by the Middle Kingdom this title had become a specific priestly rank and by the Late Period had seemingly become equated with that of the lector (Ritner 1993: 231-2). Parkinson (2009: 142) notes that Quibell described the jackal as 'roughly drawn' and in a simpler interpretation suggests that the image was simply added as a funerary motif when the box was placed in the tomb.

Lorand (2009: 40), however, states that the *Wörterbuch* (*Wb* IV: 298-9) lists no fewer than twenty-three different types of individuals who commanded the title of 'Master of Secrets'. He does see a link between the various types of text as well as between the protective nature of the contents of the Ramesseum box and the priestly and medical function of the owner of the assemblage. After considering a number of possible priestly titles such as the 'Lector' *(ẖry-ḥbt)*, 'Priest of Sekhmet' *(w'b sḫmt)*, 'Controller of Serket' *(ḫrp srḳt)*, 'Priest/Prophet' *(ḥm-nṯr)*, and even such individuals as a 'Magician' *(s3w* and *hk3y)*, Lorand concluded that nothing in the contents of the tomb determines with certainty the type of practising priest who was interred there. He does concur with Ritner (1993: 232) that because such an individual would have served in a phyle and therefore did not work full-time in the temple, he would have plenty of time to practise in the community, combining the roles of 'composer, compiler and performer' of magic (Lorand 2009: 38-40).

The papyrus box does warrant some further comments as the word box (*hn*) is found in certain titles such as 'greatest of the perceivers of the box of Anubis' (*wr m3wn hn inpw*) and 'master of secrets of the box of Anubis' (*ḥry-sšt3 n hn inpw*) (*Urk* IV: 1848, l.10). Kees (1962: 131) indicates that the box of Anubis refers to a box for papyrus scrolls rather than to a coffin. The title 'Master of Secrets of the box of Anubis', as Ritner suggests, could relate to the Ramesseum box, particularly if the painted Anubis on the top of the box is accepted as a label rather than a decorative motif. Lorand notes above that over twenty different types of individual commanded the title 'Master of Secrets', but many of these were not a specific priestly rank or ritualist. A certain Iuni, living during the reign of Ramesses II, carried the title 'royal scribe, chief lector, overseer of the *wab*-priests, who knows the secret of the box (*hn*) of Bubastis' (Hayes 1959: 349-52; Kees 1962: 134). Again, this is a reference to a lector having knowledge of papyrus rolls from just such a box, in this example the sacred texts of Bastet.

Pinch considers the occupant of the tomb to have been a lector, and suggests that he may have worked with female assistants, possibly resembling the type shown by the wooden naked figurine. She also raised the possibility that the existence of the papyri in the tomb could merely indicate that they were being stored in an accessible part of the tomb by family members, a not uncommon practice in ancient Egypt (Pinch 2006: 131).

A collection of papyri of this nature would have been a valuable commodity. Was the need, therefore, to display the occupation, status and learned nature of the tomb owner by burying them alongside him, more significant than the later usage of these papyri by other individuals? It is always possible that there could have been some form of disturbance in the community which may have necessitated the temporary safe storage of the papyri, and because of their valuable nature the intention was to recover the texts at a later date, which in this case never materialised.

As regards dating the burial, palaeographic evidence from the papyri suggests a 13th Dynasty date as previously discussed. Parkinson (2009: 140) also states that further discoveries close to Tomb 5 have unearthed statues and pottery which on stylistic grounds also indicate a 13th Dynasty date.

So is it possible to come to some conclusion as to the occupation of the owner of Tomb 5? The majority of both the texts and the objects are of a healing and protective nature and, importantly, they had been used in life. Whilst it is possible that such a collection could be placed in a tomb to provide protection for a deceased person, who may not even have been the owner of the items, it seems more probable that these items record the labours of that person whilst alive.

The quality and subject matter of the papyri in the collection implies that the owner was learned and wealthy with links to the elite administrative sphere and to the temples. Perhaps it can be concluded that the various objects with their protective and magical nature, found together with the combination of ritual and magico-medical papyri, could point to their being the working implements of a practising ancient Egyptian healer, magician and literary protagonist. Overall the range of material correlates to a learned individual with ritual and scribal experience, perhaps someone like a lector. The choice of equipment from the Ramesseum assemblage would be the type of accoutrements that a lector would need in order to perform his professional duties.

Chapter 4

Remuneration

1. Introduction

The ancient Egyptian economy was based on redistribution and reciprocity, with prices and incomes set in units that referred directly to commodities, rather than to a monetary system. The lector would therefore have been paid for his services in commodities usually referred to as 'rations', consisting of foodstuffs and other items. These consumables could then be converted into 'objects of all kinds' as attested by evidence from documents derived from all periods of ancient Egypt, although conversion tables are not known to have survived (Mueller 1975: 249-63).

The remuneration or rations of the lector would have been derived from a number of separate sources or employments but detailed evidence of this is only attested for the Late and Ptolemaic Periods. However, there are certain texts that provide information about the distribution of foodstuffs to temple personnel, including the lector, during the Old and Middle Kingdoms.

2. Old Kingdom

The most important source relating to the Old Kingdom is the Abusir archive which relates to the cults and provisions of the funerary complexes of Kings Neferirkare and Raneferef (Posener-Kriéger & de Cenival 1968; Posener-Kriéger 1976). Of particular interest for this study are the accounts referring to the amounts of foodstuffs required for the daily offering cult. At the end of this ritual the food would have been divided amongst the priests and temple personnel, representing the final stage of the 'reversion of offerings' (*wḏbw*) (Posener-Kriéger 1976).

Account 94A of the archive provides details of the distribution of rations to temple staff during the reign of King Teti (Posener-Kriéger 1976: 322; table 5). This table lists amounts of meat offered in the cult which were then later divided up amongst temple staff. The account does not provide details concerning the frequencies of such distributions. The quantities of meat distributed to the *wab*-priests and the *ḫntiw-š* is a total amount which refers to all the officiants in these classes and there is no indication of how many worked in the temple or what each of these would have obtained. The porter who is recorded as receiving only two measures of meat is given the same quantity as the lector, perhaps an indication of the status accorded to the lector at that time, although he is placed at the top of the list. It is also possible that other factors such as the number of hours spent working or the extent of the work carried out could have affected the distribution.

A further accounting document from the archive also appears to reflect the daily allocation of temple meat, but this is merely a list of names and provides no indication of the quantity or quality of the meat being distributed. Over a period of three consecutive days, forty-two individuals are recorded as being recipients. The document does provide the names of the individuals, four of whom are lectors, but as two names are duplicated, only two separate individuals are mentioned *W3š-k3* and *ḫw-n-k3* (Posener-Kriéger 1976: 317-18, account 65; table 6).

'The Year following the first complete account (Year 2 or 3 of Teti), 3rd month of Shemu, day 3
Were made the offerings of the meat...'

Position		Measures
Lector	*ḫry-ḥbt*	**2**
Inspector of priests	*sḥḏ ḥmw-nṯr*	**10**
imy-ḫt **priest**	*imy-ḫt ḥmw-nṯr*	**10**
***wab*-priests**	*wˁbw*	**20**
ḫntiw-š	*ḫntiw-š*	**20**
Porter of the meat		**2**
Total		**64 measures**

Table 5: Temple accounts from the reign of King Teti (Posener-Kriéger 1976: 322, account 94A)

From the information provided on the duty rosters, Posener-Kriéger (1976: 573-4) has estimated that the total personnel attached to the temple of Neferirkare was some 250-300 individuals. However, many of these individuals would have been part of the phyle system and so functioned on a part-time basis.

The lectors were not listed as part of this phyle system and were presumably employed full time in the temple. Lack of evidence prevents the determination of how many lectors would have actually been operating in the complex on a regular basis. There are other fragmentary documents in the archives relating to the distribution of rations, but none are complete enough to permit any further conclusions concerning remuneration.

3. Middle Kingdom

The tomb of the 12th Dynasty nomarch, Hapidjefa, provides information about additional sources of remuneration for the lector, other than the rations that were provided for temple service. Inscribed on the tomb chapel walls are a series of ten contracts made by Hapidjefa with the temple priests to secure regular ceremonies and cult offerings after his death (these contracts are discussed further on page 130).

[IVe MOIS DE *ꜣḫt*, **jour 24 ?]**

(4) .... [le *ḫntj-š Nfr*] - *ḥtp*

(1) Le chargé d'affaires du roi *sḫm-kꜣ*

(2) L'attaché au palais *sꜥnḫ-w(i̓)-Ptḫ*

(3) Les *ḫntj-š*

IVe MOIS DE *ꜣḫt*, **jour 25**

(5 et 6) Le *i̓mi̓-ḫt ḥmw-nṯr Wr-kꜣ*, **l'attaché au palais** *Nj-kꜣw-Rꜥ*

(9) La Mère Royale *ḫnt-kꜣw.s*

(10) Le *sḥḏ hmw-nṯr Mri̓-nṯr-nswt*

(11) Le *i̓mi̓-ḫt hmw-nṯr Wr-kꜣt*

(12) Le prêtre lecteur *ḫw-n-kꜣ*

(13) Le prêtre lecteur *Wꜣš-kꜣ*

(14) Le pédicure du palais *Rwḏ*

(15) Le prêtre lecteur *Wꜣš-kꜣ*

(16) Les attachés du palais

(17) Le médecin du palais *Ni̓-špss-nswt*

(18) Le chef des scribes des équipes *Nfr*

(19) Le *wr-ꜥ Mn-ḥtpwt-kꜣkꜣi̓* : **morceau** *swt*

(20) Le chargé des huiles du palais *Ptḥ-ḥtp*

(21) Le juge et administrateur *ṯi̓*

(22) Le juge et chef des scribes *spdw-ḥtp*

(23) Le juge et chef des scribes *Ni̓-ḥst-ḫnmw*

(24) Le sous-chef de la maison des archives (?) *kꜣkꜣi̓-ꜥnḫ*

(25) Le chargé d'affaires du roi *sḫm-kꜣ*

(26) L'ami *Bb-i̓b*

(27) Les *ḥnti̓w-š* : **morceau** *sḫn*

IVe MOIS DE *ꜣḫt*, **jour 25**

(28) L'attache au palais *Nj-kꜣw-Rꜥ*, (29) **le juge et scribe** *Nfr-sšm-Rꜥ*

(30) ... *Nfr-sšm-Rꜥ* **(31)** *Nfr-ḥtpwt*

(32) La Mère Royale *hnt-kꜣw.s:* **morceau** *swt*

(33) Le *sḫḏ ḥmw nṯr Mri̓-nṯr-nswt:* **morceau** *swt*

(34) Le *i̓mi̓-ḫt hmw-nṯr Wr-kꜣ:* **cuisse** *ḫpš*

(35) Le coiffeur du palais *Wšr-kꜣ.f-ꜥnḫ:* **morceau** *i̓wꜥ*

(36) Les attachés au palais: morceau *i̓wꜥ*

(37) Le chef de magasin *Ni̓ ...Rꜥ*

(38) Le médecin du palais *Ni̓-špss-nswt:* **morceau** *swt*

(39) Le prêtre lecteur *Wꜣš-kꜣ:* **morceau** *sḫn*

(40) Le juge et administrateur *ṯi̓*: **haut de** *ḥpš*

(41) Le juge et chef des scribes *spdw-ḥtp*: **haut de** *ḥpš*

(42) Le juge et chef des scribes *Ni̓-ḥst-ḫnmw*: **haut de** *ḥpš*

TABLE 6: ACCOUNTING DOCUMENT INDICATING A DAILY LIST OF MEAT PIECES DISTRIBUTED TO TEMPLE PERSONNEL (POSENER-KRIÉGER 1976: 317-18, ACCOUNT 65)

In contract 3 a lector is listed as one of the ten officiants who was to receive daily rations of bread, beer and meat on the occasion of the *wag*-festival, as payment for services undertaken for the cult of Hapidjefa. Nine of these officiants, who include the lector, were to receive two days of offerings whilst the chief priest was to receive double this amount. In return these officiants had to give bread and beer as offerings to the statue of Hapidjefa (table 7).

A list of offerings distributed among the temple personnel at Lahun is another document often cited in connection with remuneration and the redistribution of daily temple offerings (P. Cairo JE 71580 [previously Berlin 10005]; Borchardt 1902-1903: 113-17; Haring 1997: 9). The text relates to the funerary temple of Senwosret II and lists the daily income of the temple as 410 units of assorted breads *(tꜣ šbn)*, 63 units of *(sṯꜣ)* beer and 172 units of *(špnw)* beer. Of these amounts 70 units of bread, 35 units of *(sṯꜣ)* beer and 115½ units of *(špnw)* beer were distributed among 20 staff members. Table 8 shows the allocation of bread (1), *sṯꜣ* of beer (2) and *špnw* of beer (3) given to each individual as a calculation based on the total offerings of the temple that day, divided by the fixed share allocation of each member of the temple personnel. Other than the chief priest who receives ten shares, the chief lector at six shares and the ordinary lector in his month at four shares are the two individuals who receive the next highest allocations. This enhanced distribution may reflect the increased work load undertaken by the lectors, but it is more likely to be an indication of the rank and status that the lector had in the temple hierarchy at that time.

4. New Kingdom

Despite rich evidence concerning the redistribution of offerings in the New Kingdom, the reference to lectors appears to be restricted to one occurrence, the Megiddo Text of Tuthmosis III (translated Gardiner 1952: 6-23). This text is very patchy but includes a brief mention of lectors:

> (62) ... born (?) in offices, causing very [man to know] his duty, namely god's fathers, scribes, lectors, managers, those carrying ... (63) temple-priesthood of my father Amun-Re in Beneficent-of-Monuments in conjunction with the regular temple-priesthood of the House of Amun ...'

In lines 70-5 a distinction is made between the hour-priesthood (*wnwt*) and the mortuary (*kꜣ*) priests (*ḥm-kꜣw*) as recipients of the redistributed offerings:

> 'My Majesty to give 20 ...; beer ... jugs; vegetables, 4 bundles; out of what is placed on the altar [of Re] ... which goes forth for his ka priests ... my temple-priesthood'.

Regrettably, the fragmentary nature of this inscription results in too little of the context remaining for a coherent narrative to be reconstructed. This and the lack of other textual evidence from the New Kingdom prevent any additional conclusions concerning remuneration of the lector from being made during this period.

5. Late and Ptolemaic Periods

However, in the Late and Ptolemaic Periods this changes, and now there is more frequent mention in the texts of the income obtainable from such offices. There was extensive buying, selling and leasing of 'days of endowment' (*hrw n sꜥnḫ*), in which the buyer or lessee agreed to fulfil the liturgical responsibilities attached to the office, in exchange for the income which goes with it (Johnson 1986: 78). A certain Patiatum of Asyut is recorded as purchasing one-twelfth of the office of lector of Asyut in 198 BC. Additionally, he received income: from his one quarter of the office of lector of the necropolis of Shashotep (Deir Rifeh) and its neighbourhood; income from his one-twelfth share of scribe of the divine books of the necropolis of Asyut; and rations from two temples, as well as monthly meat and oil rations (P. BM 10575; Thompson 1934: I, 12, 1.37).

Other sources of income for the lector were those obtained from the performance of burial rites, and remuneration obtained by servicing the funerary chapels on behalf of members of the community (El-Amir 1959; Pestman 1963: 8-23). A number of Demotic documents record the sale of tomb chapels with their attendant responsibilities and the resultant income attached to them. Papyrus Berlin 3112 provides details of the sale of almost ninety tombs in Western Thebes (Grunert 1981).

Evidence indicates that during this period the priestly classes were a major land-owning class and much of the private statuary and funerary stelae that were manufactured was commissioned for this section of society. The signing of marriage contacts, common at that time, included a high proportion of this group (Johnson 1986: 72). Johnson (1986: 70-84) analysed a wide range of documents which involved leases, sale documents, loans, marriage agreements and various other agreements relating to economic matters from the Theban area, the town precincts of the Karnak complex and other geographical areas - an archive totalling 122 documents (table 9). Johnson included the lector among the priestly contingent and arranged the documents into four categories:

A. In which both parties were priests.
B. In which one party or several parties on one side were priests, but the other party or parties were not.
C. In which one or both sides involved people associated with a temple, but not priests.
D. In which neither party consisted of priests or others associated with a temple.

These results together with an analysis of 160 property contracts by Zauzich (1968) from different locations in Egypt indicate that priests and other temple personnel were more likely to be involved in the conveyancing of property rather than other members of society (Johnson 1986: 75). Such evidence indicates that the priestly classes, to which the lector has been included, had multiple sources of income and were one of the high status, wealthier groups in society at that period.

6. Conclusion

Evidence would suggest that the lector would have derived his income from a number of sources. There are indications of wealth and high status in the Late and Ptolemaic Periods but the sketchy evidence from other periods of ancient Egyptian history prevents a coherent or reliable picture of the remuneration of the lector from being established.

List of the same	*kby* Jars of beer	Rolls of *kfn*-bread	Rolls of white bread
Chief priest	4	400	10
Announcer	2	200	5
Master of mysteries	2	200	5
Wardrobe-keeper (*šnḏwty*)	2	200	5
Store-keeper	2	200	5
Master of the wide-hall	2	200	5
Overseer of the sanctuary	2	200	5
Scribe of the temple	2	200	5
Scribe of the altar	2	200	5
Lector	2	200	5
(Totals, not in text	22	2200	55)

Table 7: Contract 3 - amounts of bread and beer given by the listed individuals as offerings to the statue of Hapidjefa on the day of the Wag-festival
(Reisner 1918: 83)

Position		N	P	1 (bread)	2 (*sṯ3* beer)	3 (*špnw* beer)
Chief overseer of the temple	*ḥ3t imy ḥwt-nṯr*	1	10	16⅔	8⅓	2[7] ⅔
Controller of the phyle in his month	*mty n s3 imy 3bd.f*	1	3	5	2½	8 $^{1/5}$+ $^{1/10}$
Chief lector	*ḫry-ḥbt ḥry-tp*	1	6	10	5	16 ½+ $^{1/10}$
Temple scribe in his month	*sš ḥwt-nṯr imy 3bd.f*	1	1⅓	2$^{1/6}$+ $^{1/18}$	1 $^{1/9}$	3⅔+$^{1/45}$
Ordinary lector in his month	*ḫry-ḥbt ʿš3 imy 3bd.f*	1	4	6⅔	3⅓	11$^{1/15}$
wt-priest/embalmer in his month	*wt imy 3bd.f*	1	2	3⅓	1⅔	5 ½+ $^{1/30}$
Assistant priest (acolyte)	*imy-st-ʿ 3bd.f*	1	2	3⅓	1⅔	5 ½+ $^{1/30}$
ibḥ-priest in his month	*ibḥ imy 3bd.f*	3	2	10	5	16 ½+$^{1/10}$
wab-priest of the king in his month	*wʿb nsw imy 3bd.f*	2	2	6⅔	3⅓	11$^{1/15}$
m3ḏw	*m3ḏw*	1	1	1⅔	⅔+$^{1/6}$	2⅔+$^{1/10}$
Doorkeeper	*iry-ʿ3*	4	⅓	2$^{1/6}$+ $^{1/18}$	1 $^{1/9}$	3⅔+$^{1/45}$
Night doorkeeper	*iry-ʿ3 nty m ḫ3wy*	2	⅓	1 $^{1/9}$	½+ $^{1/18}$	1½+⅓ $^{1/90}$
Builder's workman of the temple	*k3wty nt ḥwt-nṯr*	1	⅓	½+ $^{1/18}$	¼+ $^{1/36}$	⅔+ ¼+ $^{1/180}$

N = number P = share allocation

Table 8: Priestly income from the funerary temple of Senwosret II
(Borchardt 1902/3: 114-15)

Category	Deir el Medina	Karnak	Other	Total
A	33%	21%	16%	25%
B	35	49	66	48
C	4	26	3	11
D	27	18	19	22

Table 9: Percentage of Theban documents involving priests or temple personnel
(after Johnson 1986: table 1)

Chapter 5

Temple and Festival Ritual

1. Introduction

Ritual

The concept of ritual centred on expected results; emphasis was on the intention of the performer, based on their understandings of the ancient Egyptian Universe. Ritual facilitated the relationship between the gods, the king, the deceased and the living. Rituals were intrinsic to the daily services observed in the temples as well as to the various periodic festivals celebrated in the Egyptian calendar. The lector had an important role to play in these ceremonies, as recitation was an important element in ritual practices (Shafer 1997: 18-22; Bell 2009). For the successful performance of ritual the lector would have had to possess ritual knowledge, speaker competence, be endowed with the power to do what was required and be in a state of purity.

Purification

Before exploring the various temple and festival rituals it is important to examine purity and purification rites, as purity was central to ancient Egyptian religion. (Meeks 1979: 430-52; Gee 1998). Gee (1998) defines purity as 'those things required to enter a ritual space' and he demonstrates them as both behavioural and ritual requirements. Autobiographies indicate that behavioural requirements were considered in the lives of officials and purification rituals consisting of washing, censing, dressing and anointing were performed. Purity is formulated explicitly in the Late Period instruction text of Onkhsheshonqi (P. BM. 10.508 8/18):

> 'Purity (*wꜥb*) is the essential (*rnnt*) of a temple (*ḥwt-nṯr*)' (translated Dieleman 2005: 212).

Purification rituals preceded all religious ceremonies and everyone who approached a deity or entered a sacred place had to be ritually pure; this not only included the priests but also the king himself. Purification ceremonies were also performed on the body of the dead king and on the bodies of all deceased persons. The ceremony of purification developed from ancient beliefs, one of which originated in Heliopolis. This myth states that in the beginning the sun-god, Re, emerged from the primeval ocean Nun, and then each morning was reborn when the sun reappeared in the sky, following which he washed in the Fields of Iaru (Sethe 1912: 121; Černý 1952: 99). Purification rituals are to be found in the Pyramid Texts such as the utterances relating to the purification of Horus (§22, §24, §27; Faulkner 1969: 6-7). Purification was symbolically not only represented by water; reliefs frequently depict the symbols of life and dominion issuing from the vases which were intended to transfer the powers of the gods to the king (Fairman 1958: 79). The king had to undergo a ritual purification before officiating in a temple and inscriptions from temples such as those at Edfu and Philae indicate that this ceremony was performed in the 'House of the Morning' *(pr-dwꜣt)* (Dümichen 1877: 10; Kees 1914: 4; Blackman 1918a: 148; fig. 54). Blackman (1918b) noted a close association in the Old Kingdom between the title 'Supervisor of the Mysteries of the House of the Morning' *(ḥry sštꜣ n pr-dwꜣt)* with the titles of sole companion *(smr wꜥty)* and that of vizier. The suggestion is that the title of supervisor was borne by persons of high rank, who would have been important functionaries and who were in close contact with the king. A number of these individuals also carried the title of chief lector or lector, such as Debhen and Iunmin from Dynasty 4, Sekhemkare and Weshptah from Dynasty 5, and Mereruka, Meriteti, Ihymhoref and Meryrenefer all from Dynasty 6.

The lector was involved in these ritual purification ceremonies as attested by an inscription on the 25th Dynasty Victory Stela of the Kushite king, Piy (Cairo JE 48862), which was erected at Gebel Barkal to celebrate his successful invasion of Egypt. The passage describes how after defeating a coalition of various Egyptian factions at Herakleopolis, Piy entered the shrine at Heliopolis in triumph (*Urk* III: 103):

> 'Going in procession to the temple of Re. Entering the temple with great praise. The chief lector praising god that rebels might be repelled from the king. The House of the Morning was visited, that the sedeb-garment be fastened on; he was purified with incense and libations …' (*ii m wḏꜣ r pr Rꜥ ꜥḳ r ḥwt-nṯr m iꜣw sp sn ẖry-ḥbt ḥry-tp nṯr dwꜣ ẖsf sẖdy r nsw irt pr-dwꜣt ṯs sdb swꜥb.f m snṯr ḳbḥ*)

Lichtheim (1980: 83, n. 74) considers that the lector's action of 'repelling the rebels' was a symbolic act, with Ritner (1993: 208, n. 958) suggesting it to be an execration ritual, with purity being a key theme in this text.

Gardiner lists thirty two scenes of royal purifications dating from the time of Hatshepsut until the Ptolemaic Period (Gardiner 1950: 3-12). The context of the depictions is not always clear as some scenes are from isolated blocks, but others are known to be from coronation ceremonies and *Sed*-festival rites. In each of these scenes it is mainly the deities Thoth, Horus and Seth who are the officiants at the ceremonies. These are three of the four gods of the cardinal points who are mentioned in the Pyramid Texts.

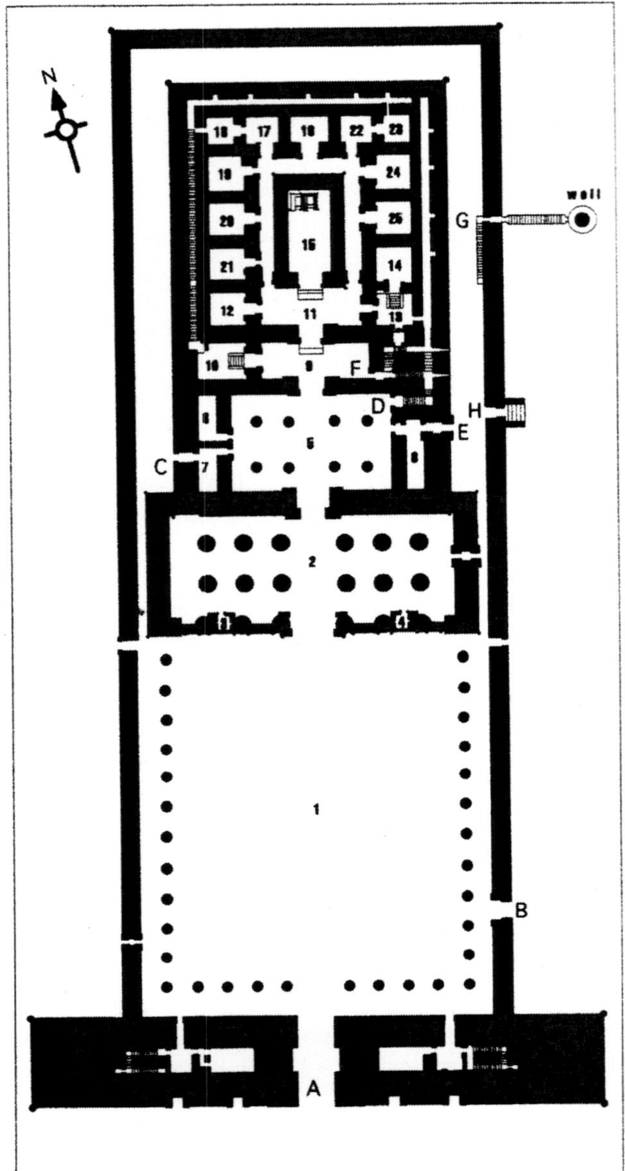

Plan of Edfu Temple: Key

1. Forecourt
2. *Pronaos*
3. The House of the Morning
4. The House of Books
5. The Great Hall
6. Laboratory
7. Antechamber-The Room of the Nile
8. Treasury
9. Hall of Offerings
10. Antechamber to Western Stairway
11. Central Hall
12. Chapel of Min
13. Food Altar
14. The Pure Place
15. Sanctuary
16. Mesen (Harpoon) Room
17. Sokar Chamber
18. Mansion of the Prince
19. Privy Chamber
20. Throne of the Gods
21. Menhet (Raiment) Mansion
22. Mansion of the Leg
23. Chapel of Hathor
24. Chapel of the Throne of Re
25. Behdet (Throne) Room

Fig. 54: Plan of the Temple of Horus at Edfu
No. 3 is the House of the Morning, No. 4 is the the House of Books
(after Chassinat)

A possible further example of an earlier royal purification is represented in a fragmentary relief from the 5th Dynasty sun-temple of Niuserre at Abu Ghurob (Borchardt 1905: fig. 42; fig. 55). In front of what appears to be a seated figure of the king are two attendants, one of whom, 'a companion' (*smr*), appears to be pouring water over Niuserre's foot. The presence of the lector behind the companion would suggest that this is a ceremonial washing or purification ritual (Blackman 1918b: 120).

An example of a non-royal ritual purification is that of the 12th Dynasty nomarch, Djehutyhotep ii (Bersha 2 = R20), whose reliefs in his tomb-chapel at El-Bersha depict him being purified by his sons and other officiants (Newberry 1895: pl. 10; fig. 56). Djehutyhotep is depicted standing between two individuals each of whom pours water from a *ḥst*-vase over him. In the second register below this a lector reads from a papyrus roll, and the partly damaged inscription alongside him, which has been restored by Blackman (1918a: 119), reads: 'Unite for you your bones. What belongs to you is complete'. This formula is regularly attributed to the lector as the officiant who recited this at similar ceremonies such as the sprinkling of water on the statue during the 'Opening of the Mouth' ceremony (see chapter 8 of this publication), the lustrations performed on the statue of the god during the daily temple service, and the ritual purification of the king mentioned above (Kees 1914: 8; Altenmüller 2010: 6).

FIG. 55: RELIEF FROM THE SUN-TEMPLE OF NIUSERRE DEPICTING A POSSIBLE PURIFICATION SCENE (BORCHARDT 1905: FIG. 42)

A scene from the 18th Dynasty tomb of Sennefer (TT 96) depicts a chief lector, a *sem*-priest and two further lectors performing a ritual purification on the deceased (Virey 1900: pl. 25; fig. 57). A comparison of representations in other scenes suggests these officiants represent the deities Horus, Seth, Thoth and Dunanwi, gods, as previously mentioned, who personify the four cardinal points (Gardiner 1950: 9-11). This evidence is supported by Utterance 35 from the Pyramid Texts §27:

> 'Your purification is the purification of Horus, your purification is the purification of Seth, your purification is the purification of Thoth, your purification is the purification of Dunanwi ...' (translated Faulkner 1969: 7).

It is rather unusual for all four gods to be depicted together as most of these types of depictions show only two officiants. Gardiner (1950: 11) considers that the reason for this may be associated with the need to aesthetically balance the picture as well as the desire not to depict the gods in miniature.

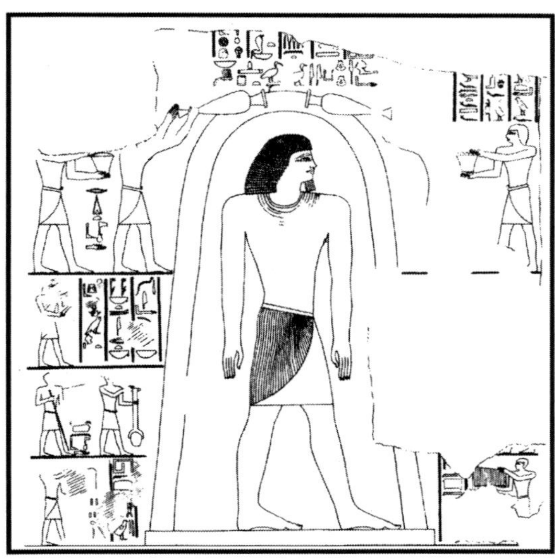

FIG. 56: THE PURIFICATION OF DJEHUTYHOTEP (NEWBERRY 1895: PL. 10)

2. Temple Ritual

Daily Temple Ritual

The Daily Temple Ritual was performed in every functioning ancient Egyptian temple and focused on the statue of the god. The ritual is considered to have its origins in Heliopolis and was carried out at dawn in a ceremony in which the god, whose power was immanent in the cult statue, was awakened, washed, clothed, and treated with unguents, before being supplied with food and divine insignia by the officiating priest (Černý 1952: 99; David 1981: 58). The full sequence of the various episodes of the morning ritual has been reconstructed by Barta (*LÄ* III: 841-4). The morning ritual was complemented by similar but more abbreviated rituals in the afternoon and evening.

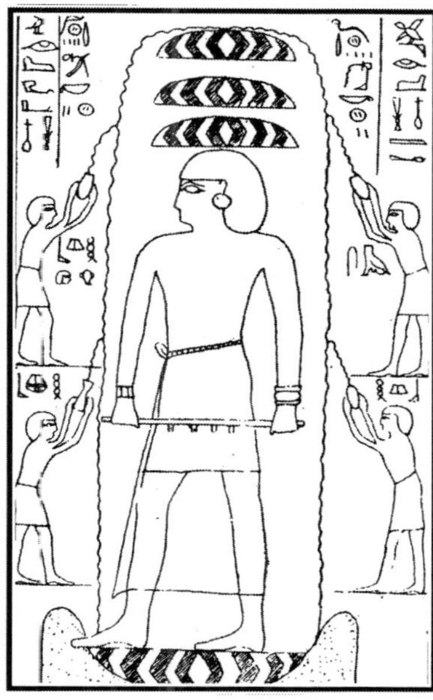

FIG. 57: THE TOMB OF SENNEFER (TT 96) (VIREY 1900: PL. 25)

Records of parts of the Daily Temple Ritual have survived for Karnak, Edfu, Dendara, Abydos and Deir el-Medina both in temple inscriptions and in papyri (Gee 2004: 102-3; Hays 2009b: 1-2). It is the scenes from the various monuments of Sety I that provide the most detailed information about these rites, depicting as they do an image, caption and a recitation, whereas most temple decorations merely display caption and image. In particular the scenes decorating the east wall of the Hypostyle Hall at Karnak and those decorating the six chapels of Ptah, Re-Horakhty, Amun-Re, Osiris, Isis and Horus at Abydos are very informative (Calverley *et al.* 1933: pls. 1-28; Nelson 1981). All the ritual scenes feature the king in the active role of priest as he performs rites for the deity. In addition various other officiants are specifically mentioned as being present at these ceremonies, such as *wab*-priests, *ḥmw-nṯrw,* lectors and god's fathers. However, in practice it is obvious that the king could not perform all these services and a deputy would stand in for him. An indication that the identity of this deputy was often a *ḥm-nṯr* is provided by an inscription at Edfu temple (Chassinat 1928: 83, 10):

> 'I am a prophet, the son of a prophet. It is the King who commanded me to see the god' (translated Fairman 1954-1955: 177).

A valuable resource for the Daily Temple Ritual is to be found in what is referred to as the 'Ritual of Amenhotep I', a text in which the role of the lector is specifically listed. The most complete copies of this ritual are two papyri dated to the reign of Ramesses II, namely Papyrus Chester Beatty 9, (P. BM 10689; Gardener 1935: 78-106), and a second papyrus, part of which is in Cairo (P. CGC 58030; Golénischeff 1927: 134-56) with the other part in Turin (P. CGT 54041; Bacchi 1942). In addition shorter and less complete versions of the Daily Ritual, which do not mention the names of Amenhotep I, are inscribed on the walls of the Hypostyle Hall at Karnak (Sety I) and the walls of the temple of Medinet Habu (Ramesses III) (Nelson 1949a: 210-32, 310-45; Fairman 1958: 75-104; Hays 2009b; Tacke 2012). Conclusions from these analyses indicate that the 'Ritual of Amenhotep I' was not used exclusively for Amenhotep I but forms part of the decorations seen in many temples, and it would be more accurate to regard it as a 'Ritual of the Royal Ancestors' (Fairman 1958: 100-4). The texts in the 'Ritual' are a selection of various rites which include not only the Daily Ritual but also a collection of spells and hymns used at different times of the day and during various festivals.

The lector is specifically mentioned in the terminal rites of the Daily Temple Ritual as illustrated in Papyrus Chester Beatty 9. The final part consists of a series of six episodes involving the return of the cult statue to the shrine, the cleansing of the shrine from evil spirits which may have entered while the shrine was open, and the final closing and bolting of the shrine after the king or officiant had left the sanctuary. The rubrics to these episodes [1]are:

> Episode 26: To be recited by the lector, bringing life to the god (section 12).
> Episode 27: To be recited by the *ḥm-nṯr*; bringing the heart of the god to him (section13).
> Episode 28: To be recited by the lector after calling out 'Hail' (section 14).
> Episode 29: To be recited by the *ḥm-nṯr*.
> Episode 30: Spell for 'bringing the foot' (section 16).
> Episode 31: Spell for fastening the doors of the shrine (section 17).
> (Translated Gardiner 1935: 85-7; Nelson 1949a: 201-32).

The rubric of the first four of these rites states that they are to be recited by the lector and the *ḥm-nṯr* alternately. In episode 30 it is the king who is depicted as 'bringing the foot'; although in non-royal funeral scenes it is the lector who is shown performing this ritual act. The lector, on most occasions, would ideally have deputised for the king in this rite, removing demons from the shrine by dragging behind him the *hdn*-plant used to brush the ground on leaving the sanctuary. Again in this capacity the king or lector would have been impersonating Thoth who was known as 'Lord of the *hdn*-plant', a plant sacred to Thoth (Davies 1915: 94-5; Nelson 1949b: 82-6). Further support for this is provided by the text associated with a similar scene in the temple of Sety I at Abydos:

> 'Thoth comes, he has rescued the eye of Horus from his enemies, and no enemy, male or female, enters into his sanctuary' (translated David 1981: 71).

During the foundation ceremonies at Edfu temple there are references to Thoth, here as master of ceremonies, where it is said of the king that he 'directs the ceremony like the Lord of the *hdn*-plant' (Chassinat 1931: 7,2, and 174, 7-8; translated Blackman & Fairman 1946: 79).

In Episode 31, after any evil spirits had been exorcised, the *ḥm-nṯr* shut the doors of the shrine and pulled the bolts across. Meanwhile the lector would recite a formula:

> 'Closing the door by Ptah, fastening the door by Thoth, closing the door and fastening the door with a bolt' (translated David 1981: 71).

Each phrase would probably accompany the movement of first one and then the other of the two bolts with which the doors of the shrine were secured (Nelson 1949a: 310).

Fig. 58: A scene from the Hypostyle Hall of the Temple of Amun at Karnak,
Seti I is elevating offerings before Amun (adapted from Nelson 1949a: fig. 34)

[1] The episodes refer to Gardiner's notation.

The Daily Temple Ritual displays some similarities to the Opening of the Mouth Ceremony as both of these rites comprise a purification ritual followed by a meal, although by the New Kingdom these ceremonies were separate rituals, each with its own particular order of episodes (Blackman & Fairman 1946: 86; David 1981: 58). As in the Opening of the Mouth ceremony the lector would have recited or chanted the sacred texts and been responsible for the correct ritual practices.

Returning to the Ritual of Amenhotep I, the later episodes numbering 42-4 also record the lector as one of the officiants. The best preserved source, for this section of the text, is a series of reliefs inscribed on the north half of the east wall of the Hypostyle Hall of the temple of Amun at Karnak. They are dated to the reign of Seti I and consist of spells recited at the Opet Festival (translated Nelson 1949a: 327-33; fig. 58). Nelson (1949a: 329) considers that the rite involved the lector supervising the 'elevation of offerings' *(f3y dbḥt-ḥtp)* and reciting the prescribed formulae, whilst the *sem*-priest and the attendants handled the food. These latter officiants would lift up and offer trays of food to the gods four times. While this ritual was being enacted the lector would say:

> 'Come O King elevate offerings before the face (of the god). Elevate offerings to Amun-Re, Lord of the Thrones of the Two Lands. All life emanates from him, all health emanates from him, all stability emanates from him, all good fortune emanates from him, like Re forever'.

However, in Papyrus Chester Beatty 9 after the rubric and the initial invocation by the lector (12, 1), the second rubric states (12, 2):

> 'Carrying of offerings by the lector (to) this god' (translated Gardiner 1935: 94, section 27).

The implication here is that the lector physically participated in the offering ritual.

Other Temple Ceremonies

The Daily Temple Ritual involved the three main services that were celebrated every day throughout the year. In addition there would have been other rituals celebrated in the temple, but for these detailed evidence is lacking. However, two inscriptions from Edfu temple do provide some insight into these services. The first of these is inscribed on the east door of the Pronaos (Chassinat 1928: 356, 1):

> 'Spells for lustrating the great sacred images of the majesty of Re in the twelve hours of the day'

The other is inscribed on the door jambs of 'The Chapel of the Throne of Re' (Chassinat 1892: 282, 12-15):

> 'The *ḥmw-nṯr* pass along its path to the palace of Behdet to uncover the face of Him-of-pleasant-life, from eventide, without ceasing through the twelve hours of the night. Provisions being in their hands in order to be laid upon its altar ... is satisfied with the offerings, and the gods and goddesses who are in his train, they eat with him' (both translations by Fairman 1954-1955: 181).

Although the lector is not specifically mentioned in these two examples, as we have seen from the Ritual of Amenhotep I, it is possible he may have been an officiant at such ceremonies.

Role of the Lector in the Foundation of the Egyptian Temple

Construction of all religious buildings in ancient Egypt began with a series of foundation rituals, and a comparison of texts and representations from many sites indicates that the complete ceremony consisted of as many as ten individual rites, although not all of these were depicted at each temple. The ceremonies were inscribed on the walls of the completed building and usually depicted the king performing the particular rituals. Representations of these rituals are evident on monuments from the Early Dynastic through to the Roman Period (David 1973: 69-73, 301; *LÄ* IV: 912-13; *LÄ* VI: 385-6). The ceremony involved the king, assisted by priests who impersonated Ptah and Thoth, and also on occasions the queen who stood in for the goddess Seshat. Possibly, among the assistants would have been a lector(s) to recite the appropriate formulae (Černý 1952: 114; Shafer 1997: 7). It is likely that the king in person would have performed at the major rites, when a new temple was to be constructed - as such foundation ceremonies would have been few in number, and a major event during the reign of a particular monarch (David 1981: 51). However, for extensions to temples and for minor religious buildings, then it would seem likely that a deputy would perform the ceremony.

Stretching the Cord

The 'stretching the cord' *(pḏ šs)* ceremony was one of the foundation rituals and is exemplified by a building inscription on the sanctuary wall of the temple of Amun at Karnak, inscribed during the reign of Tuthmosis III:

> 'A monument of fine white sandstone. The king himself performed with his two hands the stretching of the cord and the extension of the line, putting (it) upon the ground ...' (translated Breasted 1906: I, 245).

However, a building inscription dated to the reign of Senwosret I indicates that on this occasion a chief lector stretched the cord at the foundation ceremony of the temple of Heliopolis. This inscription has survived not on the original temple wall but in a later copy known as the Berlin Leather Roll (P. Berlin 3029) which was drawn up by a scribe during the reign of Amenhotep II (l. 14-19):

> 'The king appeared with the diadem and the two feathers while all the subjects were following him. The

Fig. 59: Foundation ceremony at the sun-temple of Niuserre
(Von Bissing & Kees 1923: pl. 9)

> chief lector, the scribe of the sacred book stretched the cord, he loosened the string; it was put in the earth, and made as this temple (house). Then His Majesty caused (the people) to go, the king turned back before all the subjects …' *(nsw ḫʿt nṯr m sšd šw-ty rḫyt nbt m-ḫt.f ḥry-ḥbt ḥry-tp sš mḏ3t nṯr ḥr pḏ šsy wḥʿw 3w3wt diw m-t3 irw m ḥwt tn rdi.in ḥm.f š3s nsw ʿnn sw n-ḫft ḥr ḥr mrwty)* (translated Gundlach 2011: 103, n. 2).

So in this instance, although Senwosret was present, he had delegated the important task of stretching the cord to a chief lector, an indication of the significance of this particular official in this setting. In the above passage the title of 'scribe of the sacred books' is appended to that of lector, a title frequently associated with the House of Life (Gardiner 1938a: 157-79). However, Goedicke (1974: 87-104) and Ossing (1992: 109-19) translate this passage as the chief lector and the scribe of the sacred books being separate individuals present at the ceremony. de Buck (1938: 53) and Lichtheim (1973: 118) disagree with this and translate the section as one individual with two titles, a view taken by this author.

Montet (1962: 74-100) in his review of the foundation rituals in a number of Egyptian temples, suggests, as do the results of this present study, that the king was designated as the actor who stretched the cord, and so the example of Heliopolis may have been an isolated instance. Kees (1962: 125) suggested that the inscription was imprecise and probably not a true representation of the events. However, the lector would have been present at the foundation ceremonies, reciting from the ritual texts as attested in the broken reliefs from the sun-temple of Niuserre (Bissing & Kees 1923: pl. 9; fig. 59).

Consecration of the Temple

The lector may also have had a role in the consecration of the temple as an inscription from Edfu does provide some indirect evidence. The text under consideration forms part of the frieze decoration on the west wall of the Outer Hypostyle Hall, and consists mainly of captions or headings to a number of formulae appointed to be recited during the performance of the ceremonies (Chassinat 1929: 330, 15):

> 'Supervision of the rite by the Lord of Hermopolis (*šsm.s ns in nb ḫmnw*) sprinkling water with the *nmst*-ewers and red pitchers …' (translated Blackman and Fairman 1946: 76).

The Lord of Hermopolis was Thoth, a figure often impersonated by the lector. Fairman (1946: 85) considers that the words of the text are 'excerpts from the directory of a master of ceremonies', a copy of the service book used at the Consecration of Edfu Temple. Such a manual would be a list of the various ceremonies comprising the rite, arranged in their proper sequence so that all might be performed in an orderly manner, and the solemn progress of the ritual not marred by mistakes or hesitations. Further evidence will be presented later in this study to support the suggestion that such tasks were performed by the lector.

House of Books

Certain temples have small rooms bearing the name 'House of Books' *(pr mḏ3t)*, and an inscription on the exterior façade of the *pr-mḏ3t* at Edfu temple has a reference to the activities of the lector in this library (Chassinat 1928: 339, l. 9-10):

> 'The chief lector did his duty in it the twelve hours of the day' *ir ẖry-ḥbt ḥry-tp irw k3t m-ḫnt m wnwt 12 nwt hrw*

As the *pr-mḏ3t* in late temples were usually fairly modest-sized rooms, with that at Edfu being only about two metres square, it would seem likely that they functioned as repositories for ritual scrolls which were in repeated use during temple ceremonies.

No papyri were found in the *pr-mḏ3t* at Edfu but inscriptions on the walls of the room provide details of the texts stored there, many of which were used in temple services (appendix 3). The walls are decorated with scenes offering book chests to Horus Behedeti (the main god of Edfu temple). In the east and west walls of this room there are several niches, which seem to have once been furnished with wooden book chests, often depicted in tomb reliefs from all periods (Matthey 2002: 16-18). The lector would have served in the role of a librarian or custodian, providing information regarding their contents to other officiants of the temple as well as being responsible for the safe-keeping of these valuable papyrus rolls.

Texts relevant to the construction of the temple, the Building Texts, were inscribed on the main temple walls, and papyrus copies of these were probably stored in the 'House of Life' *(pr-ʿnḫ)*. An example of one of these texts is the 'Book for Planning the Temple' *(šfdw n sšm ḥwt-nṯr)* which is inscribed on the west side of the inner face of the enclosure wall of Edfu. The actual composition, writing out and copying of these texts would have occurred in the House of Life which may also have been the primary library of the temple. At Edfu, although the House of Life has not yet been discovered, an inscription on the outer enclosure wall provides an indication of its existence:

> '…the description of their walls, which have been decorated most perfectly by the master craftsmen of the House of Life. All the decoration of them was carried out in accordance with the writings; its floor was laid as it should be' (translated Kurth 2004: 56).

At Edfu the *pr-mḏ3t* and the *pr-dw3t* are mirror images of each other on opposite sides of the pronaos and it is possible to recognise a connection between the two rooms. The king, or more likely the acting priest, would have firstly entered the *pr-dw3t* where among the attendants would have been a lector, and here he would have been ritually purified. Then on his way to fulfil his duties in the temple he would have collected the sacred rolls from the nearby *pr mḏ3t* (Zinn 2011: 194).

There is a similar *pr-mḏ3t* in the temple of Philae, situated in the east colonnade of the Isis temple forecourt. As in Edfu the *pr-mḏ3t* and the *pr-dw3t* are closely connected, here being next door to each other. Consequently, it would appear logical to store the texts needed for the ritual very close to the area of preparing for the ceremony. There is no book 'catalogue' written on the walls of Philae, as at Edfu, but an inscription on the doorjamb marks the room as the *pr-mḏ3t* and also states that the scrolls inside the room are connected with the *pr-ʿnḫ* (Zinn 2011: 196). Elsewhere in Egypt there are seemingly few remains of such repositories, but recent work at Tanis and at the Ramesseum has brought to light evidence of possible libraries. At the Ramesseum there is an illustration of Seshat, the goddess of writing and notation, and nearby on a column is the inscription 'Mistress of the House of Books' *(ḥnwt pr-mḏ3t)* (Brissaud 1993: 79-94; Leblanc 2004: 95-8).

Sacred Drama

A text from the Ptolemaic temple at Edfu depicts the lector as one of the chief participants in a dramatic performance. Only one complete version of the text, which is known to modern scholarship as the Triumph or Victory of Horus, has survived, and that is the copy engraved on the inner surface of the outer western enclosing wall of the temple (Chassinat 1931: 60-90, and 1960: pls. 146-8). The text has been referred to as a sacred drama and is thought to have been staged beside the temple's Sacred Lake. The drama forms part of a collection of works comprising the Festival of Victory, and celebrates the struggle of Horus against his enemies, led by Seth. The theme of the play is kingship, especially the renewal of the victorious power of the reigning king (Drioton 1948; Alliot 1954: 677-804; Fairman 1974; Quack 2006a: 76; Gillam 2009: 114-16).

The reliefs were carved during a period of civil war between Ptolemy X and Ptolemy XI, about 110 BC, but there are quotations from the text scattered throughout the temple, and on parts that were constructed before the enclosure wall. Additionally, some grammatical forms in the text suggest an earlier New Kingdom date and the text itself includes the section (Chassinat 1931: 14, 12-13):

> 'This wall is inscribed in conformity with the souls *(b3w)* of Re' (translated Derchain 1965: 55, 140 and Quirke 1996: 397-8).

The souls of Re is a reference to material derived from ancient books; this, together with the previous evidence, would suggest that some form of the drama had been in existence from at least the time of the New Kingdom.

Drioton (1948) and Alliot (1954) considered that the Edfu text did not represent a play, although they did recognise certain 'dramatic' elements in the work. However, Fairman, who helped to stage a modern performance of the play in 1971, likened the text to 'a primitive religious drama' and believed from its form that it was a play. He suggested that the text falls readily into acts and scenes without any manipulation of the reliefs or their order. Among the principal participants in the play was the chief lector whose task was to introduce the characters as they appeared on stage and bring coherence to the performance. Blackman and Fairman (1942: 37) considered that the players who impersonated Horus, the divinities and the demons, would have been located on a boat on the sacred lake during the performance, whilst the other characters were at the water's edge. The lector would have had a prominent position on land between the players and the audience.

In the relief of the last scene of Act 3, it is Imhotep who is portrayed as the chief lector. However, Imhotep, although known to possess the title of chief lector, is not mentioned in the drama and his appearance may be due to the veneration in which he was held at that time (Blackman & Fairman 1942: 36). Imhotep is also mentioned on the inner side of the enclosure wall, where there are inscribed references to a number of Building Texts; one of these is 'The Book of Planning the Temple', mentioned above. This text is recorded as being composed by the chief lector, Imhotep, son of Ptah (Chassinat 1931: 10, 8-10). Such an attribution of authorship from the Old Kingdom, an example of archaism, carries with it reliability, authority and trustworthiness. Imhotep is also mentioned on the Famine Stela where again he is specified as a chief lector and son of Ptah (see pages 118-19).

Summary and Conclusion of Temple Evidence

The above review of the evidence indicates that the lector had an important role in many temple activities. One of the key sources for the Daily Temple Ritual, the Ritual of Amenhotep I, specifies that it was the lector who recited the various terminal rituals, and evidence suggests that he may have had a similar role in other parts of this daily ceremony. The final parts of this text which relate to the Festival of Amun suggest that the lector not only recited the prescribed formulae during the 'elevation of offerings' but was one of the officiants physically lifting them up.

In royal scenes it is the gods who are depicted pouring water over the king in the rites of purification, whereas in the non-royal scenes, the lector and *sem*-priest are depicted fulfilling this role. In reality the lector would have been involved in the ritual purification of the king as is evidenced from the victory stela of Piy, with this ritual being performed in the 'House of the Morning'. In the Old Kingdom the 'Supervisor of the House of the Morning' was often a lector.

At the Ptolemaic temple of Edfu, the lector is depicted as overseeing one of the temple libraries, the 'House of Books', which is in keeping with his literary and scribal knowledge. The close relationship between these two ritual chambers is seen both at Edfu and Philae temples where the two rooms are of similar size and in close physical proximity to each other.

The foundation rituals associated with the construction of religious buildings normally involve the king as chief officiant, but in one instance the lector is cited as performing the rite of 'stretching the cord'. The lector was also the officiant reading from the ritual texts during the ceremony, and after the completion of the temple there is some evidence to suggest that the lector may have been associated with the consecration ritual.

Finally, at Edfu the lector is recognised as being the reader during the performance of the sacred drama, 'The Victory of Horus'. Here he was a prominent participant in the performance commentating upon and explaining some of the scenes to the audience.

3. Festival Rituals

Introduction

Festivals can be defined as extraordinary events which are usually observed at determined intervals and within which ritual and a sense of occasion play an important part. They are staged to celebrate some unique aspect of the local or national community (Handleman 1990: 10-11; Serrano 2002: 17). Ancient Egyptian festivals typically involved a joyful procession centred on the transportation of an image of the god in its sacred bark and were an important part of the cultic religion. The procession would have involved a number of active participants: such as priests who bore the processional bark containing the cult statue; standard bearers who carried the symbols representing the other gods present at the festival; the lector whose recitations would have played an important part of the ceremonies; the *sem*-priest; musicians, singers and dancers, as well as the king or his representative. The main purpose of the festivals was to honour the gods and to further the well-being of the king as the divine exponent of public life, on the occasion of established calendrical, astronomical or agricultural events (Bleeker 1967: 25).

Festivals are attested throughout ancient Egyptian history and also played an important role in the life of the people, as historically festivals have always been celebrated as a high day, an escape from the monotony of daily life and an opportunity for feasting and celebration. In ancient Egypt, the festivals were structured around religious practice and many of them provided the opportunity for the ordinary people to participate in cult celebrations, an activity from which they were usually excluded. However, the processions of the divine statues sometimes only occurred within the temple precincts where the public were not allowed to enter or where limited public presence may only have been permitted on certain occasions (Fairman 1954-1955: 174).

The majority of Egyptian festivals called the 'festivals of the times' (*ḥbw tp-trw*) were celebrated according to the calendar of three four-monthly seasons, with the remainder, 'the festivals of the sky' (*ḥbw nw pt*) being governed by phases of the moon (Murnane 1980: 26). The sources of information about ancient Egyptian festivals are many and varied and include calendar and festival lists in temples; inscriptions on stelae, statues, tombs and papyri, as well as graffiti on monuments (Schott 1950, 1952; Fairman 1954-1955; Gaballa & Kitchen 1969; *LÄ* I: cols. 172-91; Krauss 1985; Serrano 2002; Eaton 2007).

In theory, the king led all festival celebrations but in practice his representative would have presided at most non-royal events. From the Middle Kingdom onwards a festival organiser was appointed to manage the activities and in the New Kingdom this official was known as 'festival leader of the god' (*šsm-ḥb nṯr*) (*LÄ* II: 192). A Late Period inscription on the statue of an unknown vizier records one of his duties (Philadelphia, University Museum E. 16025; de Meulenaere 1982: 139):

> 'One who gave instructions for the temples in the conducting of the month-festivals and the festivals of the fifteenth day of the month' (translated Lorton 1999: 146).

At the temple of Edfu the inventory inscribed on the walls of the 'House of Books', relates to a papyrus (Chassinat 1928: 351):

> 'Every ritual related to (the god's) leaving his temple on festival days' (translated Sauneron 2000: 135).

The festivals not only involved large logistical exercises but also presented economic challenges. The first three sections of the Great Harris Papyrus (P. BM 9999) dated to the reign of Ramesses IV describe the very large donations Ramesses III made to the gods of the temples of Thebes, Heliopolis and Memphis. The list relating to Thebes alone includes 309,950 sacks of grain as well as vast quantities of meat, vegetables, metals and precious stones. In just under three years Ramesses presented nearly five million floral bouquets to the Temple of Amun at Thebes (Grandet 1994: I, 326-32).

Because of the large number of ancient Egyptian festivals that are recorded it would be impossible to study all of these within the remit of an examination of the role of the lector in ancient Egyptian society. However, it is worth investigating a small number of the more well-known festivals in order to understand the function of the lector during these festival celebrations.

Feast of Sokar

Sokar was an ancient falcon god of the Memphite region, a chthonic deity related to the cycle of death and resurrection. Sokar possessed the potential for life and was a god of vegetation and the earth. The Festival of Sokar, one of the major festivals of ancient Egypt, was celebrated on the 26th day of the fourth month of *Akhet*, the inundation season when the Nile flood was receding and the earth was ready for planting.

An early reference to the Festival of Sokar is to be found inscribed on the Palermo Stone (Bleeker 1967: 69; Serrano 2002: 92). However, Gaballa and Kitchen (1969: 13) consider that this may refer to a precursor of this later attested annual festival. Entries listed in the Abusir Papyri describe a Festival of Sokar in the fourth year of the reign of Neferirkare. The archives indicate that the king was not present at this particular festival, but describe the *henu*-bark containing the cult statue of Sokar as being welcomed by courtiers holding emblems, whilst a lector chanted appropriate hymns. The lector is not mentioned in the phyle which recorded the priests and officiants who took part in the rite (Fragment 13-14, text 1; Posener-Kréiger 1976: I, 59-76 & 549-52). This would suggest that the lector was a permanent member of the temple personnel.

By the Middle Kingdom the Festival of Sokar was increasingly being integrated into the Osirian Festival which was also being celebrated at that time. During the New Kingdom the Festival of Sokar is attested as being observed in many temples throughout Egypt. The festival was still being celebrated in the Ptolemaic and Roman Periods, but by now it had been entirely assimilated into the Khoiak Festival of Osiris (Bonnet 1952: 723; Gaballa & Kitchen 1969: 33).

Perhaps the best preserved and most detailed evidence relating to this festival is to be found inscribed on the walls of the mortuary temple of Ramesses III at Medinet Habu and so these scenes will be examined in order to determine the role of the lector during these events (Epigraphic Survey 1940: pls. 196, 218-26). The scenes occupy the upper register of the south wall of the Second Court and continue onto the second half of the east wall. The movement of the actors is from east to west and is usually divided into six scenes (Bleeker 1967: 81-92; Gaballa & Kitchen 1969: 1-76; Gillam 2009: 79-80). The festival commenced at dawn on the 26th day of *Akhet* when Sokar was woken in his shrine and the morning rites of the Daily Ritual were performed.

Scene I:

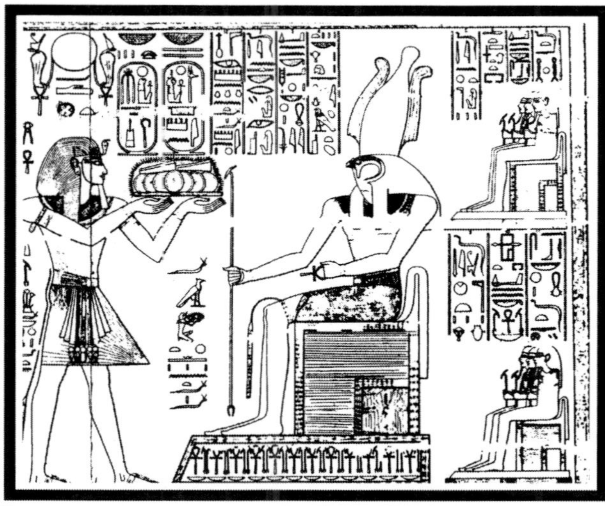

Fig. 60: The king presents offerings to Sokar (adapted from the Epigraphic Survey 1940: pl. 218)

The king presented offerings to Sokar which included products of the field, and in return Sokar promised him 'a life span like Re with earthly kingship like Harsiese'. Behind Sokar sit two groups of three deities (fig. 60).

Scene II: The king performs a censing for Khnum, Her-remenwy-f(y) and Shesmu; these gods in return promise him kingship, victory, health and joy (fig. 61).

Scene III: The king performs a 'Litany of Offerings to Sokar in all his forms' (fig. 62).

Scene IV: Next the king sets off 'Following the god at his promenade when he goes round the walls'. The bark of Sokar is being carried by groups of priests in front of the king (fig. 63).

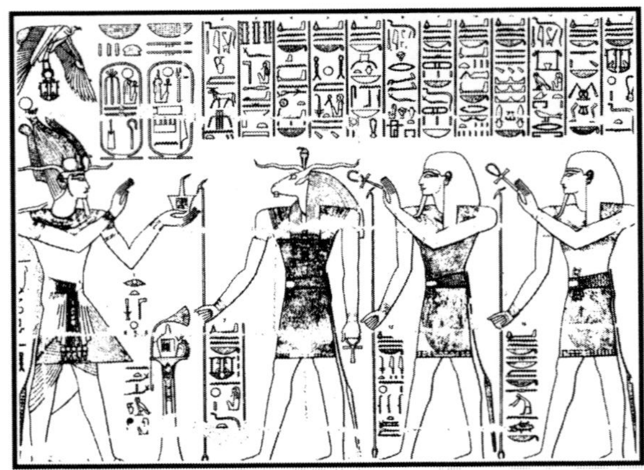

FIG. 61: THE KING PERFORMS A CENSING FOR DEITIES (ADAPTED FROM THE EPIGRAPHIC SURVEY 1940: PL. 218)

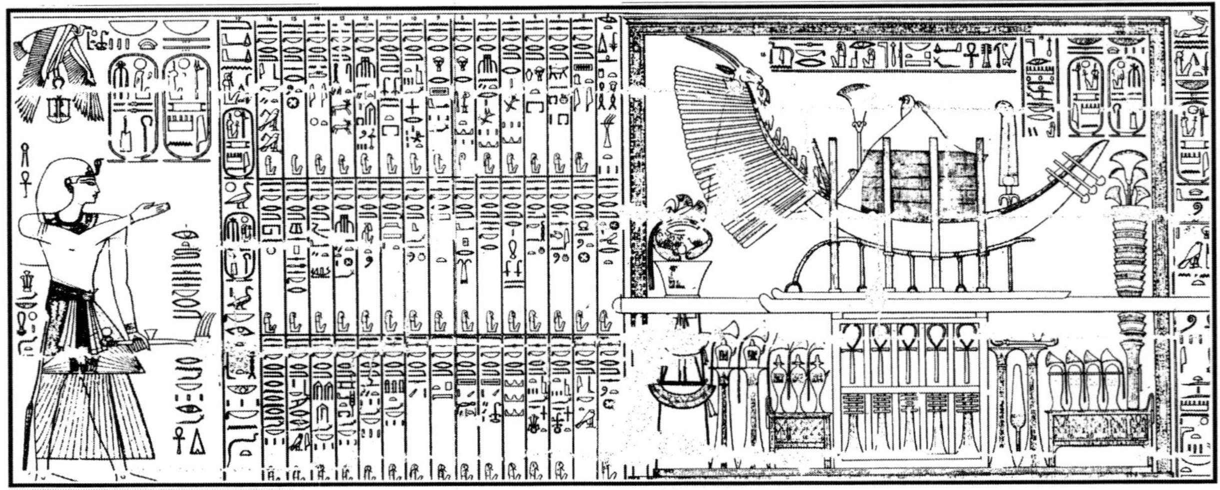

FIG. 62: THE KING PERFORMS A 'LITANY OF OFFERINGS TO SOKAR IN ALL HIS FORMS' (ADAPTED FROM THE EPIGRAPHIC SURVEY 1940: PL. 221)

FIG. 63: THE KING FOLLOWS THE BARK OF SOKAR IN PROCESSION (ADAPTED FROM THE EPIGRAPHIC SURVEY 1940: PL. 223)

Fig. 64: The lector reciting from a scroll whilst following the symbol of Nefertum (adapted from the Epigraphic Survey 1940: pl. 224)

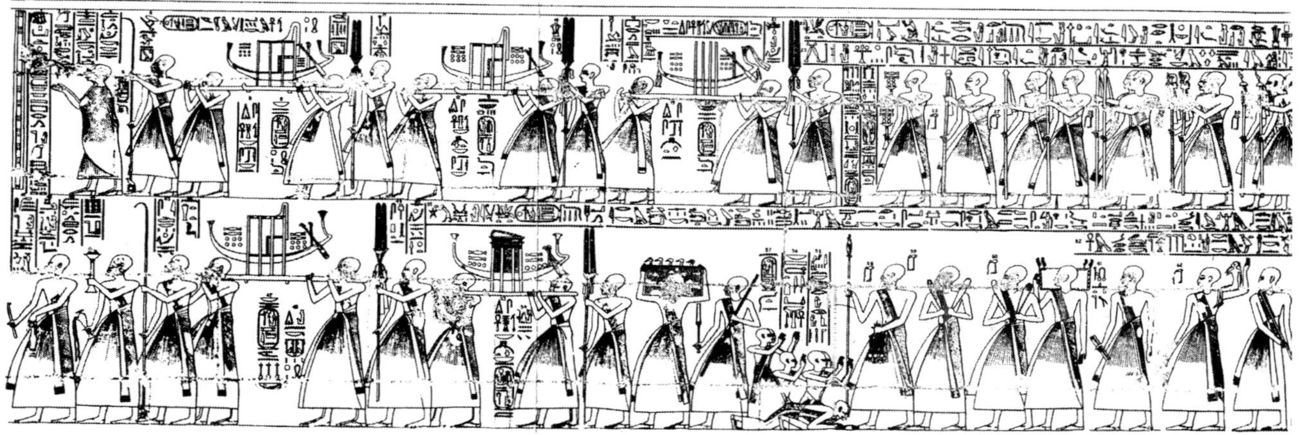

Left Side

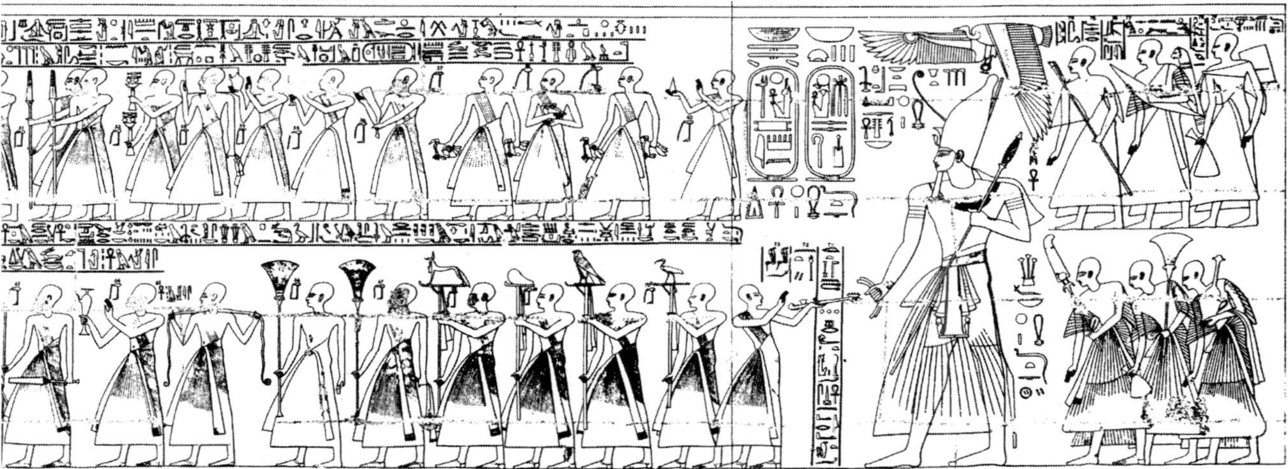

Right Side

Fig. 65: The ceremonies of the feast of Sokar (adapted from the Epigraphic Survey 1940: pl. 226)

Scene V: At the beginning of the next scene there is a depiction of the symbol of Nefertum being carried by two groups of priests whilst a *sem*-priest walks between them. Behind them a priest carries a falcon on a standard, labelled 'Horus upon his papyrus-staff'. Following them are two lines of courtiers, princes and *ḥm-nṯrw* holding the long ends of a chord, the mid-point of which is being held by Ramesses III. In front of the courtiers is a lector reciting from a scroll the main text of this scene (Epigraphic Survey 1940: pl. 218; fig. 64):

> 'Hail! Be triumphant, triumphant. O Sovereign!
> Hail! How sweet is the fragrance which you love.
> Hail! Behold, I perform the things which you love.

Hail! I shall do what praises you.
Hail! (I) kiss the earth, I open the way, (O) favoured ones of Abydos.
Hail! Fiery of eye (?), son of a prophet.
Hail! Protection is according to what you say.
Hail! I love your face when thou rest in the god's broad hall within the temple.
Hail! Abydos has, for name, 'Abydos'; Abydos has, for name, 'Abydos'.
Hail! How pleasant is the fragrance of Abydos, Abydos is protected, protected.
Hail! God, hearken you to worship!
Hail! Pray, be joyous, hearken you to worship that comes from the mouth of Egypt.
Hail! As for a servant who follows his lord, Bastet shall not have power over him.
Hail! Come, drive out, pray, the rebels. Come, instruct, pray, the child!
Hail! Put the fear of thyself into the disaffected!
Hail! Be seated and come, O weary-hearted one.
Hail! The son of the prophet (it is) who reads the ritual.
Hail! Enduring of name in Upper Djedu!
Hail! Mayest you live, may you live forever.
Hail! Thy festivals shall be everlasting.
Hail! The lord (?) Upper Djedu has come, he has smitten the disaffected ones.
For the good god, beloved of Sokar, that he may grant very numerous jubilees to Usermaatre Meryamun'.

At the end of the text the rubric is:

'To be recited sixteen times and make music. Lo, the chief lector recites the words, and (it is) the courtiers who reply to him' (translated Gaballa & Kitchen 1969: 6-8).

Scene VI: This is the largest scene and is divided into an upper and a lower row (fig. 65). At the front are priests who are pouring libations and censing the processional route. Behind them the miniature barks of the attending gods (Hathor, Wadjet, Shesmetet, Bastet and Sekhmet) are carried on the shoulders of priests. Additional priests accompany the procession carrying standards, offerings, a mace and symbols. The offerings being carried consist of birds, incense, libation-vessels, plant products and a haunch of beef. These may reflect the fertility aspect of the festival and may be intended as a final rite of offerings to Sokar whose image has been returned to the shrine, following the procession around the walls. Alternatively, they may have been intended as offerings by the *k3*-priests at the private tombs in the necropolis, since there is evidence that the procession of Sokar visited these tombs during the festivals celebrated both at Thebes and at Memphis (Blackman 1917: 128, pl. 28). That the occasion was a major celebration is evidenced in records from the village of Deir el-Medina, which detail that the festival was a public holiday when the people were able to feast and watch the procession (Sadek 1987: 171).

The chief lector is thus a key actor in the ritual, reciting the text which invokes Sokar and praises Osiris. The lector would presumably have read or chanted out a line of the invocation and the following courtiers would repeat it after him in unison as they drew on the rope (Gaballa & Kitchen 1969: 56). The passage ends with a warning that the faithful will be saved but the irreverent ones shall be in peril of death (Faulkner 1937a: 12). That the text was inscribed on the wall indicates the importance of the inscription, and suggests that this was one of the key texts recited during the procession as it travelled around the temple walls.

Papyrus Louvre N. 3176 (S), dated to *c.* 300 BC, indicates that this same text, 'Be triumphant, triumphant, O Sovereign', together with the 'Litany of Offerings to Ptah-Sokar-Osiris in all his forms' and other rituals were recited during the Festival of Ptah-Sokar-Osiris at the *Akhmenu*, the 18th Dynasty temple of Tuthmosis III at Karnak (Gaballa & Kitchen 1969: 44). The Louvre papyrus states that it was the chief lector, Pa-Hery-Khonsu, who recited the words of the 'Litany' (P. Louvre N. 3176 (S) 3, l.19-32 and 4, l.1-30 in Barguet 1962: 9-13).

In addition to P. Louvre N. 3176 (S), further versions of these same texts mentioned above are found in a number of later Ptolemaic manuscripts, the Bremner-Rhind Papyrus (P. BM 10188), translated by Faulkner (1937: 12-16), P. Schmidt (Berlin 3057), and P. BM 10252. These additional documents demonstrate the continuing importance of this ritual some eight hundred years after Ramesses III's text was inscribed on the temple walls at Medinet Habu.

The significance of the festival involves a number of themes. The texts speak of triumph and victory over foes while the presence of Horus on his papyrus staff (scene V) has overtones of new life and protection against evil (Gaballa & Kitchen 1969: 58-60). The importance of the circumambulation of the bark of Sokar was to activate the potential creative power of Sokar and to renew the life of the god for the coming growing season (Bleeker 1967: 86-90). The festival also involves funerary aspects and the falcon standard suggests connections with kingship (Gaballa & Kitchen 1969: 45-8).

The Opet Festival and Beautiful Feast of the Valley

Introduction

One of the major sources for our understanding of both the Opet and the Beautiful Feast of the Valley Festivals are scenes inscribed on the walls of the shrine for the bark of Amun at Karnak, the so-called *Chapelle Rouge*, built by Hatshepsut. Although the shrine was dismantled soon after her death and used as filling material in the 3rd Pylon at Karnak, recent reconstructions of the blocks have permitted certain inferences to be made. Troy (2006: 141) suggests that the placement of the depictions of the two festivals on corresponding positions on the north (Deir el-Bahri, Beautiful Feast of the Valley) and south (Luxor, Opet) walls suggests that they were seen as parallel celebrations to the god Amun. Haeny (1997: 103) notes many similarities between the two sets of depictions from which he tentatively suggests that the ritual aims of both processions may have been the same.

Opet Festival

The Opet Festival, an important annual festival at Thebes, was celebrated in the second month of *Akhet* (*p(3)-n-ipt*) from which it derived its modern name. The ancient Egyptian name of the festival, *ḥb-Ipt*, relates to that of Luxor Temple *Ipt-rsyt*. Its earliest attestation was during the reign of Hatshepsut (Lacau & Chevrier 1977-1979: 158, pl. 7). By the mid-18th Dynasty, during the reign of Tuthmosis III, the festival lasted for a period of eleven days and by the end of the reign of Ramesses III it had stretched to twenty-seven days (Schott 1950: 84-5). There is late evidence of the festival being celebrated in Roman times (Herbin 1994: 151-3).

As well as the *Chapelle Rouge* mentioned above, other ancient sources for the events of the Opet Festival are the various inscribed scenes located within Karnak and Luxor temples (Darnell 2010: 2). The core of the early festival at the time of Hatshepsut was the procession along a land route, pausing at six bark shrines, before travelling to Luxor Temple. The portable bark of Amun was carried on the shoulders of priests, accompanied by fan bearers and *sem*-priests. The return journey back to Karnak was by water. By the time of Tutankhamun the barks of Amun, Mut, and Khons, along with a statue of the king, took part in the festival (Darnell 2010: 4). Now both outward and inward journeys were by river with each bark travelling in a separate barge.

The rituals of the festival were celebrated at Luxor Temple, a temple which seems primarily to have existed to create a suitable monumental setting for the rites of the annual Opet Festival (Kemp 1989: 206). These ceremonies inside the enclosed chambers of the temple involved the sacred marriage of Amun (with whom the king merged) to Mut, resulting in the transmission of the royal *ka*. The individual's right to rule was thus reconfirmed which ensured the maintenance of kingship (Darnell 2010: 10). Little is recorded regarding the events that took place inside the temple after the bark of Amun had arrived. However, a lector may have been present at these rites in order to recite the relevant incantations necessary for the transformation of the king into a divine being (Bell 1985: 251-94). After the ceremony the king would appear in public, his person transformed into a divine being; unlike the Festival of Sokar which the king may not have attended, the Opet Festival centred on the presence of the king in person.

The safe return of the cult statue in procession to Karnak saw the performance of a number of ritual acts confirming the unity of Egypt, such as 'Striking the *Meret*-Chests' and 'Running the Course' (Egberts 1995; Troy 2006: 140). A scene from the *Chapelle Rouge* depicts some of the celebrants in the procession; amongst them are a group of female singers with sistra, acrobatic dancers and a number of *ḥmw-nṯr*. Also among the group is one lector and possibly another, but the poor preservation of the block restricts detailed analysis of this scene (Lacau & Chevrier 1977-9: 203-4, pl. 9, block 130; Burgos & Larché 2006, pls. 303-5).

Beautiful Feast of the Valley

The Beautiful Feast of the Valley, another Theban festival, was also associated with the god Amun whose cult statue travelled in procession from Karnak across the Nile to Deir el-Bahri (Schott 1934: 63-90 and 1952; Karkowski 1992: 155-66; Bell 1997: 136-7, 286). There is evidence that the festival was celebrated from the 11th Dynasty onwards with the temple of Mentuhotep II being the destination for the procession at that time (Arnold 2005: 137). A number of graffiti on the cliffs overlooking the temple provide this early evidence. They were left by temple priests, many of them lectors, who recorded watching for a procession leaving the east bank. An inscription by the *wab*-priest, Nerferibed, provides a date for the procession:

> 'Giving praise to Amun, kissing the ground before the Lord of the Gods on his festivals, the First Day of *Shemu* shining, on the day of voyaging to the valley of Nebhepetra, by the *wab*-priest of Amun, Neferibed' (translated Winlock 1947: 84 & pl. 40, 1).

Of the 86 priestly inscriptions recorded by Winlock, many of which are able to be dated to the reigns of Mentuhotep II and Mentuhotep III, nineteen of them are of lectors or chief lectors, an indication perhaps of the high numbers of lectors officiating in the temple of Mentuhotep at that time. The inscriptions are also an indication of their literacy as many are in different hands and presumably were inscribed by the lectors.

Another important source of graffiti in ancient Egypt is on the roof of the temple of Khonsu at Karnak. A study by Jacquet-Gordon (2003) of 334 of these graffiti, mostly dating between the end of the New Kingdom and the Ptolemaic era, concluded that they were entirely private and unofficial in nature. The majority were written by the *wab*-priests and god's fathers of Khonsu, with only five having a reference to a lector. Many of the inscriptions included outlines of the feet along with the names and titles of the author. Jacquet-Gordon (2003: 5) considers that the authors were generally of the lower ranks of the priesthood and probably did not have the right or wealth to places statues in the temple precinct as did members of the temple hierarchy. She considers that their footprints were a substitute for themselves so that they would remain in the presence of the god and under his protection. As previously mentioned (page 12) there were fewer lectors attested for the New Kingdom compared to earlier periods and this low number of lectors' graffiti may be a reflection of this.

The Beautiful Feast of the Valley was also popular in the New Kingdom with inscriptions in many private tombs referring to partaking in the festival and there is late evidence of the festival being celebrated during the reign of Ptolemy VIII in 117 BC (Traunecker *et al.*1981: 136).

Other than the *Chapelle Rouge* mentioned previously depictions of the festival are also to be found at Hatshepsut's temple, *Djeser-djeseru*, at Deir el-Bahri (Naville 1895-1908; Karkowski 1979: 359-64 and 1992: 155-66). The scenes depict the usual pageant of the bark being accompanied by processions of priests, courtiers, soldiers, dancers and musicians as well as depictions of butchery and presentation of offerings on small offering tables.

In the procession the priests carry a variety of objects, among which is a statue, a number of divine emblems and various ritual vessels. All the priests appear to have a sash across their shoulders but due to the damaged nature of the wall scene and the absence of captions, it is impossible to isolate possible lectors from amongst this procession.

Evidence of the feast in other Theban temples is not clearly represented due to the vague character of most of the depictions. Many of these are reduced to simplified scenes of navigation and procession with little reference to any of the activities of the lector (Karkowski 1992: 155).

The inscription on a stela, originally located in the mortuary temple of Amenhotep III at Kom el-Hetan, but later reused in the temple of Merenptah, provides some information about the function of the festival. The text describes the architectural features of the Temple of Amenhotep III and amongst the detail is the following passage (*Urk* IV: 1650, 6-10):

> 'It is a resting-place of the Lord of the Gods at his festival of the Valley in Amun's procession to the west to visit the gods of the West when he will reward his majesty with life and dominion'

The suggestion is that during the ceremony the spirit of the king was revived and the union of god and king would ensure the king's eternal existence (Teeter 2011: 68). Studies by the Polish team who have excavated at Deir el-Bahri over many years conclude that the essence of the feast was the reconfirmation of kingship. This is based on their interpretation of partly preserved scenes depicting rituals taking placing inside the temple, which in Pharaonic times were hidden from the public (Karkowski 1992: 155-66). One scene depicts priests carrying ritual books, bows and divine standards, and although there is no clear reference to a lector, it could be imagined that he may have recited from the texts during the ceremonies of confirmation and renewal of kingship.

The Feast of the Valley was also closely associated with funerary beliefs; families would cross the Nile to the West Bank and gather at tombs to venerate their dead ancestors. It was an occasion of banqueting, festivities and a night vigil at the tombs. The distinctive offering of the festival was a burnt sacrifice consumed entirely by flames (Bell 1997: 136). Significant numbers of inscriptions and painted scenes in private Theban tombs such as those of Haremheb (TT 78, 18th Dynasty) and Pairy (TT 139, 18th Dynasty) vibrantly record these events (Schott 1952; Teeter 2011: pls. 9, 10).

Summary and Conclusion of Festival Evidence

Many of the ancient Egyptian festivals provide evidence for the presence of a lector, with perhaps the earliest example being at the Festival of Sokar celebrated during the 5th Dynasty reign of Neferirkare. Here the lector is attested as chanting appropriate hymns. During the 19th Dynasty, inscriptions on the walls of the Temple of Ramesses III at Medinet Habu depict the lector reciting or chanting the main text at the festival of Sokar: 'Be triumphant, triumphant, O Sovereign'. Various later papyri such as Papyrus Bremner-Rhind, Papyrus Schmidt and Papyrus BM 10252 dating through to the Ptolemaic Period record this particular hymn as well as other passages that were recited during the Festival of Sokar. The indication is that it was the lector who was the appropriate person to recite these ritual texts.

The Beautiful Feast of the Valley and the Opet Festival do not provide the same direct evidence for the activities of the lector, although one scene from the *Chapelle Rouge* does depict lectors in the procession. Two minor pieces of evidence relate to the presence of the lector. First, during the reign of the 5th Dynasty ruler, Neferirkare, the lector, although recorded as being present at the Sokar Festival, was not listed in the temple phyle, possibly suggesting that he was a full-time member of the temple personnel. Secondly, 11th Dynasty graffiti on the cliffs that overlooked the temple of Mentuhotep II record numbers of lectors watching the procession during the Beautiful Feast of the Valley.

Chapter 6

Royal Involvement

1. Introduction

The lector came into contact with the ruler through his command and knowledge of ritual practices. This chapter provides such evidence for lectors being associated with the royal palace, having an involvement with the composition of the royal titulary, and having an important role to play during the celebration of the king's *Sed*-festival.

2. The Lector in the Royal Palace

There are a number of examples of lectors possessing the title 'Lector of a King' (*ḫry-ḥbt of a king)* (see page 15). An indication of the function that a lector to the king would have had can be determined from an inscription on an 11th Dynasty statue of the officiant Nebhepetre[1]:

> 'Great lector in the king's house, in charge of the mysteries in the august chamber, priest assigned to making offerings, the lector Nebhepetre' (translated Allen 1923: 51).

Thus Nebhepetre, who significantly has the same name as the prenomen of Mentuhotep II (the ruler at that period) would appear to have been responsible for ritual practices in the throne room, a role which would have included the provision of offerings.

3. The King and the Sons of the King Acting as Lector

A Ptolemaic inscription in the first hypostyle hall of Edfu temple dating to the reign of Ptolemy IV Philopator records the king as a lector. The reference is listed immediately after full cartouches (Chassinat 1928: 141, l.15; Otto 1975: *LÄ* I: 940-3):

> 'The excellent god, the lector who is in his year' (*pꜣ nṯr mnḫ ḫry-hbt n imy rnpt*)

In the Old Kingdom there are examples of kings' sons taking the titles of lector and chief lector such as Iunre, Iunmin and Ankhmare, the sons of Khafre (Baud 1999: I, 266, tb. 16). These royal sons who did not succeed to the throne may have assisted the monarch in his ritual duties. In the New Kingdom Seti, son of Ramesses I, before he succeeded to the throne, was sent to Tanis for the 400-year-celebration of the god Seth. For this festival he was appointed high priest of Seth and chief lector of Wadjet (O'Connor & Silverman 1995: 195)

[1] A polished haematite statue in the Oriental Institute, University of Chicago, 10.239 (Allen 1923: 51)

4. Role of the Lector in Establishing the Royal Titulary

There is evidence to suggest that at least on one occasion the lector was associated with proclaiming the titulary of the new monarch. An inscription from the temple of Hatshepsut at Deir el Bahri states (Naville 1892: pl. 62; *Urk* IV: 261, 2-3):

> His majesty (Tuthmosis I) commanded that the lectors be brought in order that her great names be acclaimed (*wḏ ḥm.f int ḫry-ḥbwt r mꜣṯ rnw.s wrw*)

The text also mentions that the titulary had been determined by the gods, but presumably the lectors and court advisors would have established this.

5. Role in Royal Purification

As discussed on pages 51-3 the king had to undergo a ritual purification before officiating in a temple. Evidence for the involvement of the lector in the rites of purification is possibly offered by a fragmentary relief from the 5th Dynasty sun-temple of Niuserre at Abu Ghurob, with more positive evidence being provided by the 25th Dynasty stela of Piy and the royal purification scenes collated by Gardiner (1950: 3-12).

6. The *Sed*-Festival

Introduction

The *ḥb-sd* or *Sed*-festival is regarded by many authors as one of the most important events in a king's reign with many references to this festival throughout Egyptian history. The festival has been extensively studied by Wilson (1936), Frankfort (1948), Uphill (1963 and 1965), Bleeker (1967), Hornung & Staehelin (1974), Murnane (1981), Kemp (1989), Gohary (1992), Galán (2000), Serrano (2002) and Lange (2009).

Attempting to reconstruct and understand the festival and the role of the lector at this festival presents a number of difficulties, as although there is an abundance of fragmentary material on this celebration, there is no one text which describes the various rituals in their entirety. The relevant material is derived from the reigns of kings that are widely separated by many centuries. It is uncertain if the various sources portray the complete ritual or are merely representations of certain scenes. The extent and number of episodes portrayed would have depended on such factors as amount of wall space available and the need to include certain scenes in order to fulfil the ritual requirements. Also have the scholars who arranged the fragments of reliefs in a set order succeeded in reconstructing the correct sequences? (Bleeker 1967: 97; Gohary 1992: 16).

Definition

The *Sed*-festival is often described as a jubilee, but the ritualised event was more than a celebration of the king's accession. It was a renewal of the king's potency and the reaffirmation of the divine descent of the king, and thus a confirmation of his right to the throne (Serrano 2002: 43). Lange (2009: 218) considers that the emphasis was not on the physical powers of the king but a renewal of the special abilities and rights ascribed to the king by virtue of being legitimate successor of the divine royal line, these having been bestowed on him at the coronation ceremonies. However, against this argument is that one of the traditional events in the *Sed*-festival ceremonies was running between boundary markers (albeit in a ritual sense), an activity which does emphasise physical abilities.

Although it was often celebrated thirty years after accession to the throne, several rulers celebrated the event repeatedly and at shorter intervals. Tuthmosis IV had two festivals within ten years, whilst Amenhotep III waited the full period of thirty years. Sethe (1898: 64) suggested that the period started from the proclamation of the future king as crown prince. However, the deciding factor could have been the state of the king's health rather than the passage of a set number of years (Frankfort 1948: 79; Uphill 1963: 124). Godron (1990: 183) notes that on the Rosetta stone, *ḥb-sd*, '*Sed*-festival' is rendered in Greek as *triakontaeteris* 'a thirty-year festival'. However, Bleeker (1967: 114) considers that the Greek term should be translated as 'lord of the *Sed*-festivals', implying that the king is wished a very long reign.

History

Serrano (2002: 42) suggests that the origin of the festival may lie in the Predynastic era, but the first time it is recognised is during the reign of Narmer. Some of the earliest attestations are from the 1st and 2nd Dynasties, but the majority of these depictions are hardly more than single icons, showing the king seated in a *Sed*-festival pavilion. Many of these have come from dockets and jars unearthed at locations such as Hierakonpolis and Saqqara. The first major piece of evidence comes from various architectural elements found in the 3rd Dynasty Step Pyramid complex of Djoser at Saqqara. A comprehensive list of the kings who celebrated *Sed*-festivals together with the relevant supporting evidence can be found in *Studien Zum Sedfest* (Hornung & Staehelin 1974: 16-42).

Sources

There are four main surviving series of representations of the ceremony which are sufficiently comprehensive to be used as a basis for understanding the meaning and purpose of the festival, as well as determining the involvement of the lector in the various rituals. These sources are:

> The reliefs from the chapel of the 5th Dynasty sun-temple of Niuserre at Abu Ghurob.
>
> The reliefs in the 18th Dynasty temple of Amenhotep III at Soleb in Nubia.
>
> The *Sed*-festival scenes of Amenhotep IV inscribed on the Karnak *talatat*.
>
> The reliefs from the 22nd Dynasty temple of Osorkon II at Bubastis.

Additionally, there are some minor sources to which reference will be made.

Niuserre

The scenes from the sun-temple of King Niuserre at Abu Ghurob are the earliest known detailed representations of the *Sed*-festival, but being very fragmentary the information obtainable and the conclusions from them concerning the festival are somewhat limited. The scenes have been copied and published by von Bissing & Kees (1922, 1923 and 1928) and later interpreted by Borchardt (1926), Kaiser (1971), Gohary (1992) and Serrano (2002).

From the inscriptions and interpretations of the above scholars it is possible to reconstruct a sequence of the main ceremonies of the festival. This arrangement then forms a basis for the major rites of the other *Sed*-festivals discussed in this study:

1. Foundation rituals.
2. Inspection of festival building works and census of the cattle.
3. Start of the procession (the king wears the *Sed*-cloak).
4. Lion furniture procession for the rebirth and regeneration of the king.
5. People from all over the country pay homage to the king.
6. The second homage scene.
7. A Min procession.
8. Wepwawet scene incorporating the running sequence.
9. Driving the cattle and presentation to the gods.
10. Bringing the palanquin (carrying-chair).
11. The king takes his place in the palanquin.
12. Closing palanquin procession.

The lector is in evidence in many of the scenes at Abu Ghurob standing in close proximity to the king being one of his principal officiants, as illustrated in figure 66, where he stands with the *sem*-priest and the sole companion. Here, as in all the scenes of the *Sed*-festival of King Niuserre, the lector is depicted with empty hands by his side not holding a papyrus roll. In the later sources of the festival the lector is depicted carrying a roll. As discussed on pages 10-11 these are some of the earliest depictions of a lector with there being little evidence of his activities before this period. Possibly, the ritual practices were not as complex at this time as later and it was not deemed necessary for him to carry a ritual roll. Alternatively, this could relate to ranking, with perhaps lower ranks of lectors not holding a scroll.

FIG. 66: THE KING WEARING THE *SED*-ROBE ACCOMPANIED BY HIS ATTENDANTS AND PRIESTS
(VON BISSING & KEES 1928: PL. 13)

FIG. 67: ANOINTING/PRESENTING THE STANDARDS IN FRONT OF THE KING
(VON BISSING & KEES 1928: PL. 6)

FIG. 68: ENTHRONEMENT OF THE KING IN THE PAVILIONS OF UPPER AND LOWER EGYPT
(VON BISSING & KEES 1928: PL. 16)

FIG. 69: UPPER EGYPT PROCESSION SCENE
(VON BISSING & KEES 1928: PL. 19)

Figure 67 is a scene common in many of the portrayals of the *Sed*-festival, depicting the Wepwawet standard being anointed. The lector, who is standing before the king, speaks whilst his arms are outstretched. It is probable he is announcing this event but the inscription is too damaged to determine this for certain.

The episode central to figure 68 is the enthronement of the king in the pavilions of Upper and Lower Egypt. In the register below this scene the lector faces towards a *was*-sceptre, behind which are the 'Great Ones of Upper and Lower Egypt'. The caption next to the lector is:

> 'Words spoken: accepting and causing the *was*-sceptre to be taken to Horus in the shrine of Lower Egypt' (*ḏd-mdw šsp di in ḥr pr nw*).

To the right of this event there is a procession in the middle of which there is another lector.

Figure 69 is a procession scene in which there are three separate episodes where the king is depicted wearing the crown of Upper Egypt and being carried in a palanquin. In two of these episodes the lector is present. In the first of these (1), the lector faces the king and the caption is:

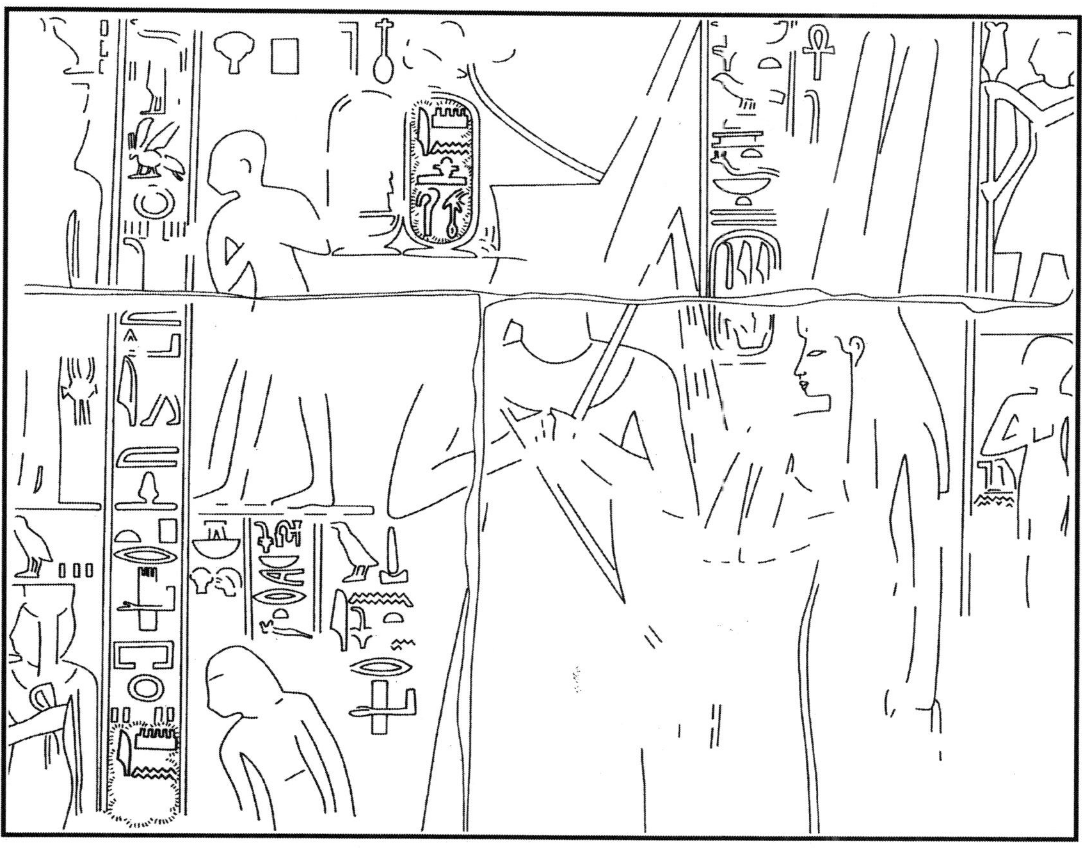

Fig. 70: The king and queen going to the palace preceded by the chief lector, Nebmerutef (adapted from Giorgini *et al.* 1998: pl. 95)

Fig. 71: Chief lector reciting the *ḥṯp-ḏỉ-nšw* formula before the king (adapted from Giorgini et al. 1998: pl. 104)

> 'Words spoken by the lector, carrying the sandals of Niuserre' (*ḏd-mdw ḫry-ḥbt n ꜥḥr ṯbt N-wsr-rꜥ*).

In the second of the episodes (2) a lector presents a bow and quiver of arrows to a *sem*-priest who then passes them on to the king.

At Abu Ghurob the lector can be considered a frequent participant in many of the episodes of the *Sed*-festival. On a number of occasions a lector is labelled as announcing an event or being involved with ritual practice, but at other times the lector is portrayed in procession with other priests and attendants. At no time is he depicted carrying or reading from a papyrus scroll.

Amenhotep III

The surviving inscriptions of the *Sed*-Festival from the temple of Amenhotep III at Soleb are more complete than those at Abu Ghurob, although the festival is not represented in its entirety. The relevant scenes are to be found on the pylon and on the gateway between the court and the outer hypostyle. The scenes have been studied by Lepsius (1849-1859), Breasted (1908), Wilson (1936), Gohary (1992) and Giorgini *et al.* (1998).

On the pylon of the temple is depicted the 'Illumination of the Thrones' ceremony (*hf tnṯ3t*), which Gohary (1992: 12) considers was an initial purification rite prior to the commencement of the festival proper. In this ceremony the king is portrayed as being assisted by various priests and officiants, these being named as: the *sem*-priest and high priest of Amun, Merire; the chief lector, Nebmerutef; and the lector of the phyles and second priest of Amun, Simut, (*ḫry-ḥbt s3w ḥm 2-nw n imn*). A further group of officials is designated the council (*ḏ3ḏ3t*), but the remainding part of the inscription is destroyed and so no further details of this group are able to be determined.

The 'Illumination of the Thrones' ceremony can be split up into four parts as described and translated by Wilson (1936: 293-6):

> Scene A – The beginning of the rite consisting of a number of actors carrying torches, but as this section is badly damaged the content is not clear.
>
> Scenes B and C – These next two scenes appear to be identical and show Amenhotep III and Queen Tiye facing an elaborately decorated shrine which has open doors and a throne inside. Before them a *sem*-priest holds a torch, whilst the chief lector, Nebmerutef, recites:
>
> > 'O *sem*-priest, let a flame be brought and given to the king. O King, take a light from the torch which illuminated (the baldachin)'.
>
> Scene D - Nebmerutef then distributes the flame to the individuals in the procession, each of whom is carrying a torch. Meanwhile the lector recites a formula which is repeated six times:
>
> > 'O *X* let a flame be brought and given to *Y*. O *Y* take a light from the torch which illuminated the baldachin'.

It is not clear what happens to the distributed flame at the end of the ceremony but the reference to the various gods in the text, suggests that the flame is then to be carried to various temples or chapels (Wilson 1936: 296).

On the gateway of the temple arranged in eight registers are the main scenes of the *Sed*-festival. The first and lowest register depicts a procession in which the king is borne in a palanquin. He later leaves the palanquin and proceeds to the palace on foot accompanied by the queen and the chief lector, Nebmerutef (fig. 70). The caption above this scene is:

> 'The chief lector, Nebmerutef. The proceeding to the royal palace' (*ḫry-ḥbt ḥry-tp Nb-mrt.f wḏ3 in nsw r ꜥḥ*).

The second register depicts the king standing beside an offering table with a *sem*-priest censing him and a group of officiants in attendance. Alongside the group stands the chief lector reciting the 'offering formula' (*ḥtp-di-nsw*) to Osiris (fig. 71). In the next register the king proceeds to another shrine to perform a ceremony, again accompanied by the lector and various other priests, before then returning to the palace to rest.

The remaining scenes at Soleb are similar, with the king making offerings to various deities in different shrines, preceded by a standard bearer, priests and other attendants. Some of these scenes are damaged and so the actors cannot always be identified, but a lector is recognised in the fifth register standing alongside the king who is facing towards three rows of men, all of whom carry standards (fig. 72).

Another scene depicts Nebmerutef offering an enigmatic object, the so-called 'clepsydra' (*šbt*), and passing it to the king (fig. 73). The king is shown in a later scene offering the clepsydra to the goddess Nekhbet (fig. 74). The clepsydra which is not depicted before the New Kingdom appears to represent a primate in front of a vertical trunk and is usually considered to be a water clock. This might symbolically relate to the renewal of the king's reign for a future period of time. Cauville (2012: 177) in a recent interpretation suggests that the trunk may have been a container for magical scrolls, with the primate denoting Thoth in the form of a baboon protecting the container (figs. 75, 76).

There is no record at Soleb of the foundation ceremonies, cattle inspection, lion-headed furniture sequence or census, but these could well have been represented on adjacent walls that are now destroyed. Additionally, nearly a thousand years separates the Soleb scenes from those at Abu Ghurob and so factors such as differing artistic convention, style and religious iconography could all influence the choice of material (Gohary 1992: 16).

Fig. 72: Chief lector, Nebmerutef before the king
(adapted from Giorgini *et al.* 1998: pl. 127)

Fig. 73: Chief lector, Nebmerutef holding a clepsydra before the king
(adapted from Giorgini *et al.* 1998: pl. 81)

FIG. 74: THE KING OFFERING THE CLEPSYDRA TO NEKHBET (ADAPTED FROM GIORGINI *ET AL.* 1998: PL. 79)

FIG. 75: IMAGE OF A 'CLEPSYDRA' - KARNAK (COURTESY OF CAUVILLE 2012: 177)

FIG. 76: IMAGE OF A 'CLEPSYDRA' - DENDERA (COURTESY OF CAUVILLE 2012: 177)

In addition to the *Sed*-festival scenes at Soleb there are some depictions of the ceremony in the funerary temple of Amenhotep III at Kom el-Hettan, but these scenes are very fragmentary (Borchardt 1926: 41-4). The title of lector can be recognised on a number of the blocks but other details concerning these depictions are sparse and so there is little in the way of additional information to be obtained.

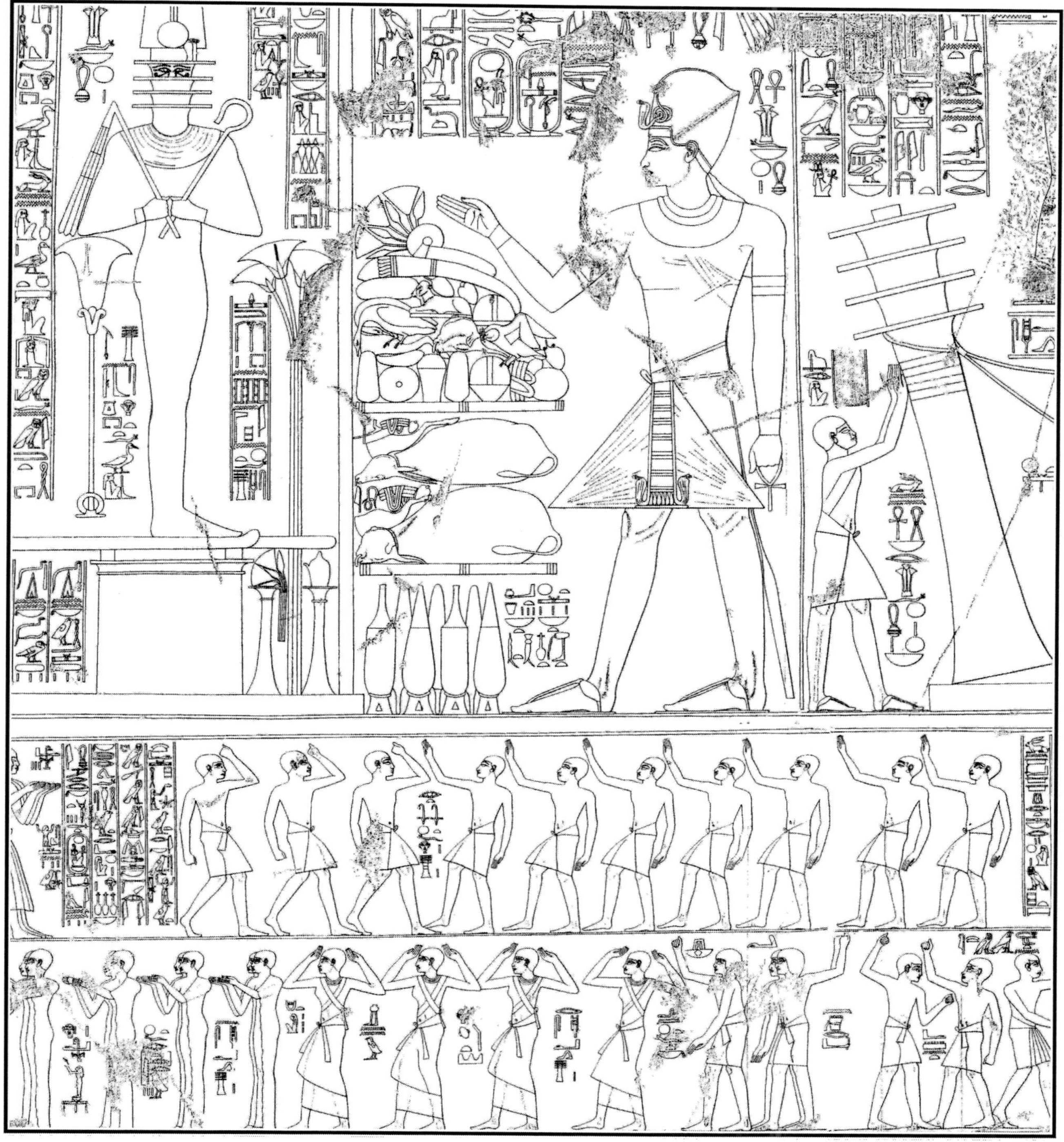

Fig. 77: A scene from the tomb of Kheruef (TT 192) showing the *Sed*-festival of Amenhotep III. A lector is depicted in the lower register, in a dancing pose (adapted from the Epigraphic Survey 1980: pl. 47)

The Theban tomb of the official Kheruef (TT 192) has scenes relating to both the first *Sed*-festival in Year 30 and the third festival in Year 37. These particular scenes are an abbreviated illustration of parts of the festival and seem to be restricted to ceremonies in which Kheruef himself had an active role (Gohary 1992: 17). In the first festival one of the scenes depicts Kheruef standing with the king alongside the chief lector and two viziers. In the third festival one of the scenes depicts the 'Raising of the *Djed*-pillar', a ceremony considered to be another preliminary rite to the main festival.

Below this rite are two registers showing dancing girls and musicians, and next to a troupe of four female dancers is a lector (Fakhry 1943: 483; fig. 77). He appears to be in a dancing posture as his right arm is half-raised with fist closed, possibly in the *hnw* gesture, but the caption alongside him is damaged so the scene cannot be completely interpreted.

Amenhotep IV

The temple of the Aten at Karnak, the *Gem-pa-Aten,* ('the sun disk is found') was built by Amenhotep IV and was constructed from small sandstone blocks known as *talatat*. The temple was dismantled at the end of his reign and the blocks were subsequently reused by later kings in other structures at Karnak, such as foundations for the hypostyle hall and filling material in the Second, Ninth and Tenth Pylons (Gohary 1992: 26).

Many of these blocks have subsequently been recovered and the Akhenaten Temple Project has been able to recreate many of the lost scenes, including the partial depiction of a *Sed*-festival being celebrated by Amenhotep IV (Smith & Redford 1976). The ceremony is considered to have occurred early in his reign, possibly by year 2 or 3, as all the scenes display the name of Amenhotep rather than that of Akhenaten, a name he took by Year 6 of his reign.

Scene Number	Plate Number
58	27
64	30
68	32
69	32
72	32
73	33
74	34
79	35
92	37
93	39
94	39

Table 10: Scenes which include a depiction of the lector with relevant plate numbers (modified from Gohary 1992)

Photographs of all the talatat blocks have been published in *Akhenaten's Sed-Festival at Karnak* by Jocelyn Gohary (1992). From an examination of these images it is possible to identify the lector in the following scenes:

1. Scene 3 (Gohary 1992: pl. 3): The chief lector is shown bowing before the king and queen as they leave the palace.
2. There are a number of 'offering-kiosk' scenes in which the king wearing the *Sed*-festival robe makes an offering before an offering table in a roofless kiosk, before then moving off in procession to another kiosk to repeat this ritual. Above each offering table, the sun-disk of the Aten is depicted, the rays of which terminate in hands directed towards the table. In each of these episodes the king is assisted by three officiants: the 'Greatest of Seers of Re-Horakhty in the House of Aten in Southern Heliopolis' (*wr m3w n Rʿ-ḥr3hty m pr ʿitn m ʿiwnw šmʿw*), a lector who precedes him, and a priest who carries the title the 'Chamberlain and First Prophet of the King' (*imy-ḫnt ḥm nṯr tpy n Nfr-ḫprw-Rʿ wʿ-n-rʿ*). (Table 10 lists the scenes depicting the lector with the relevant plate numbers).
3. In Scene 157 (Gohary 1992: pl. 63) there is a depiction of a lector but few other details of this scene are discernable.
4. There are a number of other individual blocks that are considered repeats of episodes described in scenes 1-165 (plates 1-66). These either show the presence of a lector or just his title, and they are listed in Table 11.

Plate Number	Block Number
67	9
68	20
69	7
74	1
103	7, 14, 15

Table 11: Repeated episodes (modified from Gohary 1992)

There are some marked differences between the *Sed*-festival of Amenhotep IV and those of other rulers. The only god mentioned at the *Sed*-festival of Amenhotep IV is the Aten; the major deities that were present in the *Sed*-festivals of other rulers are absent. There is no procession of the gods and their emblems to their shrines, and the shrines that are present are not of traditional design but roofless kiosks into which the rays of the Aten could penetrate (Aldred 1988: 266; Reeves 2001: 97). Importantly, the scenes of the festival suggest the acceptance by Amenhotep of the event even though he had rejected the presence of the traditional Egyptian gods at the ceremony.

However, there are also some close similarities to other festivals such as the king wearing the short jubilee cloak, wearing the crowns of Upper and Lower Egypt, and being accompanied by various officiants, one of these being the lector. The lector is dressed similarly, has the same hair style as in previous ceremonies, and carries the papyrus roll ready to recite the prescribed liturgy. As in other scenes relating to the reign of Amenhotep IV, the lector similar to other officials, is depicted bowing deeply in the usual submissive attitude. An example is a limestone relief showing Amenhotep IV making offerings to the Aten, preceded by a deeply bowing lector (Cambridge E.GA.2300.1943).

Importantly, although the study of the *Sed*-festival *talatat* indicates a state of transition from the traditional religious views of previous generations to the more developed monotheistic religion of the Amarna Period, the lector is still depicted in scenes performing the usual ritual acts and is present in close proximity to the king as one of his principal attendants. This continuity of the role of the lector at the *Sed*-festival during the reign of Amenhotep IV contrasts strongly with the lack of depictions of the lector in funerary art during this period (see page 103 for funerary rituals in the Amarna Period).

Amenhotep is considered to have celebrated another *Sed*-festival later in his reign after his change of name, but there are no surviving inscriptions of that festival that would be helpful in this present discussion on the role of the lector (Aldred 1959: 26-7).

Osorkon II

The scenes of the *Sed*-festival of Osorkon II at Bubastis were originally copied and published by Naville in 1892. Because of the relative completeness of the scenes, compared to those of other rulers, they have been utilised by many researchers as the main source upon which to understand and interpret the *Sed*-festival.

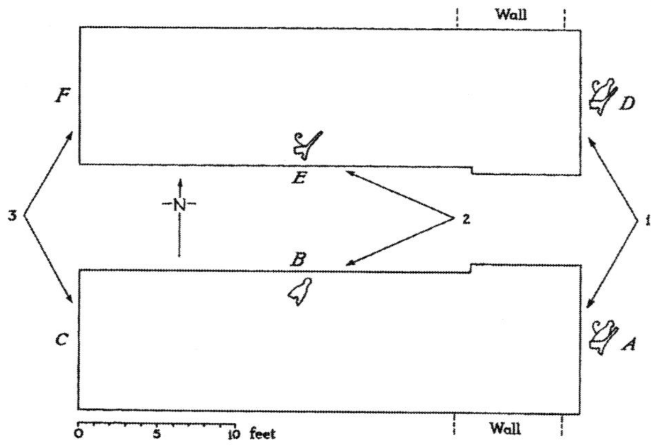

FIG. 78: SCHEMATIC REPRESENTATION OF THE WALLS OF THE FESTIVAL HALL OF OSORKON II (ADAPTED FROM UPHILL 1965: 366)

A word of caution is issued by Bleeker (1967: 103) as to the interpretation of these scenes as only about 30% of the original reliefs from the temple have survived. Uphill (1965: 367) suggests that the scenes were never intended to be a complete representation of the full rites, but merely a synopsis of the ceremony. Additionally, parts of the granite doorway, upon which the *Sed*-festival scenes are represented, had collapsed when Naville attempted his reconstruction and so later scholars have come to question his sequence of the various episodes (Bleeker 1967: 103; Gohary 1992: 18).

For the purpose of this discussion the schematic representation of the walls of the Hall published by Uphill (1965: 366) will be referred to. Each wall is discussed in turn, commencing with the lower register. Only the relevant scenes that include the presence of a lector are commented on (fig. 78).

Walls A and D

The beginning of the ceremony is recorded on the lower register of Wall A where Osorkon is shown offering to a number of deities. The register above this depicts the king, accompanied by the Queen, offering a clepsydra to the Goddess Nekhbet (Lange 2009: 205). A figure standing behind the queen passes the clepsydra to the king, and although the identity of this actor is not certain, parallels with other scenes suggests him to be a lector (fig. 79; also see previously on page 70). A similar scene is to be found on wall D (fig. 80).

FIG. 79: SHOWING A FIGURE (ASSUMED TO BE A LECTOR) PASSING A CLEPSYDRA TO THE KING (WALL A) (NAVILLE 1892: PL. 3)

FIG. 80: SHOWING A FIGURE (ASSUMED TO BE A LECTOR) PASSING A CLEPSYDRA TO THE KING (WALL D) (NAVILLE 1892: PL. 16)

Fig. 81: The lector in front of the king, shown bent slightly forwards (Naville 1892: pl. 2)

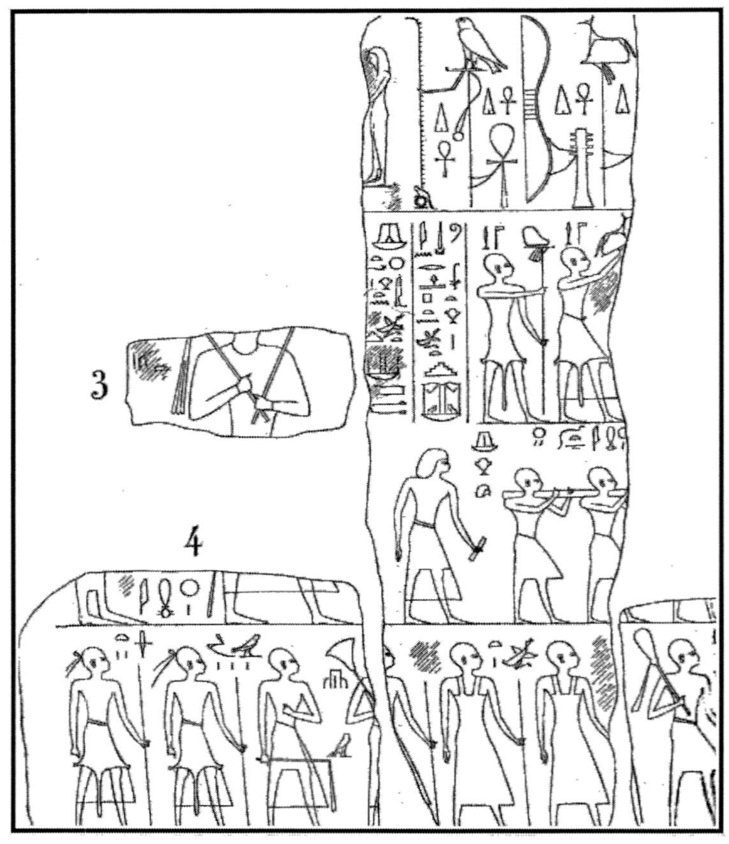

Fig. 82: The lector in front of the king (Naville 1892: pl. 1)

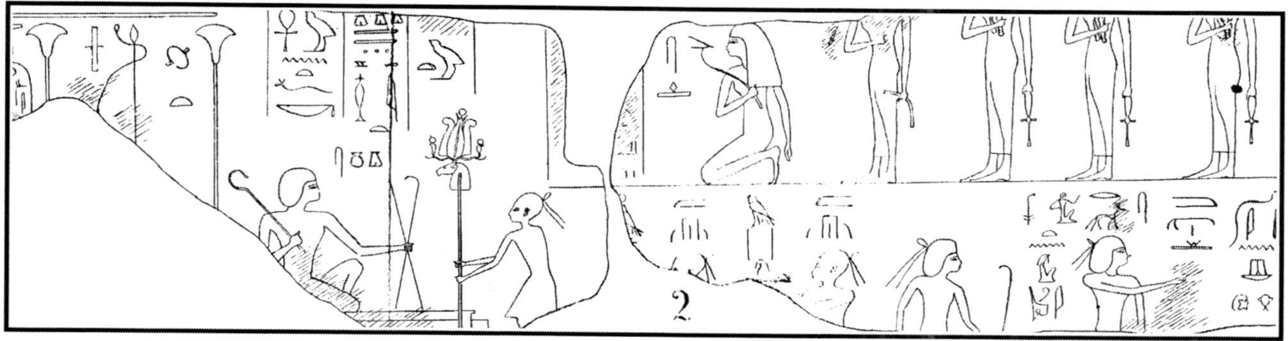

Fig. 83: The chief lector with hand outstretched (Naville 1892: pl. 1)

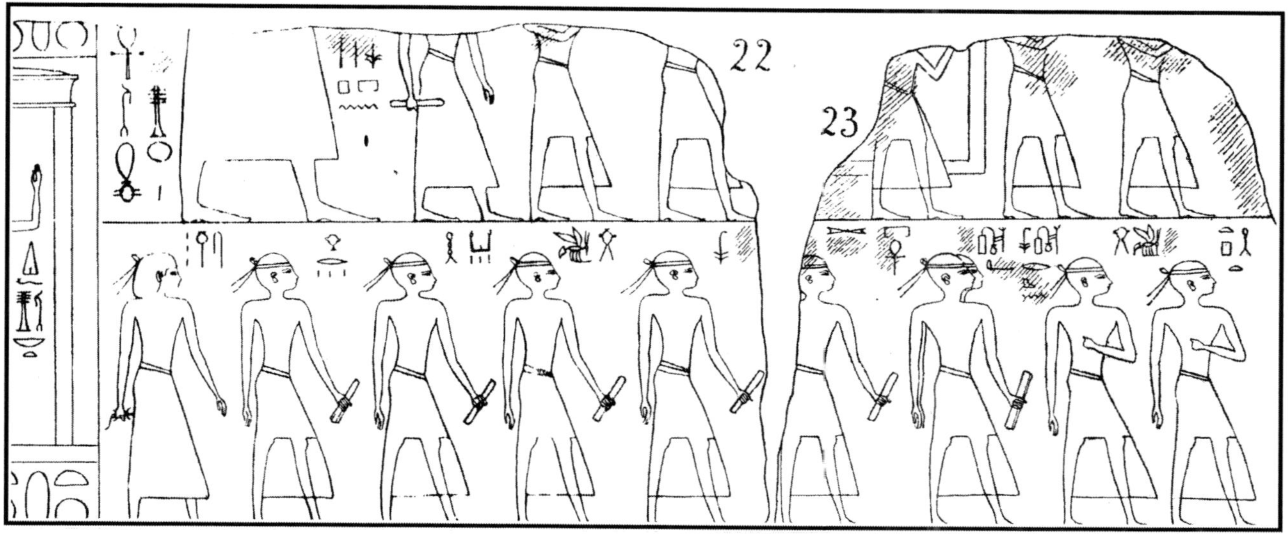

Fig. 84: The lector immediately in front of the king (Naville 1892: pl. 8)

A procession of priests led by the 'Divine Mother of Siut' (*mwt nṯr n s3ty*) then advances to the first *Sed*-festival pavilion. Following on behind are the standard bearers and six men carrying the shrine of Wepwawet. Finally, at the rear of the procession, in front of the king, is a lector who is portrayed as inclining forward and holding a papyrus roll (fig. 81).

The next register, higher up wall A, again depicts a procession scene involving priests and the lector with the king and queen (fig. 82). The inscription reads:

> 'A proceeding of the king in order to rest in the baldachin of the *Sed*-festival, the lector when he goes towards the baldachin of the *Sed*-festival reads …' (*wd3 nsw r ḥtp ḥr tnt3t ḥb-sd ẖry-ḥbt ḫtf ii(.f) ḥr tnt3t ḥb-sd*).

In the top register of Wall A the king is shown seated in a pavilion. Standing on the platform in front of the king are a number of priests and the chief lector. He has his arm outstretched and the inscription above him reads:

> 'Words spoken by the chief lector in the presence of the royal official(s)' (*ḏd.in ẖry-ḥbt ḥry-tp m-b3ḥ sr nsw in*) (fig. 83).

Walls B and C (Upper Egyptian rituals)

Wall B mainly consists of the first homage or 'appearance' scene and the visit to the assembled gods and goddesses of Upper Egypt. The only relevant register showing a lector is the procession scene of the god Wepwawet behind which can be seen the lector in his usual position, immediately in front of the king (fig. 84).

A lector is again shown in the upper register of Wall C but here there is some confusion as to the sequence of these upper episodes on both Walls B and C, with Uphill (1965: 377) and Gohary (1992: 23) choosing to read them in a different order. This particular scene shows Osorkon standing before the Great Ennead. The register also shows him being accompanied by men holding figures on statues, and a row of officiants, one of whom is a chief lector (fig. 85).

Fig. 85: The lector in a procession
(Naville 1892: pl. 10)

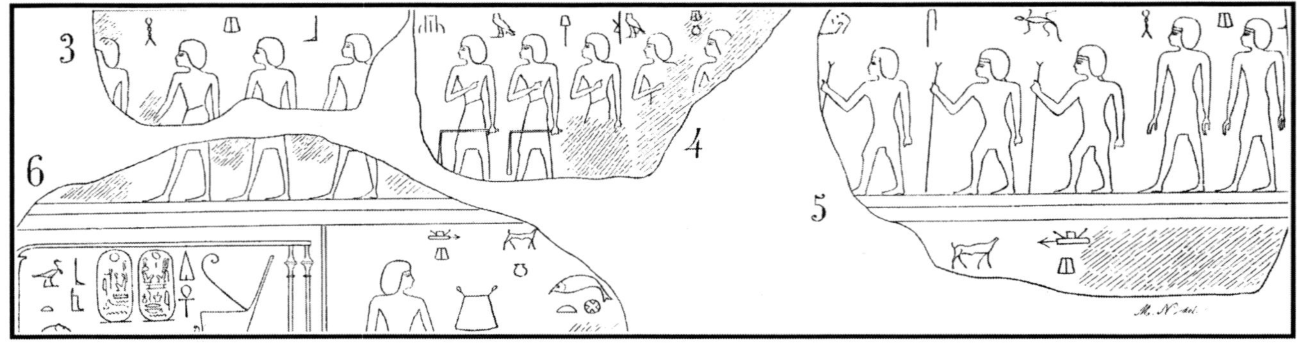

Fig. 86: Two groups of lectors, the right group is without papyrus rolls
(Naville 1892: pl. 20)

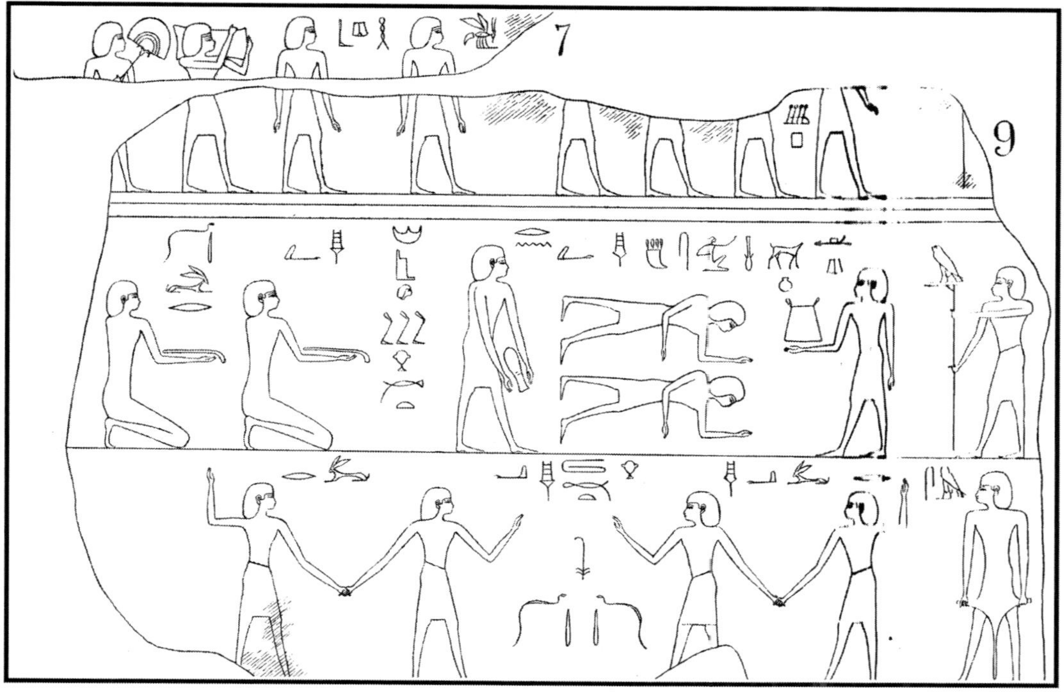

Fig. 87: Two lectors in procession without papyrus rolls
(Naville 1892: pl. 24)

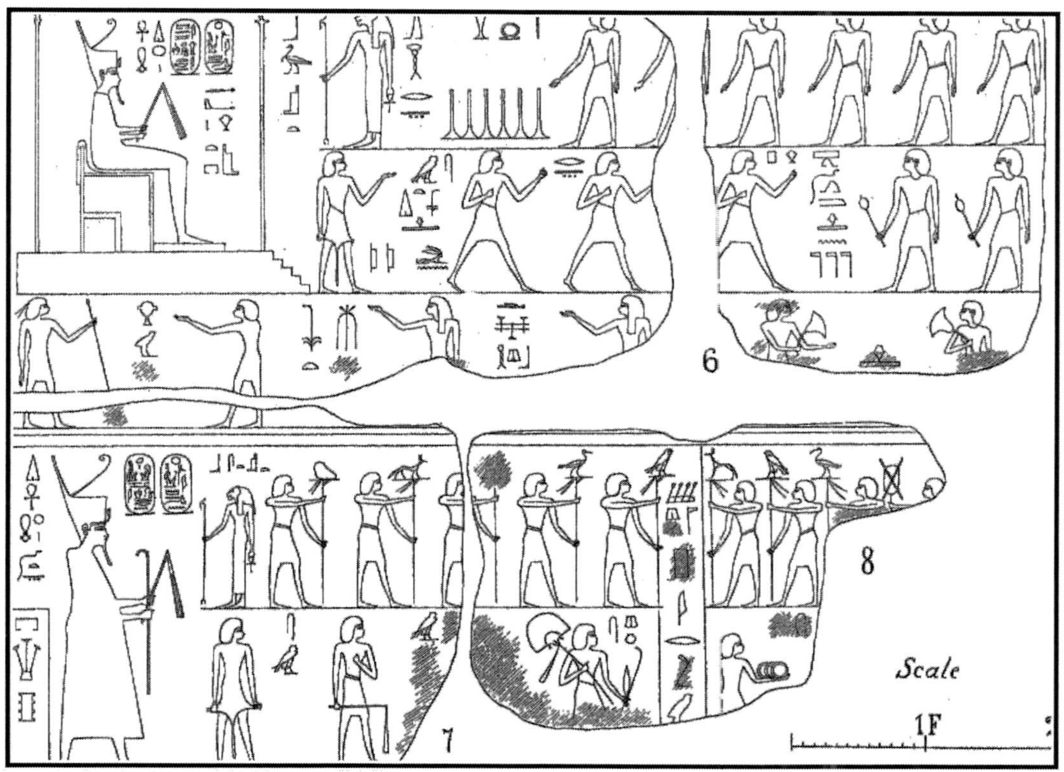

Fig. 88: Two princesses gesturing to the lector
(Naville 1892: pl. 23)

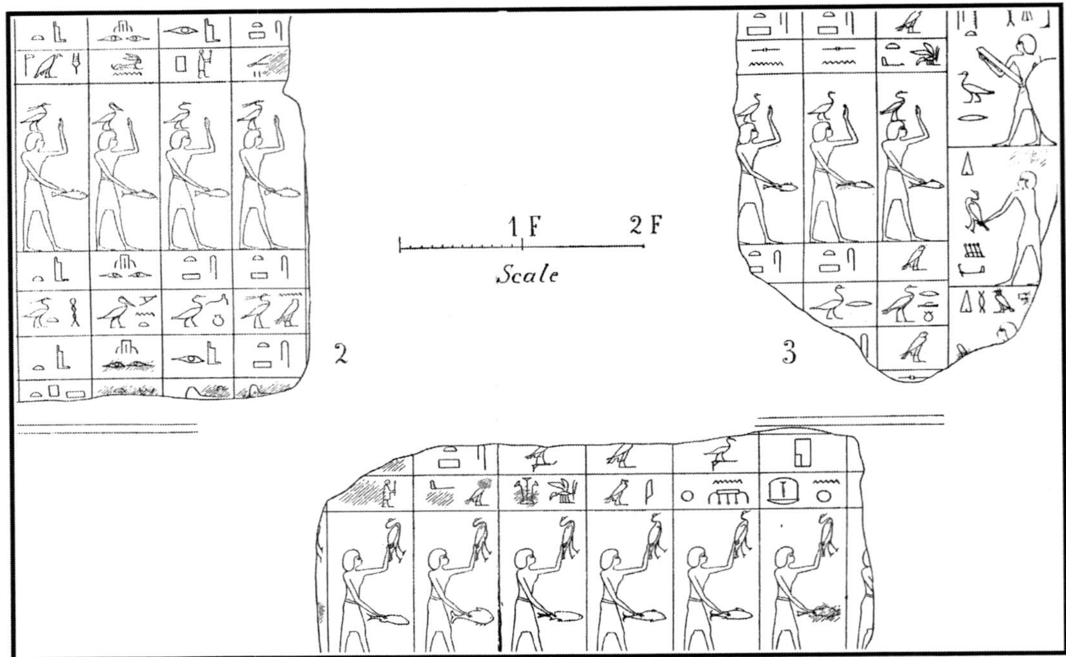

Fig. 89: The lector receiving/recording the offerings (Naville 1892: pl. 2)

Walls E and F (Lower Egyptian Rituals)

Wall E is extensively damaged with many of the inscribed blocks no longer in position. In the centre of the wall there are some traces of a scene depicting dwarfs acting as guards or police (*sꜥšꜣ*), behind whom are a group of lectors (fig. 86.5). Nearby are figures of a Headman of Pe (*ḥry Pe*), a *sem*-priest and an unnamed individual who carries a bow. An adjacent scene again shows a number of lectors (fig. 86.3).

Moving next to Wall F, the lower register again displays a procession scene with the king and his entourage leaving a building, labelled the 'House of the North' (*pr mḥw*). Amongst the officials of the entourage are the *sem*-priest and the lector (fig. 87).

Above this register there is a homage scene with the king sitting in a kiosk and below him is a lector. Here the two royal daughters are gesturing to the lector saying: 'Wait lector' (*dy ḥry-ḥb*). Naville (1892: 34) interprets this scene as gesturing to the lector to halt proceedings whilst an offering ritual is being completed (fig. 88).

Above this register is a scene which is divided into individual compartments, in each of which there is a man bringing an offering of birds or fish. Each compartment is labelled with the name of a particular god, and the suggestion is that the particular variety of bird or fish is the property of that god. These gods are then considered to be bringing these various birds and fish to the festival (Naville 1892: 33). In front of these figures is a lector holding an open papyrus roll who appears to be recording and accepting these offerings on behalf of the temple (fig. 89).

The uppermost register of Wall F has two representations of the king seated inside a kiosk, and here the inscription indicates that he sits in one before then moving on to the other. Among the usual attendants are two lectors. Above this scene is the caption 'the house of putting the fans in their places' (*pr rdi šwt ḥr swt*) which has been interpreted by Naville (1892: 35) as an indication that the fans are being put away and the festival is at an end.

Summary of the Role of the Lector in the Sed-festival Rituals

Niuserre

The lector is frequently depicted immediately before the king. He is seen announcing the anointing of the Wepwawet standard and the presentation of the *was*-sceptre to the king. He takes an active part in the ceremonies when he presents the ritual bow and quiver of arrows to the king. On other occasions a lector is shown in procession and in none of the scenes at Abu Gurob is the lector shown holding a papyrus roll.

Amenhotep III

At Soleb the lector is involved with the preliminary 'Illumination of the thrones' ceremony, initially acting as 'master of ceremonies' or 'director of ritual'. He later distributes the flame to the individuals in the procession during this rite. In the main part of the *Sed*-festival the lector accompanies the king in procession. He recites the *ḥtp-di-nsw* formula; he is portrayed as passing the clepsydra to the king, and in the tomb of Kheruef he is represented in a *hnw* or dancing pose.

Amenhotep IV

The lector has a similar role as described for the other main sources, but is shown bowed in the usual subservient Amarnan posture.

Osorkon II

Similarly, at Bubastis, as in the other *Sed*-festivals the lector is immediately in front of the king being one of the leading officiants. Again he acts as 'master of ceremonies' as is attested by two of the princesses calling on him to delay the proceedings.

Interpretation and Conclusion

The lector is seldom absent from scenes depicting the *Sed*-festival, often immediately before the king and acting as one of the principal officiants. His role is often that of ritual director, a similar function to the one he performed in the Opening of the Mouth ritual. The lector is also an active participant in the rituals, passing ceremonial regalia to the king at Abu Ghurob and distributing the flame in the 'Illumination Ceremony' at Soleb. A lector is observed in a *hnw* or dancing posture at the *Sed*-festival of Amenhotep III.

In the festival scenes from Abu Ghurob the lector is not shown carrying a papyrus roll. However, in other examples of the *Sed*-festival described above the lector is usually depicted with the roll except on the occasions when he is in procession. This could relate to the early 5th Dynasty date of the Abu Ghurob scenes, when the liturgy was less complex and the lector may have memorised the recitations or had few to recite. The function of the lector may not have been fully developed at that time.

There are a number of similarities between the various *Sed*-festival scenes of the different monarchs, particularly, the Bubastis scenes which appear to follow very closely those of Amenhotep III at Soleb, despite there being some 450 years separating these two ceremonies. Naville and subsequent researchers have acknowledged that the precise order of a number of the Bubastis reliefs is difficult to determine, but they did comment on the marked similarities with the scenes at Soleb. Gohary (1992: 25) suggested that the depictions must have been copied from a common source despite the time-period between these reliefs. In addition, the depictions of the *Sed*-festival at Soleb and Bubastis show some similarities with the much earlier scenes at Abu Ghurob. However, Lange (2009: 214) considered that the reliefs from a *Sed*-festival were not simply copies of a specific forerunner but were created independently from a collection of different sources.

Nevertheless, there could be an element of archaism in operation, a conscious return to past styles and models in order to derive inspiration from the past, provide legitimacy and emulate styles held in esteem. 18th Dynasty styles influenced the construction and decoration of the Festival Hall of Osorkon. Additionally, there are examples of statues of Osorkon II bearing distinctly Tuthmoside features (Morkot 2003: 94). It would seem quite possible that the Egyptians during the reign of Osorkon II derived inspiration from the earlier model of the *Sed*-festival of Amenhotep III.

Importantly, the lector is frequently depicted in all of the above examples of the *Sed*-festival, spanning a period of over 1600 years of Dynastic history. In all these ceremonies he performed a similar role in being a principal officiant, a director of proceedings and an active participant in a number of the rituals.

Chapter 7

Funerary Ritual and Provisioning the Dead

1. Introduction

In ancient Egypt death was conceptualised as dismemberment, a severing of the connection between the distinctive aspects of the individual. An eternal afterlife could only be achieved by various actions carried out on behalf of the dead person by the living. The physical body had to be preserved through mummification, material provision had to be made for the deceased and various magical rituals had to be performed to cause the individual to become a 'transfigured spirit', an *akh* (Assmann 2005: 23-31; Taylor 2010: 17). These ceremonies were vital in ensuring the immortality of the dead person and the lector had a key role to play in these rituals.

The necessity of having a lector at a funeral is emphasised in the inscriptions on the façade of the 6th Dynasty joint tomb of Mekhu I (QH 25) and Sabni (QH 26) at Qubbert el-Hawa. The text describes how Sabni set off on an expedition to recover the body of his father Mekhu who had died in Nubia. The king, on hearing of this, sent all the equipment required for a burial together with a number of officiants and among this group was a chief lector. The inscription reads (*Urk* 1, 138):

> 'Two embalmers, a chief lector, one who is on his annual duty, the inspector of the *wabet*, mourners, and the whole of the equipment from the *per-nefer'*[1] (translated Strudwick 2005: 337).

Probably for reasons of decorum there are virtually no depictions of a royal funeral at any time in Egyptian history apart from the Amarna Period (Gillam 2009: 36). However, depictions of private funerary ceremonies and their aftermath can be found in tombs, papyri and on coffins. Altenmüller (*LÄ* I: 745-65) lists 102 examples of funerary scenes of different individuals which vary in detail and extend from the 1st Dynasty to the beginning of the Ptolemaic Period. In this present study into the role of the lector in the funeral liturgy, the Old Kingdom will be studied in the greatest detail as the tomb scenes from this period provide the most complete picture of the various stages of the funeral procession from leaving the home of the deceased to final interment in the tomb.

2. Old Kingdom

For the Old Kingdom the decoration of any tomb is not complete enough to be able to recreate the entire funeral ceremony or to determine the extent of the involvement of the lector. Bolshakov (1991: 34-5) provides a list of all the available Old Kingdom burial scenes with the earliest and most specific representation of such ceremonies being that in the 4th Dynasty tomb of Debehen at Giza (LG 90). However, the scenes of the 6th Dynasty tombs of Mereruka and Ankhmahor from the Teti Pyramid Cemetery at Saqqara, together with those of Qar (G 7101) and Idu (G 7102) at Giza, make it possible to reconstruct an Old Kingdom funeral, containing as they do all the essential elements of the ceremony (Snape 2011: 72).

The order and number of the various funerary scenes differ from tomb to tomb and so attempting to establish a pattern is not always possible, nor is it always obvious what actual event is being portrayed. This problem of recognition and interpretation has been acknowledged in previous studies (Eaton-Krauss 1984). However, this may not be a very successful exercise as endeavouring to interpret the scenes in terms of modern concepts can be misleading, as these images were never intended to be analysed by a different culture. As regards the number of scenes being portrayed in tombs, then the availability of sufficient wall space and differing resources could explain the variation from tomb to tomb and also account for the limited number of funerary scenes noticeable in certain tombs. Equally, it is possible that not all of the funerary rituals described in some tombs were performed at every burial, so the depiction of the ideal seen in certain tombs would conform to representational convention.

Transition from Home to the River

Following death the corpse would have been embalmed without delay as the hot climate in Egypt would have soon caused putrefaction. Mummification was carried out on the western side of the Nile and in the depictions of funerary scenes of the elite, the deceased were transported across the river in a funerary procession (Assmann 2005: 304-6; Taylor 2010: 83).

The place of departure of the procession is depicted in scenes from both the funerals of Mereruka and Ankhmahor as being the house of the deceased, where groups of mourning women are portrayed (figs. 90, 91).[2] This is confirmed by the caption above the house of Ankhmahor which states:

> 'Going out from the house of the estate to the beautiful west' (*prt m pr n ḏt r imnt nfr*).

[1] *Per-nefer* or 'House of Perfection' is rendered 'House of Rejuvenation' and discussed by Donohue (1978: 143-8). It is suggested that this is the place where the deceased was prepared for burial and corresponds to the *wabet*.

[2] For a discussion of stages of grief and mourning rites during Egyptian funerary ritual see Kucharek 2005.

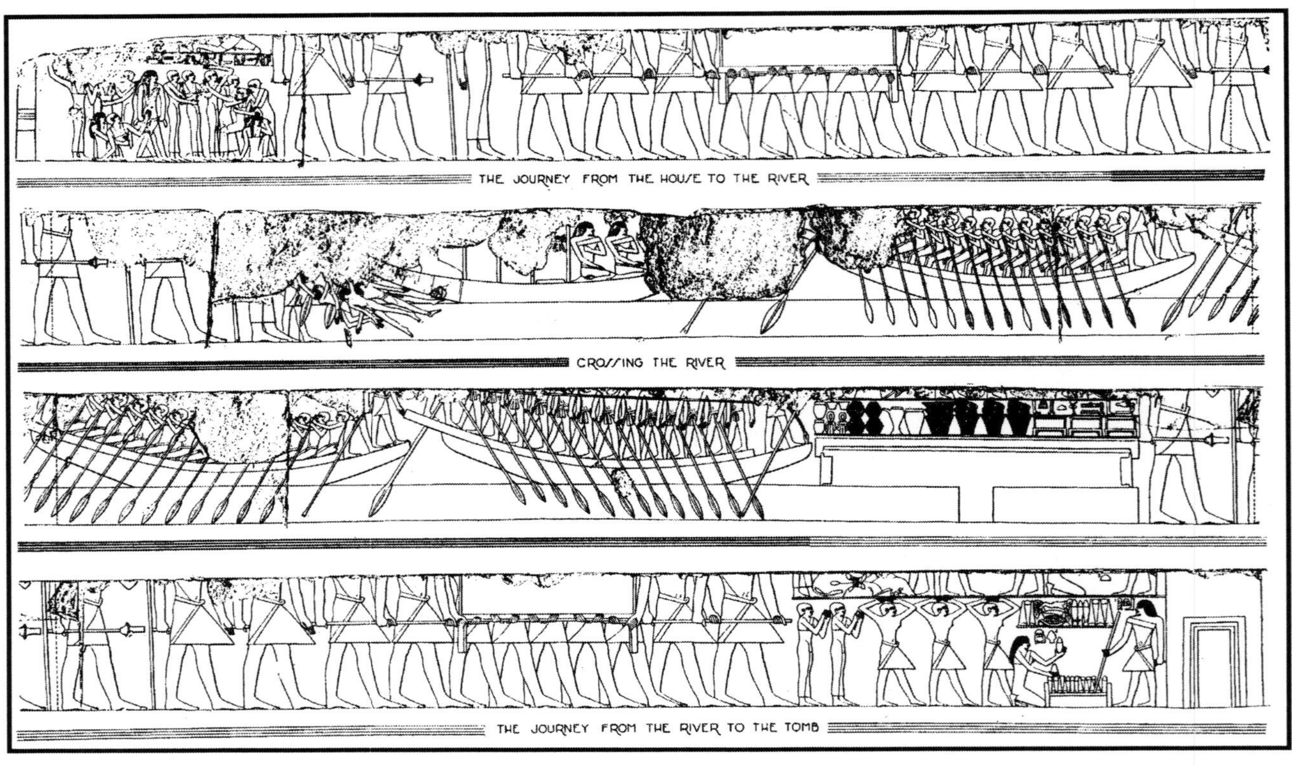

FIG. 90: FUNERAL PROCESSION OF THE VIZIER MERERUKA
(DUELL 1938: II, PL. 130)

FIG. 91: THE FUNERAL PROCESSION OF ANKHMAHOR
(CAPART 1907: II, PLS. 70-2)

The coffin carried on poles by a group of bearers was accompanied by the main celebrants of the procession, whose number and role varied from tomb scene to tomb scene. There were one or two women labelled as 'kites' (*ḏrywt*), these being identified with the goddesses Isis and Nephthys. The role of a man named 'Seal-bearer of the god and chief *wt'* appeared to be that of organising the activities associated with the funeral. This function would in later times be discharged by the *sem*-priest and the lector. Other celebrants were an individual labelled as 'the embalmer *(wt)* of Anubis', and, finally, the lector who is considered to represent the god, Thoth (Wilson 1944: 203-5; Assmann 2005: 302-3; Hays 2010: 5).

FIG. 92: THE FUNERAL PROCESSION OF QAR (ADAPTED FROM SIMPSON 1976: PL. 24)

FIG. 93: THE FUNERAL PROCESSION OF NEBKAU-HOR (HASSAN 1938: PL. 47)

In his capacity of assisting the deceased the lector resembles Thoth who cared for Osiris. In funerary texts the deceased appeals to Thoth to help him in obtaining a blessed existence in the afterlife by rendering him assistance, just as Thoth did for Osiris. Thoth 'unites' the deceased as demonstrated in Pyramid Text §639: 'He has caused Thoth to reassemble you …', and §830: 'O Thoth, reassemble me, that what is on me may cease to be' (Faulkner 1969: 121, 149).

This reunion of the body is essential for continued existence in the after-life. Thoth also washes the feet of the deceased as in Pyramid Text §1247: 'O Thoth rub my feet' (Faulkner 1969: 198). In Pyramid Text §1570 Thoth places his arms around the deceased, and in Text §157 he announces the arrival of the deceased in the after-life (Faulkner 1969: 237, 44; Bleeker 1973: 145-7).

Many of the tomb scenes depicting this part of the journey show the lector standing with his scroll rolled up in his hand, but in the mastaba of Qar the lector is depicted reciting from an unrolled scroll. The coffin is being borne on carrying-poles by a group of men who are being led by the lector and the caption is: 'Making transfigurations' (*s3ḫt*) (Simpson 1976: fig. 24; fig. 92).

Crossing the Water

The Old Kingdom scenes then usually show the coffin loaded onto a barge to cross a body of water. Possibly this was the river Nile or a canal used to transport the coffin to the edge of the desert plateau. Equally, there may have been a symbolic significance in this depiction of a water crossing, as later in Egyptian history the boat carrying the coffin is sometimes equated with the 'great ferry' that the deceased would use to facilitate the transition from the realm of the dead to the afterlife. An example of such a ferry is depicted in the 19th Dynasty tomb of Neferronpet (TT 133; Assmann 2005: 304). Bolshakov (1991: 37) suggests that depictions showing the funeral boat being hauled by a group of men trudging along the shore indicate that this was merely a symbolic cruise. However, in a practical sense water would have been the preferred mode of transportation for a coffin where a stretch of canal or river was available.

A seated lector is invariably depicted in the boats of these various scenes and evidence suggests that whilst crossing the water he is performing a ritual act (appendix 4). A damaged funeral scene from the tomb of the 5th Dynasty vizier, Ptahhotep (D 62), has a caption above the seated lector stating: 'Making transfigurations' (*s3ḫ*) (*LD* II: 101b). In a tomb scene from the 6th Dynasty funerary procession of Nebkau-Hor from Saqqara, again showing a funeral boat, there is a depiction of a booth at the rear of the scene in which a lector is reciting from his unrolled papyrus scroll (Hassan 1938: pl. 47; fig. 93). The reception group ahead of the funeral boat of Nebkau-Hor also contains two reading lectors. The 6th Dynasty tomb scenes of Sneferu-Inshetef at Dahshur (Mastaba 2) similarly show a standing lector inside a booth reading from a papyrus roll (de Morgan 1903: pl. 22; fig. 94).

Fig. 94: The funeral procession of Sneferu-Inshetef (de Morgan 1903: pl. 22)

A scene from the 5th Dynasty funeral procession of Hetepherakhti from his tomb at Saqqara (D 60) again shows the funeral barge and at the prow of the boat there is an undesignated man and women together with a seated lector. The caption above the lector reads (Rijksmuseum van Oudheden te Leiden 1905: 1, pl. 9):

> 'Sailing while the ritual is conducted by the lector' (*ḫnt šsm ḥb in ḫry-ḥbt*)

Further confirmation concerning the ritual being performed by the lector during the water-crossing is provided by the false door in the tomb of Ptahhotep at Saqqara (Quibell *et al.* 1898: pl. 39; figs. 95, 96). Ptahhotep is shown seated under a canopy facing a lector reading from his scroll, the caption being:

> 'There is performed for him the traversing of the lake. He is transfigured by the performance of a service by the lector' (*ir n.f nmit š s3ḫt.f ḥr ir ḫt in ḫry-ḥbt*).

Similarly, an inscription on the false door of the 5th Dynasty tomb of Tepemankh at Saqqara (D11) reads (*Urk* I: 190, l.15-17; Mariette 1889: 195):

> 'A procession to his tomb of the west, after rowing him in the *wrt*-boat, when a fully equipped ritual had been conducted for him according to the writing of the craft of the lector' (*šms r is.f in imntw m-ḫt ḫnwt.f m wrt sšm n.f ḥb ʿpr ḫt sš n ḥmt n ḫry-ḥbt*)

As with the procession shown in the tomb of Qar and Idu, whilst the crossing of the water was in progress the lector was reciting various texts that were designed to make the deceased a 'transfigured one' or 'blessed one' (*3ḫ*). Assmann (2005: 304-5) relates the physical crossing of the water and the ritual as effecting a spiritual crossing to another world, a transition from death to the afterlife.

In the 6th Dynasty tomb of Djau at Deir el-Gebrawi two boats are being towed. On a platform at the front of the first of these boats stands a lector who appears to be acting as a pilot when he calls out (Davies 1902: II, pl. 7; Wilson 1944: 208; fig. 97):

> 'Starboard! You have made to port' (*imy-wrt ir in t3-wr*)

This is a rather unusual scene, perhaps indicating the practical nature of the role of the lector, although the representation of the lector high in the prow of the boat could also suggest the performance of a magical act. An incantation aimed at protection against creatures in the water as well as malevolent forces.

The Harris Magical Papyrus refers to the deployment of a magically activated substance to 'the man at the front of a boat' to ward away the crocodiles (P. BM EA 10042, recto VI, 12-VII, 1):

> 'This spell is to be spoken (to/over) an egg of clay (*ḏd-tw r pn swḥt n sin*)
> which is placed in the hand of a man at the front of a boat. (*rdiw mḏrt s m-ḥ3t dpt*)
> If the one who is on the water should come out, (*ir pry nty ḥr mw*)
> it is to be thrown on the water (*ḫ3ʿ.tw ḥr mw*)' (translated Kyffin 2011: 233).

Again the Harris Papyrus refers to water spells being conducted by a chief lector (as discussed on page 20).

> 'First spell of enchanting all that is in the water concerning which the chief lector says' (*r tpy sḥsy m mw nb iw ḏd ḫry.w-tp r.f*)

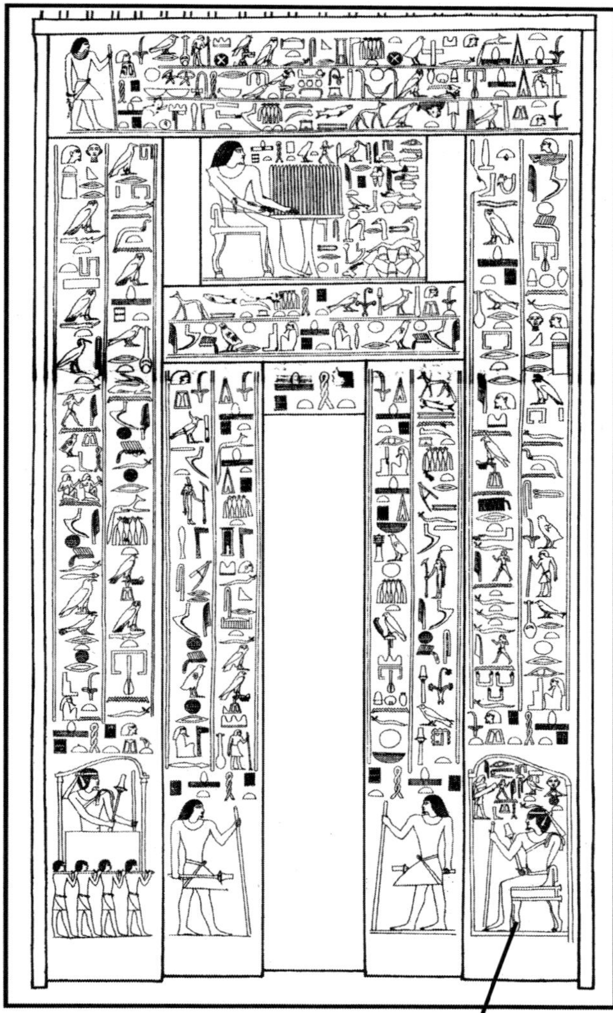

Fig. 95: The false door of Ptahhotep from his tomb at Saqqara (Quibell 1898: pl. 39)

Fig. 96: Detail from the above figure

There is another reference to water-spells in a scene from the funeral procession of Sneferu-Inshetef at disembarkation on the western river bank. Here the lector is receiving the barge whilst sacrifice and offerings are being prepared. The caption above the scene is:

> 'Conducting the water ritual by the lector Iihemenes' (*sšm ḥb nw in ẖry-ḥbt iḥmns*) (fig. 94).

The next stage of the funerary proceedings is where the coffin is conveyed to the tent of purification (*ibw*) and further rituals are performed. This is illustrated in the funeral procession depicted in the tomb of Qar, where the lector leads the procession reading from his scroll with the usual caption: 'Making transfigurations'.

Following him are the *wt* and the kite. Behind the coffin this grouping of officiants is repeated and here the caption is:

> 'Travelling in peace to the *ibw*-tent for purification by the followers of the revered one' (*sḏ3t m ḥtp r ibw r wʿb m šmsw im3ḫw*) (fig. 92).

There are also representations of the *ibw* in the tombs of Mereruka at Giza and Pepyankh (A2) at Meir, but an indication of the rituals which were performed at the *ibw* is only depicted in the tomb of Qar (Bolshakov 1991: 38).

Embalming Ritual

Following purification the body would have been conveyed to the 'pure place' (*wʿbt*) which has been variously rendered as a 'place of embalming' or 'mortuary workshop'. The latter term may be a better understanding of the activities that occurred in the *wabet* as although the core activity was the preparation of the dead body, it was also a place where a variety of funeral equipment was manufactured (Wilson 1944: 202). Part of an inscription in the tomb of Semerkheten-ankh mentions that craftsmen of the *wabet* carve and paint two false doors (Mariette 1889: 202-5; *Urk* I, 38). In the tomb of Ankhmahor, 'the painter of the southern *wabet*, Mesi', is depicted painting a statue (Capart 1907: pl. 33).

The embalming period is often considered to be a period of some 70 days as suggested by the evidence of Herodotus (II, 88) and illustrated from a stela in the 18th Dynasty tomb of the royal herald, Djehuty (TT 110):

> 'The beautiful burial, may it come in peace after your seventy days are completed in the *wabet* (translated Davies 1932: 289).

However, there is also evidence for differing periods, such as 272 days in the 4th Dynasty tomb of Queen Meresankh III (G7530 + 7540) and over a year in the 5th Dynasty tomb of the vizier Senedjemib (G2378).

The nature of the participation by the lector in the embalming procedures can be illustrated by two texts from the Middle Kingdom:

Fig. 97: Water voyage from the tomb of Djau with a lector in the first boat being towed (Davies 1902: pl. 7)

Fig. 98: Funeral procession from the tomb of Qar showing the *wabet* (adapted from Simpson 1976: fig. 24)

a) 'Further, I have contractually obligated (*ḫtm*) the chief lector, son of Montu, son of Intef, son of Tjetu, to perform the liturgy in the place of embalming and to read (*šdt*) the festival roll (*ḥ3bt*) for my majesty, at the month festival and the mid-month festival, that my name might be beautiful and that recollection of me might endure in the present day' (BM E1164, stela of Intef, son of Mait; Budge 1911: pl. 55; translated Assmann 2005: 260).
b) 'Treating in her place of embalming, that the work of the embalmer and the craft of the lector be performed for her' (*srwḫt m wʿbt.s ir n k3t wt ir n.s ḥmt ḫry-ḥbt*) (False door of Princess Inti, translated Wilson 1954: fig. 5).

This latter inscription suggests that the lector was present during the embalming procedures.

A *wabet* is depicted in the mastaba of Qar, shown after the boat carrying the coffin has crossed the water and arrived at the far river-bank (fig. 98). A schematic plan of the building shows a quantity of ritual equipment and food offerings at the top of a room, and below, an angled entry (right), a long corridor, an outer L-shaped room, a vestibule and an inner room. In the outer room stands a man holding out a jar. Above him is the caption: 'The lector attends to the house' (*iw ḫry-ḥbt ḥr pr*). In the vestibule a similar smaller figure also holds out a jar. In the inner room is a caption (Edel 1969: 5; Simpson 1976: fig. 24):

> 'Inner-room of the embalming house of attending' (*ḥrt-ib nt wʿbt ʿḥʿw*)

This evidence suggests that the lector was present in the embalming place, and as he is depicted carrying an ointment jar, he may also have been directly involved with the practical procedures of the embalming process.

In page 27 the close association of the lector and the *ibw* was demonstrated with the caption 'requirements of the lector' (*dbḥw n ḥmt ḫry-ḥbt*) being placed adjacent to the *ibw*. Consequently, it would appear that the lector may have had some involvement in the ritual washing, purification and possibly the embalming procedures themselves.

Night before the Funeral

Following the embalmment ritual the mummified body would be returned to the relatives, and the night before the funeral was then an occasion when a vigil took place. This seems to have taken the form of hourly rituals and various recitations as attested in the tale of Sinuhe where an Egyptian burial is being promised to Sinuhe should he return to Egypt (P. Berlin 3022, 191-2 in Blackman 1932: 32):

> ‘A night will be divided up for you with unguents and wrappings from the hands of Tayt’ (*wḏꜥ.tw n.k ḫꜣwy m sfwt wt(ꜣ)w m ꜥwy tꜣyt*).[3]

The night before the funeral and the division into hours is also referred to in Spell 49 from the Coffin Texts (Assmann 2005: 261; translated Faulkner 2007: 45-6).

There are a number of references in the Coffin Texts to these night rituals, and such rituals can be dated from at least 2000 BC with the rites and recitations still preserved on the walls of Ptolemaic temples, such as Edfu, some 2000 years later. The vigil is thus a long standing tradition and the lector can be seen to be involved with these various rituals as illustrated by Spell 50 of the Coffin Texts (de Buck 1935: 223-32):

> ‘Horus is king after he has played the role of the *sa-meref*-priest for him. The opponent is silent when he sees you. The *sem*-priest, the chief lector, and the embalmer: each one of them casts down the enemy. The nurse of the souls of Heliopolis has come, laden with the revenue of the All-lord. Anubis, foremost of the divine booth, offers the necessities on behalf of the chief lector. Until morning, when the day dawns, when the god comes out of the hall of embalming’ (translated Assmann 2005: 265-6).

Journey to the Tomb

Following the night vigil the coffin would be either carried or dragged on a sledge, pulled by men or oxen, to the necropolis at the desert plateau. Again there is evidence that the lector continued with his recitations during this part of the funeral journey. The tomb of Ankhmahor depicts the funeral party preceding the coffin and amongst the retinue are two lectors with open scrolls (fig. 91). In a scene from the tomb of Hetepherakhti there is a depiction of a statue of the deceased on a sledge being drawn by oxen. In front of the statue is an officiant offering incense and behind him is the lector, seemingly overseeing the ritual.

Arrival at the Tomb

The coffin and procession finally arrive at the tomb and the scenes usually depict singers, dancers and accompanying officiants in the funeral cortège. The tomb of Mereruka shows a lector standing with a staff in his hands overseeing the event.

Representations of the mummy are not seen in the Old Kingdom, but during the Middle Kingdom, with differing attitudes and altered styles of tomb decoration, this practice changed. The earliest known depiction of a mummy is in the 11th Dynasty tomb of an unknown female at Barnugi (ancient Nitria) in the Delta (Edgar 1907: 109-18). In later New Kingdom representations the mummy is taken out of the coffin or sarcophagus and set upright in the forecourt of the tomb, as illustrated in a vignette to the funerary papyrus of Hunefer (P. BM 9901/5; Faulkner 1985: 54; Assmann 2005: 310).

Services at the Tomb - Opening of the Mouth

Following arrival at the tomb, the Opening of the Mouth ceremony would be performed. Evidence is lacking for representations of this ceremony in the Old Kingdom, but Assmann (2005: 312) and Otto (1960: 1-8) consider that elements of it date to the Early Dynastic Period.

Fig. 99: Funeral scene from the tomb of Debehen at Giza (adapted from Hassan 1943: fig. 122)

Scenes from the 4th Dynasty tomb of Debehen at Giza support this suggestion, as there are depictions of rituals being conducted on the roof of the mastaba-tomb (Snape 2011: fig. 5.2; fig. 99). Offerings are presented to a statue of the deceased standing in a shrine and an embalmer is ‘Making transfigurations’. There is no evidence of the lector being involved with these rituals in the 4th Dynasty as at that period the embalmer would have pronounced the recitations and conducted the rituals. However, the embalmer is standing with a scroll in one hand, a pose later adopted by the lector.

Services at the Tomb - offering ritual

As the ancient Egyptians believed that death was a continuation, albeit on a different plane of existence, the deceased would need sustenance and this was provided by means of the offering ritual. The ritual was performed for the first time immediately after the Opening of the Mouth ceremony.

A text from the false door of the 5th Dynasty tomb of Tepemankh at Saqqara states (*Urk* 1: 190, 9-10; Mariette 1889: 195):

[3] Unguents and wrappings refer to the embalming ritual. The word divide implies the division of the night into hours, with each hour having a protective deity.

Fig. 100: Scene of the offering rite from the tomb of Kagemni
(adapted from von Bissing 1911: II, pls. 29-30 and Badawy 1981: fig. 1)

Fig. 101: Various actions performed by the officiants in the offering ritual
(Junker 1938: pl. 10)

'Causing to stand on the roof[4]; an invocation-offering is made to him; his hand is grasped by (his) *kas'* and his fathers' *(sꜥḥꜥ ḥr-tp ḳrtt prt-ḫrw n.f nḏr ꜥ.f in kꜣw in itw.f* (translated Wilson 1944: 213).

This liturgy was performed in the tomb chapel and involved the presentation of food and drink, the performance of various rites, and the recitation of the offering formula. The most important part of the ceremony was the latter, the offering formula or invocation to the gods to supply various provisions for the wellbeing of the deceased which was expressed in a standard form of words (Taylor 2001: 96; Assmann 2005: 330). The offering formula was also important in the long term as it would ensure the continued survival of the deceased. The offering formula was inscribed on stelae and other monuments in the tomb chapel with the expectation that future visitors to the tomb would pronounce the formula and thus bring benefits for the deceased.

The offering liturgy represented in the 6th Dynasty tomb of Kagemni (LS10) at Saqqara is one of the most elaborate of the Old Kingdom representations of this rite (Badawi 1981: 85-93; Harpur & Scremin 2006: 466, pls. 445-54). The scenes from this tomb depict many of the key rituals involved in the offering liturgy and so will be used as a case study to examine the role of the lector in the ceremony.

The scenes in question depict Kagemni sitting at an offering table facing an offering list. Adjacent to this is the offering rite described in two phases, the recitation of the various spells and the offering scene itself, these two being separated by the rite of 'Removing the foot' (fig. 100). The various actions of the officiants during the offering ritual have been studied by Junker (1938: 103-11) who assigned numbers to them. This system created by Junker has been accepted in a number of publications and will be used in this research and referred to on the relevant occasions (fig. 101).

The offering liturgy is in Room 7 of the tomb and depicts the funerary priests (*ka*-priests) and lectors in line, as if they were performing a continuous ceremony. However, different rites are represented, and so they are probably occurring at different times during the funeral of Kagemni. The incense, for example, is intended for Kagemni and yet it is offered some distance away from his seated figure (Harpur & Scremin 2006: 466).

The offering liturgy of Kagemni commences in the left of the scene with two 'funerary priests' *(ḥm-kꜣw),* one of whom pours water over the head of a kneeling colleague who is holding both hands together (Junker 4). Adjacent to the priests is a standing lector who is holding a rolled up papyrus in one hand and his other hand is raised up in a gesture of summoning (Junker 13). Badawy (1981: 88) considers that this attitude was inherited from that of the 'Master of Largess' *(ḥry-wḏb),* who during the 5th Dynasty called out the offerings (cf. Gardiner 1938b: 83-91).

This standing lector is followed by a second lector who is holding an open papyrus roll and is 'Reciting the transfiguration' (*šdt-sꜣḫ*) (Junker 15). Accompanying these recitations are a group of three kneeling lectors who have their left arms raised and their right arms, with fists clenched, pressed to their chests. The caption is 'Numerous transfiguration(s) by the lector' (*sꜣḫ ꜥšꜣ in ḫry-ḥb*) (Junker 16). Junker (1938: 110) suggests that the kneeling lectors are a choir accompanying the standing reciting lector, with Gardiner (1938b: 87) adding that the kneeling lectors are echoing the spells in a breast-thumping accompaniment. This action would create a muffled rhythmic sound, known in Egyptian as *hnw*, and perhaps can be best rendered in this context as an expression of emotion at the presence of the deceased person (Junker 16; Dominicus 1994: 61-5; Assmann 2005: 243; see previous discussion on the *hnw* gesture pages 8-9).

Fig. 102: Offering scene from the tomb of Antefoker (Davies 1920: pl. 28)

The rites of the first phase of the liturgy terminate with a lector 'Removing the foot' *(int rd),* a ritual which involved dragging a brush to erase the footprints of the officiants from the sandy floor of the tomb chapel (Quack 2006a: 70). In this action the lector looks at the other actors but strides in the opposite direction (Junker 17). An alternative suggestion is that the rite was aimed at removing all malign demons that might have been lurking in the tomb (Davies 1915: 93-4). The ritual is depicted at the beginning of the offering scene in the Middle Kingdom tomb of Antefoker (TT 60; fig. 102) but is usually situated at the end of the sequence as portrayed in the Old Kingdom tombs of Mereruka and Qar (fig. 103). This terminal rite is also seen

[4] The roof here would refer to the roof of the tomb and so the text suggests that the offering formula is being said as part of the final funerary rituals.

when ceremonies connected with the daily ritual of the gods in temples were concluded, as attested at the temple of Sety I at Abydos and the temple of Hatshepsut at Deir el Bahri (Davies 1915: 93; Gardiner 1938b: 87; Junker 1938: 110-11; David 1981; also see page 54 of this publication).

Fig. 103: 'Removing the Foot' in the tomb of Qar (adapted from Simpson 1976: fig. 29)

The second phase of the Kagemni scene depicts, firstly, a priest kneeling before a closed basket (Junker 6). By comparison with other similar scenes, such as that of Mereruka, the basket would appear to contain bread, cakes, beer and meat. The caption above the scene is: 'Reversion of offerings' *(wḏb ḫt tꜣ ḥnḳt)* a part of the offering formula and indicating that the ceremony consisted of presenting the food offerings contained in the basket (Badawy 1981: 89).

There are then two pairs of funerary priests, the first of whom is pouring water into a vessel held by his kneeling companion: 'Giving water by the funerary priest' *(rdi mw in ḥm kꜣ)* (Junker 4). Of the second pair of priests one is sprinkling water over the hands of his kneeling companion: 'Flowing water' (*sṯꜣ mw*). This is to provision the dead with water, an important ritual and something emphasised in the Book of the Dead. This is formulated in a late example in the 4th century BC funerary Papyri of Nesmin (P. BM EA 10209: I, 9-10):

> 'That your *ba* and *ka* may receive the offerings of food, bread, beer, water from the inundation by which the gods live, wine, milk incense and cool water' (translated Haikal 1972: II, 17).

However, Harpur & Scremin (2006: 466) place a different interpretation on this second pair of priests seeing it as cleansing an offering slab, on which offerings for the deceased would be purified and magically transformed in order to sustain the tomb owner in the afterlife

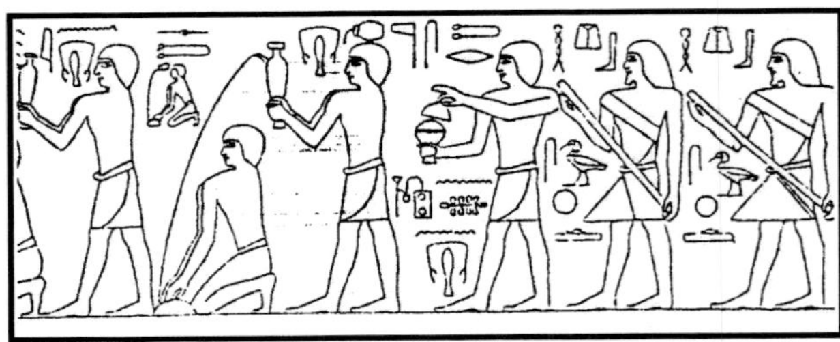

Fig. 104: A section of the offering rite from the tomb of Kagemni depicting the *ka*-priest censing (adapted from von Bissing 1911: II, pl. 30 and Badawy 1981: fig. 1)

Next there is a funeral priest who is 'Burning the incense' (*kꜣp snṯr*) (Junker 9), and below him the caption is: 'the words (writings) of protection by the *ka*-priest' *(sš n sꜣ n ḥm-kꜣ)* (fig. 104). This particular ritual is well attested in other funeral scenes such as the 5th Dynasty tomb of Rawer at Giza (G5270; fig. 105), and that of Akhethetep at Saqqara. Importantly, the caption for 'the words of protection' is next to the *ka*-priest and not the lector as might be expected, although the action that the *ka*-priest is depicted as performing is censing. Possibly the *ka*-priest is censing the protective words towards Kagmeni, as there are examples in temple cult of 'spells of incense' *(rꜥw n snṯr)* (Gardiner 1952: 16, pl. 6). Alternatively, space constraints or copyist's errors could have resulted in the transposition of the hieroglyphs.

Fig. 105: Offering scene from the tomb of Rawer (Junker 1938: pl. 46)

FIG. 106: BUTCHERY SCENE FROM THE TOMB OF MERERUKA (DUELL 1938: II, PL. 109)

The looped cord symbol used for hobbling cattle (Gardiner V16) is used as part of the hieroglyphic grouping in 'the words of protection by the *ka*-priest'. This is used as a protective symbol and is attested in the Pyramid Texts §1203:

> 'I walk quite unhindered for the ordinance of the Great Lake protects me'

and §1752:

> '... and protect yourself from him who would harm you. O beware of the Great Lake'.

Both these texts refer to water and 'ferryman' spells and are protective in nature.

The second phase of the liturgy terminates with two lectors reading out from their rolls: 'Transfiguring' (*s3ḫ*). Thus the actual transmission of offerings, the first part of the ceremony, relies on the transfiguration performed by the lectors (Junker 15; Badawy 1981: 88-90).

Another typical offering scene is in the 6th Dynasty tomb of Hetepni-Ptah at Qubbet el Hawa (G5290). Again the deceased is depicted sitting at an offering table, facing an offering list. Two lectors with open scrolls face the deceased and the caption above the first reads: 'Summoning the requirements of the offering table', and above the second is: 'Making transfigurations so that he might become a blessed one'. This distinction between the food offerings and spells to make the deceased a blessed spirit demonstrates that the lector was performing functions concerned with both the physical and spiritual aspects of the dead (Wilson 1944: 215).

A number of tomb scenes illustrating the offering ritual demonstrate the supervisory or 'master of ceremonies' role of the lector. This is particularly illustrated in scenes depicting the butchery of cattle for offerings where his duty was to initiate the service, first going into the courtyard where the butchers slaughtered the cattle to ensure the sacrifice was pure, and then returning with a foreleg of bullock to be laid on the altar. The inscription in the tomb of Rakapu at Saqqara is (Mariette 1889: 274):

> 'Give a piece of fore-flesh, the lector is coming' (*di iwf n ḥ3t ḫry-ḥbt ii*).

In the tomb of Mereruka a caption states (Duell 1938: II, pl. 109; fig. 106):

> Hurry, be eager, men! The lector is performing the service and presenting choice cuts! Hurry up, be quick and be lively!' (*wn ṯn r ḥw iw ḫry-ḥbt ḥr irt ḫt sḫp stpt wn ḥn.ṯn m ꜥnḫ*).

Later in the Middle Kingdom tomb of Ukhhotep (tomb no. 3 at Meir) a caption above a butchery scene is (Blackman 1915: 24, pl. 16):

> 'The lector comes to perform the service' (*r irt iḫt*).

Fig. 107: Tomb of Montuherkhopshef
(Davies 1913: pl. 6)

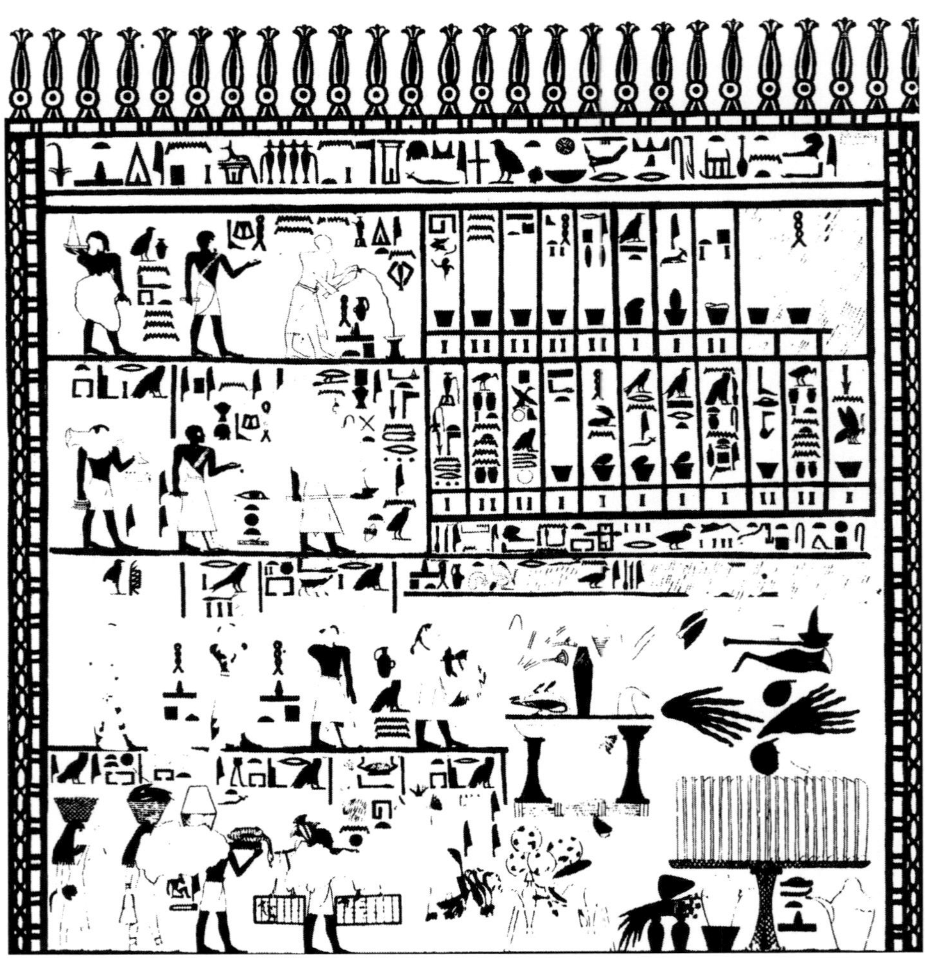

Fig. 108: Offering scene from the tomb of Amenemhat at Beni Hasan
(Newberry 1893: pl. 19)

Some of the rites that were carried out in the Old Kingdom ritual for Kagemni can be still recognised in the Ptolemaic Period. The title of a 4th century BC funerary papyrus belonging to Nesmin is (P. BM EA 10208, I, 2):

> 'To transfigure his soul and perpetuate his corpse, so that his soul may shine in heaven and his corpse endure in the underworld' (translated Haikal 1972: II, 50).

Again the role of the lector is still evident in this papyrus (I, 19):

> 'The god's servants have been purified at the opening of your mouth with the Opening of the Mouth ritual, the chief lector and the *wab* priests hold their transfiguration books in their hands' (translated Haikal 1972: II, 51).

In general the offering ritual is depicted in the uppermost register of the funeral scenes with the officiants nearest to the owner of the tomb, and preceding the offering bearers. The figures are shown as being ready to perform the offering ritual in order to ensure the everlasting provision of goods that are brought by the offering bearers, as specified in the inscribed offering list (Badawy 1981: 93).

Closure of the Tomb

With the completion of the offering liturgy the mummy would be returned to the coffin and placed in the burial chamber. Details and associated rituals concerning this final act are not known for certain, but an inscription in the tomb of Ptahhotep states that Ptahhotep descended into his house of eternity after an invocation offering. Texts from the 6th Dynasty sarcophagus lids of three officials, all from the same area of the Teti Pyramid Cemetery at Saqqara, also shed some light on this. The text from Ankhmahor called Sesi states:

> 'O eighty men, embalmers, rulers of the necropolis and every office-holder who shall descend to this place; do you wish that the king favour you, that invocation offerings be made to you in the necropolis, and that you become *imakhu* in the perfect manner in the presence of the Great God. Then you should place the lid of this coffin upon its base exactly in the excellent manner of which you are aware, in accordance with that which you should do for an excellent *akh*' (translated Strudwick 2005: 424).

Similar inscriptions are also to be found on the sarcophagus lid of Khentika called Ikhekhi and that of Kaiaper (Strudwick 2005: 424-5). The 'place' here is the burial chamber and the presence of the lector and embalmer suggests that a final ritual and recitation are being performed (Wilson 1944: 218; Snape 2011: 77).

A New Kingdom scene from the 18th Dynasty tomb of Montuherkhopshef (TT 20), mayor of Cusae, depicts a small enclosed space that could represent the sarcophagus chamber with a group of seven officiants crouching around the coffin. Among these are a *sem*-priest, a chief lector, an embalmer, and an *imy-khent*. The caption specifies:

> 'First to the west, second to the east, third to the south and fourth to the north' (translated Assmann 2005: 329; fig. 107).

Presumably this recitation was to place the coffin under the care of protective deities and drive off enemies on all four sides (Settgast 1963: 110). Finally, the officiants would leave and the sarcophagus chamber was bricked up and sealed, bringing the funerary ceremony to a close.

3. Middle Kingdom

During the Middle Kingdom the regions of Egypt were administered by local officials or nomarchs who bore the title *ḥ3ty-ꜥ*, these being directly responsible to the king. Many of these officials were able to deploy considerable resources for their own burials, resulting in fine examples of rock-cut tombs being built at the major population centres. As a result, elite tombs were now far more scattered throughout Egypt compared to the concentration at Saqqara and the Memphite regions during the court-centred Old Kingdom (Grajetzki 2006: 78-133).

The tomb scenes of the Middle Kingdom show marked differences to those seen previously, as there is now less evidence of funerary subjects, particularly the various stages of the ritual procession that were a common feature in the Old Kingdom. However, Snape (2011: 155) suggests that some scenes, such as the south wall of the tomb of Khnumhotep II (Tomb 3) at Beni Hasan, although interpreted as offering scenes, may depict funeral activity. Further evidence suggestive of funeral practices during the Middle Kingdom is to be found in a papyrus discovered beneath what was later the Ramesseum (P. Ram. E, BM EA 10753; see pages 43-4 for discussion on Ramesseum Papyri). This papyrus, although badly damaged, is a funerary liturgy describing ceremonies performed at a mastaba, and includes some details of the working practices of a lector (Gardiner 1955a: 9-17; Parkinson 2009: 146-60).

Offering scenes are still very much in evidence in the Middle Kingdom and the lector performed a similar role to that during the Old Kingdom, although the *sem*-priest now shares organisational responsibilities with the lector. The tomb of Senbi's son, Ukhhotep, at Meir (B No. 2) depicts an offering scene involving the censing and pouring of water. The *henu* rite is performed by two lectors, and at the end of the scene a lector is depicted 'removing the foot' just as in Old Kingdom scenes (Blackman 1915: II, pl.10). Comparable scenes depicting the *henu* rite and 'removing the foot' are evident in the 12th Dynasty tombs of Djehutihotep at Deir el-Bersha and Amenemhat (Tomb 2) at Beni Hasan (Newberry 1892: I, pl. 34: Newberry 1893: I, pl. 17). Also in the tomb of Amenemhat at Beni Hasan, a chief lector is depicted with a papyrus scroll in his hand and an arm outstretched with the caption 'Doing things' (*ir ḫt*) which signifies in this example 'Performing ritual' (fig. 108).

Again as in the Old Kingdom there are many instances during these ceremonies of the lector reciting from a papyrus scroll and performing ritual activities such as presenting forelegs of beef. Examples can be seen in the 12th Dynasty tombs of Ihy at Saqqara and Ukhhotep, son of Iam, at Meir (A, No. 3; Firth & Gunn 1926: pl. 39; Blackman & Apted 1953: pl. 17; fig. 109). Also at Meir in the 12th Dynasty tomb of Ukhhotep's son, Senbi, a lector is depicted 'Reciting the transfigurations' (*šdt s3ḫt*) (Blackman 1914: pl. 3; fig. 110). Here the coffin can be seen to be supported on the shoulders, unlike in the Old Kingdom scenes where the coffin was carried by a group of men.

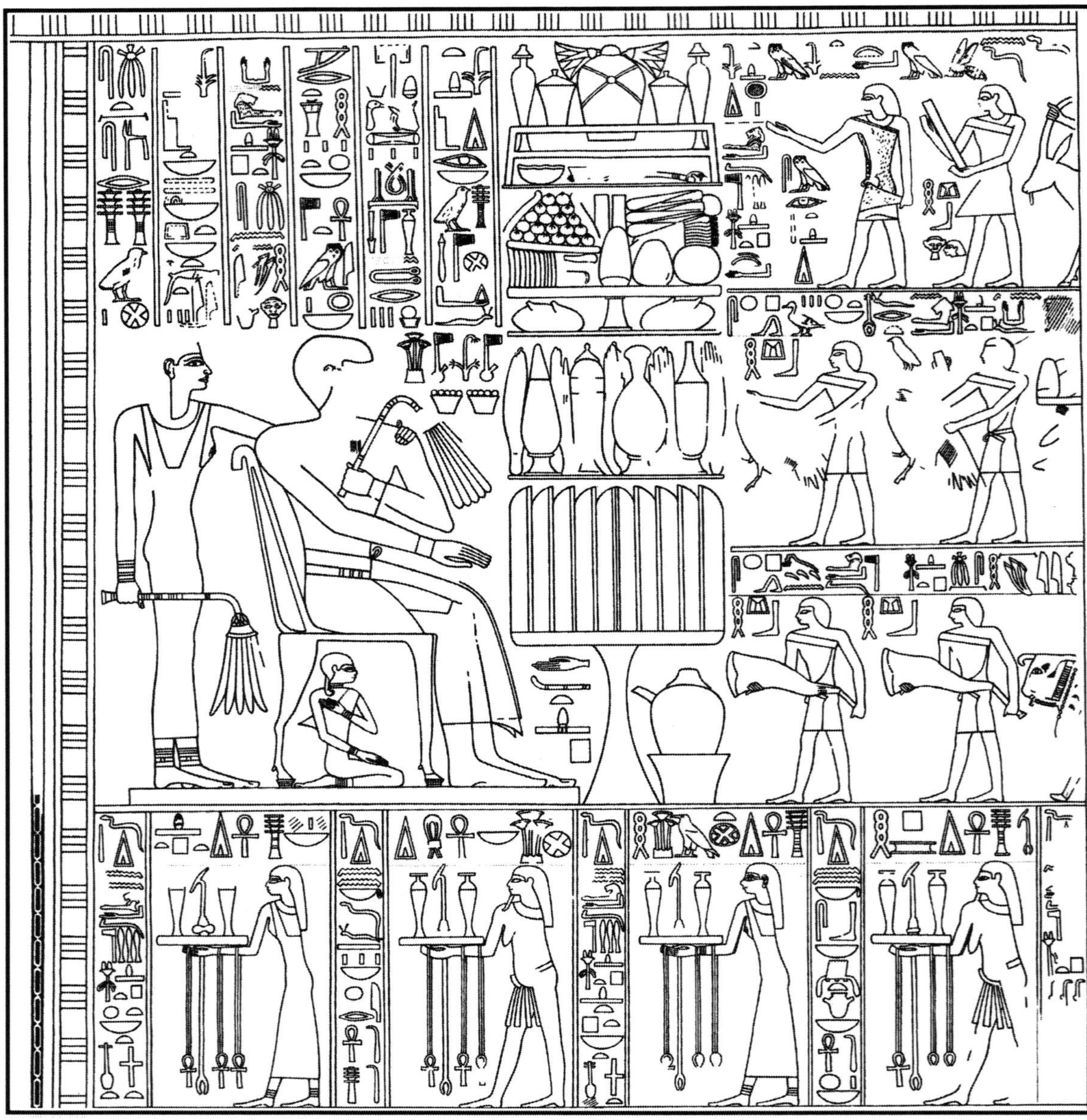

Fig. 109: Offering scene in the tomb chapel of Ukhhotep at Meir
(adapted from Blackman & Apted 1953; pl. 17)

Fig. 110: Offering scene in the tomb chapel of Ukhhotep's son Senbi
(Blackman 1914: pl. 3)

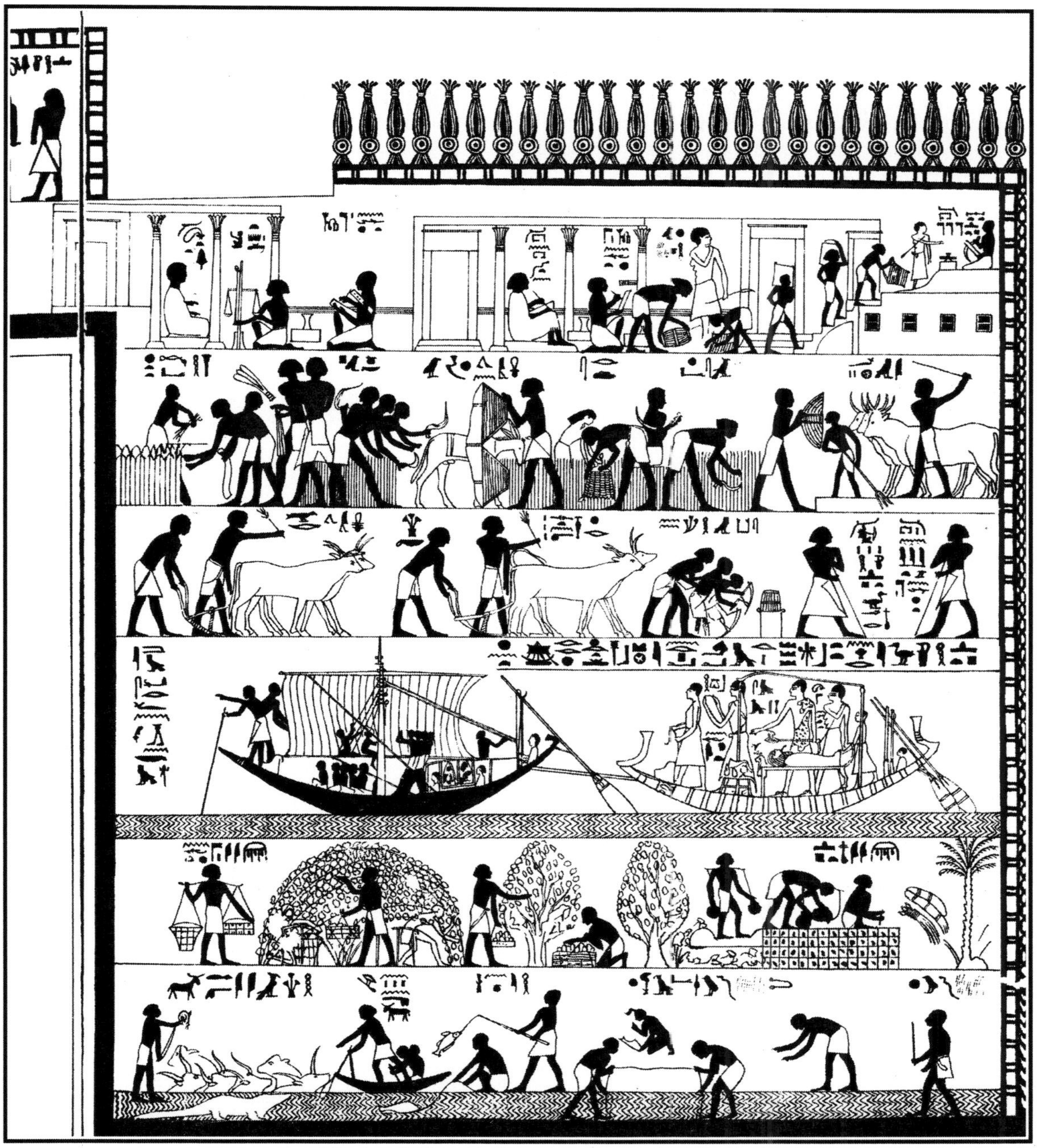

Fig. 111: Scene from the tomb of Khnumhotep II at Beni Hasan (Newberry 1893: pl. 29)

Fig. 112: Nile boat under sail towing a papyrus skiff. Detail of the scene (fig. 24a above) from the tomb of Khnumhotep II

With the new emphasis on the worship of Osiris and the prominence of Abydos as a burial site in the Middle Kingdom, it became common practice for ancient Egyptians to make a pilgrimage to this sacred place. Visitors commonly erected stelae at the site in order to preserve their identity there and thus obtain spiritual benefits by being in close proximity to the god.

This journey to Abydos was emphasised in tomb scenes either as a real or as a symbolic journey. A damaged scene, from the 12th Dynasty tomb of Daga (TT 103) at Thebes, depicts three boats travelling downstream to Abydos and among the occupants of the third boat, along with the deceased, is a lector (Davies 1913: pl. 36). The 12th Dynasty tomb of Khnumhotep II (No. 3) at Beni Hasan shows in the main chamber, adjacent to the doorway, a scene labelled (Newberry 1893: pl. 29; fig. 111):

> 'Sailing upstream in order to perform the ceremonies at Abydos by the hereditary prince, the nomarch, overseer of the Eastern desert, Khnumhotep, son of Nehri' (*ḫnt r rḫ ḫrt ꜣbdw in rpꜥ ḥꜣty-ꜥ m r iꜣbtt nhri sꜣ ḫnm-ḥtp*).

The scene depicts a Nile boat under sail which is towing a papyrus skiff, the cult barque (fig. 112). In the barque, on a lion shaped couch, is the coffin of Khnumhotep, and standing immediately in front of the coffin is the lector, Nekheti. He has both arms raised, presumably reciting, although the papyrus roll is not clear in the image. In the same tomb, above the doorway, is a scene depicting the towing of a statue of the deceased, and in front of it is the lector, Hormaakheru, reading from his papyrus scroll.

4. New Kingdom

The New Kingdom tombs, particularly those at Thebes, provide greater details of ancient Egyptian funerary rituals compared to those seen in the preceding Middle Kingdom. The lector once again had an important role to play in these ceremonies, having similar responsibilities to those seen previously. A summary of the funeral rites performed during the New Kingdom is described in a stela from the early 18th Dynasty tomb of Djeheuty (TT 110; Davies 1932: 279-90, pl. 40):

> 'The beautiful burial, may it come in peace after your seventy days are completed in the *wabet*.
> May you be placed on a bier in the house of rest and be drawn by white oxen.
> May the ways be opened with milk until you reach the entrance of your tomb.
> May the children of your children be gathered in an unbroken circle and weep with an affectionate heart.
> May your mouth be opened by the chief lector and your purification performed by the *sem*-priest.
> May Horus adjust your mouth and open for you your eyes and ears.
> May your limbs and bones all be present on you.
> May the transfiguration spells (*sꜣḫw*) be read for you, and the offering-spell (*ḥtp-di-nsw*) be performed for you' (translation after Davies 1932: 288-9 and Snape 2011: 193-4).

Scenes from the 18th Dynasty tomb of the vizier, Rekhmire (TT 100; Davies 1943) and that of the 'Accountant of grain of Amun', Amenemhat (TT 82; Davies and Gardiner 1915) illustrate these rites. These two groups of tomb scenes will be used as representative case studies to discuss the role of the lector in New Kingdom funerary rituals.

Rekhmire

1. Plate 87 of Davies depicts the funeral journey across the river and here the lector is one of the officiants in the lead boat. This boat is towing the papyrus skiff containing the coffin and to the right of this scene, there is a depiction of a lector reciting (Davies 1943: II, pl. 87; fig. 113).
2. Having arrived on the west bank, the deceased is borne firstly to the *ibw* for purification and then later to the *wabet* for the embalming procedures. The coffin is carried by nine pallbearers called friends (*smrw*). A chief lector with arm raised and holding a papyrus scroll appears to be calling, perhaps supervising the operation or reciting incantations (Davies 1943: II, pl. 89; fig. 114).
3. Following the embalming procedures the mummified corpse is then subject to the rites of the night vigil. Among these are enactments of symbolic processions and voyages, including the ritualised journey to the Delta city of Sais where the lector is one of the occupants of the ritual boat (Davis 1943: II, pl. 92; fig. 115).

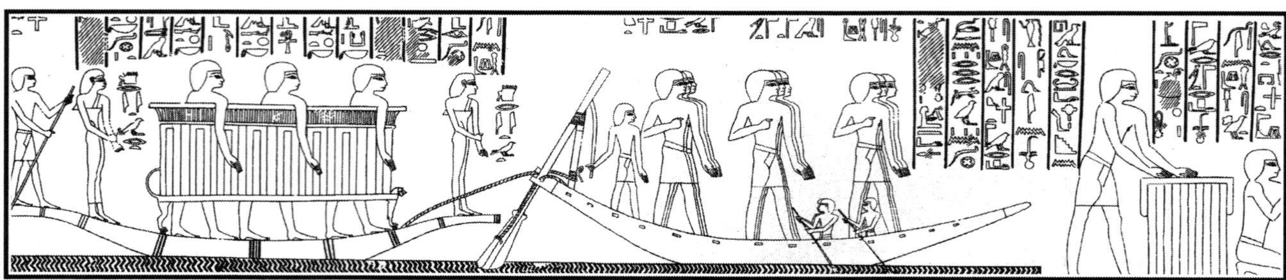

Fig. 113: Journey across the river - funeral procession of Rekhmire (Davies 1943: II, pl. 87)

FIG. 114: JOURNEY OF THE COFFIN TO THE *WABET* - FROM THE TOMB OF REKHMIRE
(DAVIES 1943: II, PL. 89)

FIG. 115: RITUAL VOYAGE TO SAIS - TOMB OF REKHMIRE
(DAVIES 1943: II, PL. 92)

FIG. 116: DRAGGING THE COFFIN TO THE TOMB OF REKHMIRE
(DAVIES 1943: II, PL. 90)

4. After the vigil the coffin is taken in procession to the tomb. In plates 90 and 93 of Davies the coffin is being dragged to the tomb and a chief lector is depicted as one of the chief officiants (Davies 1943: II, pls. 90, 93; figs. 116, 117).

5. The funeral cortège finally arrives at the tomb and is welcomed by the lector and the *mww* dancers. The lector recites from an unrolled scroll (Davies 1943: II, pl. 92; fig. 118).

Fig. 117: Dragging the coffin to the tomb of Rekhmire
(Davies 1943: II, pl. 93)

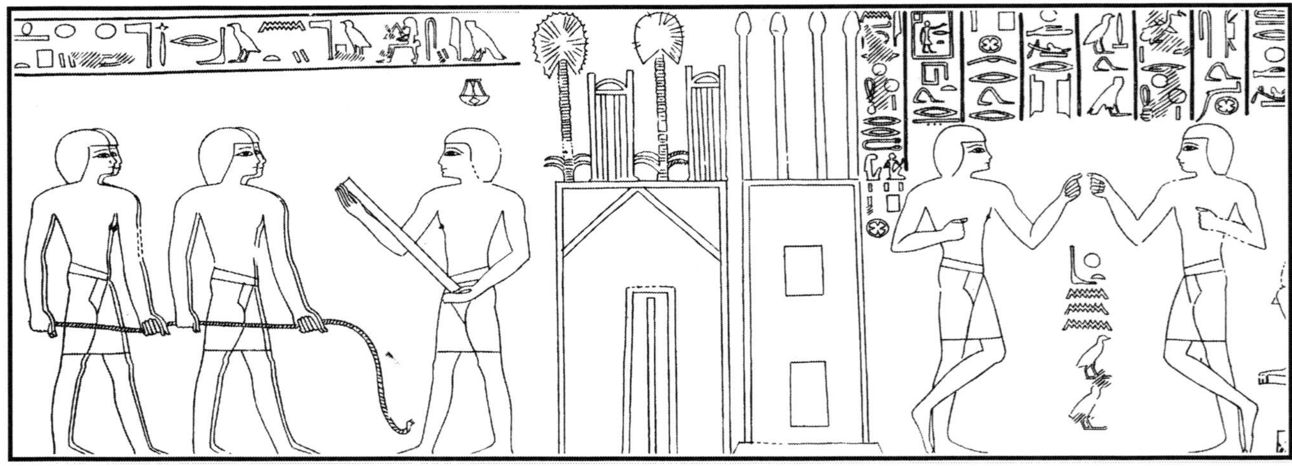

Fig. 118: The lector welcomes the funeral cortège at the tomb of Rekhmire
(Davies 1943: II, pl. 92)

Amenemhat

The funerary scenes from the tomb of Amenemhat, although not as extensive as those of Rekhmire, do provide further details of the role of the lector in these rituals, although there is some uncertainty as to the sequence of some of the scenes.

1. In plate 12 of his publication, Davies suggests that the officiant following behind the men who are dragging the bier to the tomb is a lector. However, the caption here is damaged, and as in many of the scenes from the tomb of Amenemhat, the lector is not depicted wearing a sash. He is shown without a scroll but is shown censing and pouring libations (Davies 1915: pl. 12; fig. 119).

2. In another scene in which a sledge containing the coffin is being dragged, the lector stands in front of the procession and the caption is:

'O people of Pe, Dep, Unu, Neter, Sais and Hut-weru. You thousand of Pe, you thousand of… all common folk; the god comes, do him reverence' *(rmṯw p dp wnw nṯr s3w ḥwt-wrw ḥ3 p ḥ3 … rḫyt nbt nṯr ii s3-t3 sp2).*

The men carrying the coffin are considered to represent the inhabitants of certain cities concerned with the mythical burial of Osiris (Davies 1915: 50, pl. 11; Assmann 2005: 308; fig. 120, middle register). The inscription continues:

> 'Your hands upon the ropes' (*ʿ.wy.tn r nwḥw.ṯn*).

There is a comparable scene to this in the 18th Dynasty Theban tomb of Ahmose Humay (TT 224) (Settgast 1963: 38).

In the upper register of this same scene a lector sits in the bows of a skiff containing a naos and a burning lamp. This is probably a representation of the ritualised voyage to Sais since in the middle register of this same plate, there is another image of a boat with the caption:

> 'Travelling to go downstream, accompanying the steward of the vizier, Amenemhat, to Sais' (*pḫr m ḫd šms imy-r pr n ṯ3ty imn-ḥ3t n s3w*).

Here the lector is depicted with a staff in his left arm and a folded cloth in his right hand, heading a party of men who are towing a boat with a structure upon it. In the lower register on the right of this scene the lector welcomes the funeral cortège at the entrance to the tomb and reads a hymn of praise from his papyrus roll:

> "Words spoken by the lector: 'Receive … …
> 'Arrival after (?) they have done reverence to the scribe who reckons the grain of Amun, [Amenemhat, justified].
> Praise … in joy, for chief of the weavers [of Amun], Amenemhat, justified.
> Hail (?) to thee, O god, in raising him (?) to the steward of the vizier Amenemhat, justified.
> The god arises in his palace and shines as Re himself, Amenemhat, justified.
> Prostration is pure unto thee, arising in …, Amenemhat, justified.
> O how the Ennead rejoices at thy beauty, to the overseer of the ploughed lands, Amenemhat, justified.
> The gods on their banners arise for thee in the Broad-Hall, for the scribe of the vizier, Amenemhat, justified.
> Hail to thee, O great Ennead, for the steward who counts the people, Amenemhat, justified' (translated Davies 1915: 51, pl. 11).

3. The upper register of Plate 13 from Davies has a scene which is also common to the tomb of Rekhmire (Davies 1943: II, pl. 87), in which a man is depicted bending over a receptacle for offerings. The caption states that the lector along with other officiants are pronouncing transfigurations and recitations for Amenemhat (fig. 121, upper register on right). The far left of this same register has a damaged section depicting three lectors, one of whom is reading from a scroll.

FIG. 119: DRAGGING THE HEARSE - TOMB OF AMENEMHAT
(DAVIES 1915: PL. 12, LOWER REGISTER)

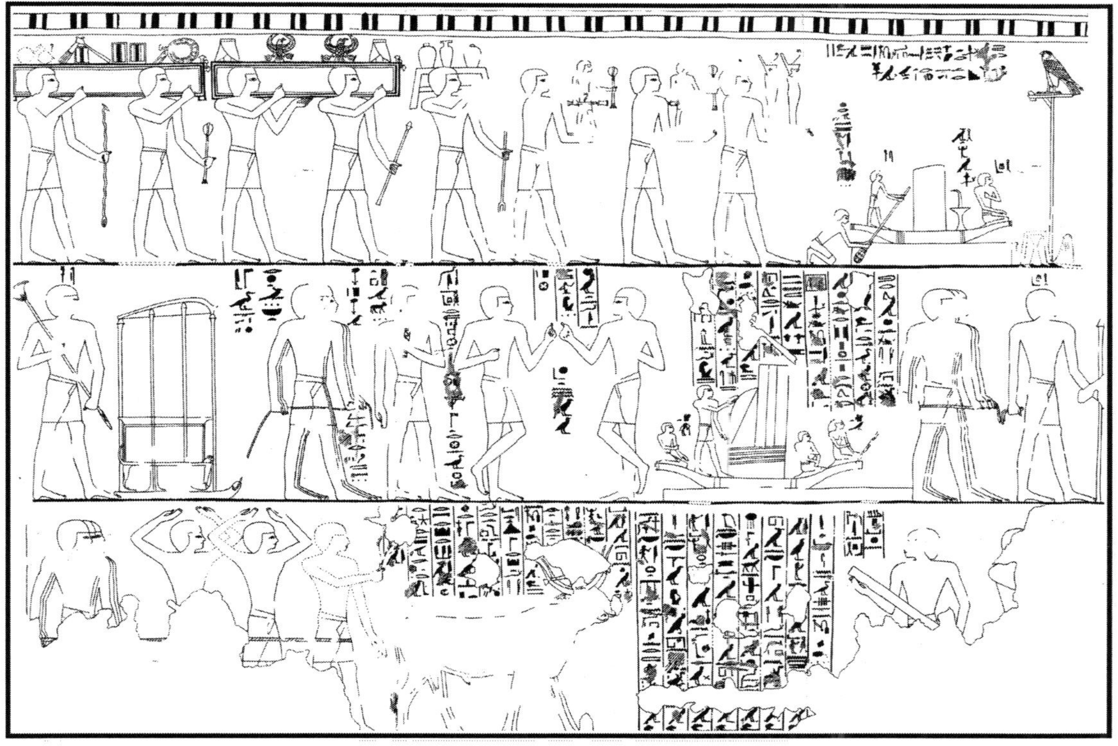

FIG. 120: FUNERAL SCENES FROM THE TOMB OF AMENEMHAT
(DAVIES 1915: PL. 11)

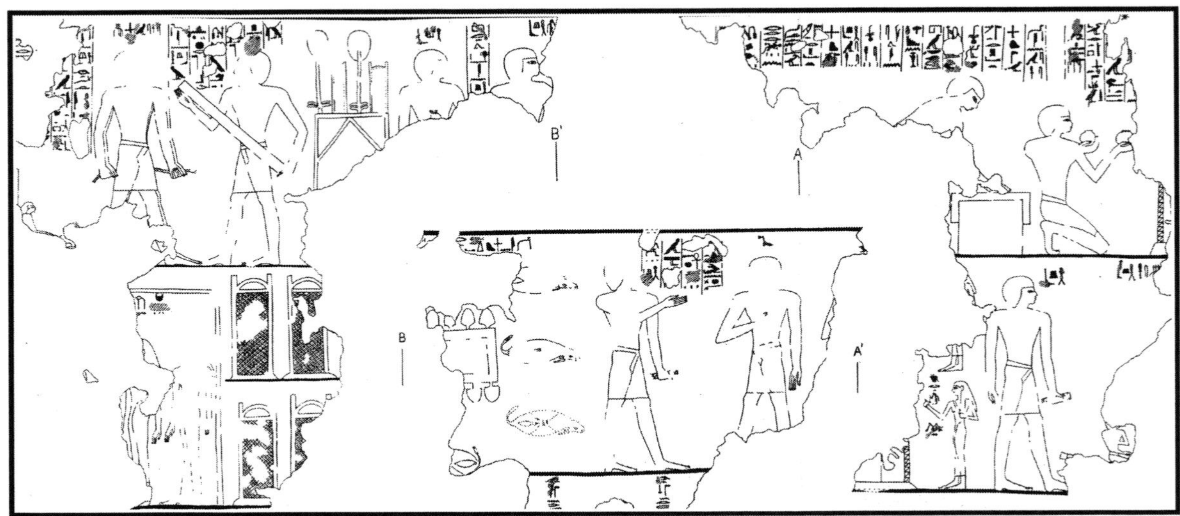

FIG. 121: LECTOR AND OTHER OFFICIANTS OFFERING TRANSFIGURATIONS AND RECITATIONS IN THE TOMB OF AMENEMHAT (DAVIES 1915: PL. 13)

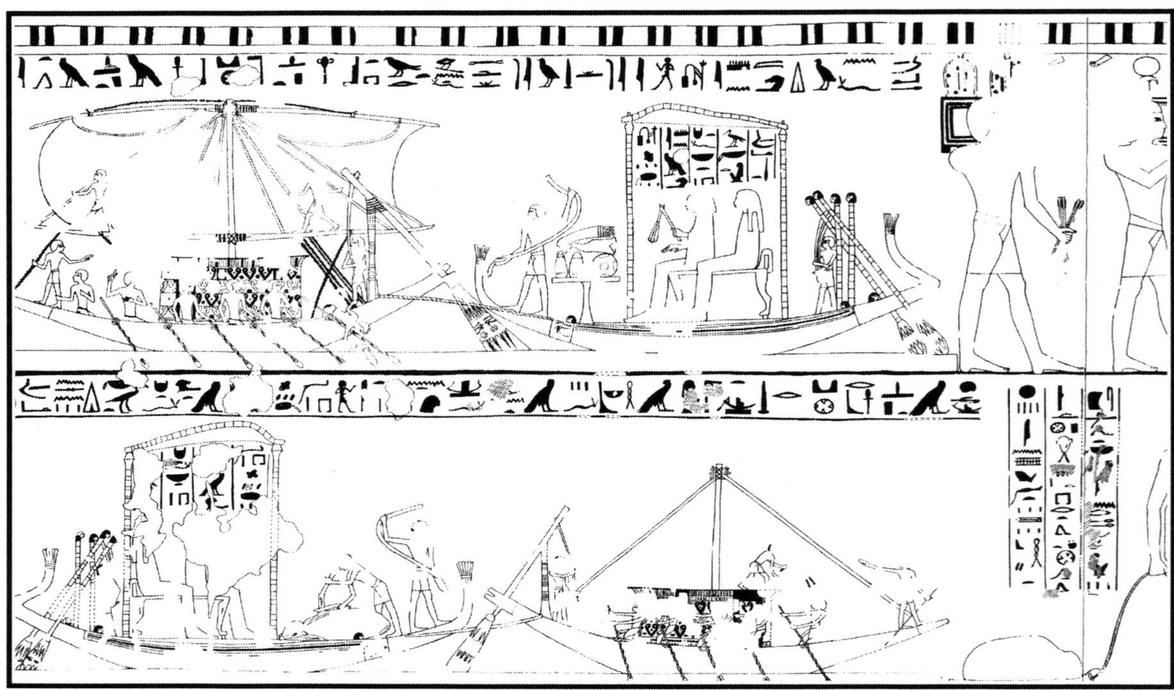

FIG. 122: VOYAGE TO ABYDOS FROM THE TOMB OF AMENEMHAT (DAVIES 1915: PL. 12, UPPER TWO REGISTERS)

The tomb of Amenemhat also has a depiction of the water-borne journey to Abydos, the pilgrimage to the sacred site of the tomb of Osiris, a pilgrimage that every Egyptian aspired to make, a theme commonly displayed in Middle Kingdom tomb scenes. It is not clear if a lector is present on this voyage. It is possible that this was a mere representation of the voyage as many people may well not have undertaken such a pilgrimage, although many do appear to have expressed a desire to be associated with the main cult centre of Osiris (Davies 1915: 48, pl. 12; Wegner 2001: 248; fig. 122).

Finally, in another 18th Dynasty tomb, that of Neferhotep (TT 49), one of the scenes depicts the funeral procession arriving at the tomb and within the accompanying text is:

> "Words spoken by the chief lector - 'I perform incense and libation for your ka, O Osiris, the chief scribe of Amun, Neferhotep'" (*ḏd mdw ḫry-tp ḥry-ḥbt ir snṯr ḳbḥw n k3.t wsir šs sr imn nfr-ḥtp*) (translated Davies 1933: I, pl. 24).

Here the lector is actively involved in the rites and not merely reciting from his scroll.

Fig. 123: Funeral scene from the tomb of Huya (Davies 1905: III, pl. 22)

Amarna Period

In the early Amarna Period the lector is attested during the *Sed*-festival of Amenhotep IV at Karnak performing the same ritual duties as in the festivals of previous rulers (see pages 74-5). However, at Amarna there are no apparent depictions of the lector either in the private or the royal tombs. Priests and officiants are portrayed, all bowing subserviently, but none are shown with a papyrus roll in their hands, nor are there any captions referring to a lector (Davies 1903-8; Martin 1974, 1989b).

However, one funeral scene is depicted in the tomb of Huya, where a typical Egyptian funeral procession is portrayed and large numbers of mourners are evident (Davies 1905: III, 16-17, pl. 22; fig. 123). Some of the male mourners wear a sash, similar in appearance to the lector's attire. However, captions associated with the scenes are not clear and the individuals appear to be pouring dust on their heads in a token of sorrow, and bear little resemblance to the typical portrayal of lectors.

5. Post-New Kingdom

Following the demise of the New Kingdom, the subsequent eras mainly comprised internal fragmentary rule and foreign conquests. Few high-quality elite tombs were constructed and decorated tomb chapels were rare. Essential scenes and texts were transferred to coffins, funerary papyri and stelae. A reorganisation of funerary iconography seems to have occurred at the end of the 20th Dynasty resulting in a new repertoire of scenes. The emphasis was now on rebirth, drawn from Osirian and solar mythology and the journey of the deceased into the underworld. Comprehensive funerary scenes were no longer the norm and the lector was rarely represented. Coffin scenes sometimes did depict an individual reading from a scroll, who is presumed to be a lector, but not labelled as such (see the example of Mutirdies page 7).

6. Transfiguration and the Nature of Texts used by the Lector

As demonstrated above, the chief function of the lector in the funerary liturgy was to perform 'transfiguration rites' (*s3ḫ*) for the deceased. These were recitations, the words of the ritual that were uttered at the time of the funeral and burial. The word *s3ḫ* is a causative form of the verb *3ḫ* 'to become an *akh* or spirit' or 'to transfigure'. The ancient Egyptian did not become an *akh* merely by dying; there was a considerable amount of physical and ritual activity involved in making the deceased a fully effective spirit. The concept of transfiguration is recognised throughout Egyptian history with references in the Pyramid Texts, the Coffin Texts and the Book of the Dead. Pyramid Text §833 states:

> 'You have departed that you may live, you have not departed that you may die: you have departed that you may be an *akh*, the foremost among *akhs*, that you may have power at the head of the living' (translated Faulkner 1969: 149).

The *akh* or spirit was acquired after death as demonstrated in Pyramid Text §474:

> 'The *akh* is bound for the sky; the corpse is bound for the earth' (translated Faulkner 1969: 94; Badawy 1981: 90).

These mortuary liturgies or transfigurations that were utilised during the funeral have a ritual context and a textual coherence and were intended to be carried out on behalf of the deceased. The mortuary liturgies are not individual spells but rather a series of utterances (Assmann 2005: 237-59).

The transfigurations that were recited by the lector can best be described as a wish that expresses an intense appeal and are thus not descriptive but appellative, as for example in the Pyramid Texts §654-§656:

> 'Raise yourself Osiris N, take your head, gather your bones, collect your limbs, wipe the earth of your flesh, take your bread, which does not grow mouldy, and your beer which cannot go sour' (translated Assmann 2005: 331).

Where an imperative is lacking, the statement is formulated as a wish, as illustrated in a mortuary spell linked to the Opening of the Mouth ritual found inscribed in both the 19th Dynasty tombs of Tjay (TT 23) and Neferrenpet (TT 115):

> 'May you stand up on the sand of Rosetau, may you be greeted when the sun shines on you, and may your purification be carried out for you as a daily performance' (translation based on Hofmann 1995: 62 and Assmann 2005: 323).

Assmann (2005: 297-8) describes the division of the mortuary liturgies into Liturgy A and Liturgy B. Both are recognised in the Coffin Texts which were ultimately derived from the Old Kingdom Pyramid Texts. Liturgy A did not appear in the later mortuary literature but Liturgy B became chapter 169 of the Book of the Dead. Liturgy A was aimed at entry into the next world and was a ritual intended to compensate for the helplessness of the deceased and referred to the social aspect of the salvation of the deceased. Liturgy B centres on the themes of physical restoration and the provision with offerings.

The lector would thus employ speech as his main instrument and the uttering of prescribed words was essential to accomplish the purpose of the ritual. The lector is usually depicted reading from a papyrus roll rather than reciting from memory, indicating the importance and authority of the written word. Writing represented power and prestige, reinforcing the status of the lector. Although the actual communication was the oral performance, using the papyrus roll would guarantee the exactitude of the recitation and confer decorum on the ritual act. Assmann (2005: 246) considers that the transforming power of the recitations, enabling the deceased to become an ancestral spirit, was derived from the speech in the mouth of the lector which, at the moment of cultic action, would become divine speech. The lector did not utter it as speech from himself, but the sacred recitations were divine speech with all the power that went with this concept.

7. Interpretation and Conclusion

There was some variation in the funerary rituals between different chronological periods, but the practical steps following death and the main stages of the ritual procedures remained largely unchanged. These involved the taking of the corpse to the place of embalming, the process of embalming, conveying the deceased to the tomb, and the interment. Common to all periods was the funeral procession which consisted of dragging the sledge and the deceased by bearers or cattle. Accompanying the procession were the mourners and officiants (among them the lector).

A study of the scenes depicting the funeral liturgy suggests that the importance of certain officiants varied during different periods. The embalmer or *wt*-priest was the earliest major officiant in Old Kingdom funeral liturgies, and he performed a range of activities as illustrated by his frequent appearance in the 4th Dynasty tomb of Metjen (*LD* II: 4-6). From the Middle Kingdom onwards the *sem*-priest had assumed the role of the *wt*. However, the lector from his first appearance in the 5th Dynasty tomb scenes remained a central figure in funeral liturgy throughout the time span of Dynastic Egypt.

The major role of the lector at the funeral ceremonies was that of reciting the transfiguration spells from the papyrus scrolls. He would often be accompanied by other lectors who were depicted, crouching down and rhythmically thumping their chests, in the *henu* gesture. The transfiguration rites were undoubtedly of major importance as without the correct recitations, the deceased would not become an *akh*, regarded perhaps as an ideal form of the individual after death. At every stage of the transportation of the deceased, including the water crossings and the symbolic voyages, the lector was present. In this role of assisting the deceased to obtain the afterlife, the lector represents the god Thoth who in the mythical past provided assistance for Osiris.

In Old Kingdom scenes, captions describe the lector as 'Making transfigurations' (*s3ḫt*), but from the Middle

Kingdom onwards this caption is less frequently seen. The sash worn by the lector across his shoulder, whilst being present in virtually every Old Kingdom scene, is far less often depicted in the New Kingdom.

Although this role of reciting transfiguration spells is more frequently represented than any other activity, the lector did engage in other ritual acts. In the New Kingdom tombs of both Amenemhat and Neferhotep the lector is depicted pouring libations and censing. The function of these actions would have been aimed at purification as well as providing offerings to the deceased. The lector is frequently seen presenting fore-legs of beef such as in the 12th Dynasty tombs of Ihy and Ukhhotep son of Iam. In the tomb of Qar the lector is depicted both in the outer room and in the embalming hall holding an ointment or water vessel, suggesting that he may have had some practical role in the embalming procedures. It is always the lector who is depicted brushing the floor of the tomb in the rite of 'Removing the foot', one of the last ceremonies before leaving the tomb chamber.

There is evidence for the lector performing the role of ritual director or acting as master of ceremonies organising the various elements at the funerary rituals. In the tomb of Rekhmire the lector is depicted as one of the major officiants in the funeral procession; in the tomb of Amenemhat the lector orders the bearers of the sledge to haul upon the ropes, and in the Mereruka and Amenemhat scenes the lector is depicted at the tomb waiting for the arrival of the funeral cortège to welcome it. In a voyage scene from the tomb of Djau the lector sits in the front of the lead boat possibly piloting the funerary vessels, although an alternative suggestion is that the lector is reciting magical spells for protection and to ward off crocodiles.

Finally, in this supervisory role the lector can be seen to have authority and to command respect. In the butchery scenes in the tomb of Mereruka, the overseer of the butchery team cautions his men to work quickly as the lector is approaching. In the tomb of Amenemhat the lector orders the pallbearers to show reverence to the coffin of the deceased.

Chapter 8

The Opening of the Mouth Ceremony

1. Introduction

The Opening of the Mouth Ceremony *(wpt-r)* consists of a series of rituals in which the lector is not only observed in his customary role of ritualised recitations but can also be identified as having a close participation in the rites themselves. The ceremony has attracted much scholarly attention, chiefly from Blackman (1924), Baly (1930), Otto (1960), Goyon (1972), Schulman (1984), Roth (1992, 1993, 2001), Smith (1993), Fischer-Elfert (1998), Lorton (1999), Assmann (2005), Quack (2005, 2006a) and Altenmüller (2010).

The Opening of the Mouth has been described variously as 'arguably the most important ancient Egyptian ritual' by Roth (2001: 605), and as 'the most important part of the funeral ceremony' by Schulman (1984: 171). The rite was originally intended to animate an inanimate person and as such was performed on the mummy and/or the statue of a deceased individual, as well as on the statue of a deity. By the New Kingdom the ceremony had developed further and was now being applied to all sacred objects. There is even evidence of the rite being carried out on mummified Apis bulls and there is an example of the ritual being performed on the figurehead of the prow of the barque of Amun (Goyon 1972: 90, no. 1). During the Ptolemaic Period there is explicit evidence for the ceremony being carried out on the whole temple itself as a future living receptacle of the divine essence – 'Opening of the Mouth of Throne-of-the-Protector-of-his-Father'[1] (Blackman & Fairman 1946: 75; Assmann 2001: 45 and 2005: 312).

The Opening of the Mouth consisted of touching the body parts of the deceased or the statue using various 'implements'. The purpose of the ceremony was to allow the mummy or statue to eat, breathe, see, hear and partake of the provisions offered by the cult. Otto (1960: I, 10) considers the ritual as an amalgamation of material drawn from several different sources. Within these he distinguishes: an early ritual performed on statues; the various embalming and burial rites carried out on a deceased person; a temple ritual; rites of slaughtering animals; and offering practices. He suggests that the ritual was never edited into a harmonious whole, which would thus explain the repeated scenes in the ceremony, although it was structured in a way that was meaningful. Smith (1993: 13) also recognises these different rites and he considers that they centre around two separate themes:

> 'the animation or reanimation of the statue or mummy (opening the mouth, eyes, ears, and nose, knitting together the bones, assembling the limbs, attaching the head, establishing the heart in its place), and the purification and presentation of offerings (food, drink, clothing) to ensure the continued survival of the newly (re)animated being.'

Roth suggests a different interpretation of the ceremony; she considers that it is derived from a ritual sequence of actions and spells that ensure the ability of new-born and developing children to partake of nourishment. As the ancient Egyptians considered that birth and rebirth after death were dangerous transitions, they attached great importance to these events, and believed that a variety of complicated rituals, symbols and implements were necessary to ensure successful completion of the ceremony (Roth 1992: 147).

Roth (2001: 606) further proposes a different reconstruction of the ritual's origins from that of Otto, basing her opinion on an analysis of Old Kingdom texts. She notes that the ritual changed and evolved over the centuries of its use. She suggests that it was not until the 6th Dynasty that the statue ritual was incorporated into the Opening of the Mouth Ceremony, a rite which had previously developed independently as part of the funerary ritual.

2. History and Development of the Ritual

The earliest known reference to the rite of Opening the Mouth is found in the 4th Dynasty tomb of the royal official Metjen at Saqqara (LS6) where the ceremony occurred in conjunction with censing and the ritual of transforming the deceased into an *akh*. Inscriptions on both the 5th Dynasty Palermo Stone and from the sun-temple of Niuserre contain the formula (Brovarski 1977-8: 1-2; Helck 1977: pl. 3):

> 'Fashioning and Opening of the Mouth in the workshop' (*mst wpt-r m ḥwt-nbw*)

Again in the 5th Dynasty Pyramid Texts of Unas is spell 30B: 'Osiris Unas, I open for thee thy mouth' (Piankoff 1968: 78). In later collections of Pyramid Texts there are various references to Horus opening the mouth of Osiris with his little fingers (Spells 1329-30) and the Sons of Horus opening the mouth with fingers of meteoric iron (Spell 1984) (Faulkner 1969: 209, 286; Roth 2001: 605-8).

The ceremony is attested in later private tombs of both the Old and Middle Kingdoms, and with the development of the Coffin Texts in the Middle Kingdom, a different version of the ritual appears, as illustrated in CT I, 265 (Faulkner 1973: 58). Here Horus and Ptah open the mouth of the deceased; Ptah and Thoth perform the ritual of transfiguration, and Thoth replaces the heart in the body.

[1] Throne-of-the-Protector-of-his-Father is the name for Edfu Temple.

FIG. 124: THE STELA OF RAMOSE FROM DEIR EL-MEDINA (TT 250)
(BRUYÈRE 1927: PL. 6)

FIG. 125: STELA, LOUVRE E 25496, UNKNOWN PROVENANCE.
ONLY THE LOWER PART OF THE STELA COMPRISING TWO REGISTERS IS PRESERVED AND EACH OF THESE HAS AN OPENING OF THE MOUTH SCENE WITH THE UPPER REGISTER A DOUBLE SCENE.
(COURTESY OF THE MUSEÉ DU LOUVRE)

In none of the various Old and Middle Kingdom examples is there an actual pictorial representation of the ceremony, and neither is there much detail provided about the procedures of the various rites (Smith 1993: 13; Eaton-Krauss 1984: 70). There is therefore no confirmation that the lector was involved in the ceremony at this time.

3. New Kingdom Version of 'Opening of the Mouth'

By the New Kingdom this changes and detailed descriptions and representations are to be seen in both royal and private tomb scenes. The Coffin Text spell of the Middle Kingdom has developed into Spell 23 of the *Book of Going Forth by Day* (Faulkner 1985: 51-2).

Additional gods are now involved in the various rites and an enlarged list of funerary implements are utilised (Roth 2001: 607). The ceremony is depicted as being divided up into a number of scenes or episodes with each scene depicting a ritual act. In the more complete versions of the ritual texts, descriptions of each ceremony are arranged in columns next to the illustration.

Otto (1960: I, II) published an account of the textual and pictorial sources of the New Kingdom rite, examining seven sources with the longest scenes and most extensive textual accounts, together with a further eighty shorter versions. These sources involved not only inscriptions from tombs and stelae but also from coffins and papyri. The seven major sources are:

1. Tomb of the Vizier Rekhmire at Thebes, 18th Dynasty, (TT 100).
2. Tomb of King Seti I at Thebes, 19th Dynasty, (KV 17).
3. Tomb of Queen Tausret, 19th Dynasty, (KV 14).
4. Coffin of Butehamun from Thebes, 20th/21st Dynasty, Scribe of the necropolis (E 5288, Turin Museum).
5. Tomb of Amenirdis I, 23rd Dynasty, God's Wife of Amun at Thebes (Medinet Habu).
6. Tomb of Pediamenopet, 26th Dynasty, Chief Lector (TT 33).
7. Funerary Papyrus of Sais. This papyrus relates to a woman who lived during the Roman Period and was buried in the Memphite Necropolis (Louvre N 3155).

This combination of scenes from various sources permitted Otto to distinguish seventy-five separate episodes of lustrations, censings, libations and ritual procedures, which he was then able to group into six separate themes:

1. Episodes 1-9: preliminary rites, which involve purification of the statue with libations, natron and incense.
2. Episodes 10-22: animation of the statue involving the sleeping/trance of the *sem*-priest, and discussions with the sculptors.
3. Episodes 23-42: presentations relating to Upper Egypt.
4. Episodes 43-46: presentations relating to Lower Egypt.
5. Episodes 47-71: funerary meal.
6. Episodes 72-75: closing rites.

(Otto 1960: I, 34-171; http//.digitalegypt.ucl.ac.uk?religion/wpr.html).

Schulman (1984: 169-96) studied the Opening of the Mouth Ceremony, primarily in the New Kingdom, and has published a comprehensive list of known references to the ritual which include both royal and private tomb wall scenes, temple scenes and papyri references. He studied in detail the ceremony on various New Kingdom stelae identifying twenty-six as containing references to this rite. (Figure 124, the stela of Ramose, and figure 125, a stela of unknown provenance, are examples of these).

The pictorial representations and texts of the episodes collected from these various sources, mentioned above, have permitted a reconstruction of the ceremony and a meaningful understanding of the main events of the rite. The location for the performance of the ceremony varied as to whether it was a deceased person or a statue being animated. For a statue, the ceremony commenced in the workshop where the statue was being fashioned, before then being transported to the funerary chapel or other display location. For a deceased individual, the ceremony was performed at the conclusion of the funeral ceremony at the entrance to the tomb.

In a number of instances the ritual was depicted on more than one mummy within a single family. Although it is possible that there were multiple deaths at the same time, it would seem more likely that the scene illustrated the funeral of the deceased and the symbolic re-enactment of a previous funeral of the relative(s) of the deceased (Schulman 1984: 176). Additionally, when the second coffin is that of the wife of the tomb owner, then the wife plays a double role in these depictions. She appears in the role of the widow mourning her husband and she is also represented as being deceased, standing mummiform next to her husband (Assmann 2005: 312).

4. Actors/Officiants

The main episodes of ritual activity comprising the statue ceremony were performed by a distinct group of officiants which involved craftsmen as well as priests, some of the officiants being identified with divinities. The *sem*-priest usually, but not always, performed the ritual actions. The lector's main role was to recite the incantations and in some earlier publications he was considered here as an ancillary figure. Davies (1943: 77) referred to him as a minor officiant and Otto (1950: 166) considered that his role was unnecessary 'as he is not performing a role essential to the action, but he serves, here as elsewhere, simply to recite the ritual'. However, this study proposes that the lector had a more active role in the ceremony and had an involvement in the important ritual actions.

Other officiants who were engaged in the ritual were the '*imy-ḫnt* priest', the 'friend' *(smr)*, the 'hereditary noble' *(iry-pꜥt)*, the '*imy-is* priest', the 'attendant of Horus' *(imi-ḫt-ḥr)*, the 'beloved son' *(sꜣ mr.f)* or 'pillar of his mother' *(iwn mwt.f)*, and the 'sculptors' (*gnwtyw*). A female officiant, the 'great kite' (*ḏrt wrt*), is represented in the ritual in the tomb of Rekhmire, whilst in the tomb of Pediamenopet and the Louvre Papyrus of Sais it is the 'small kite' who is present. Stelae often depict grieving family members at the funerary ceremony and on occasions the lector is accompanied by a troop of 'professional mourners' (*wšbt. iw*) (Bruyère 1927: 67-72; Otto 1960: I, 11-16; Schulman 1984: 172-3).

5. Ritual Implements

The ritual implements used in the Opening of the Mouth Ceremony have been analysed in detail by Otto (1960: I, 6-26) and Roth (1992, 1993) and only a summary will be provided here. In the burial chamber of Unas the inscriptions record two blades of meteoric iron (*ntrty*) being used to open the mouth. In the Pyramid Texts, the *dwꜣ-wr*, thought to be a chisel, is used, and in Spell 1329b an unknown instrument (*ssꜣ*) is used (Faulkner 1969: 209). In the New Kingdom version of the ceremony the *ntrty* or one of the adze-shaped instruments such as the *nwꜣ*-blade or the ram-headed, snakelike implement called 'great of magic' (*wr-ḥkꜣw*) were used. Also in episode 32 the beloved son is depicted opening the mouth with a *mḏtft*-tool and a finger of gold. In episode 37 the *psš-kf*-knife is used, this consisting of a flake of flint broadening to a fork at one end, and finally in episode 46 the *msḫtyw* blade of iron is used.

6. Choice of Scenes in Stelae and in Tomb Depictions

In the case of stelae, where space is usually restricted to the depiction of one scene, the same stock scene is not shown on every stela. An individual choice from the various episodes of the Opening of the Mouth ceremony appears to have been selected for each stela. Although a depiction of a single episode of the rite is sometimes shown, equally two or more episodes conflated within a single scene can be recognised. When this does occur the scenes are shown in the correct chronological sequence. Similarly, the choice and extent of the text chosen can vary from a simple caption to a longer section of text (Schulman 1984: 174-7).

A key question arises as to the rationale for the inclusion of a particular scene in preference to another, particularly by the New Kingdom when there were a large number of distinct stages. It might be assumed that the more episodes represented, then the more effective and the better able the ritual is to achieve its purpose. But as indicated by the tomb evidence, not every episode is represented in the various Opening of the Mouth ceremonies. Perhaps only those actually intended to take place would have been depicted. Availability of resources and importantly wall space would have been a factor here as the number of stages able to be represented would depend on the amount of wall area available in each tomb. A parallel is the *Book of the Dead* where different versions of the text vary considerably in their choice of spells.

Ayad (2004: 113-33), in a study of the selection and layout of the various 45 scenes in the tomb chapel of Amenirdis I at Medinet Habu, suggests that the various episodes were carefully selected and thoughtfully arranged on the various walls. Her research indicated that there was a 'thematic continuity between adjoining walls and a distinct parallelism between the content of the East and West walls of the tomb'.

7. Case Study:

The Opening of the Mouth Ceremony in the Tomb of Rekhmire

The tomb of Rekhmire dating to *c.*1400 BC records the earliest pictorial representation of the ceremony (fig. 126). The tomb also shows the greatest number of scenes with 51 being depicted, and here it is possible to obtain some conception of the part the lector played in the ritual. The following account describes the various scenes in which the lector is present with 'Sq' representing the sequence number of that scene in the tomb of Rekhmire with Otto's episode number indicated by 'Ep' alongside.

Sq. 1 (Ep. 8) The lector with an *imy-khent* priest goes to the *is*-chamber (burial/shrine) where the statue is being prepared, and both officiants are depicted standing facing each other. The lector, who is not holding a papyrus roll, announces 'I enter to see him'. Otto recognises this scene as Episode 8, but Rekhmire placed the scene at the beginning of the sequence, perhaps wishing to introduce the key actors at this stage in the ceremony.

The lector is then not involved with the next ten scenes which consist of the initial purification ceremonies and the 'sleep/trance' of the *sem*-priest (as discussed on pages 9-10).

Sq. 12 (Ep.14) The lector is next shown behind the *sem*-priest who is touching the mouth of the statue with his finger. In this scene the *sem*-priest is standing in for the 'loving son'. He is identified with Horus and is thus seen as son and avenger of the murdered Osiris. The 'loving son', who is later introduced into the workshop, is the deceased's son who was entrusted with the duties of arranging the funeral as well as the continuance of the mortuary cult (Lorton 1999: 149-56).

Sq. 13 (Ep. 13) The *sem*-priest and lector address the sculptors ritually questioning them as to who is 'striking' or 'violating' the statue that is now seen as the father (Rekhmire) of the son. The statue is no longer considered

Fig. 126: Opening of the Mouth Ritual as seen on the chapel north wall of the Tomb of Rekhmire (adapted from Davies 1943: pls. 97-102, 105-107 and Otto 1960: I, pl. 1)

a block of stone and so any further preparation of the stone would be construed as violating the 'body' of Rekhmire.

Sq. 15 (Ep. 16) The *sem*-priest and lector address the statue cutter, calling upon him to cease the carving of the statue.

Sq. 16 (Ep. 17) The lector addresses the *sem*-priest, the *imy-khent* priest and members of the entourage of Horus, announcing the end of sculpting.

Sq. 17 (Ep. 18) The lector faces the *sem*-priest, who is standing in for 'the beloved son' and invites him to 'Go to see your father'.

Sq. 18 (Ep. 19) The lector announces 'untying the qeni-mat *(ḳni-šsp)*, putting on the panther skin'. The *sem*-priest is not shown in this scene but it is assumed that it is him to whom the lector is referring. The *sem*-priest would wear the panther skin so that he could symbolically utilise the physical power of the animal in order to enhance his performance in the ensuing ritual (Lorton 1999: 159).

Sq. 20 (Ep. 21) In this scene the lector states: 'I have marked your eye for you, your *ba* (to be) in it'. Whilst the literal meaning of this statement may be uncertain, the implication is that the utterances of the lector are designed to empower the *sem*-priest to perform the rites.

Sq. 21 (Ep. 22) Here there is a change of scene from the interior to the outside of the chamber where the lector, with two companions standing behind him, faces both the *sem*-priest and the *imy-khent* priest. The text describes the actions but there is no dialogue.

Sq. 22 (Eps. 23,II; 23,III; 24,II) In this combined scene, the great kite speaks briefly into the ear of the bull and the lector then recites the remainder of the text. The *sem*-priest holding up a *kherep*-sceptre gives the order for a goat and goose to be slaughtered. Then a foreleg of the ritually slaughtered bull is brought. In the second part of the scene the lector states: 'Receive the foreleg; the eye of Horus, the heart is brought to you with it. Do not approach that god!'

Sq. 23 (Eps. 25; 23,I; 24,I) The description of this scene is 'the rite of Opening of the Mouth and eyes at the offering of the sacrificial bull'. So this is the crux of the whole ceremony and here the lector has his arm outstretched and announces that he has opened the mouth and eyes. In the butchery part of the scene, the butcher or grappler (*imnḥ*) states that he is giving the foreleg to the lector and the heart to the companion and requests that they place them in front of the statue of Rekhmire. As the foreleg has been freshly cut from the bull, it would still be twitching and bleeding and thus the statue is being symbolically endowed with living matter.

The ensuing part of the ceremony is primarily concerned with touching the mouth of the statue with various objects.

Sq. 24 (Ep. 27) The *sem*-priest is in front of the statue. The lector again with arm outstretched announces the opening of the mouth with the '*ntry*-blade'. A figure dressed as a *sem*-priest performs the ritual, but the label above the figure identifies a lector, possibly a copyist's error. The *imy-khent* priest stands behind the statue.

Sq. 25 (Ep. 26) The lector announces the opening of the mouth with the *nwꜣ* blade and the *msḫtyw* blade. The *sem*-priest performs the ritual and an *imy-is* priest stands behind the statue.

Sq. 26 (Ep. 28) The lector with arm outstretched presents the statue to the hereditary noble (*iry-pꜥt*) who stands behind the statue.

Sq. 28 (Ep. 30) Here in a duplication of an earlier scene the lector, with arm outstretched, addresses the facing sculptors, ordering them to cease sculpting. The *sem*-priest and the companion stand behind him.

Sq. 29 (Ep. 31) In two combined episodes the lector firstly announces that the *sem*-priest is bringing the beloved son to the statue and then in the second part the lector announces the arrival of the son.

Sq. 30 (Ep. 32) The lector declares the Opening of the Mouth with the *mḏtft*-blade and the finger of the *kherep*-sceptre by the beloved son, who is now wearing the panther skin.

Sq. 31 (Ep. 33) The lector then announces the Opening of the Mouth with the little finger of the *sem*-priest.

Sq. 32 (Ep. 36) The lector proclaims the Opening of the Mouth with the four *abet*-tools *(ꜥbwt)* by the beloved son.

Sq. 33 (Ep. 43) In this, the second butchery scene, the great kite speaks while the lector is seen facing the bull holding up a *kherep*-sceptre. The lector then gives the order for the butchery to commence.

Sq. 35 (Ep. 45) A similar scene to sequence 23/episode 25 above, in which the lector announces the Opening of the Mouth.

Sq. 36 (Ep. 46) The lector with an arm outstretched proclaims the Opening of the Mouth with the *nwꜣ*-blade and the *msḫtyw* blade of iron.

Sq. 37 (Ep. 50) A double scene with, firstly, the lector announcing the rite of clothing the statue. The second part of the scene (50C) has a similar figure to the lector who is shown holding a scroll, but in this instance he is labelled a *sem*-priest. Again, possibly a copyist's error as the *sem*-priest is shown further forward in the scene clothing the statue.

Sq. 38 (Ep. 39) The caption to this scene is stated as 'adorning the statue with an ostrich plume'. Although the actor is labelled as a lector, he is dressed as a *sem*-priest and again, as in Sq. 24, this may be an error in transmission of scenes or texts from the original papyrus copy. In addition there is a lector standing in the usual position at the right of the scene. Otto (1960: II, 21) in his analysis of the scene suggests that the ostrich plume may infer a fan indicating that the statue is now able to breathe. Otto, however, does caution as to the tentative nature of this conclusion.

Sq. 39 (Ep. 37) Again there is possible confusion in this scene as the labelling indicates two *sem*-priests, but the figure on the right is dressed as and has the usual pose of a lector[2] The sequence involves the rite of touching the mouth with the *peseshkef* blade *(psš-kf)*.

Sq. 40 (Ep. 38) The lector with arm outstretched announces the giving of grapes to the statue, possibly prefiguring the later offerings (Lorton 1999: 171). The *sem*-priest is the officiant.

Sq. 41 (Ep. 41) The lector with arm outstretched proclaims the offering of water. The *sem*-priest is the officiant.

Sq. 42 (Ep. 47) The lector with arm outstretched announces the rite of censing. The *sem*-priest is the officiant.

Sq. 43 (Ep. 59) The lector with arm outstretched announces the rite of censing and litany to all the gods. The *sem*-priest is the officiant.

Sq. 44 (Ep. 65) The lector with arm outstretched announces the rite of taking the offerings.

Sq. 45 (Ep. 69) The lector proclaims the recitation of formulae for transfiguration which is performed by other lectors. Meanwhile the *sem*-priest and a *ḥm-nṯr* perform the ritual, in front of an offering list.

Sq. 46 (Ep. 73) The lector in standard pose announces the transportation of the statue to the chapel which is depicted being carried by the companions.

Sq. 47 (Ep. 74C) The lector announces the installation of the statue inside the chapel.

Sq. 48 (Ep. 74A + B) The lector announces the opening of the shrine doors and the placing of a garland on the consecrated shrine by the *sem*-priest.

Sq. 49 (Ep. 75) The lector declares the statue is complete. The *sem*-priest is standing in front of the statue with his hands turned outwards.

Sq. 50 (Ep. 71) The lector announces the offering of incense to Re. A *ḥm-nṯr* is the officiant in this scene.

Sq. 51 (Ep. 72) The lector proclaims that the Opening of the Mouth has been performed. The lector is the sole officiant and he is shown standing in front of an offering table which is set before the statue.

Analysis of the Opening of the Mouth Scenes in the Tomb of Rekhmire

In the 51 scenes displayed in the tomb of Rekhmire, the lector is present in 37 of these. The scenes from which he is absent are mainly the initial purification scenes where the companion recites the utterances. Of the episodes where the lector is present he is shown in 11 scenes with his arm at his side and in 26 scenes with an arm outstretched indicating a ritual action (Dominicus 1994: 92; figs. 127, 128). In none of the scenes is he depicted wearing a sash, which is not unusual for the New Kingdom.

In Sq. 1 (Ep. 8) the lector travels to the workshop (*is*) with the *imy-khent* priest and here he is shown without a papyrus roll and without his arm raised in a ritual gesture. Similarly in Sq. 29 (Ep. 31) the lector is shown without the roll when he accompanies the *sem*-priest and beloved son to stand before the statue. However, in Sq. 25 (Ep. 26) again he has no papyrus roll, but here the lector would be expected to carry a roll as the text indicates that he is performing recitations. There seems to be no apparent reason for this and so again this could be an error in transmission of the scene from the papyrus copy.

In Sq. 22 (Eps. 23,II; 23,III; 24,II), the first butchery scene, the *sem*-priest holds a *kherep*-sceptre and gives the order

[2] It is interesting to note that in three separate scenes (Sq. 24, Sq. 37 and Sq. 39) the lector is mislabelled.

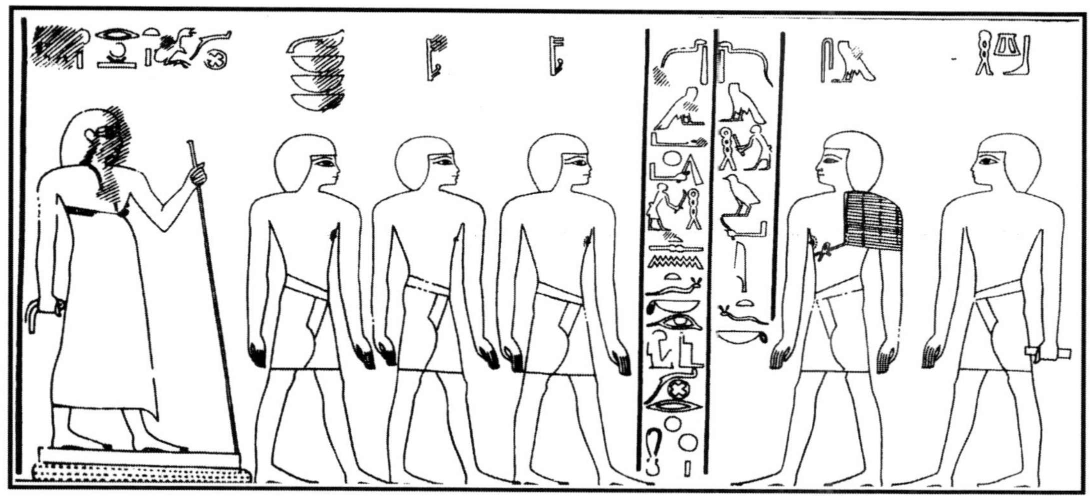

Fig. 127: Depiction of the lector with arms at his side from the Tomb of Rekhmire (Sq. 14, Ep. 15) (Davies 1943: II, pl. 107)

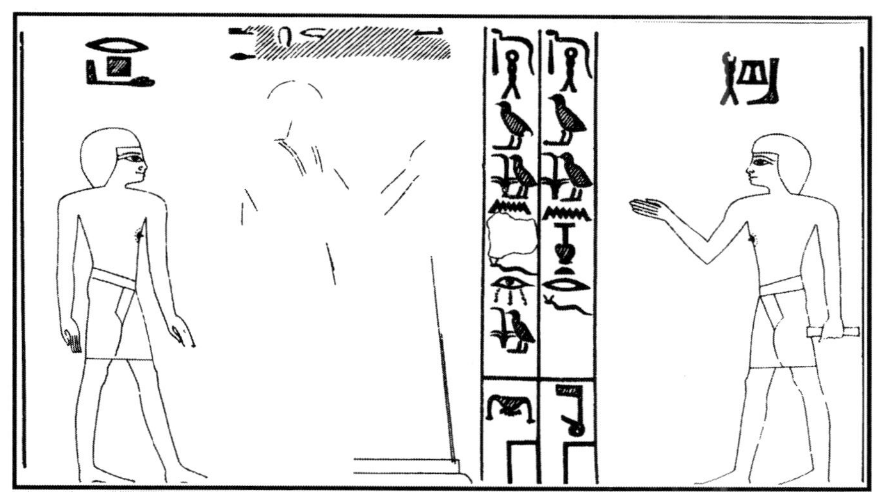

Fig. 128: Depiction of the lector with an arm outstretched from the tomb of Rekhmire (Sq. 26, Ep. 28) (Davies 1943: II, pl. 105)

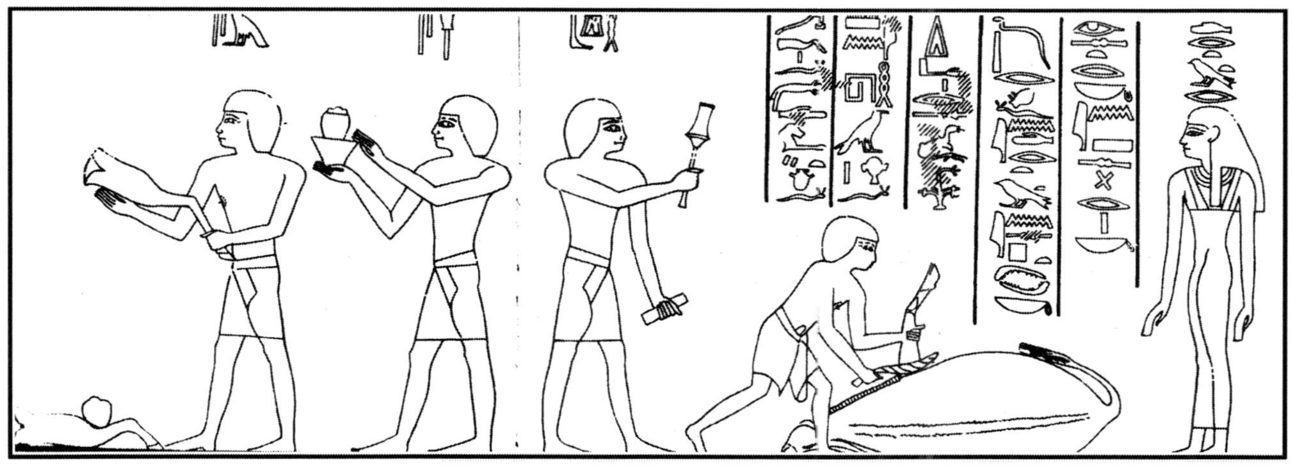

Fig. 129: Depiction of the lector holding a *kherep*-sceptre and giving the order for the slaughter of a bull of Upper Egypt (Sq. 33, Ep. 43) from the tomb of Rekhmire (Davies 1943: II, pl. 106)

for the slaughter of the bull. In Sq. 33 (Ep. 43), the second butchery scene, there is no *sem*-priest present and it is the lector who now holds a sceptre and gives the order for the slaughter of the bull of Upper Egypt (fig. 129).

Importantly, in Sq. 23 (Eps. 25; 23,I; 24,I) a foreleg of the bull is given to the lector and he is requested by the butcher to present it to the statue, so the lector is now directly involved in the ritual action. The butchery scene is crucial to the Opening of the Mouth ceremony and the presentation by the lector of the bleeding, twitching foreleg of the bull, indicative of the very essence of life, can be considered as a defining moment of the ritual (Lorton 1999: 165). The statue is now symbolically endowed with physical strength. Additionally, the lector being present at both slaughter scenes indicates the ritualisation of the Opening of the Mouth ceremony through the various recitations.

In several of the scenes a degree of authority and control is shown by the lector since by the use of the imperative tense he orders the *sem*-priest and other officiants to perform their tasks. Such an example is Sq. 7 (Ep. 18) where the lector tells the *sem*-priest who is standing in for the beloved son:

> 'Words spoken; go and see your father' (*ḏd-mdw is m33n.k it.k*).

Again in Sq.28 (Ep.30) he orders the sculptors to cease carving the statue.

In Sq. 20 (Ep. 21) the utterances of the lector are designed to empower the *sem*-priest, underlining the significance to the ritual of the words spoken, and also the importance of the lector as the one speaking the words. In Sq. 49 (Ep. 75) the lector and the *sem*-priest declare that the statue is complete, but in the final scene of Rekhmire, Sq. 51 (Ep. 72), the lector as sole officiant stands facing the statue announcing that the Opening of the Mouth has been performed.

8. Opening of the Mouth in Other Tomb Scenes

It is also important to consider the depictions of the lector in other source materials showing the Opening of the Mouth ceremony. Appendix 5 lists all the episodes from Otto's major and minor sources in which it is possible to identify the presence of the lector. However, this is obviously not a true representation of the number of scenes in which the lector was originally depicted due to weathering and deterioration that has subsequently occurred to many such scenes. Appendix 6 lists the presence or absence of the various episodes of the Opening of the Mouth rites in the seven major versions of the ceremony (from Otto 1960: II, 189-90).

A comparison of the order of the episodes in the major sources indicates some minor variations between these. The scenes in the tomb of Rekhmire demonstrate the greatest variation in this order compared to other sources but as this is the earliest known pictorial record of the ceremony, a standard might not yet have been established at that time. Variations in order could be choice on the part of the tomb owner or a record of the ritual as it was hoped for, as mentioned previously (on the topic of tomb selection cf. van Walsem 2008). However, Rekhmire being vizier, conspicuously wealthy, and a member of the elite may well have wanted a large number of scenes in his tomb as an outward display, an indication of his status during life.

The choice of officiant performing the various ritual activities also shows a degree of variation. In the tomb of the royal domain administrator, Nebsumenu, dated to the reign of Ramesses II, it is a chief lector and not a lector who is the officiant working alongside the *sem*-priest. In this version the caption to the important episode 24 (repeated 44) emphasises the significance of both the chief lector and the *sem*-priest when presenting the foreleg of the bull:

> 'Sem-priest and chief lector priest: Taking the leg, opening the mouth and eyes' (translated Assmann 2005: 325).

The initial purification scenes in the various Opening of the Mouth sources were suggested by Baly (1930: 176) as not belonging to the ritual but rather as later appnded to it. However, this distinction is not made by researchers in later analyses who generally consider the purification scenes as a prelude to the main core of the ritual. Purification scenes such as these are also to be seen in the daily temple cult ritual where the offering ritual is preceded by purification with incense and water. In addition the latter part of the Opening of the Mouth ritual and the latter part of the daily cult ritual also contain a significant amount of shared material. However, the purpose of the Opening of the Mouth ritual was quite different to that of the daily cult ritual, with the former being associated with animation or reanimation whilst the latter was directed at the awakening of the cult statue (Lorton 1999: 153; Assmann 2005: 313).

9. Conclusion

Although, as stated earlier, the lector was considered in some early publications as a minor actor in the ceremony, the evidence presented above demonstrates that he plays a more active role. He is present in more than 75% of the scenes decorating the tomb chapel of Rekhmire and in the Funerary Papyrus of Sais. The lector orders and directs the various ritual actions and his recitations empower the *sem*-priest. He presents the foreleg of the bull in the important animation scene and in the second butchery scene he holds a *kherep*-sceptre whilst giving the order for the slaughter of the bull. In the last scene of the ceremony it is the lector who announces the end of the ritual.

The lector can thus be seen as a central performer in the ritual, which not only involves recitations but also ritual actions. Without the relevant recitations the ritual would be incomplete and deemed invalid. Eyre (2002: 188) suggests he might be considered as a master of ceremonies and, because of his direct involvement in the ritual activities, his role is one of being a key figure and an active officiant.

Chapter 9

The Involvement of the Lector in Healing

1. Introduction

In the archaeological and textual record of ancient Egypt there are many references to disease and the various agencies which cause disease processes. As in many ancient societies, Egyptians would have sought assistance from others in an attempt to obtain relief from these ailments. Inevitably, certain members or groups in the community would emerge who would claim to possess certain skills and healing abilities.

The textual record indicates that the practice of healing was not restricted to a single class of individuals, but that various categories of healers were involved in treating illness. The physician (*swnw*), the *wab*-priest (*wꜥb*), the priest of Sekhmet (*wꜥb sḫmt*), the controller of Serket (*ḫrp srkt*), the magician (*sꜣw*), and the local healer all had some involvement in healing practices. In addition there is certain evidence to suggest that the lector had a role in healing.

Many approaches and treatment strategies to cope with infirmity were pursued by these various healers, but discussions about healing often distinguish between rational therapy on the one hand, and the use of magical incantations and performative ritual on the other. However, reason and magic harmoniously coexisted in ancient Egypt and so an alternative viewpoint is to consider the two methodologies as complementary to one another with boundaries, if they existed at all, being rather blurred. The physician would often treat a patient with medicaments and remedies listed in the medical papyri, some of which stand up to scrutiny today, whilst delivering a ritual incantation. The 'Controllers of Serket', who treated snake bites and scorpion stings, not only analysed snakes by description and toxicity but also considered the reptile's divine associations, and as a result used incisions and topical applications as well as invocations to divinities (Ritner 2001a: 326).

To explore the extent of the lector's engagement in healing activities, the relevant source materials such as the medical papyri, the temple evidence, together with the extant historical and literary records all need to be examined.

2. Medical Papyri

There are approximately twelve important medical papyri, and these are the written records of medical procedures and treatments that have been handed down to us from ancient Egypt. There is some duplication amongst the content of these papyri and translational difficulties restrict our understanding of some of the prescriptive elements, but nevertheless they are an invaluable insight into medical practice in ancient Egypt. The association of the lector with healing practices is directly attested in three of these documents, the London, Berlin and Chester Beatty papyri.

The London Medical Papyrus (P. BM 10059) which is in a poor state of preservation has been dated by Leitz (1999: 1) on palaeographic grounds to the 18th Dynasty. Ritner (2001: 354) considers that it could have been composed during the Ramesside Period due to the presence of several incantations in foreign languages incorporated within the document. The manuscript consists of sixty-two separate treatments covering essentially four groups of ailments: skin disease, ophthalmic problems, haemorrhages (principally against miscarriage) and burns.

There is a reference to a lector in section 15, lines 8-13 (Wreszinski 1912: 149, No. 25):

> 'Another [conjuration] for [repelling] *nsy*-disease and *tmyt*-disease,[1] which [Isis] did for her father... … … …This amuletic protection was found at night, descended into the broad court of the temple of Coptos as a secret of this goddess, by the hand of this lector of this temple, while this land was in darkness. It is the moon-god who shone on this book on all its way. It was brought as a marvel to the king of Upper and Lower Egypt…' (*kt šntw dr nsy tmyt ir.n ꜣst n it.s … … gm.n tw wdꜣw pn m wḫ sꜣw m wsḫt h nt ḥwt-nṯr m gbttw sštꜣ n nṯrt tn m dt ḫry-ḥbt n r pr pn m kkw in iꜣḥ wbn ḥr mḏꜣt tn ḥr wꜣt.s int.tw.s m bi(ꜣ)yt n ḥm n nsw-bit*) (translated Leitz 1999: 81).

In this text the lector is noted as the agent who discovered the amuletic protection, and although there is this mention of the lector, this does not directly confirm his involvement in the treatment of these diseases.

Another direct reference to a lector is in the Berlin Papyrus (P. Berlin 3038). The provenance of this papyrus is also uncertain but on palaeographic grounds it has been dated to the 19th Dynasty (Nunn 1996: 37). The papyrus comprises 204 paragraphs or treatments, some of which are paralleled in the Ebers Papyrus. These paragraphs encompass a variety of conditions such as treatments for various worms, management of venomous bites, provision of ointments, the usage of fumigations and various other ailments. The lector is referred to in section 10, lines 10-11 (Wreszinski 1909: 19, No. 100):

[1] The translation of *nsy*-disease and *tmyt*-disease is uncertain, but it has been suggested that the terms refer to unknown illnesses perhaps caused by disease demons, see Leitz 1999: 80; Nunn 1996: 225; *Wb* II: 324 & V: 306.

'Another ointment to dress a wound: Pork grease. To be coated by an excellent lector, who knows this ointment' (*ky gsw wḫdw srf sḏf mrḥt gsw s im in ḫry-ḥb(t) ikr rḫ pn gsw*).

The concept that pork was to be avoided, a suggestion put forward by Herodotus (II, 47; Selincourt 1996: 104) and accepted by early Egyptologists, has now largely been discounted. There is considerable evidence of pig having been consumed throughout the dynastic age as pig bones have been found at many archaeological sites. There is, however, a scarcity of pigs in the artistic records of many tombs, due perhaps to their cultural association with Seth, or that they may have been taboo in certain situations, localities and in different time periods (Darby *et al.* 1977: 171-209: Ikram 2001: 390-1).

In Papyrus Chester Beatty (P. BM. ESA 10695) there is evidence of a lector knowing about a particular remedy (P. Chester Beatty 15, l.5-8; von Deines et al. 1958: 170; Grapow 1958: 297; Bardinet 1995: 478):

'Remedy for the driving out of thirst (illness?) from the mouth [...] a (book?) relating to (the activities) of a lector. Acacia leaves; leaves of the Arou tree; panther skin... ...' (*pḫrt nt dr ibbw m r iry ḫry-ḥbt ḏrḏw šndt ḏrḏw n ʿrw inm n ȝby*).

These three prescriptions are some of the few references to a lector having knowledge of a particular compound or protection in order to treat a medical condition. Also they are rare instances where a particular professional is named as being the person to administer a medicament; the overwhelming majority of the remedies are not addressed to a particular category of healer or individual.

Unusually, in the Ebers Papyrus (Ebers 855u) there is mention of a lector having the power to cause illness, which is in contrast to his normal healing and ritual role in society. The paragraph in question is within the section providing information about the cardiovascular system (Wreszinski 1913: 211 [102, l.4-5]; von Deines *et al.* 1958: 5):

'As to vanishing of the heart (*ib*) and forgetfulness: it is the breath of the (harmful) doing of the lector that does it. It enters the lung several times and the heart *(ib)*[2] becomes confused through it' (*ir ȝk ib mht ib in ṯʿw n r di ḫry-ḥbt irr.st ʿk.f m smȝ m sp snw prr ib th ḥr.s*).

It is not certain why the lector should choose to use his recitations or magic in such a manner, but by invoking malevolent powers to cause illness, he is not conforming to the perception of the healer conveyed in the other medical papyri. However, contrary to the above, another of the remedies listed in the Ebers Papyrus (Ebers 227) is a treatment for, among other complaints, 'forgetfulness of the heart' (Wreszinski 1913: 68 [45, l.7-8]; von Deines et al. 1958: 148; Grapow 1958: 260):

'Another to eliminate the evil influence on the heart, expel forgetfulness of the heart, flight of the heart, stiches of the heart: inst plant part 8; figs part 8; celery part 16; [ochre] part 32; *šȝšȝ* part 8; honey part 32; water likewise' (*kt nt dr ʿȝʿ ib ḥr ḥȝty dr mht ib wʿr dmwt ib inst 8 r dȝbw 8 r mȝt 16 r .... 32 r šȝšȝ 8 r bit 32 mw mitt*) (translated Ghalioungui 1987: 77).

There is one other reference in the Ebers Papyrus (Ebers 855h) to similar malevolent activity, but on this occasion the action is being performed by a wab-priest (Wreszinski 1913: 209 [100, 18 - 101, 2]; von Deines et al. 1958: 4; Grapow 1958: 6):

'As to every kind of bitterness. It penetrates into the left eye; it goes out of the navel. It is the breath of the (noxious) doing of a wab-priest. It is the heart that causes it (the bitterness) to penetrate into his vessels. It cooks a cooking[3] in his whole flesh...' (translated Ghalioungui 1987: 223).

3. Temple Evidence

There is evidence to suggest that the ancient Egyptian temple had an association with healing practices, an activity that may well have been centred on the House of Life (*pr-ʿnḫ*). Confirmation of medical practices being part of temple activity was attested following the discovery of over 30,000 papyrus fragments from the Ptolemaic temple of Tebtunis (Strouhal 1997: 241; Sauneron 2000: 136; Pinch 2006: 94). These fragmentary texts have been translated and published in a series of volumes, *The Tebtunis Papyri, Vol. I-IV* (1902-76), and are the subject of continuing research at the 'Center for the Tebtunis Papyri, University of California, Berkeley' (www.tebtunis.berkeley.edu). The texts are dated from approximately 800 BC to after AD 300 and are written in a variety of languages. Their subject matter includes contents of the temple library and notary office as well as a number of family archives from the dignitaries residing in the surrounding village.

Among the many categories of text which have been published to date are fourteen medical texts, three of which were discovered within the temple enclosure (P. Tebt. II: 676, 677, 679). During excavations undertaken by an Italian team during the 1930's, artefacts which were interpreted as possibly relating to the preparation and administration of medicaments were discovered within the temple precinct. Many of the Tebtunis texts and artefacts relate to the Ptolemaic and Roman periods, and it is not certain that temple libraries were similar to this in earlier periods but there may well have been similarities.

Another possible link between healing practices and temple activities can be construed from a scene carved on the north-

[2] The heart is considered to refer to the mind as the ancient Egyptians recognised the heart as the centre of emotions, memory and intelligence.

[3] Ghalioungui interprets this as active cooking.

western corner of the inner aspect of the outer enclosure wall of the Graeco-Roman temple of Kom-Ombo (Nunn 1996: 163; fig. 130). The relief appears to be a depiction of nearly forty surgical instruments, being presented to the god Haroeris by the Roman emperor Trajan, in his role as king of Egypt. Ghalioungui (1963: 101-4) believes that these instruments appear to be too large and clumsy for practical use in surgery and considers that they represent a votive offering of foundation instruments, whereas Weeks (1980: 102) considers some of these instruments may have been used in dental surgery. Another opinion is that they might depict goldsmith's tools or possibly general artisan's implements (Sigerist 1951: 345). However, as Worth Estes (1993: 54) and Forshaw (2009: 484) indicate, several of the items shown are contemporary with many well-authenticated depictions of Roman and Greek surgical instruments, either found in medical locations or shown in the tombs of surgeons (see Tabanelli 1958; Bliquez 1981: 11-17; Jackson & La Niece 1986: 267-71).

FIG. 130: 'INSTRUMENTS' CARVED ON THE ENCLOSURE WALL OF THE PTOLEMAIC TEMPLE AT KOM OMBO
PHOTOGRAPH: AUTHOR

Further evidence of an association between the House of Life and healing practices is provided in an inscription on the restored green basalt naophorous statue of Udjahorresnet. This statue was originally set up in the temple of Neith at Sais during the reign of Darius I and it is now located in the Vatican Museum. The inscription on the statue is an important biographical text as it forms the only preserved Egyptian account relating to the Persian conquest in 525 BC and its aftermath (Posener 1936: 1-26; Gardiner 1938a: 157-9; Otto 1954: 169-73; Lichtheim 1980: 36-41; Lloyd 1982: 166-80; Baines 1996: 83-92).

The biographical inscription describes how Udjahorresnet's career began during the Saite Period when he was a naval officer. Following the Persian invasion of Egypt, Udjahorresnet was appointed priest of Neith and chief physician. Udjahorresnet explains how he was able to expel the foreigners from the temple of Neith at Sais and arrange for its reconsecration. He further describes how he helped the people of Sais to recover from the effects of the Persian invasion. On the back of the plinth of the statue is an important statement concerning the command he received from Darius to restore the establishment of the House of Life which had fallen into decay:

'His majesty did this because he knew the worth of this craft for causing the sick to live and in making to endure the names of all the gods, their temples, their offerings, and the conduct of their festivals for ever...'(translated Lichtheim 1980: 41).

This passage outlines the various activities of the House of Life and provides some evidence of healing practices that were being engaged in. It is also perhaps significant that a physician was given the important task of restabilising the House of Life. Udjahorresnet seems to have attached considerable significance to the title of chief physician as it is mentioned on his statue no fewer than eleven times, far more than any other title he possessed.

A group of three statues, attested to Peftuaneith and dated to the same period, provide similar evidence. Peftuaneith was a hereditary prince, administrator of the palace and chief physician during the reign of King Apries. The objects identified with Peftuaneith are a broken basalt statue discovered at Heliopolis and now in the British Museum (BM EA 83; fig. 131); a grey granite naophorous statue discovered at Abydos and now located in the Louvre (A 93), and a statue uncovered and located at Memphis (No. 545) (Piehl 1894: 118-22; Breasted 1906: IV, 514-7; Bakry 1970: 325-33, pls. 35-7; Lichtheim 1980: 33-6).

The biographical inscription on the Abydos statue (Louvre A 93) describes how Peftuaneith carried out extensive restorations to the city of Abydos, how he gave a donation of land to the temple of Osiris and how he restored the House of Life:

> 'I put in order the House of Life after (its) ruin. I established what is good for Osiris; I caused the execution of all its utterances (procedures) to be in order' (translated Piehl 1894: 119, l. 6-7 and Lichtheim 1980: 35).

As with Udjahorresnet, described above, Peftuaneith was also a chief physician and so again a physician was entrusted with the important task of restoring the House of Life. Although in this particular text there is little detail concerning the activities of the House of Life, Petftuaneith does claim that he reinstated all the different procedures of the institution, which again would have included those relating to healing practices.

Thus a link between the House of Life and healing practices can be established and from a number of sources of evidence it is also possible to explore a connection between the lector and the House of Life. Such an association is to be recognised in the various statues and monuments of Nakhthorheb, a high official during the reign of Psamtek II (BM EA 1646, fig. 132; Louvre A94; with further monuments in museums in Rome, Copenhagen and Cairo). Both the British Museum and Louvre statues show Nakhthorheb kneeling with his hands flat on his thighs in an act of reverence. The texts inscribed around the bases of the statues are recitations to the god Thoth, whilst on the back pillars of the statues are inscribed the many titles that Nakhhorheb possessed. These include 'sole companion' and 'chief lector' whilst his association with the House of Life is attested with the title of 'controller of the Masters of Magic of the House of Life' (*ẖrp ḥryw ḥkȝt m pr ˁnḫ*) (Gardiner 1938a: 166; Pierret 1978: 51-2; Andreu *et al.* 1997: 185-6, 255, no. 92; Russman 2001: 239-40).

FIG. 131: BASALT STATUE OF PEFTUANEITH 26TH DYNASTY, BM EA 83 (COURTESY OF THE BRITISH MUSEUM)

A connection between the lector and the House of Life can be found in the wording of the inscription carved on the celebrated Famine Stela, located on the island of Sehel in the Nile, some 4 km south of Aswan. The text describes an account of a major famine that struck Egypt during the reign of Djoser. The stela purports to be from the Old Kingdom but is usually considered to have been raised during the Ptolemaic Period. This later date is indicated by the vocabulary, grammar, orthography and divine affiliation accorded to Imhotep. The suggestion is that it was composed by the priesthood of Khnum, on the island of Elephantine, who had resided there for centuries, and who were now attempting to establish their prior ownership of the land in the face of an encroaching claim from their much newer, but increasingly prestigious neighbour, the temple of Isis at Philae (Lichtheim 1980: 94-103; Goedicke 1994; Ritner 2003b: 386-91).

FIG. 132: QUARTZITE STATUES OF NAKHTHOREB 26TH DYNASTY, BM EA 1646 (COURTESY OF THE BRITISH MUSEUM)

To try and alleviate the famine, the text describes how Djoser had consulted with one of the priests of Imhotep, who in addition to being an architect was also chief priest of Heliopolis:

(2) 'Hapy had failed to come in time. In a period of seven years, grain was scant, kernels were dried up, scarce was every kind of food ... ...
(4) I directed my heart to turn to the past; I consulted one of the staff of the Ibis[4], The chief lector Imhotep...'

The statement 'directed my heart to turn to the past' is the typical ancient Egyptian concept of reaching back in time for inspiration. It is a worshipful attitude for their antecedents, a belief in the wisdom of past documents, an example of archaism[5]. So Djoser dispatched a chief lector to Hermopolis, an officiant qualified to investigate the archives of the temple of Thoth:

(5) 'He stood: 'I shall go to the Mansion-of-the-Net,
[It is designed to support a man in his deeds]
I shall enter the House of Life,
Unroll the Souls of Re,
I shall be guided by them ...'[6]
(translated Lichtheim 1980: 96).

There the chief lector discovered that the god Khnum, who presided over the region of the First Cataract and controlled the flow of the Nile, was angry, and as a result had not allowed the Nile to flow properly. However, by conciliating him with a share of the revenue derived from trade at the border region and by giving a donation of land, Khnum was pacified and so restored the normal flow of the Nile (Lichtheim 1980: 94).

Significantly, a chief lector was entrusted with this important work, which involved consulting the 'Souls of Re'. This key statement describing how these papyrus scrolls were unrolled and examined by the chief lector is an assertion of his literacy and draws attention to his ability to interpret these ancient texts, a statement, in fact, highlighting one of his fundamental roles. This image that is evoked is a representation of the lector that is repeatedly depicted on tomb and temple wall scenes, a lector consulting and reading from an unrolled papyrus scroll.

The Famine Stela also provides information concerning the contents of the texts held by the House of Life. Columns 7-15 list mythological compendia for each nome, lexical texts and geographical descriptions (Haiying 1995: 517).

The Bentresh stela, similar to the Famine stela, is also considered to be propagandist in nature. This black sandstone stela, now in the Louvre in Paris (C 284) was discovered in a small Ptolemaic chapel that formerly stood beside the Khonsu temple at Karnak (Kitchen 1979: 284-7; Lichtheim 1980: 90-4; Ritner 2003a: 361-6). It is believed to have been composed by priests in the Late Period, but was disguised as a royal inscription dating to the time of Ramesses II. The stela describes how a princess of Bakhtan (identified as the land of the Hittites) was possessed by a demon, and how help was sought from Ramesses. Ramesses consulted with the personnel of the House of Life and Thothemheb, described as a learned man and royal scribe was dispatched to Bakhtan in an attempt to free the princess from the malevolent spirit. Thothhemheb does not specifically possess the title of lector, but it is possible that the description of 'a learned man' from the House of Life could relate to such an individual.

Gardiner (1938a: 178) notes an association between the lector and the House of Life in a magical papyrus (Cairo 58027) dating to the Roman Period which is aimed at affording protection to the king during the hours of night. One of the few individuals permitted to view this work is the lector, in his role as a liturgical specialist (Golénischeff 1927: 126 [3, 14]):

'(The book) must not be seen by any eye save (that of) the king himself or the chief lector or the myrrh-keeper of the House of Life' (translated Gardiner 1938a: 178).

In the same papyrus there is a rare reference to a medicament used in the House of Life, which thus provides additional evidence of healing practices/medicine being an integral part of the activities of the House of Life (Golénischeff 1927: 128 [4, 1]):

'the great mysterious ointment of the House of Life' (translated Gardiner 1938a: 178).

This text then proceeds to describe the remedy as effective 'for a man in danger by night' and among the ingredients listed are fragrant plants (*ꜥnḫ-imyw*), fine oil (*tpt*), honey (*bit*) and goose fat *(gbr)*.

4. Documentary Evidence

Documentary evidence of the lector's role in healing is attested in a number of textual and inscriptional sources. One of these is an inscription in the Old Kingdom mastaba tomb of Washptah who was a vizier, chief judge, chief lector and chief architect to king Neferirkare. This highly fragmentary text is inscribed on a series of blocks (CG 1569, 1570, 1674, 1702, JE 55937; Aberdeen 1560, 1558a-c) that originally formed part of the tomb of Washptah at Abusir (D38), and which are now located in the Egyptian Museum, Cairo and in the Marischal Museum, Aberdeen (Breasted 1906: I, 111-13; Sethe 1933: 40-5, No. 27; Grdseloff 1938: 353-4; Ghalioungui 1983: 74; Strudwick 2005: 318-20; Picardo 2010: 93-104).

The tomb inscription provides information about the development of tomb biography and also contributes to an understanding of early healing practices during the Old Kingdom (Picardo 2010: 93). The text describes how King Neferirkare was inspecting progress on some building work that was being overseen by Washptah, in his role as chief architect. On turning to commend Washptah for his good work, Neferirkare found that his chief architect

[4] The 'staff of the Ibis' designates the profession of scribes whose patron was Thoth (Lichtheim 1980: 100-1).

[5] For further comments on archaism in relation to Imhotep see page 58.

[6] The *Mansion-of-the-net* is thought to be the temple of Thoth at Hermopolis and the *Souls of Re* are the temple books kept in the House of Life, see Lichtheim 1980: 101, Notes 6 and 8.

had collapsed. The text is not completely clear as to what occurred next but it would seem that, initially, 'emergency treatment' or bandaging *([ḫr]-ʿw iḫr)* was provided for Washptah. The king then summoned both his lectors and chief physicians to attend to Washptah, and had a chest of papyrus rolls brought so that these specialists could consult them. Neither the lectors nor physicians were able to revive Washptah and had to pronounce him dead, although Grdseloff (1938: 354) interpreted the text by suggesting that Washptah had merely fainted.

The papyrus rolls that were consulted, presumably of a medical and magical nature, could have been the precursors of the later medical papyri. Most medical papyri are traditionally dated to the New Kingdom but on palaeographic grounds are sometimes considered to be copies of earlier works (Breasted 1906: I, 112 f; Strouhal 1997: 245; Nunn 1996: 27).

In this account Neferirkare entrusted the important task of trying to revive Washptah to lectors and physicians. The summoning of both these groups of individuals emphasises the multifaceted nature of ancient Egyptian healing practices with lines of demarcation between the activities of such personnel not always obvious[7].

This participation of both the lector and a physician can again be seen in an event that occurred during the reign of Ramesses II. The evidence is furnished from the Hittite archives of Boghazköy, a collection of clay tablets inscribed in Akkadian and found within the palace at the Hittite capital. Among these are three fragments which constitute a letter sent by Ramesses II to Hattusili III, the Hittite ruler, and are dated to the middle of the 13th century BC (652/f + 28/n + 127r = text KBO 28.30; Edel 1976: 67-70).

Hattusili wrote to Ramesses requesting that Egyptian physicians prepare drugs to help his married sister, Matanzi, to have children. Ramesses replied in a rather undiplomatic manner:

'Now see (here), as for Matanzi, my brother's sister, the king your brother knows her. Fifty is she? Never! She's sixty for sure! ...No-one can produce medicine for her to have children. But of course, if the Sun-God and the Storm-God should will it ...But I will send a good lector and an able physician, and they can prepare some birth drugs for her (anyway)' (translated Edel 1976: 69 and Ghalioungui 1983: 77).

Again treatment of the patient involves both magical incantations by the lector and the preparation of drugs by the physician. This passage and similar communications between the Egyptians and the Hittites illustrates the reputation that Egyptian medicine had in the ancient world.

Another inscribed clay tablet is a communication between Hattusili and Ramesses again requesting medical help (NBC 3934, Goetze 1947: 241-51). Full translation of this tablet is difficult due to its fragmentary nature, but what is obvious is that the Hittites had repeatedly requested an Egyptian physician to be sent to the Hittite court and only after the third attempt did they claim to have obtained a response. However, Ramesses replied by saying he had agreed to this request on three previous occasions, and that a physician had already been dispatched along with the relevant medicines that were required. The fragmentary parts of the text indicate that there were other individuals in the party sent to Hatti and it is possible a lector was among them, as was the case described above in text KBO 28:

> 7 [................I have consented one, two and three times to send.
> 8 [..................] I have sent you a certain physician.
> 9 [..................] Leya went with him.
> 10 [................] to you and I have sent you
> 11 [rich presents] through the hand of my envoys.
> 12 [................] to you among them
> 13 [.......I consented to] send a physician to you.
> 14 [...........................] all the good herbs
> (translated Goetze 1947: 245)

The above examples again illustrate the lector and physician working together and there are also a number of physicians who held the additional title of lector (appendix 7):

1. Mereruka, the vizier to King Teti, carried a very large number of titles. However, with his position among the elite of society, it seems likely that his titles of physician and lector may well have been honorary (Nunn 1996: 125-6).
2. A 19th Dynasty chief physician, Amenhotep, carried the title of chief lector and is known from his tomb at Deir Durunka, near Asyut (Hayes 1959: 349).
3. A 22nd Dynasty physician, Huy is known from two graffiti in the temple of Sety I at Abydos (Frankfort *et al.* 1933: I, 88 l. 6 and II, pl. 88; Ghalioungui 1983: 33).
4. Horakhbit, who also lived during the 22nd Dynasty, was a chief physician and a lector of the king. He is known from a number of artefacts which include a sarcophagus discovered at Sais (Gauthier 1922: 202-4) and two fragments of a basalt statue in the Graeco-Roman Museum of Alexandria (Accession No. 20950, 26532, Bakry 1970: 333-41). An unprovenanced travertine ointment jar, now located in the Metropolitan Museum of Art, New York, can also perhaps be attributed to Horakhbit, as it displays an inscription identical to that shown on the basalt statue (Accession No. Rogers Fund 42.2.2; Ghalioungui 1983: 34):

[7] For a discussion on ancient Egyptian healing practices see Forshaw 2014.

'Controller of the Red-crown Enclaves, Chief Physician, Horakhbit' (*ḫrp ḥwwt-nt wr swnw ḥr-ꜣḫbt*).

Of the many inscriptions that were carved by ancient Egyptian mining expeditions, one in particular also provides information about the healing activities of a lector. As to be discussed later, graffito 12 from the travertine quarries of Hatnub is an autobiography by the lector, Tutnakhtankh (see expedition inscriptions on pages 124-5).

5. Literary Evidence

There is a reference to a lector in a New Kingdom manuscript of 'love poems', the well preserved Papyrus Chester Beatty 1 (P. BM 10681). Among the texts in the papyrus are three collections of love poems, with the poem in question being a cycle of seven stanzas entitled 'Beginning of the Sayings of the Great Happiness' (Gardiner 1931: 27-34; Lichtheim 1976: 181-6; Mathieu 1996: 25-30; Tobin 2003b: 322-7). The poem is a poignant tale of a young man enraptured with a beautiful young lady who is unable to think of little else, so much so that his love causes him to become unwell. In the final stanza he complains that physicians and their remedies are unable to cure him, and nor are lectors able to make him well:

'And sickness invaded me;
I am heavy in all my limbs,
My body has forsaken me.
When the physicians come to me,
My heart rejects their remedies;
The lectors (magicians) are quite helpless,
My sickness is not discerned'
(translated Lichtheim 1976: 185).

Although the choice of words may be rather rhetorical, the reference to the consultation of a lector in an attempt to improve the young man's condition is again an indication of the respect and purported abilities of the lector. Additionally, there is again a reference to the administrations of both a physician and a lector in attempting to effect a cure.

6. Summary and Conclusion

The evidence presented and discussed in this chapter helps to provide some insight into the lector's association with healing practices. The references to the lector in the medical papyri indicate that he was directly involved with dispensing some of the remedies, suggesting that he had a 'hands on' approach to healing practices as well as a more traditionally perceived role in that of a narrator of healing incantations and ritualist. These particular prescriptions are some of the few remedies in the medical papyri where a particular professional is named as being the individual to administer a medicament.

The temple evidence indicates that healing practices were part of the activities of the House of Life, with the lector being active in this institution. There is also a record of a particular remedy being produced there, with the strong possibility of this being one of many. Finally, the references in both the Old and New Kingdoms to a lector and a physician working together suggest the importance in the healing regime of the incantations recited by the lector and the medical skills of a physician, an illustration of the multifaceted nature of ancient Egyptian healing practices.

Chapter 10

The Title of Lector Recorded in Expedition Inscriptions

1. Introduction

Inscriptions were frequently left on rock faces and stelae by members of state organised expeditions, who travelled outside the Nile valley. A number of these inscriptions included the title of lector within their subject matter. The purposes of such expeditions were trading, military missions and mining and were a major feature of state activity (Seyfreid 1981; Eichler 1993; Hikade 2001). They are attested from as early as the Predynastic Period and can be found through to the 30th Dynasty (Eichler 1993: 269; Blumenthal 1977: 87). These are found not only within the boundaries of Egypt but also at sites such as Sinai, the Eastern Desert regions and Nubia (Enmarch 2011: 97-8). The texts range from simple inscriptions which merely list a name and title(s), often with a *ḥtp-di-nsw* formula, to more elaborate texts which may include self-laudatary epithets, biographies and appeals to the living. Certain of the larger inscriptions include details concerning the nature of the expedition, ruler at that time and numbers of expedition members (Shaw 2001: 99; Enmarch 2011: 98).

2. Trading and Military Expeditions

Trading missions included among their expedition members a variety of occupational categories ranging across the whole of Egyptian society. There are instances of high ranking members and leaders of trading expeditions carrying the title of lector such as that of Harkhuf in the Old Kingdom. Inscriptions also listed the presence of other lectors on these missions but included few biographical details.

Numerical and occupational data for the Egyptian army is not frequent and its interpretation can be difficult (Faulkner 1953; Spallinger 2005: 155-8). There are few known references to the lector being present on wholly military missions, although it is possible that the lector may have accompanied such expeditions to officiate at burial rituals that may have fairly common during warfare. Military personnel were known to accompany mining expeditions and there is evidence that generals of the army commanded mining expeditions to Sinai in the Old Kingdom (inscriptions 1, 2 and 16 of Gardiner, Peet & Černý 1955). An expedition to the Wadi Hammamat dated to the time of Ramesses IV included a full division of the army (Faulkner 1955: 42). However, as Endmarch (2011: 99) indicates it is relevant that the Egyptian term *mšꜥ* (*Wb.* II, 155.12) encompassed both military and non-military expeditions.

3. Mining Inscriptions

The overwhelming number of inscriptions that include a reference to a lector relate to mining activities. There is evidence of mining as early as 35,000 years ago with the inhabitants of Nazlet Khater, a desert area some 25 km north of Sohag in Middle Egypt, quarrying chert by open-air trenches, galleries and bell pits, using methods that were precursors to modern mining techniques (Vermeersh *et al.* 1984: 285). From predynastic times onwards the mountains and desert regions adjacent to the Nile valley both in Egypt and in Nubia as well as the Sinai Peninsula were exploited for stone, metal ores and various gems.

There is a considerable body of surviving archaeological and inscriptional evidence that provides an insight into how these mining and processing operations were undertaken. Unlike modern mining techniques, where long-term mining communities are the norm, Pharaonic mining was predominately short-term with the concept of the 'expedition' being the overriding impression of mining activities (Seyfried 1981: 4).

Other than inscriptional evidence, additional information about such mining enterprises is provided by paintings and texts. A scene in the 4th Dynasty mastaba tomb of Queen Meresankh III at Giza includes depictions of melting and hammering copper (fig. 133). Similarly, the 6th Dynasty autobiography of Weni and the 18th Dynasty transportation of the obelisks of Hatshepsut are all important in understanding the methods employed and the significance that the ancient Egyptians attached to mining.

From this evidence it is possible to create some impression of the organisation and manpower that went into coordinating a Pharaonic mining expedition. Much of the information relating to personnel and social organisation of such an expedition comes from the inscriptional records left behind at the extraction sites by the various mining crews. Such evidence is mainly centred on the four important localities of Sinai, Hatnub, Wadi Hammamat and Wadi el-Hudi, although a few inscriptions can be found at some smaller mining sites.

Sinai

Turquoise, copper and malachite were mined in the Sinai although much of the epigraphic evidence relates to the extraction of turquoise (Ogden 2000: 149). The inscriptions found in the Sinai have been studied by Petrie (1906); Gardiner and Peet (1917); Gardiner, Peet and Černý (1952, 1955); Giveon (1974, 1978); Pinch (1993); Valbelle and Bonnet (1996), and Tallet (2003: 470-3). In total over 500 inscriptions from the areas of Magharah, Wadi Nasb, Wadi Kharig, Rod el-`Air and Serabit el-Khadim have been recorded to date.

FIG. 133: EAST WALL OF THE MAIN ROOM OF THE MASTABA OF QUEEN MERESANKH III AT GIZA SHOWING ILLUSTRATIONS OF COPPER WORKING (ADAPTED FROM DUNHAM & SIMPSON 1974: FIG. 5)

The composition of the various expedition personnel fluctuated from one period to another with the amount of detail supplied by each inscription also varying significantly. Prior to the 6th Dynasty the majority of the inscriptions merely recorded details of the reigning monarch with little other information about expedition members. During the remainder of the Old Kingdom there is reference to leaders and the more important members of the expedition but little mention of the ordinary individuals. The Middle Kingdom expeditions include the most detail about the composition of the personnel, whereas in the New Kingdom again details are lacking about individual expedition members.

As regards size of workforce, there is one Old Kingdom reference to an expedition numbering 1,400 (inscription no. 19 of Gardiner, Peet & Černý 1955: 65, pl. 9). However, all the Middle Kingdom expeditions contained far fewer personnel, the largest lists 734 members (inscription no. 23 of Gardiner, Peet & Černý 1955: 65, pl. 9). Shaw (1998: 247) considers that an average expedition would comprise 300 men and 400 donkeys. In the Middle Kingdom there are at least 39 expeditions to the mines in Sinai with an average interval of 31 years between each expedition (Shaw 1998: 251).

There is reference to only one lector in the Sinai inscriptions, the chief lector, Werkherephemut, who additionally bears the titles of 'dignitary' (*s3b*), priest and scribe. He is referred to on the west wall of the Shrine of Kings in the temple of Serabit el-Khadim, an inscription that has been dated to the reign of Amenemhat IV. Although the inscription is incomplete, Werkherephemut appears to be performing an offering ritual (inscription no. 123B of Gardiner, Peet & Černý 1955: 128, pl. 46). In the remainder of the temple, and indeed in all the inscriptions in Sinai, there are few references to priests, with only two *wʿb* priests and three *ḥm-nṯrw* being recorded.

Medical care seems to have been considered as four of the expeditions to Sinai record a physician (*swnw*) as being present. Snakes and scorpions were a threat in the desert conditions of the Sinai and a controller of Serket (*wʿb sḫmt*) was present on four of the expeditions and a further five included a scorpion remover (*ḫrp srḳt*) among the expedition personnel.

Hatnub

The travertine quarries of Hatnub are located in the Eastern Desert some eighteen kilometres from the el-Amarna plain. Early studies investigating the archaeology of this region were carried out by Blackden and Fraser (1892), Newberry (1895) and Petrie (1894), although the main epigraphic work was carried out by Anthes in 1928. Some fifteen inscriptions and fifty-two graffiti were documented by Anthes, with subsequent researchers publishing additional unprovenanced material (Simpson 1959; Goedicke 1959; Posener 1968). More recent research at Hatnub has been carried out by Shaw (1986, 1987, 2010).

The quarries appear to have been worked from the Old Kingdom through to the New Kingdom (Shaw 1986: 201). Again most of the texts relate to expedition leaders although there are some references to labourers and lower ranking members of the undertaking. The sizes of the expeditions vary but many of them seem to have been fairly large-scale. Two First Intermediate Period inscriptions (Hieratic graffiti 6 of Anthes 1928: 21-2, pl. 11; Hieratic graffiti 9 of Anthes 1928: 23-4, pl. 13) list expeditions that numbered some 1600 men. A stela dated to the reign of Senwosret III mentions over 1400 men with further numbers of 'necropolis workers' (Goedicke 1959: 56). The inscriptions that list lectors are (see appendix 8):

1. Graffito 7 dates to the Old Kingdom and mentions Ankhy whose titles were recorded as sole companion, overseer of the Southern lands, lector and overseer of the priests. In the same inscription there is a reference to Khnumankh, the father of Ankhy, who was seal bearer, sole companion, lector and chief priest (Anthes 1928: 22-3, pl. 12-12a).
2. Graffito 12 dates to the Middle Kingdom/Second Intermediate Period and is an autobiography by the scribe of the god's book, the lector, Tutnakhtankh. Amongst the usual self glorifications, are the following statements:

> (5) '... Moreover I was an excellent lector, skilled in (6) judgement concerning an illness... (*ink gr ḥry-ḥbt ikr ḥmww m wpt ḫ3t*).
> (13) ... I performed magic on the afflicted face.

(14) I exorcised the bad odours…' (*iw ḥkꜣ.n(.i) ḥr ind šnt.i n sṯ*) (Anthes 1928: 28-9, pl. 14).

These statements would appear to be a reference to the healing capabilities of the lector, one of only a few direct indications in the texts from ancient Egypt to this ability. There are a few other inscriptions at Hatnub relating to healing both by priests of Sekhmet and by physicians, but no others relate to a lector.

3. Inscription 15 is a weathered royal decree inscribed on the façade of an Old Kingdom tomb in the Wadi Nakhla close to Deir el-Bersha, but is listed by Anthes amongst the Hatnub inscriptions (Anthes 1928: 18, pl. 2). The tomb has been dated to the 5th Dynasty reign of Neferirkare (De Meyer 2011: 57-64).

The owner of the decree is identified as Ia-ib who amongst his titles is recognised as a lector. The recent translation by De Meyer indicates that the inscription basically consists of a title string of high rank titles, typical for an *Ernennungsurkunde,* a kind of decree in which the king elevates the addressee to a higher rank. Although the text supplies limited information, its mere presence indicates that Ia-ib must have been a man of exceptional merit, in that he was granted the privilege of been able to carve this decree on his tomb.

Wadi Hammamat

The Wadi Hammamat was another important area for Pharaonic mining activity where the principal stone extracted was a sedimentary rock varying from sandstone to siltstone (Harrell 2002: 239). It has one of the longest records of activity amongst the quarries of ancient Egypt, spanning as it does the late Predynastic through to the Roman Period. Again, many inscriptions have been left on the wadi walls by the ancient mining crews, although a number of these were carved by traders passing through the desert (Harrell 2002: 232). The main work of recording these texts was carried out by Couyat and Montet (1912) who documented some 266 inscriptions. Later research by Debono (1951), Goyon (1957), Simpson (1959), Bernand (1972), Seyfried (1981: 241-83), Gundlach (*LÄ* VI: 1099-113), Peden (2001: 35-7), and Harrell (2002: 232-43) has resulted in a number of further inscriptions being added to this corpus.

A feature of many of the mining expeditions to the Wadi Hammamat was the considerable size of the work force involved, perhaps necessitated by the requirement to quarry and transport very large blocks of stone back to the Nile. An inscription dated to the reign of Senwosret I, (inscription no. 61 of Goyon 1957: 81-5, pls. 23, 24), notes that in year 38 a work force of over 17,000 men, one of the largest ever assembled, quarried 60 sphinxes and 150 rough-hewn statues. Immense resources would have been necessary to mount such an undertaking, and the numbers of workers assembled are considered comparable with those sent on military campaigns. The inscriptions that list lectors in the Wadi Hammamat are (see appendix 8):

6th Dynasty lectors:

1. Inscription 107 records Merptahankhmeryre who was a senior lector and who was sent to Hammamat as an overseer of works (Couyat and Montet 1912: 74, pl. 27; inscription 21 of Goyon 1957: 55). Two biographical inscriptions relating to the same individual are known from the tomb-complex of the Senedjem-ib family at Giza (Reisner 1913: 53; Sethe 1932: 215-21; Dunham 1938). Merptahankhmeryre was primarily an overseer of builders and carried a number of other associated titles. However, his title of senior lector was near the end of his long list of titles and was therefore not as important to assert in that context.
2. Inscription 27 is for Nibu-nesu, who was sole companion, lector and overseer of priests but few other details are known about him (Goyon 1957: 61, pl. 10).
3. Inscription 28 concerns Rekey who was sole companion and lector, but again there is no further autobiographical information (Goyon 1957: 62, pl. 10).

Middle Kingdom lectors:

1. Inscription 74 records Djedu who carries the title of 'lector of the court'.
2. Inscription 149 mentions Putiker, a hereditary prince, lector and governor (Couyat & Monet 1912: 91, pl. 35; Breasted 1906: I, 225c). The inscription describes how he was not present on the expedition but that he had commissioned stone to be cut for him.
3. Inscription 152 again includes a reference to Putiker, describing how he commissioned a further expedition to cut stone (Couyat & Monet 1912: 92, pl. 34).
4. Inscription 150 consists only of an 'appeal to the living' formula, for Shemai, a treasurer, sole companion and senior lector (Couyat & Monet 1912: 91, pl. 35).

Wadi el-Hudi

The final major site yielding inscriptions is the Wadi el-Hudi, an extensive region some 35 km south east of Aswan. This area was exploited from at least the early second millennium for its minerals which included mica, barites, gold and amethyst. The major period of mining activity was during the Middle Kingdom when amethyst extraction was at its peak (Shaw & Jameson 1993: 81). A total of fifteen expeditions have been recorded for the Middle Kingdom with an average of seventeen years between each expedition (Shaw 1998: 251). The key epigraphic survey of the inscriptions was carried out during the 1940's by Fakhry (published 1952), with later research by Sadek (1980), and Shaw and Jameson (1993).

To date over 150 inscriptions have been recorded, but few of these texts contain any relevant details with only inscription no. 6, dated to the reign of Senwosret I, including any substantive information. This inscription records 1510 men present on an expedition and includes a breakdown of types of personnel present (Fakhry 1952: 24, fig. 20, pl. 9).

There are a number of references to Middle Kingdom lectors in the inscriptions:

1. Inscription 48 records part of the 'offering formula' for Intef, a lector, born of Iby, but includes few other details (Fakhry 1952: 51, fig. 49, pl. 29, B).
2. Inscription 53 lists four individuals, one of whom is another Intef, son of Ita, who is recorded as a ruler of a domain and a lector (Fakhry 1952: 53, fig. 54, pl. 31, A).
3. Inscription 54 seems to refer to the Intef mentioned in no. 53 above (Fakhry 1952: 53, fig. 52).
4. Inscription 148 is a lengthy partial text on a sandstone stela which is now located in the Neues Museum, Berlin. Although this stela was found some distance from the Wadi el-Hudi, it is considered by Sadek (1980: 92-5) to have originated from this location. The text includes a list of members of that expedition, one of whom is recorded as Se, the lector of Ptah.

4. Interpretation

A review of the above data indicates that although lectors were present on a number of the mining expeditions, lack of evidence makes it difficult to accurately determine their numbers or to precisely explain their role. Goyon (1957: 21) suggests that the presence of dignitaries and officials, among who are included lectors, were, by their mere presence, confirming the authority of the expedition.

Undoubtedly, the presence of a substantial work force travelling and working in a hostile environment in Egypt's desert regions, sometimes far from centres of civilisation, would be a hazardous operation and there would be a need for some form of medical care. The occasional *swnw* is documented and there were a number of controllers of Serket, particularly in the Wadi Hammamat where snakes and scorpions would be an ever present threat. It is possible that healing may have been one of the responsibilities of the lector on these expeditions. As previously recognised one of the primary roles of the lector was in reciting incantations from the sacred papyrus rolls, some of which have been identified as being of a healing nature. Additionally, as mentioned above, graffito no.12 from Hatnub refers to the lector's skill in treating ailments.

Evidence suggests that the mortality rate on such expeditions was high. The second stela erected at the Wadi Hammamat during the reign of Ramesses IV mentions an expedition of 8,368 men of which 900 lost their lives (inscription no. 12 of Couyat & Montet 1912: 34-9, pl. 34). It is recognised that the ancient Egyptians wished to be buried within the borders of Egypt and had a fear of being buried abroad.

In *The Tale of Sinuhe* the royal decree attempting to entice Sinuhe to return home to Egypt describes a death in a foreign country, comparing the uncleanliness and impermanence of being buried in a ram's skin to the security and magnificence of an Egyptian burial:

> 'Your death will not happen in a foreign country;
> Asiatics will not lay you to rest;
> You will not be put in a ram's skin when your coffin is made (translated Parkinson 1999: 34).

Again in the tale of *The Shipwrecked Sailor* the importance of dying in Egypt is explicitly mentioned. The inscriptions in the tombs of the Old Kingdom expedition leaders, Sabni (*Urk.* I: 135, 17-140, 11) and Pepinakht (*Urk.* I: 131, 15-135, 7), state that both went on a journey to recover the bodies of Egyptians who died far from home on expeditions (Köp-Junk 2013: 10).

In reality it would seem unlikely that many bodies were conveyed back to Egypt, particularly in view of the large number of deaths involved and the distance some of the expeditions were from Egypt. Therefore, burials on such expeditions would probably not have been uncommon and the lector may have been called upon to officiate at funerary ceremonies. However, none of the excavation reports make any reference to finding cemeteries and recent work at some of these short term mining sites has not uncovered any evidence of burials (Elizabeth Bloxham, personal communication 2013). Additionally, there is little textual and archaeological data relating to mortuary practices in such situations. Cremation is unknown from pre-Roman Egypt and little is reported of sub-formal or non-formal disposal of bodies (Baines and Lacovara 2002: 13).

At El-Harageh in the Fayuum cemeteries, probably dating to the Middle Kingdom, that had proper burials but no tomb structure or grave goods, illustrate how large numbers might be treated formally (Englebach 1923: 2-3). Possibly burials on these mining expeditions were superficial in nature and have not withstood the ravages of time.

As referred to in chapter 5 the lector had an important role to play in temple ritual and as temples were known to have been constructed in the mining regions of Sinai, both at Serabit el-Khadim and Timna, then it would seem likely lectors would have had a function there. As previously mentioned, there is a reference to chief lector Werkherephemut at Serabit el-Khadim.

With regard to the other major sites, there are remains of a Middle Kingdom fortress at Wadi el-Hudi and although no evidence of a temple has so far been discovered, it is possible that such a structure may have once existed there. Certainly, among fortresses of comparative size, such as Semna South, temples were known to have existed within the fortified walls (Wilkinson 2000: 230).

Additional evidence has been put forward by Fakhry (1952: 2) who describes the discovery of two small

Fig. 134: A scene from the tomb of Khnumhotep (Tomb No. 3 at Beni Hasan) depicting the lector Hormaakheru reciting, whilst a group of workers pull a statue of the tomb owner (Newberry 1893: pl. 29)

obelisks and an offering table that may have originated from a temple at Wadi el-Hudi. Espinel (2005: 60) refers to a short autobiographical inscription on a stela (Cairo JE 86119), considered to have originated from Wadi el-Hudi and which describes a certain Sareru performing rituals in the temple. At the Hatnub quarries Shaw (1986: 204) describes cairns which he considers may be forms of religious expression, but evidence for possible ritual activity occurring there is lacking. It is possible that there were temples at some of the other major mining sites for which evidence no longer exists and within which there may have been a ritual role for the lector.

A number of mining inscriptions dwell at some length on the difficulties encountered on their missions, followed by how such difficulties were eventually overcome. A late 12th Dynasty inscription from Sinai attributed to Harwerre (inscription no. 90 of Gardiner, Peet & Černý 1952-5: II, 97-9); an inscription from the Wadi Hammamat by an expedition leader Mery (inscription 19.2-12 of Couyat & Montet 1912: 41, pl. 5; Goedicke 1964: 48-50) from the reign of Amenemhat III; and another inscription left in the Wadi Hammamat by the expedition leader, Intef (inscription 199.6-10 of Couyat & Montet 1912: 101, pl.38; Goedicke 1964: 44-5) all illustrate this well. The solution to the encountered problem is either brought about as a result of the inititive of the individual, as in the case of Mery, or more usually it involved invoking divine assistance. Harwerre urged reverence to the local deity whereas Intef, who had difficulty in locating good quality stone, entreated divine aid, and then on successfully finding stone gave thanks to 'Montu, lord of this quarry' (Seyfreid 1981: 233-4; Enmarch 2011: 107-11). It is possible that the services of a lector may be sought when entreating the deity in order that the correct incantations and effective ritual procedures were performed.

Another possible function of the lector on these mining expeditions could be the reciting of incantations and the performance of ritual actions during the quarrying, preparation and transportation of rough blocks of stone that were to be used for statuary. Subsidiary activity associated with statue transport is recognised, as attested by the celebrated scene in the tomb of the Middle Kingdom nomarch, Djehutyhotep, at Deir el-Bersha. Here the transportation of a statue is accompanied by officiants lubricating the statue's path with water which can be likened to ritualised libation whilst others are depicted burning incense, a sensory allusion to cultic action (Newberry 1895: 16-26, pls. 12-15; Eaton-Krauss 1984: 66-9; Price 2008: 115).

Again in the main chamber of Tomb No. 3 at Beni Hasan, a scene depicts the lector Hormaakheru reading from a papyrus roll, whilst a group of workers pull a statue, the captions is (Newberry 1893: pl. 29; fig. 134):

> 'accompanying the statue to the temple' (*šmswt twt r ḥwt-nṯr*).

In another scene from the tomb of Ptahhotep at Saqqara (D64) there is a depiction of the tomb-owner's son who is designated as a lector, censing a statue of his father (Eaton-Krauss 1984: 67, pl. 20).

Returning to the mining expeditions, final completion of statuary would probably have been carried out in workshops rather than in the quarries that were situated many miles from the final location of the statue. However, rough hewing of the stone was often carried out on site, as attested by examples of incomplete statues from the Wadi Hammamat. The partially prepared statue was by then an intended receptacle for the ka of the owner and so ritual activity, as described above, could well have been an integral part of the journey from the quarry to the final destination of the statue. As such the lector would have been involved in this ritual movement and a required member of such mining expeditions.

Chapter 11

The Lector and the Law

1. Introduction to the Ancient Egyptian Legal System

Although there are known collections of Sumerian, Akkadian, Hittite and Neo-Babylonian laws, for much of the dynastic period there is a lack of similar compilations for ancient Egypt (Théodoridès 1971a: 291). There are some indications of an official judicial system with the setting up in the Old Kingdom of a Royal Archive containing records of land-ownership, civil actions and texts of royal decrees (Grimal 1992: 91; Redford 2001: 105). Additionally, the districts or nomes were controlled by local administrators who would also carry the title of 'judge' and sit on a local assembly concerned with legal matters known as the *ḏ3ḏ3t* (Kruchten 2001: 279). From the Middle Kingdom a 12th Dynasty papyrus is a register of criminals from an Egyptian prison at Thebes and refers to five *hpw* 'laws' dealing with fugitives (P. Brooklyn 35.1446; Hayes 1955: 49-52).

Only during the New Kingdom is there is sufficient evidence to be able to reconstruct in detail some aspects of the Pharaonic legal practice (Lorton 1977). The chief sources of information for this are derived from ostraca found at the workmen's village at Deir el-Medina, some of which relate to the activities of the local *ḳnbt*. The *ḳnbt* was a legal and administrative council whose members met when required and was concerned with local matters involving private disputes over economic transactions, property arrangements and wills. Crimes such as murder, assault and rape are rarely documented, possibly because the ostraca were private records and it would not be desirable to record and retain such crimes and their aftermath (McDowell 1999: 165).

Records indicate that the composition of the *ḳnbt* consisted of 'officers/magistrates' *(srw)* who at Deir el-Medina were local members of the community, the workmen, together with outside officials such as scribes of the vizier and chief policemen. The ostraca provide details about the workings of the *ḳnbt* which include plaintiffs' statements of the cases, the court's verdicts, names of judges and names of witnesses. These records may have been written up to be cited later, as the power of the written word would have authority, particularly, as some were fairly elaborate and were augmented with further judicial texts or memoranda (Allam 1968: 121-8). However, Jansen (1975: 295-6) and McDowell (1990: 6), consider that these were not official documents, and although some may have been notes upon which a later official record could be based, others may merely have been kept by interested parties.

These ostraca from Deir el-Medina as well as papyri found in the precinct of the temple at Medinet Habu also attest to the existence of a 'Great Qenbet' (*ḳnbt ˁ3t*) at Thebes. The inscription of Mes, dated to the reign of Ramesses II, which is inscribed in his tomb at Saqqara, relates to five lawsuits over land, and here a 'Great Qenbet' at Heliopolis is mentioned (Gardiner 1905; Allam 1991: 111). A study of the inscription of Mes is instructive concerning the workings of Pharaonic justice as it describes an entire case from beginning to end and also indicates that in ancient Egypt, legal decisions were made on the basis of documentary proof supported by witnesses' statements, and that evidence was not referred to as a necessity (Théodoridès 1971a: 311).

During the New Kingdom a further development was the use of divine oracles for legal decision making. Legal disputes could also be referred to the vizier and evidence from Deir el-Medina indicates that the lines between these various legal authorities were very fluid (McDowell 1990: 245). For serious cases such as the Harem Conspiracy and the Great Tomb Robberies (see below) special commissions were set up to investigate and adjudicate, and these bodies were given considerable powers and had extensive authority (Peet: 1930; Kruchten 2001: 280; VerSteeg 2002: 62).

Sources for later periods are not as extensive as for the New Kingdom but by the 26th Dynasty specialised courts and *n wptyw* 'judges' sitting in permanent rooms are known to have been established. These superseded the *ḳnbwt* and perhaps are closer to modern courts of justice. These courts continued to exist and function into the Ptolemaic Period (Allam 1991: 126).

At the heart of the ancient Egyptian legal system was the principle of *maat*, a concept that embraces order, harmony, truth and justice (Allam 2007: 263). *Maat* was the embodiment of a just administration and associated with *Maat* is the word *hp* which begins to appear in the language during the Middle Kingdom and is usually translated as 'law'. In later Demotic texts the plural *hpw* encompassed other terms such as rules, decrees, customs and even contracts (Nims 1948: 243; Kruchten 2001: 278). Examples of this usage are two Demotic papyri that refer to the law or rules adopted by a group. The word is used referring to 'regulations for a cult association' and in these instances lectors (P. Leiden 374 I, 12 & 374 II, 15):

> '...according to the *hpw* of the lectors' (translated Nims 1948: 244-5).

These two texts date to the rule of Ptolemy XII Neos Dionysos, and are almost identical texts written on the same papyrus. They relate to four gods' seal-bearers, who also carried the title of 'lector' and who were giving up their rights to the revenues from the funerary endowment of an oil and wine merchant in favour of their colleagues.

2. The Role of the Lector on Temple Councils

From the Middle Kingdom onwards there is evidence of *ḳnbt* councils being associated with many of the temples in ancient Egypt. The members of such councils were drawn from the priests of the particular temple as well as auxiliary staff employed by the temple. A 19th Dynasty papyrus which is a record of a court settlement that took place in year 46 of Ramesses II shows the composition of a typical *ḳnbt* and includes a lector amongst its various members (P. Berlin 3047, 4-7, Helck 1963: 66):

> 'The *ḳnbt* of the day - chief priest of Amun, *Bꜥk-n-ḫnsw*; priest of Amun, *Wsr-mntw*; priest of Amun, *Rꜥm*; priest of the temple of Mut, *Wnn-nfr*; priest of the temple of Khons, *Ỉmn-m-ḥb*; .... of the temples of Amun, *Ỉmn-m-ipt*; *wꜥb*-priest and lector of Amun, *Ỉmn-ḥtp*; *wꜥb*-priest (and) lector of Amun, *ꜣnii*; *wꜥb*-priest of the temple of Amun, *ḥꜥyꜥ*; scribe of the accounts of the court, *ḥꜥyꜥ*'.

Additional evidence that the lector sat on the temple *ḳnbt* is provided by a series of Middle Kingdom legal contracts. Surviving legal documents from ancient Egypt that provide detailed information about contracts and civil law are quite rare, but one such document, that also sheds light on the political and social conditions during the Middle Kingdom, is to be found in the tomb of Hapidjefa. Hapidjefa was a nomarch, chief priest and chief lector during the reign of Senwosret I, and inscribed on the walls of his tomb chapel at Asyut (Tomb No. 1) are a series of ten contracts (see also in relation to the remuneration of the lector on pages 47-8). These contracts were made between himself and various religious officials and other personnel associated with the local temples of Wepwawet and Anubis at Asyut. The purpose of the contracts was to secure for Hapidjefa certain ceremonies and offerings to honour his statue that were to be performed on a regular basis.

The basis of Hapidjefa's wealth that made such disbursements possible is specified in the inscriptions, which discloses the division between office-held property and personal property and reveals the complexity of the system. Details emerge of income derived from what he had inherited as a nomarch, income from lands, cattle and tenants that he had inherited from his father, and also payments for the duties he performed at the Wepwawet temple (Spalinger 1985: 7-20).

Hapidjefa arranged ten separate contracts in order to provide for ceremonies and offerings to be presented at various festivals throughout the calendar year. Numbers 1-6 of the contracts relate to the Wepwawet temple, where Hapidjefa was high priest, and the remaining four (7-10) involve the Anubis temple. Information provided about the individual payments that were made by Hapidjefa for these services are very detailed and quite specific. They include a conveyance of land, a quantity of barley, and part of a bull as well as loaves and beer. Additionally, the conveyance of 'temple-days' is listed, a term referring to all the produce that entered the temple of Wepwawet on a daily basis. Hapidjefa's claim to such produce was based on his hereditary office of *wꜥb*-priest of Wepwawet (Griffith 1889: pls. 1-10; Breasted 1906: I, 258-71; Reisner 1918: 79-98; Théodoridès 1971b: 108-251; Spallinger 1985: 7-20).

Contract 3 illustrates how Hapidjefa gave twenty-two temple days of produce to the *ḳnbt* of the temple so that the *ḳnbt* would make offerings of bread and beer for the mortuary cult on the day of the *Wag*-festival (table 7). The individual members of the *ḳnbt* are recorded in this contract and the last of these on the list is a lector. The second part of contract 4 is similarly an agreement made with the *ḳnbt*, whereas the other eight contracts that Hapidjefa established were with single groups of officials that included hour priests, the great *wꜥb*-priest of Anubis, cemetery workmen and overseers of the desert.

The *Wag*-festival in which the lector is mentioned was one of the great festivals on which offerings were brought to honour the dead, and at this festival the lector together with the remainder of the *ḳnbt* would have presented offerings of bread and beer to the statue of Hapidjefa. The lector is at the end of the list of the officials, whilst the chief priest, the most senior of the *ḳnbt*, provides double the amount of the other officials and is at the head of the list. This is also supported by noting that the scribe of the temple, a more senior role, is listed above the scribe of the altar.

These contracts indicate that the lector was a member of the temple *ḳnbt*, and the agreements also provide information about the workings of such a council. The *ḳnbwt* can thus be seen to be responsible for the organisation of temple affairs, as well as being concerned with the administration of justice for its personnel and for the population retained by them (Allam 1991: 110-11).

Temples, particularly in the New Kingdom, were large landowners and important centres associated with agriculture, commerce and various industries, and as such they would have employed large numbers of the local population. The Great Harris Papyrus (P. BM 9999) which includes a list of temple endowments as well as being a brief summary of the reign of Ramesses III records 86,486 individuals working at the temple of Amun at Thebes and the estates owned by the temple throughout Egypt. The comparable figure for the mortuary temple of Ramesses III at Medinet Habu is 62,626 (Breasted 1906: IV, 124-6; Grandet 1994: 89, 235). The temple *ḳnbwt* being responsible for the administration of justice for such large numbers of individuals may well, therefore, have been fairly active bodies.

3. The Lector as a Judge

A fragmentary Demotic Papyrus which provides evidence of the possible role of the lector as a judge was discovered in the vicinity of the Pyramid of Unas (El-Khouli 1978: 35-43 & 1980: 46-8). The papyrus, in which only two columns of text are preserved, was translated and studied by H. S. Smith who considered that it was of Ptolemaic origin and part of a journal or day-book containing legal or administrative records. Column 2 of the papyrus provides some information as to the nature of the content (P. Saqqara No. 17489.2, 1-12):

> 2/1 'Year 20, first month of 'winter', day 28:
> 2/2 they …according to the evil manner of the troubles which have happened to…
> 2/3 (they) seize the men, (but) they do not bring them to him; the man who is brought them…
> 2/4 (if) they do not wish to leave him, they do not leave him: they do not enter so as to pass by… does not…
> 2/5 a stater (?) which disappeared in his possession remains over; … bring them…
> 2/6 punish a man by the service of a lector priest. The…has produced/procreated…
> 2/7 and he will leave him. The one against (lit. after) whom there is not yet (?) any word, let them seize him…
> 2/8 she listens (?) to your (m.) heart. Do you (m.) cause them to be done, and write about them. …does not happen (?)
> 2/9 and it will happen that you (pl.) do not send saying: "There is no man of the manner of … Let…
> 2/10 in their presence. And the lector priest (?) shall cause them to be judged (?) …day so as to cause to happen…
> 2/11 when the matter of this service occurs, you shall not send concerning…
> 2/12 Harempe, I have spoken it concerning it" (translated H. Smith in El-Khouli 1980: 47).

Smith stated that further study of this papyrus was needed as this was merely a preliminary report; however, there does not appear to be an improved translation of this Demotic text yet published. Although the meaning of the passage is not clear, certain facts can be determined. It would appear that this is correspondence relating to an account of certain troubles that occurred and includes instructions of action to be taken concerning these events in the future. Smith states that this same theme is repeated in section 1 of the papyrus and his suggestion is that the text could be a file of correspondence copied out for the purpose of some legal or administrative process, but he made few other comments regarding the content of the text.

A lector is mentioned in the text on two occasions, the first of these is in line 2/6 where the implication is that as a result of the professional duties of a lector, a man is to be punished, suggesting either the giving of evidence or the passing of judgement by the lector. In line 2/10 the meaning is clearer with a statement that the lector is judging certain individuals. Extant evidence is very limited for the lector acting in a judicial role and so further conclusions relating to this are not possible.

4. The Harem Conspiracy

The so-called Harem Conspiracy was a plot against the life of Ramesses III towards the end of the New Kingdom. The reign of Ramesses III was a time that saw political instability, work strikes, foreign invasion and the loss of external possessions (Cline & O'Connor 2012). Social instability and conflict of this nature are often preconditions for some form of challenge to the legitimate rule in a country. Such a challenge to Ramesses III's rule did occur and took the form of a conspiracy in which Queen Tiye together with the aid of a number of court personnel, including lectors, attempted to murder the reigning monarch.

Historical Records
Judicial Papyrus of Turin (the arraignments: accused and crimes)
Papyrus Rollin (first case of magic)
Papyrus Varzy (embezzlement of the king's cattle)
Papyrus Lee I (second case of magic); II (third case of magic)
Papyrus Rifaud I (A, B, and C)
Papyrus Rifaud II (E)

Table 12: The primary sources for the conspiracy against Ramesses III

The primary sources of information about this conspiracy are a series of fragmentary documents once thought to be a single papyrus roll (table 12). These documents are the trial records of an attempt on the life of Ramesses III, the context of which suggests the illegal or malign use of magic. They have been extensively translated and studied by Breasted (1906: II, 208-21); de Buck (1937: 152-64); Sauneron & Yoyotte (1952: 107-17); Goedicke (1963: 71-92); Posener (1976: 435-42); Kitchen (1983: 360-6); Ritner (1993: 192-9); Redford (2002), and Vernus (2003).

From the trial records it would appear that thirty-two men and an undetermined number of women were indicted for their part in the conspiracy. The papyrus lists stewards, inspectors, a general, a military commander, women of the harem and a number of others. By its very nature the attempted murder of a ruling monarch would be fraught with many problems. Not only would the ruler be heavily guarded but he was deemed to be under the protection of the gods. The conspirators considered that there would be little hope of success in this venture without the use of magic, and to that end they enlisted the help of a number of individuals versed in the use of magical practices. It is these individuals who are listed in the second arraignment and who are relevant to this study (Turin Judicial Papyrus 5:4, 5 in Kitchen 1983: 357-8):

> 'Persons arraigned because of their crimes, in colluding with Paibakamana, Pasai and Pentawere. They were placed before the magistrates of the Court of Examination; they found them guilty; they left them in their own hands in the Court of Examination; they took their own lives; nobody laid a hand on them:

The great criminal, Pasai, formerly commander of the army;
The great criminal, Messui, formerly scribe of the House of Life;
The great criminal, Prekamenef, formerly lector;
The great criminal, Iyroy, formerly overseer of the priests of Sekhmet;
The great criminal, Nibjatfe, formerly butler;
The great criminal, Shotmaadje, formerly scribe of the House of Life;
Total 6' (translated de Buck 1937: 155-6 and Redford 2002: 16).

The individuals listed above, except for Pasai and Nibjatfe, had links to magical practices. Although Prekamenef is the only recorded lector in the trial documents, a limestone door lintel from the tomb of Iyroy at Qantir contains the following inscription (Kitchen 1983: 425; see page 12 of this publication):

'May the king give an offering to Atum, lord of the House of Life [on ... behalf of] for the ka of the royal scribe, his truly beloved, the chief lector, the overseer of the priests of Sekhmet, the one who foretells the festivals from day to day, pure of hands, Iyroy of Bubastis' (translated Redford 2002: 80).

A second inscription on the door jamb again refers to Iyroy as chief lector and in both inscriptions the title of lector is placed before that of overseer of the priests of Sekhmet (Habachi & Ghalioungui 1971: 61). The indication is that at Bubastis Iyroy favoured the title of chief lector above that of overseer of the priests of Sekhmet. Iyroy was thus a royal scribe and chief lector although in the court documents he is referred to on three occasions as a priest of Sekhmet:

'He acted in the capacity of overseer of the priests of Sekhmet' (P. Rifaud B, l. 4).

Whilst the Judicial Papyrus of Turin contains a summary of the trial proceedings, listing the accused, their crimes (in a general way), their trial and the verdicts, it is the descriptions found in Papyrus Rollin and Papyrus Lee that provide some insight into the details of the conspiracy. For convenience the relevant parts of both papyri are translated here, based on the hieroglyphic transcription of Kitchen (1983: 360-2) and the translations of Goedicke (1963: 71-92), Ritner (1993: 193-8) and Redford (2002: 19):

Papyrus Rollin
[*name of accused missing*] 'He began to prepare writings of magic (*ḥk3w*) for the purpose of confusing/exorcising (*stwh3*) and disturbing (*sẖnnw*), to make waxen (figures) of gods (*ir.n h3w n nṯrw n mnh*) [and] some potions (*pẖrwt*) for laming (*dit gnn*) the limbs of people. They were placed into the hands of Paibakamana – Re did not allow him to be butler – and the other great criminals saying, "Take them inside", and they took them inside. Now after he allowed the ones who did the evil to enter – which he did but which Re did not allow him to be successful in'.

Papyrus Lee (column 1)
[*name of accused missing*] '...was made to swear an oath of the lord, l.p.h. of undertaking fealty by swearing at every [time, saying "I have not given] any [document/roll] of the office in which I was to anyone on earth". But when Paibakamana who was (formerly) overseer of cattle said to him, "Give to me a roll for giving to me terror and respect", he gave to him a writing of the scrolls of Usermaatre Meryamun, l.p.h. the great god, his lord. And he began to petition the god to delude the people, and he penetrated the side of the harem and this other great deep place. And he began to use inscribed waxen figures in order to cause that they be taken inside by the hand of the agent Idrim for the confusing/exorcising of the crew and the disturbing of others'.

So from Papyri Rollin and Lee it is possible to obtain some understanding of the magical practices that were utilised in this conspiracy. Use was made of written magical spells (*sẖw n ḥk3w*), inscribed wax figurines and potions (*pẖrwt*). Such a combination, the word (spell), the act (manipulation of wax figures) and the use of a magical material (potion), conforms to the tripartite nature of magic in ancient Egypt (Ritner 1993: 72, 198). These elements were intended to exorcise/confuse (*stwh3*), to disturb (*sẖnn*), to lame (*dit gnn*) and to enchant (*ḥk3w*). It may be imagined that the aim was to immobilise the king's guards to allow access to the king's person and to have a direct negative impact on the health of the king.

Papyrus Lee I also states that an unrecorded defendant used inscribed figurines in the magical practices, a form of an execration rite. The defendant was accused, despite his oath to the contrary, of providing Panhayboni with a text from his office. Redford (2002: 81) suggests that the defendant was probably Prekamenef, the lector, but it is also possible that Messui or Shotmaadje, scribes of the House of Life, could have passed over the documents to Panhayboni. The document was likely to have been a sacred magical scroll from the House of Life, written specifically for the king's protection. It was believed that the removal and unauthorised use of these documents would overturn the royal protection and make the king vulnerable to attack.

The fate that befell the accused of the second arraignment provides some important information about the status of the lector and the part social status played in the legal system of ancient Egypt. Whilst all of the accused of the first arraignment were executed, the conspirators of the second arraignment were allowed to commit suicide. These included Pasai, commander of the army, and Iyroy, overseer of the priests of Sekhmet, men of high status at court. Also, because it was recognised that four of the six conspirators possessed an expertise in magical procedures, they may have been prosecuted with some trepidation.

Indeed, insertions were made in the court records to nullify any potent effects the written word might produce. Details of Paibakamana's tenure in office together with that of the other co-conspirators was removed, and the malicious deeds they carried out were obliterated from the records by statements that the god Re did not sanction them (Redford 2002: 18, 130).

Right-hand column
(4) Chief guard and scribe of the prison Dhoutemhab of the army.
(5) Chief guard Hori, son of Dhoutnakht, of the army.
(6) Deputy Neskhons of the army.
(7) Overseer of the stable Mensenu of Kheni...
(8) Groom Bekenese of [the temple].
(9) The scribe Dhoutmose of the necropolis.
(10) The scribe Efenkhons of the necropolis.
(11) The chief workman Bekenmut of [the necropolis].
(12) The lector-priests of the temple.
(13) The prince Nesamenōpe.
(14) The scribe of the quarter Nesamenōpe.
Left-hand column
(15) The chiefs of Mazoi of the necropolis.
(16) The controller Amenkhau of the West of Nō.
(17) The controller Pekhal of the West of Nō.
(18) The controller Pnekhtōpe.
(19) The controller Amenhopte.
(20) The controller Amenōpenakht.
(21) The controller Ankhtuemdiamūn.

TABLE 13: LIST OF WITNESSES RELATING TO THE MARRIAGE CONTRACT OF AMENKHAU (ČERNÝ & PEET 1927: 33)

Also the name of each conspirator was deformed as a magical *damnatio memoriae*, to identify them with forces of chaos and evil. The name of Paibakamana was changed from 'the servant of Amun' to 'the blind servant', whilst Prekamenef was given the name 'the sun blinds him' thus symbolically applying a punishment (Ritner 1993: 194).

The records of the Harem Conspiracy provide direct evidence of the involvement of the magical practices of a lector in a conspiracy against the legitimate rule of a monarch. The co-conspirators deemed it necessary to have a magical element in their attempt on the life of the monarch in order for the undertaking to become a viable proposition. Two of the conspirators of the second arraignment carried the title of lector and a further two were scribes of the House of Life. Finally, this group were allowed to commit suicide rather than suffer the humiliation of a public execution, an indication of their higher status and perhaps a fear that the magic that they were deemed to possess could be turned against the judges and executioners.

5. The Lector as a Witness - 'A marriage settlement'

Among the witnesses to a late 20th Dynasty marriage settlement are listed lectors of the temple (table 13). The agreement is recorded in a fragmentary hieratic papyrus now located in Turin (P. 2021). The case involves a certain Amenkhau who was a 'god's father' *(it̠-nt̠r)* and who had been married on two occasions. His first wife, by whom he had children, had died and Amenkhau was arranging his affairs so that his children by his first marriage and his wife by his second marriage would receive part of his possessions. This process of arrangement was carried out in the presence of the vizier and representatives of his children, and this particular document is a record of those proceedings prior to the writing of the contract (Černý & Peet 1927: 30-9).

Černý and Peet (1927: 37) consider that because there was a list of witnesses at the end of the document, the proceedings were not carried out before a fully constituted court where such witnesses would have been unnecessary, but was merely a declaration in front of the vizier. Amenkhau would probably have served in the Temple of Ramesses III at Medinet Habu, where a record of the contract was to be store (P. 2021: 4, 2):

> 'The vizier gave instructions to the *wꜥb*-priest and scribe of accounts Ptahemhab of the *ḳnbt* of the temple of Usermatre Meryamun' (translated Černý & Peet: 1927: 33).

The position of the lector is midway down the list and significantly no *ḥm-nt̠r* or *wꜥb*-priests are listed as witnesses. The lector is operating outside the temple and priestly sphere and is listed with other officials.

6. 'Great Tomb-Robberies of the 20th Dynasty'

The final years of the 20th Dynasty were an unsettled time in ancient Egypt and at Thebes the population experienced starvation, incursions of Libyan tribesmen, and there is evidence of increasing breakdown in public order and safety. All these factors contributed to the violation and plunder of the royal tombs in the Valley of the Kings and of the mortuary temples in Thebes. The unrest which had commenced during the reign of Ramesses IX continued into the reign of Ramesses XI (Kitchen 1996: 247; Goelet 2001: 417-18). Eventually the authorities decided that the integrity of the tombs was no longer secure and so removed the royal mummies, restored them and then reburied them in two large caches.

The account of the investigations into the looting of the royal tombs and mortuary temples, together with the subsequent trials of the miscreants, is documented in a series of texts known as the Tomb Robbery Papyri (P. Abbot; P. Amherst, BM 10053, 10054, 10068, 10383, 10403; P. Mayer A & B; P. Ambras). These papyri provide evidence of an extensive cover-up, of negligence, corruption and complicity of many high officials in the Theban area. The texts record the manner of the investigations, the taking of evidence during the trials and the varying punishments meted out to the guilty (Peet 1930).

Most of the tomb robberies appear to have been instigated by various craftsmen from the workmen's village at Deir el-Medina as well as their associates from the wider community at Thebes. These papyri also record details of the robbery of the Theban mortuary temples, and here, not surprisingly, the priests were complicit in these desecrations. In part 3 of the recto of P. BM 10054 there are records of the gold foil being stripped from the shrine of Nefertum in the Ramesseum. The majority of the perpetrators of this crime appeared to be the priests who stole the gold from the shrine and later melted it down to divide it up amongst themselves.

P. BM 10053 and 10383 are concerned with further robberies to the mortuary temples and again the Ramesseum is mentioned. The indication is that the temple of Ramesses II was being systematically robbed, primarily by the priests of the temple, of precious metals, copper and valuable wood. P. BM 10383 details how a vase-stand weighing 86 *deben* of silver was stolen from the Ramesseum and how the scribe of the treasury, the gods' fathers, the *wꜥb*-priests and the lectors all cut off a portion of the silver from the stand, and then returned it to the temple hoping that the missing silver would not be noticed (P. BM 10383 1, 1-10; translation after Peet 1930: 124-5; Appendix 9).

Although this is the only direct reference to lectors in the Tomb Robbery Papyri, the fact that the plundering of the tombs and temples was quite widespread among the priests and temple personnel may suggest further involvement by lectors for which no records survive.

7. Summary and Conclusion

The evidence for the direct involvement of the lector in the legal system in ancient Egypt is not strong, although one Ptolemaic text found at Saqqara (mentioned above) refers to a judgement passed by a lector. The lector may on occasions have sat on the local *ḳnbt*, and both P. Berlin 3047 and the contracts of Hapidjefa provide direct evidence for the lector sitting on a temple *ḳnbt*. With the large work forces being employed by the temples and their estates, particularly in the New Kingdom, the temple *ḳnbwt* may have been fairly active organisations.

The lector is called upon to witness legal proceedings as attested in a 20th Dynasty marriage settlement, an indication, perhaps, of his being recognised as a respected member of the community. So although the primary role of a lector was not that of an expert in legal affairs, his involvement in temple life, his literacy and status indicate some association with the legal processes of ancient Egypt which were focused on the authority of the documents. In contrast to upholding the law, there is also evidence that lectors were involved with breaking the law as attested in major criminal investigations such as the 'Harem Conspiracy' and the 'Great Tomb Robberies of the 20th Dynasty'.

Chapter 12

Literary Evidence

1. Introduction

Within the surviving literary corpus from ancient Egypt there are a number of literary texts which include the lector as one of the principal characters. These works emphasise the lector's use of magical practices and his engagement with books and ritual texts. An analysis of these texts is useful for this study as they provide further information about the workings of the lector as well as indicating the esteem with which society regarded him.

2. Papyrus Westcar (tales of wonder at the court of King Khufu)

A significant source of information about the purported magical powers of the lector is to be found in the stories comprising the Papyrus Westcar (P. Berlin 3033; Lichtheim 1973: 215-22; Simpson 2003: 13-24; Quirke 2004: 77-89). This papyrus has been dated on palaeographic grounds to the 15th Dynasty, but the subject matter is thought to have been composed as early as the 12th Dynasty, whilst the events relate back to the Old Kingdom (*LÄ* IV: 744-6). In the story cycle, the sons of King Khufu attempt to entertain him with tales of the magical deeds of famous magicians, most of whom carry the title of lector.

The first tale relates to a marvel performed by a lector, possibly Imhotep, during the reign of King Djoser. Only a few lines of the conclusion have survived, and it is not possible to know how extensive the composition originally was, although Parkinson suggests that as many as seventy verses may have been lost from the beginning of the story (Parkinson 1997: 102). It is the second tale that provides more detailed information about the working practices of the lector, with the account of the chief lector Webaoner and his unfaithful wife. The narrative describes that in revenge for her infidelity Webaoner sent for his electrum and ebony box which contained magic scrolls and equipment needed for spells. He then fashioned a wax crocodile which he had thrown into a pond where his wife's lover was bathing. The wax figure grew into a real crocodile and seized this individual dragging him under the water. Seven days later, when the king was present, Webaoner ordered the crocodile to reappear and changed it back into a wax model, merely by the touch of his hand. The king condemned the lover for his actions, and the crocodile, which once again had reached full size, was allowed to escape for good with its unfortunate victim (Simpson 2003: 14-16).

This passage contains the earliest reference to a wax image of a reptile and demonstrates a number of points concerning the operating practices of the lector. There is a mention of an electrum and ebony casket containing the working implements and/or scrolls, a rare reference to the apparatus of the lector (see discussions relating to the equipment of the lector in chapter 3). The actions that the lector performed demonstrate the immense power the lector is credited with. Eyre (1992: 280) equates Webaoner ordering the crocodile to release the lover as equivalent to resurrection, with Webaoner briefly bringing the man back to life.. Additionally, being able to tame a crocodile, a reptile known to destroy without pity and one that does not willingly disgorge its prey, again demonstrates great magic:

> 'Webaoner is the magician who controls the uncontrollable: the power of death and resurrection' (Eyre 1992: 280-1).

In this tale the wax crocodile is an instrument in the hand of a chief lector. There are other references to wax being utilised in this manner which concern even more dangerous creatures, some of a cosmic nature, such as the rituals aimed at the destruction of the serpent-like creature, Apep (see execration rituals on page 25). In Spell 7 of the Book of the Dead, the deceased is identified with Atum in order to overcome Apep, who is obstructing the progress of the solar bark. Apep is challenged with the reminder that he is merely 'one of wax':

> 'O you waxen one who takes by robbery and who lives on the inert ones…' (translated Faulkner 1972: 36; Raven 1983: 20).

The power credited to a chief lector is again demonstrated in the third of the tales of the Papyrus Westcar. Here the chief lector Djadjaemankh is able to part the waters of a lake, challenging the power of the elements, in order to recover a pendant that had been accidently dropped into the water (Simpson 2003: 13-24, §6, l.8-13). The fourth narrative describes a certain Djedi who although experienced in magic is not listed as a chief lector but as a commoner (*nḏs*). However, section 8, line 3 mentions:

> 'Let me have a *kakau*-boat that it may bring (my) students (*ẖrdw*) and my writings' (translated Simpson 2003: 19).

As Djedi possesses books and teaches students, the suggestion is that Djedi is a learned individual with perhaps priestly training and is a man of recognised status (Ritner 1993: 222). Eyre (1992: 280) considers him as a 'contemporary' chief lector, again having considerable powers in being able to bring the dead back to life and being able to control fierce animals (Simpson 2003: 13-24, §7, l. 4-5 & §8, l. 26-29). Also similar to Djadjaemankh in the third tale, he is able to manipulate water on the sandbanks.

The tales represent a series of wonderful episodes, in which there are elements of parody combined with some underlying serious topics (Parkinson 1997: 102-5). Simpson (2003: 13) considers that the real substance of the composition lies in the final tale which deals with the prophecy of the birth of the kings and suggests that the other tales merely lead up to it. Eyre (1992: 280) recognises a structural parallelism in the Westcar stories all relating as they do to powerful chief lectors and magicians, in which the power of these individuals is demonstrated. Additionally, Papyrus Westcar provides insight into one of the functions of the chief lector - that of attending and protecting the king at court (Pinch 2006: 51; see pages 15 and 65 of this publication).

3. Papyrus St. Petersburg (the prophecies of Neferty)

This text (P. St. Petersburg 1116B) is an example of a poetic lament, a style of literary work characteristic of the Middle Kingdom. The setting of the text is the court of King Sneferu to which the lector Neferty is summoned to entertain the king by means of his eloquent speech. At the request of the king, Neferty foretells the future and relates the destruction of Egypt during the First Intermediate Period followed by the subsequent rise of Amenemhat I who restores order to the land. The original work was actually composed during the reign of Amenemhat I and was intended as a glorification of Amenemhat used for propaganda purposes (Posener 1956: 21-60; Helck 1970; Tobin 2003c: 214-20).

After the initial introduction, it is Neferty who relates the pessimistic prophecy, and as in many of these literary works it is he, the lector, who is the chief character and whose magical powers are central to the story. Again, similar to Papyrus Westcar, the lector is portrayed as an exceptional character, an individual who has earned his position by merit (9-11):

> 'Our sovereign Lord, there is a great lector of Bastet, whose name is Neferty. He is a citizen strong of arm, a scribe of outstanding skill, and a rich man whose wealth is greater than that of any of his peers' (translated Lichtheim 1973: 140; Tobin 2003c: 215).

4. Papyrus Vandier (the tale of Meryre)

In the fragmentary hieratic papyrus, Papyrus Vandier, dated to the late 6th or early 5th century BC, the hero of the tale is a certain Meryre who carries the title of chief lector or 'magician' (*ḫry-tp*) (abbreviated from *ḫry-ḥbt ḫry-tp*), scribe (*šs*) and general (*imy-r mšꜥ*) (P. Lille 139; Posener 1985). Posener (1985: 17) notes that Meryre is also mentioned as an excellent scribe (*nfr šs*) and comments that in demotic literature the association of the two words possesses a particular connotation. In the Setna Khaemwase cycle, 'good scribe' implies 'skilful magician' and the scribal excellence of Meryre implies a similar term.

In this tale King Sisobek learns that he is dying. After the royal magicians (*ḫry-tpw*) fail to cure him, Meryre descends into the underworld to petition Osiris to grant the king extra years on earth, a task in which he is successful. After becoming trapped in the underworld, the jealous magicians encourage the king to seize Meryre's wife and kill his son. In revenge Meryre magically creates a man of clay, whom he then sends back to earth, to order the king to burn the magicians in the furnace of the goddess Mut at Heliopolis (Pinch 2006: 96). The destruction by fire of the enemies of Osiris can be traced back to the Coffin Texts and is a recurrent theme in the literature of the New Kingdom and later (Leahy 1984: 199-206). The creation of the model figure and the burning of the magicians on a brazier are typical of the execration rituals in which the lector was known to be involved.

5. Papyrus Cairo 30646 and Papyrus British Museum 604 (Setna Khaemwase Cycle)

This is a sequence of two stories dating to the Ptolemaic and Roman Periods which have as their main character the historical figure of Khaemwase, son of Ramesses II (Griffith 1900). The principal title used for the historical Khaemwase was '*sem*-priest of Ptah', and in these demotic tales the title is rendered as 'Setna' and used as a personal name. The two texts do not make reference to one another but follow the same pattern in which Setna comes face to face with the spirit of a powerful magician of the distant past (Lichtheim 1980: 125-6). The events described are of a miraculous nature with similar characteristics to those related in Papyrus Westcar.

Setna I (P. Cairo 30646) has as its main characters Setna and Naneferkaptah who were both royal children, trained to read the texts of the House of Life. Naneferkaptah is referred to as having performed acts by means of 'his skill as a good scribe' (*wp.t n sš nfr*) (Setna I, col. 4.23). This terminology is discussed by Posener (1985: 17) and Ritner (1993: 222) who both consider that this is a derivation of the late understanding of a chief lector. Setna II (P. BM 604) links three magician heroes: Setna, who carries the title of *sem*-priest; Setna's son Si-Osire; and Horus-son-of-Punesh. The tale reveals that Si-Osire is a reincarnation of Horus-son-of Punesh who carries the title of chief lector. These tales are useful as they demonstrate the vocabulary of magic used by a chief lector as written in the Ptolemaic/Roman Periods:

Written Spells and Magical Books

Both tales have references to spells with the word for a written spell appearing as a 'law or custom of writing' (*hp n sš*) (Setna I, col. 3.12-14 and 3.104-5; Setna II, col. 6.15). Scrolls of spells or magical books are referred to as 'books of taking security' (*dmꜥ.w nṯ-iwy.t*) (Setna I, col. 4.32).

Recitation of Spells

> Setna II, col. 2.26: 'Setna recited [a protective spell from] the book of exorcising spirits' (*mḏy n sḫr iḫy*),

after a visit to the underworld' (translated Lichtheim 1980: 142; Ritner 1993: 48).
Setna II, col. 2.27: 'recite spells of taking security' (*ʿš sẖ nt ṯ-iwyt*).

Performance of Magic

There are a number of examples in the text of different phrases employed to describe the performance of magic, indicating that it was 'a thing done' rather than merely a recitation of spells:

Setna II, col. 6.13: 'who now performs magic against me' (*ir ḥkꜣ*).
Setna II, col. 6.15: 'made a magical formula' (*hp-n-sẖ*).
Setna II, col. 6.16: 'made another spell of magical writing' (*sp-n-ḥyḳ-sš*) (translated Ritner 1993: 68 and 2003c: 486-7).

'Consumption of Magic'

The consumption of magic by swallowing or engorging is mentioned in Setna II, col. 6.5:

'He flew up to Egypt engorged with magic' (*iw.f ʿm m ḥyḳ*) (translated Ritner 2003c: 486).

The suggestion here is that the papyrus, upon which the magical spells were written, was physically swallowed. The rationale was that the consumption of the papyrus entails the absorption of the material and the acquisition of its benefits, which in this case refers to the spells written on the papyrus. An example in Setna I, col. 4. 1-4 describes this in detail:

'I read another formula of writing …though I cannot write. I was speaking with regard to my elder brother Naneferkaptah, who is a good scribe and a very wise man. He caused that a new sheet of papyrus be brought before him. He wrote it down every word that was on the papyrus, completely. He burned it with fire; he dissolved it with water. He recognised that it had dissolved; he drank it and knew that which was in it' (translated Lichtheim 1980: 131; Ritner 1993: 108).

This link between ritual swallowing and absorption can be recognised from references in the earlier Pyramid Texts 273-4 (the 'Cannibal Hymn'):

§403c: It is the king who eats their magic (*ḥkꜣw*), swallows their spirits (*ꜣḫ*)[1]
§410b: The king feeds (*wšb*) on the lungs of the wise.
§410c: He is satisfied (*ḥtp*) with living on hearts and their magic.
§411b: He is replete (*wꜣḥ*) their magic is in his belly.
(Translated Faulkner 1969: 81-2 and Eyre 2002: 118-34).

[1] The spirits or souls seem to refer to the divine force or 'magical power' (Eyre 2002: 118).

These Ptolemaic and Roman examples make explicit what is implied in earlier material: namely that magic involved both the recitation of spells as well as a performative element. The power of the lector could be enhanced by the physical ingestion of papyri upon which had been written magical spells.

6. Papyrus Chester Beatty

There is a reference to lectors on the recto of Papyrus 4 of the Chester Beatty Papyri. The papyrus is described as a student's miscellany and its content relates to a Ramesside scribe's education (P. BM 10684; Gardiner 1935: 37-44). The theme of the literary work is the glorification of the scribe's profession. In addition the text emphasises the superiority of written texts inscribed in a tomb as a memorial to a deceased person, rather than expecting one's children to relate one's biography. The papyrus illustrates this theme by exalting the memory of eight celebrated 'writers of knowledge' (*ir nꜣ n sšw rḫt*) or 'authors' of previous generations. Of the eight names mentioned several are known from other surviving compositions such as Hordedef {the instruction of prince Hordedef (Lichtheim 1973: 58-9)}, Neferty (see above), Khety {possibly identified from the Satire of the Trades as Dua-Khety (Simpson 2003: 431-7)}and Khakheperraseneb {the lament of Khakheperraseneb Ankhu (Quirke 2004: 173-5)}. Both Imhotep and Neferty are recorded as being lectors.

'Is there anyone here like Hordedef?
Is there another like Imhotep?
There is no family born for us like Neferty,
and Khety their leader.
Let me remind you of the name of Ptahemdjehuty
Khakheperraseneb.
Is there another like Ptahhotep?
Kaires too?
Those who knew how to foretell the future,
What came from their mouths took place,
and may be found in their utterances (*ṯsw*)
They are given the offspring of others
as heirs as if their own children.
They concealed their magic *(ḥkꜣw)* from the entire world,
to be read in their teachings (*sbꜣyt*) .
They are gone, their names might be forgotten,
but writing lets them be remembered'
(translation based on Gardiner 1935: 39 and Digital Egypt for Universities 2003-6).

The text thus refers to the power of the magic of these 'authors', a power that involves prophesies and teachings. The main proposal is that the 'authors' will be remembered through their writings. The text is important in that the authors are listed as trained scribes and two are recorded as lectors. They have control over magic (*ḥkꜣw*), which again highlights the power of the written word and that of the lector.

Summary and Conclusions

The lector is first attested during the 2nd Dynasty but only appears as a regular officiant at ritual performances during the 5th Dynasty as demonstrated in many temple and funerary scenes. Different ranks are evident and some understanding of the wide range of functions that the lector undertook is apparent from the many additional names that were appended to the title of 'lector', ranging from that of funerary workshop to particular temples and deities. The lector is predominately portrayed with an unrolled papyrus scroll in his hand, wears a broad sash from his shoulder across his chest, and is recognised throughout the time span of Pharaonic Egypt.

Literacy and knowledge of ritualistic use were his principal qualifications and his primary role was that of reciting from a papyrus scroll the various liturgies that were a feature of ancient Egyptian ritual practices. These narrations would have incorporated a performative element that may have necessitated the use of accessory equipment. A study of the burial assemblage of an individual, possibly considered to be a lector, excavated from beneath the Ramesseum has revealed the types of implements that a lector may have used.

The lector is recognised as being closely associated with 'magic' where his knowledge of spells and performative ritual define him as a leading protagonist in this field. This expertise in magic is acknowledged in the literary texts of ancient Egypt where he is portrayed not only as a sage but also a magician with extensive powers.

He was an important officiant at funerary ceremonies where, as a symbolic representative of Thoth, his delivery of the 'transfigurations' (*s3ḫw*) enabled the deceased to become an *akh,* a 'transfigured being'. In the Opening of the Mouth ceremony he was, similarly, a key actor where along with the *sem*-priest he would perform the rite of animation.

In the temple sphere he not only performed recitations and executed a variety of ritual actions but he directed ritual practices. He had a role in the royal palace as attested by the title 'lector of the king'. Lectors helped to compose the titulary of Hatshepsut, and the lector is an officiant seldom absent from scenes representing the royal *Sed*-festival.

The lector had an involvement in healing where he recited therapeutic incantations and there is some evidence that he had knowledge of and prepared remedies for the sick. He accompanied state organised military, trading and mining expeditions where his role is considered one of healing, conducting funerary ritual, and performing ritual incantations during the rough carving and transportation of stone blocks intended for future statues. There is some limited evidence of his role sitting on legal assemblies, both temple-based and in the community.

The aim of this study has been to elucidate the role of the lector in ancient Egyptian society by examining relevant textual and iconographic sources. The evidence presented demonstrates the wide range of activities in which the lector was involved, which encompassed many aspects of ancient Egyptian life. Conclusions relating to these various activities have been discussed at the end of each chapter.

Of necessity many of these conclusions have been based on representation both in the iconographic and the textual sources. As with all ancient Egyptian source material the preserved record will have been subject to a number of biases. The interpretation of the wide range of evidence presented here has attempted to recognise such distortions, but despite the analysis of the considerable data, the reality of the role of the lector may still have varied from that postulated.

A number of key issues relating to this study have become evident. There is a certain degree of ambiguity in the office and rank of lector as demonstrated by the varying importance of the bearers of this title which range from viziers and sons of the monarch to 'scribes of the ship's watch'. The title could be honorary, merely appended to a number of other titles, but it could also signify a working professional. His status in society could therefore vary greatly and monuments subsequently left by the lector range from a short statement on a collective stela at Abydos to a large tomb such as that of Pediamenopet on the Assasif at Thebes.

The lector has been demonstrated, in this publication and in previous studies, to be a specialist in ritual practices but his role as a 'ritual director' or 'master of ceremonies' perhaps needs to be emphasised further. During the course of many ritual performances in the funerary, temple and royal spheres the evidence suggests that it is the lector or chief lector who is guiding and directing proceedings.

Much of the literature relating to ancient Egypt refers to this title as a 'lector-priest', but this labelling of him as a priest does not fully define his role. The activities of the lector were not restricted merely to the temple sphere but he fulfilled a number of other functions and performed ritual activities in many areas of ancient Egyptian life. The role of the lector in ritual practice outside the temple can be underestimated as has been demonstrated in this study. Perhaps to understand him as a ritualist and refer to him as a 'lector' may be a more appropriate appreciation of his role in society.

Appendix 1

The objects comprising the burial assemblage of Tomb No. 5 at the Ramesseum

- Squatting faience baboon statuette (Manchester 1835, Quibell 14).
- Small faience squatting baboon statuette (Manchester 1837, Quibell 6).
- Upright lion statuette (Manchester 1839, Quibell 5).
- Left fragment of an apotropaic wand (Manchester 1798, Quibell 2a).
- Two fragments of an apotropaic wand, the left fragment is in three sections and has been repaired in antiquity (Manchester 1799, Quibell 2b).
- An apotropaic wand in two pieces (Manchester 1800, Quibell 3).
- Two fragments of an apotropaic wand, both of which have been repaired in antiquity (Manchester 1801, Quibell 1).
- Wooden figurine of a naked woman (Manchester 1790, Quibell 12).
- Bronze serpent wand (Fitzwilliam Musem E.63.1896, Quibell 4).
- Blue, faience female figurine (Manchester 1787, Quibell 11).
- Bottom half of a limestone female figurine (Manchester 1788, not illustrated by Quibell).
- Limestone female figurine (Manchester 1789, Quibell 10).
- Top half of a limestone female figurine (Manchester 1794, Quibell 13).
- Flat wooden preformal figure (paddle doll) (Manchester 1832, Quibell 9).
- Ivory statuette of a naked dwarf with a calf on his back (Pennsylvania Museum of Archaeology and Anthropology E13405).
- Miniature faience cup (Manchester 1791, Quibell 16).
- Model faience cucumber (Manchester 1792, Quibell 7).
- Faience bunch of grapes or body part of an animal (Manchester 1841, not listed by Quibell).
- Left-hand ivory clapper in two pieces (Manchester 1796.a-b, Quibell 17).
- Right-hand ivory clapper in two pieces (Manchester 1797 a-b, not mentioned by Quibell).
- Section of an ivory magical rod (Manchester 1795, Quibell 18).
- Group of beads (location unknown).
- Ivory Djed column (Manchester 1838, Quibell 15).
- Ivory burnisher (Manchester 1834, Quibell 8).
- Bundle of 118 reeds (Manchester 1882).
- Wooden papyrus box (location unknown).
- Seeds of doum-palm and of balanites (mentioned in Quibell's report).

Appendix 2

The papyri from the burial assemblage of Tomb No. 5 at the Ramesseum

1. P. Ram. A (P. Berlin 10499): *Recto text:* The Eloquent Peasant. *Verso text: Sinuhe.*
2. P. Ram. B (P. BM EA 10610): *Recto text:* Dramatic festival ritual. *Verso text:* Sketch plan of a building.
3. P. Ram. C+18 (P. BM EA 10752+10771): *Recto text:* Dispatches from the Nubian fortresses. *Verso text:* Magical texts including an incantation against ghosts + a strengthening strip with accounts.
4. P. Ram. D (P. Berlin 10495): *Recto text:* Onomasticon listing cereals, birds, animals as well as Nubian fortresses and Upper Egyptian towns. *Verso text:* Accounts list.
5. P. Ram. E (P. BM EA 10753): *Recto text:* A funerary liturgy for ceremonies at a mastaba. *Verso text:* An account list for granaries.
6. P. Ram. I (P. BM EA 10754) *Recto text:* The Discourse of Sasobek. *Verso text:* Later accounts list.
7. P. Ram. 2 (P. BM EA 10755) *Recto text:* Compilation of moral pronouncements on various topics. *Verso text:* Continuation of the text from recto.
8. P. Ram. 3 (P. BM EA 10756) *Recto text:* A magico-medical text for mother and child and also eye complaints. *Verso text:* Dated accounts list.
9. P. Ram. 4 (P. BM EA 10757) *Recto text:* A magico-medical text associated with pregnancy, birth and conditions associated with mother and child. *Verso text:* Accounts list.
10. P. Ram. 5 (P. BM EA 10758) *Recto text:* Medical prescriptions dealing with 'vessels' with muscular complaints, rheumatic troubles and stiffness generally, having parallels with the Ebers Papyrus. *Verso text:* Very short 'jottings'.
11. P. Ram. 6 (P. BM EA 10759) *Recto text: Hymns to Sobek* (the most complete and finest in the collection). *Verso text:* None.
12. P. Ram. 7 (P. BM EA 10760) *Recto text:* Spells for gaining respect from men? *Verso text:* Later accounts.
13. P. Ram. 8 (P. BM EA 10761) *Recto text: The Banquet of Hedjhotep* (magical text with incantations against headaches). *Verso text:* None.
14. P. Ram. 9 (P. BM EA 10762) *Recto text:* Rituals to protect a house from magic, ghosts and serpents. *Verso text:* None.
15. P. Ram. 10 (P.BM EA 10763) *Recto text:* 'Spell for protection of the limbs against any male and female serpent'. *Verso text:* Continuation of the text?
16. P. Ram. 11 (P. BM EA 10764) *Recto text:* Magical text, possibly love texts. *Verso text:* None.
17. P. Ram. 12 (P. BM EA 10765) *Recto text:* Invocations to demons against fever. *Verso text:* Later jottings?
18. P. Ram. 13 (P. BM EA 10766) *Recto text:* Healing texts? *Verso text:* Diary of embalmment.
19. P. Ram. 14 (P. BM EA 10767) *Recto text:* Magical healing text. *Verso text:* Continuation of the text.
20. P. Ram. 15 (P. BM EA 10768) *Recto text:* Spells to protect the body. *Verso text:* Continuation of the text.
21. P. Ram. 16 (P. BM EA 10769) *Recto text:* Spells for protection including a number against evil dreams. *Verso text:* Continuation of the text.
22. P. Ram. 17 (P. BM EA 10770) *Recto text:* Protection against the dangers of the epagomenal days at the turn of the year and other miscellaneous matters. *Verso text:* Continuation of the text.
23. P. Ram. 19 (P. BM EA 10772) *Recto text:* Ritual/magical texts. *Verso text:* Continuation of the text.
24. P. Ram 1/ 'Ramesseum Wisdom Fragment' *Recto text:* The Discourse of Sasobek. *Verso text:* Some later accounts.

Appendix (P. Berlin 10131) Six fragments containing administrative entries which may have belonged to the Ramesseum group (Parkinson 2012).

Appendix 3

List of the books inscribed on the walls of the 'House of Books' *(pr-mḏ3t)* at Edfu Temple

(Based on Sauneron 2000: 135)

The books and the great rolls of pure leather that enable the smiting of the demon,
the repelling of the crocodile,
the protection of the hour,
the preservation of the barque,
and of carrying the barque.
(The book of) bringing out the king in procession.
(The book of) conducting the ritual…
The protection of the city, the house, the White Crown, the throne, and the year...
The book of appeasing Sekhmet…
(The book of) driving away lions, repulsing crocodiles, and repelling reptiles.
Knowing all the secrets of the laboratory.
Knowing the divine offerings in all their details... and all the inventories of the secret forms (of the god), and all the aspects of the associated deities, which are copied daily for the temple, every day, each one after the other, so that the 'souls' of the deities will remain in (this) place and will not leave (this) temple, ever…
The book of the inventory of the temple.
The book of the capture (of enemies).
The book of all the writings of combat.
The book of the conduct of the temple.
Instructions for decorating a wall.
Protection of the body.
The book of magical protection for the king in his palace.
Spells for repelling the evil eye.
Knowing the periodic returns of the two heavenly bodies (i.e. the sun and the moon).
List of all the (sacred) places, and knowing what is in them.
Every ritual related to (the god's) leaving his temple on festival days.

Appendix 4

Occurrences of a lector performing rituals during water crossings

Name	Location of tomb	Tomb number	Dyn.	Action
Ptahhotep	**Saqqara**	**D 62**	**5th**	**Damaged scene above a seated lector stating: 'Making transfigurations'** (*s3ḫ*).
Ptahhotep	**Saqqara**	**D 62**	**5th**	**Inscription on the false door shows Ptahhotep seated under a canopy facing a seated lector reading from his scroll, the caption being: 'There is performed for him the traversing of the lake. He is transfigured by the performance of a service by the lector'** (*ir n.f nmit š s3ḫt.f ḫr ir ḫt in ḫry-ḥbt*).
Tepemankh	**Saqqara**	**D 11**	**5th**	**An inscription on the false door : 'A procession to his tomb of the west, after rowing him in the** *wrt*-**boat, when a fully equipped ritual had been conducted for him according to the writing of the craft of the lector'** (*šms r is.f in imntw m-ḫt ḫnwt.f m wrt sšm n.f ḥb ʿpr ḫt sš n ḥmt n ḫry-ḥbt*).
Hetepherakhti	**Saqqara**	**D 60**	**5th**	**'Sailing while the ritual is conducted by the lector'** (*ḫnt šsm ḥb in ḫry-ḥbt*).
Nebkau-Hor	**Saqqara**		**6th**	**Reciting from his unrolled papyrus scroll.**
Sneferu-Ishetef	**Dahshur**	**Mastaba 2**	**6th**	**Standing lector on the shore inside a booth facing the funeral boat reading from a papyrus roll.**

Appendix 5

Episodes in the Opening of the Mouth Ritual in which it is possible to identify the presence of the lector

(From the list as per Otto 1960. The seven fullest versions 1 – 7 are listed by name, and the minor sources are listed by number only. The key at the end of the list provides the names of the minor souces).

Episodes	Rekhmire	Sety I	Tausret	Butehamun	Amenirdis	Padiamenopet	Salis	Minor sources
1								51, 83
2				/				27, 41, 53, 78, 80
3								27
4								
5								49
6					/			
7								
8	/	/	/	/	/	/		26, 83
9								
10								
11								
12								
13	/							
14	/							83
15	/							
16	/							
17	/							
18	/	/	/		/		/	83
19	/				/			
20		/					/	
21	/	/			/		/	62, 83
22	/	/	/					
23	/				/	/	/	62, 83
24	/	/	/	/	/	/	/	62, 83
25	/	/			/	/		49, 62
26	/	/			/	/		26, 27, 29, 45, 49
27	/	/			/	/	/	26, 27, 35, 45
28	/	/		/	/	/	/	
29								
30	/				/	/	/	62
31	/	/			/	/	/	46, 47, 79
32	/	/			/	/	/	62
33	/	/			/	/	/	47
34					/	/	/	
35		/			/	/		
36	/	/			/	/		49
37					/	/	/	22, 47, 79
38	/				/	/	/	
39	/				/	/		26
40						/	/	
41	/							
42						/	/	
43					/		/	
44		/				/		45, 79
45	/	/			/	/		
46	/	/				/	/	26
47	/	/					/	26
48		/				/	/	26
49								
50	/					/		26
51								
52							/	
53							/	
54							/	
55							/	45
56						/	/	
57							/	
58							/	
59	/						/	
60							/	
61								
62							/	
63								
64								
65	/					/	/	
66								
67							/	
68							/	
69	/					/	/	
70							/	26, 15
71	/						/	
72	/						/	26, 81
73	/					/	/	58
74	/					/	/	
75	/							22

Tomb owner's names for the minor sources of the Opening of the Mouth ritual

15	Amenemhat (TT 82) *c.* 1479 – 1425 BC
22	Horemheb (TT 78) *c.* 1450 – 1350 BC
26	Nebamun (TT 17) *c.* 1911-1877 BC
27	Userhat (TT 56) *c.* 1427 – 1400 BC
29	Amenemhat (TT 97) *c.* 1427 - 1400 BC
35	Paser (TT 106) *c.* 1294 – 1213 BC
41	Huy (TT 54) *c.* 1400 - 1352 BC
45	Amenemhat (also called Surer)(TT 48) *c.* 1390 – 1352 BC
46	Khaemhat (TT 57) *c.* 1390 – 1352 BC
47	Amenmose (TT 89) *c.* 1390 – 1352 BC
49	Pairi (TT 139) *c.* 1390 - 1352 BC
51	Nebamun and Ipuky (TT 181) *c.* 1550 – 1295 BC
53	Ramose (TT 55) *c.* 1352 – 1336 BC
58	Paser (TT 106) *c.* 1294 – 1213 BC
62	Nebsumenu (TT 183) *c.* 1279 – 1213 BC
78	Hunefer (vignette in P. BM EA 9901) *c.*1295 – 1186 BC
79	Harwa (TT 37) *c.* 664 – 332 BC
80	Wenamun (temple wall of Umm el-Ebeida, Siwa Oasis) *c.* 664 - 525 BC
81	Petosiris (Tuna el-Gebel) *c.* 300 BC
83	Setjawetawedjat (P. Cairo 36803, JE 40803) *c.* 550 BC

Appendix 6

Presence of the episodes of the Opening of the Mouth ceremony in the seven major sources

Indicated as (P) present, (D) an area destroyed in that source, (T) traces of, or blank, indicating that the episode was not included in that source.

Table adapted from Digital Egypt UCL website: http://www.digitalegypt.ucl.ac.uk/religion/wpr.html

Episodes	Rekhmire	Sety I	Tausret	Butehamun	Amenirdis	Padiamenopet	Sais
1	P	P		P	P	D	D
2	P	P	P	P	P	D	D
3	P	P	P	P	P	D	D
4	P	P	P	P	P	D	D
5	P	P	P	P	P	D	D
6	P	P	P	P	P	D	D
7	P	P	P	P	P	D	D
8	P	P	P	P	P	T	
9	P	P	P	P	P	T	
10	P	P	P	P	P	T	T
11		P	P	P	P	T	T
12	P	P	P	P	P	D	D
13	P	P	P	P	P	D	D
14	P	P	P	P	P	D	D
15	P	P	P	P	P	D	D
16	P	P	P	P	P	D	D
17	P	P	P	P	P	D	P
18	P	P	P		P	D	P
19	P	P	P		P	D	P
20	P	P	P		P	D	P
21	P	P	P		P	D	P
22	P	P	P			D	
23	P	P	P	P	P	P	P
24	P	P	P	P	P	P	P
25	P	P	P	P	P	P	P
26	P	P	P	P	P	P	P
27	P	P		P	P	P	P
28	P	P		P	P	P	P
29	P	P		P	P	P	P
30	P	P		P	P	P	P
31	P	P		P	P	P	P
32	P	P		P	P	P	P
33	P	P		P	P	P	P
34				P	P	P	P
35		P		P	P	P	P
36	P	P		P	P	P	P
37	P			P	P	P	P
38	P			P	P	P	P
39	P			P	P	P	P
40						P	P
41	P			P	P	P	P
42		P		P	P	P	P
43	P	P		P	P	P	P
44	P	P		P	P	P	P
45	P	P			P	P	P
46	P	P		P		P	P
47	P	P					
48		P		P		P	P
49				P			P
50	P	P		P		P	P
51				P		P	P
52				P			P
53							P
54							P
55		P		P		P	P
56				P		P	P
57		P		P			P
58				P			P
59	P	P		P			P
60				P			P
61				P			P
62				P			P
63				P			P
64				P			
65	P	P		P		P	P
66				P			
67				P			P
68				P			P
69	P			P		P	P
70				P		P	P
71	P			P		P	P
72	P			P		P	P
73	P			P		P	P
74	P					P	P
75	P					P	P

Appendix 7

Lectors who additionally carried the title of physician

Name	Dynasty	Relevant Titles	Sources
Mereruka	**6th Dynasty**	**'Overseer of the two sides of the boat of the physicians of the great house'** (*imy-r gs-wy dpt swnw pr-ꜣꜥ*) **and 'Chief lector'** (*ḫry-ḥbt ḥry tp*)	**Tomb in the Teti cemetery at Saqqara (LS 10)**
Amenhotep	**19th Dynasty**	**'Chief physician'** (*wr swnw*) **and 'Chief lector'** (*ḫry-ḥbt ḥry tp*)	**Tomb at Deir Durunka (near Asyut)**
Huy	**Late Period**	**'Physician'** (*swnw*) **and 'Lector'** (*ḫry-ḥbṯ*)	**Grafitto in the temple of Sety I at Abydos**
Horkhebet	**Late Period**	**'Chief physician'** (*wr swnw*) **and 'Lector'** (*ḫry-ḥbt*)	**Sarcophagus from Sais and offering table**

Appendix 8

Lectors present on mining expeditions

A. Hatnub

Name	Period	Inscription Details	Rank
Ankhy	OK	Graffito 7 (Anthes 1928: pl. 12-12a)	Lector
Khnumankh	OK	Graffito 7 (Anthes 1928: pl. 12-12a)	Lector
Tunakhtankh	MK/2IP	Graffito 12 (Anthes 1928: pl. 14)	Lector
Ia-ib	Unknown	Graffito 15 (Anthes 1928: pl. 2)	Chief Lector

B. Sinai

Name	Period	Inscription Details	Rank
Werkherephemut	MK	Inscrip. 123B (Gardiner *et al.* 1955: pl. 46)	Chief Lector

C. Wadi Hammamat

Name	Period	Inscription Details	Rank
Merptahankhymeryre	6th Dyn.	Inscrip. 21 (Goyon 1957: 55)	Senior Lector
Nibunesu	6th Dyn.	Inscrip. 27 (Goyon 1957: 61, pl. 10)	Lector
Rekey	6th Dyn.	Inscrip. 28 (Goyon 1957: 61, pl. 10)	Lector
Djedu	MK	Inscrip. 74 (Goyon 1957: 94, pl. 22)	Lector of the Court
Putiker	MK	Inscrip. 149 (Couyat & Monet 1912: pl. 35)	Chief Lector
Shemai	MK	Inscrip. 150 (Couyat & Monet 1912: pl. 35)	Senior Lector
Putiker (same as above)	MK	Inscrip. 152 (Couyat & Monet 1912: pl. 34)	Chief Lector

D. Wadi el-Hudi

Name	Period	Inscription Details	Rank
Intef (1)	MK	Inscrip. 48 (Fakhry 1952: fig. 49)	Lector
Intef (2)	MK	Inscrip. 48 (Fakhry 1952: fig. 52)	Lector
Intef [same as Intef (2)]	MK	Inscrip. 53 (Fakhry 1952: fig. 54)	Lector
Se	MK	Inscrip. 148 (Sadek 1980: 92-5)	Lector of Ptah

Appendix 9

Papyrus BM 10054

Recto p.3 (Pls. VI-VII); Translation after Peet (1930: 62-3)

(7) Year 18, second month of the inundation season, day 24. Taking the deposition of the *wab*-priest Penwenhab. His statement was heard. They said to him, what have you to say concerning the gold foil of Nefertum (8) belonging to King Usermatre-Setepenre, the great god. He said, I went with the divine father Hapiwer, and the divine father Sedi, and the divine father Perisen, son of Hapiwer, and the divine father Pekheru. (9) We stripped this gold-covered column-drum (?) of Nefertum. We brought away 4 *deben* 6 *kite* of gold, and I melted it down, and the divine father Hapiwer divided it up (10) between himself and his companions. They gave me 3 *kite* of gold and they gave 3 *kite* to the divine father Pekheru, son (?) of ... and they took the remainder. (11) Now the goldsmith said, The god of Pharaoh remains stripped to this day, it is not covered. And ... also said ... You went to the shrines (?) (12) of this god and brought away 4 ox-amulets (?) of silver and broke them up. And I made copies in wood... and put them in their place. (13) The 4 ox-amulets (?) weighed 6 *deben* of silver. They divided them among themselves. (14) Men along with the divine father Pekheru and the *wab*-priest Penwenhab to whom the god of Nefertum was given: to the (15) *sem*-priest Khaemope 1 *deben* of gold, to the scribe of the royal records Setekhmose 6 *kite* of gold, to the divine father Hapiwer 3, to the divine father Sedi 3 *kite*, to the divine father Pekheru 3, (16) to the *wab*-priest Penwenhab 3 *kite*, to the *wab*-priest Pesen son of Hapiwer 3 *kite*, to the *wab*-priest Setekhmose 1 *kite* of gold: amount (still) covering the god 8 *kite*; total 4 *deben* of gold. (17) Said the divine father Pekheru. The coppersmith Khonmose and the coppersmith Usermarenakht brought away 150 *deben* of copper (from?) the great statue of the Lord which stands (in) the court. It is in their possession.

Bibliography

Al-Ayedi, A. R. (2006), *Index of Egyptian Administrative, Religious and Military Titles of the New Kingdom* (Ismalia, Egypt: Obelisk Publications).

Aldred, C. (1959), 'The beginning of the El-Amarna Period', *Journal of Egyptian Archaeology,* 45, 19-33.

--- (1988), *Akhenaten: King of Egypt* (London: Thames & Hudson).

Allam, S. (1991), 'Egyptian law courts in Pharaonic and Hellenistic Times', *Journal of Egyptian Archaeology,* 77, 109-27.

--- (2007), 'Law', in T. Wilkinson (ed.), *The Egyptian World* (London & New York: Routledge), 263-72.

Allen, J. P. (2005), *The Art of Medicine in Ancient Egypt* (Metropolitan Museum of Art Series; New York: The Metropolitan Museum of Art).

Allen, T. G. (1923), *A Handbook of the Egyptian Collection* (Chicago: Oriental Institute of the University of Chicago).

--- (1974), *The Book of the Dead of Going Forth by Day: Ideas of the Ancient Egyptians Concerning the Hereafter as Expressed in their Own Terms* (Studies in Oriental Civilisation, vol. 37; Chicago: Chicago University Press).

Alliot, M. (1954), *Le culte d'Horus à Edfou au temps des Ptolémées*, 2 vols. (Bibliothèque d'Étude, 1; Le Caire: Imprimerie de l'Institut Français d'Archéologie Orientale), 677-804.

Altenmüller, H. (1979), 'Ein Zauberspruche zum 'Shutz des Leibes'', *Göttinger Miszellen,* 33, 7-12.

--- (1983), 'Ein Zaubermesser aus Tübingen', *Die Welt Des Orients,* 14, 30-45.

--- (1986), 'Ein Zauberspruch des Mittleren Reiches', *Studien zur Altägyptischen Kultur,* 13, 1-27.

--- (2010), 'Totenliturgie und Mundöffnungsritual: Bemerkungen zur vermuteten "Vision von der Statue im Stein"', in H. Knuf *et al.* (ed.), *Honi soit qui mal y pense: Studien zum pharaonischen, griechisch-römischen und spätantiken Ägypten zu Ehren von Heinz-Josef Thissen.* (Orientalia Lovanensia Analecta 194; Leuven: Peeters), 3-14.

Andreu, G., Rutschowscaya, M-H. & Ziegler, C. (1997), *Ancient Egypt at the Louvre* (Paris: Hachette).

Andrews, C. A. R. (1994), *Amulets of Ancient Egypt* (London: British Museum Press).

--- (2000), *Egyptian Treasures from the British Museum* (Santa Ana: The Bowers Museum of Cultural Art).

--- (2001), 'Amulets', in D. B. Redford (ed.), *Oxford Encyclopedia of Ancient Egypt* (1; Oxford: Oxford University Press), 75-82.

Anthes, R. (1928), *Die Felseninschriften von Hatnub, nach den Aufnahmen Georg Möllers* (Leipzig: J. C. Hinrichs).

Arnold, D. (2005), 'The temple of Hatshepsut at Deir el-Bahri', in C. Roehrig (ed.), *Hatshepsut, from Queen to Pharaoh* (New York: Metropolitan Museum of Art), 134-46.

Assmann, J. (1990), 'Egyptian mortuary rituals', in S. Israelit-Groll (ed.), *Studies in Egyptology* (1; Jerusalem: The Magnes Press, The Hebrew University), 1-45.

--- (2001), *The Search for God in Ancient Egypt*, trans. D. Lorton (Ithaca & London: Cornell University Press).

--- (2005), *Death and Salvation in Ancient Egypt,* trans. D. Lorton (Ithaca and London: Cornell University Press).

Assmann, J., Bomas, M. & Kucharek, A. (2002-10), *Altägyptische Totenliturgien,* 4 vols. (Heidelberg: Universitätsverlag Winter).

Ayad, M. F. (2004), 'The selection and layout of the Opening of the Mouth scenes in the Chapel of Amenirdis at Medinet Habu', *Journal of the American Research Center in Egypt,* 41, 113-33.

Bacchi, E. (1942), *Il Rituale di Amenhotep I* (Pubblicazioni Egittologiche del Museo di Torino 6, Torino: Museo di Torino).

Badawy, A. (1978), *The Tomb of Nyhetep-Ptah at Giza and Ankhmahor at Saqqara* (Berkeley: University of California Press).

--- (1981), 'The spiritualisation of Kagemni', *Zeitschrift für Ägyptische Sprache und Altertumskunde,* 108, 85-93.

Baer, K. (1960), *Rank and Title in the Old Kingdom: The Structure of the Egyptian Administration in the Fifth and Sixth Dynasties* (Chicago: University of Chicago Press).

Baines, J. (1990), 'Restricted knowledge, hierarchy, and decorum: Modern perceptions and ancient institutions', *Journal of the American Research Center in Egypt,* 27, 1-23.

--- (1996), 'On the composition and inscriptions of the Vatican Statue of Udjahorresne', in P. Der Manuelian (ed.), *Studies in Honor of William Kelly Simpson* (1; Boston: Museum of Fine Arts), 83-92.

--- (2006), 'Display of magic in Old Kingdom Egypt', in K. Szpakowska (ed.), *Through a Glass Darkly* (Swansea: Classical Press of Wales), 1-32.

--- (2007), *Visual and Written Culture in Ancient Egypt* (Oxford: Oxford University Press).

Baines, J. & Eyre, C. (1983), 'Four notes on literacy', *Göttinger Miszellen,* 61, 65-96.

Baines, J. & Lacovara, P. (2002), 'Burial and the dead in ancient Egyptian society: Respect, formalism, neglect', *Journal of Social Archaeology,* 2 (5), 5-36.

Bakry, H. S. K. (1970), 'Two Saite monuments of two master physicians', *Oriens Antiquus,* 10, 325-41.

Baly, T. J. C. (1930), 'Notes on the ritual of Opening the Mouth', *Journal of Egyptian Archaeology,* 16 (3/4), 173-86.

Bardinet, T. (1995), *Les Papyrus Médicaux de l'Égypte Pharaonique* (Lyon: Fayard).

Barguet, P. (1953), *La stèle de la famine à Séhel* (Bibliothèque d'Étude; Le Caire: Institut Français d'Archéologie Orientale).

--- (1962), *Le Payrus N. 3176 (S) Du Musée Du Louvre* (Institut Français d'Archéologie Orientale. Bibliothèque d'Étude; Le Caire: Institut Français d'Archéologie Orientale).

Barns, J. W. (1956), *Five Ramesseum Papyri* (Oxford: Oxford University Press for the Griffith Institute).

Baud, M. (1999), *Famille royale et pouvoir sous l'Ancien Empire égyptien,* 2 vols. (1; Le Caire: Institut Français d'Archéologie Orientale).

Bell, C. (2009), *Ritual Theory, Ritual Practice* (Oxford: Oxford University Press).

Bell, L. (1985), 'Luxor temple and the cult of the royal *ka*', *Journal of Near Eastern Studies,* 44 (4), 251-94.

--- (1997), 'The New Kingdom 'divine temple': The example of Luxor', in B. E. Shafer (ed.), *Temples of Ancient Egypt* (Ithaca, New York: Cornell University Press), 127-84.

Bergmann, von, E. (1887), 'Inschriftliche denkmäler der sammlung ägyptischer alterthümer des österreichischen Kaiserhauses', *Recueil de travaux relatifs à la philologie et à l'archéologie égyptiennes et assyriennes* (9), 32-63.

Bernand, A. (1972), *De Koptos à Kosseir* (Leiden: E. J. Brill).

Bissing, F. W. von (1905-11), *Die Mastaba des Gem-ni-kai,* 2 vols (2; Berlin: A. Dunker).

Bissing, F. W. von & Kees, H. (1905-28), *Das Re-Heiligtum des Königs Ne-Woser-Re (Rathures): Die kleine Festarstellung,* 3 vols. (2; Leipzig: J. C. Hinrichs'sche Buchhandlung).

--- (1922), *Untersuchungen zu den Reliefs aus dem Re-Heiligtum des Rathures* (Munich: Verlag der Bayrischen Akademie der Wissenschaften).

Blackden, M. W. & Fraser, G. W. (1892), 'Collection of Hieratic Graffiti from the Alabaster Quarry of Hatnub', (Private Circulation).

Blackman, A. M. (1917), 'The funerary papyrus of Ankhefenkhons', *Journal of Egyptian Archaeology,* 4 (2/3), 122-29.

--- (1918a), 'The House of the Morning', *Journal of Egyptian Archaeology,* 5 (3), 148-65.

--- (1918b), 'Some notes on the ancient Egyptian practice of washing the dead', *Journal of Egyptian Archaeology,* 5 (2), 117-24.

--- (1924), 'The rite of Opening the Mouth in Egypt and Babylonia', *Journal of Egyptian Archaeology,* 10 (1), 47-59.

--- (1932-1948), *Middle-Egyptian Stories* (Bruxelles: Fondation Égyptologique Reine Élisabeth).

Blackman, A. M. & Apted, M. R. (1914-1953), *The Rock Tombs of Meir,* 6 vols. (London: Kegan Paul, Trench, Trübner & Co).

Blackman, A. M. & Fairman, H. W. (1941), 'A group of texts inscribed on the façade of the sanctuary in the temple of Horus at Edfu', *Miscellanea Gregoriana: Raccolta di scritti pubblicati nel I Centenario dalla fondazione del Museo Egizio (1839-1939)* (Vatican City: Tipographia Poliglotta Vaticana), 397-428.

--- (1942), 'The myth of Horus at Edfu: II. C. The triumph of Horus over his enemies. A sacred drama', *Journal of Egyptian Archaeology,* 28, 32-38.

--- (1946), 'The consecration of an Egyptian temple according to the use of Edfu', *Journal of Egyptian Archaeology,* 32, 75-91.

Bleeker, C. J. (1967), *Egyptian Festivals: enactments of religious renewal.* (Studies in the History of Religions 13; Leiden: E. J. Brill).

--- (1973), *Hathor and Thoth: two key figures of the ancient Egyptian religion.* (Studies in the History of Religions 26; Leiden: E. J. Brill).

Bliquez, L. J. (1981), 'Greek and Roman Medicine', *Archaeology,* 34 (2), 11-17.

Blumenthal, E. (1977), 'Die textgattung expeditionsbericht in Ägypten', in J. Assmann, E. Feucht, & R. Grieshammer (ed.), *Fragen an die altägyptische Literatur.* (Wiesbaden: L. Reichert), 85-118.

Bolshakov, A. O. (1991), 'The Old Kingdom representations of funeral procession', *Göttinger Miszellen,* 121, 31-54.

--- (1997), *Man and his Double in Egyptian Ideology of the Old Kingdom* (Wiesbaden: Harrosswitz Verlag).

Bonnet, H. (1952), *Reallexikon der Ägyptischen Religionsgeschichte* (Berlin: Walter de Gruyter & Co.).

Borchardt, L. (1902-1903), 'Besoldungsverhältnisse von priestern im mittleren reich', *Zeitschrift für Ägyptische Sprache und Altertumskunde,* 40, 113-17.

--- (1905), *Das Re-Heiligtum des Königs Ne-woser-re (Rathures)* (ed.), F. W. von Bissing (Bd. 1; Leipzig: A. Dunker).

--- (1910-1913), *Das Grabdenkmal des Königs Sahure,* 2 vols. (Leipzig: J. C. Hinrichs).

--- (1911-1936), *Catalogue général des antiquités égyptiennes du Musée du Caire: Statuen und Statuetten von Königen und Privatleuten* 5 vols. (Berlin: Reichsdrukerei).

--- (1926), 'Jubiläumsbilder', *Zeitschrift für Ägyptische Sprache und Altertumskunde,* 61, 30-51.

--- (1937), *Denkmäler des Alten Reiches (ausser den Statuen)* (Berlin: Reichsdruckerei).

Borghouts, J. F. (1987), "Akh and Heka' Two basic notions of ancient Egyptian magic, and the concept of the divine creative word', in A. Roccati and A. Silotti (ed.), *La Magia in Egitto ai Tempi dei Faraoni* (Milan: A. Siliotti), 29-46.

Bosse-Griffiths, K. (1977), 'A Beset amulet from the Amarna Period', *Journal of Egyptian Archaeology,* 63, 98-106.

Bourriau, J. (1988), *Pharaohs and Mortals: Egyptian Art in the Middle Kingdom* (Cambridge: Cambridge University Press).

--- (1991), 'Patterns of change in burial customs during the Middle Kingdom', in S. Quirke (ed.), *Middle Kingdom Studies* (New Malden, Surrey: SIA Publishing), 3-20.

Boylan, P. (1922 (this edition 1979)), *Thoth, the Hermes of Egypt* (London: Humphrey Milford (reprinted Chicago: Ares 1979)).

Breasted, J. H. (1906 (this edition 2001)), *Ancient Records of Egypt*, 5 vols. (Champaign, Illinois: University of Illinois Press).

--- (1908), 'Oriental exploration fund of the University of Chicago. Secondary preliminary report of the Egyptian expedition', *The American Journal of Semitic Languages and Literatures,* 25 (1), 1-110.

--- (1930a), *The Edwin Smith Surgical Papyrus: Hieroglyphic Transliteration, Translation and Commentary V1* (Chicago: The University of Chicago Press).

--- (1930b), *The Edwin Smith Surgical Papyrus V2: Facsimile Plates and Line for Line Hieroglyphic Transliteration* (Chicago: The University of Chicago Press).

Brissaud, P. (1993), 'Mission Française des fouilles de Tanis: rapport sur la XIe campaigne de fouilles -1993', *Bulletin de la Société Française des Fouilles de Tanis,* 7, 79-94.

British Museum Collection Database. http://www.britishmuseum.org/collection, British Museum. Online. Accessed 19.06.2013.

Brovarski, E. J. (1977), 'The doors of Heaven', *Acta Orientalia,* 46, 107-15.

--- (1977-1978), 'Hor-aha and the Nubians', *Serapis. The American Journal of Egyptology,* 4, 1-2.

Brugsch, H. (1871), 'Bau und Maafse des Tempels von Edfu', *Zeitschrift für Ägyptische Sprache und Altertumskunde,* 9 (1871), 42-5.

Bruyère, B. (1927), *Rapport sur les fouilles de Deir el Médineh (1926)* (Le Caire: Institut Français d'Archéologie Orientale).

de Buck, A. (1935), *The Coffin Texts, v. 1* (Chicago: Oriental Institute of the University of Chicago).

--- (1937), 'The Judicial Papyrus of Turin', *Journal of Egyptian Archaeology,* 23, 152-64.

--- (1938), 'The building inscription of the Berlin leather roll', *Analecta Orientalia,* 17, 48-57.

Budge, W. E. A. (1911), *Hieroglyphic Texts from Egyptian Stelae in the British Museum* (1; London: British Museum).

Burgos, F. & Larché, F. (2006), *La Chapelle rouge. Le sanctuaire de barque d'Hatshepsout. Vol. 1 Facsimilés et photographies des scènes / sous la direction de N. Grimal* (Paris: Éditions Recherche sur les Civilisations).

Calverley, A. M. & Broome, M. F. (1933), *The Temple of King Sethos I at Abydos*, (ed.), A. H. Gardiner, 2 vols. (London & Chicago: Egypt Exploration Society & the Oriental Institute of the University of Chicago).

Capart, J. (1907), *Une rue de tombeaux à Saqqarah*, 2 vols. (2; Bruxelles: Vromant & Co.).

--- (1940), 'Avant-Propos', in G. Posener (ed.), *Princes et pays D'Asie et de Nubie* (Bruxelles: Fondation Égyptologique Reine Élisabeth Parc du Cinquantenaire), 1-9.

Carnarvon, G. E. & Carter, H. (1912), *Five Years Exploration at Thebes: A Record of Work Done 1907-1911* (London: Henry Frowde).

Cauville, S. (2012), *Offerings to the Gods in Egyptian Temples* (Leuven, Paris & Walpole MA: Peeters).

Center for the Tebtunis Papyri Collection Database. "http://tebtunis.berkeley.edu/, The Center for the Tebtunis Papyri, the Bancroft Library, University of California, Berkeley. Online. Accessed 14.07.2011.

Černý, J. (1952), *Ancient Egyptian Religion* (World Religions; New York, Melbourne, Sydney, Cape Town: Hutchinson's University Library).

Černý, J. & Peet, T. E. (1927), 'A marriage settlement of the Twentieth Dynasty', *Journal of Egyptian Archaeology,* 13 (1/2), 30-9.

Chabân, M. E. (1903), 'Nécropole de la VIe dynastie à Koçeir el-Amarna', *Annales du Service des Antiquités de l'Égypte,* 3, 250-53.

Chassinat, É. (1892-1960), *Le Temple d'Edfou*, 14 vols. (Mémoires Publiés par les Membres de la Mission Archéologique Français du Caire; Le Caire: Institut Français d'Archéologie Orientale).

Cline, E. H. & O'Connor, D. (2012), *Ramesses III: The Life and Times of Egypt's Last Hero* (Ann Arbor: University of Michigan Press).

Couyat, J. & Montet, P. (1912), *Les inscriptions hiéroglyphiques et hiératiques du quâdi Hammâmât* (Le Caire: Imprimerie de l'Institut Français d'Archéologie Orientale).

Crompton, W. M. (1916), 'Two clay balls in the Manchester Museum', *Journal of Egyptian Archaeology,* 3, 128.

Darby, W. J., Ghalioungui, P. & Grivetti, L. (1977), *Food: The Gift of Osiris*, 2 vols. (1; London, New York, San Francisco: Academic Press).

Daressy, G. E. J. (1905), 'Une Statue d'Aba', *Annales du Service des Antiquités de l'Égypte,* 5, 94-96.

--- (1906), *Catalogue général des antiquités égyptiennes du Musée du Caire: (Nos. 38001-39384), Statues de divinités* (Le Caire: Imprimerie de l'Institut Français d'Archéologie Orientale).

--- (1916), 'La nécropole des grands prêtres d'Héliopolis sous l'ancien empire', *Annales du Service des Antiquités de l'Égypte,* 16, 193-212.

--- (1917a), 'Inscriptions du mastaba de Pepy-Nefer à Edfou', *Annales du Service des Antiquités de l'Égypte,* 17, 130-40.

--- (1917b), 'Monuments d'Edfou datant du Moyen Empire', *Annales du Service des Antiquités de l'Égypte,* 17, 237-44.

Darnell, J. C. (2010), 'Opet Festival', in J. Dieleman & W. Wendrich (ed.), *UCLA Encyclopedia of Egyptology* (Los Angeles: http://digital2.library.ucla.edu/viewItem.do?ark=21198/zz0025n765).

Dasen, V. (1993), *Dwarfs in Ancient Egypt* (Oxford: Oxford University Press).

David, A. R. (1973), *Religious Ritual at Abydos (c. 1300 BC)* (Warminster: Aris & Phillips Ltd.).

--- (1981), *A Guide to Religious Ritual at Abydos* (Warminster: Aris & Phillips Ltd.).

--- (1996), *The Pyramid Builders of Ancient Egypt* (London: Routledge).

--- (2002), *Religion and Magic in Ancient Egypt* (London: Penguin).

Davies, N. de Garis. (1902), *The Rock Tombs of Deir el Gebrâwi at El Amarna*, 2 vols. (2; London: Egypt Exploration Fund).

--- (1903-8), *The Rock Tombs of El Amarna*, 6 vols. (Archaeological Survey of Egypt; London: Egypt Exploration Fund).

--- (1913), *Five Theban Tombs* (London: Egypt Exploration Fund).

--- (1920), *The Tomb of Antefoker, Vizier of Sesostris I, and his Wife, Senet (No. 60)* (The Theban Tomb Series, Memoir 2; London: G. Allen & Unwin).

--- (1926), *The Tomb of Huy, Viceroy of Nubia in the Reign of Tutankhamūn (No. 40) / copied in line and colour by N. de Garis Davies and with explanatory text by A. H. Gardiner* (London: Egypt Exploration Society).

--- (1932), 'Tehuti: Owner of Tomb 110 at Thebes', in S. R. K. Glanville (ed.), *Studies Presented to F. Ll. Griffith* (London: Oxford University Press), 279-90.

--- (1933), *The Tomb of Nefer-Hotep at Thebes*, 2 vols. (1; New York: Metropolitan Museum of Art).

--- (1943), *The Tomb of Rekh-mi-re*, 2 vols. (Publications of the Metropolitan Museum of New York, 1; New York: Metropolitan Museum of Art).

--- (1948), *Seven Private Tombs at Kurnah*, 2 vols. (Mond Excavations at Thebes, 2; London: Egypt Exploration Society).

Davies, N. de Garis & Gardiner, A. H. (1915), *The Tomb of Amenemhet* (London: Egypt Exploration Fund).

Debono, F. (1951), 'Expédition archéologique royale au désert oriental (Keft-Kosseir). Rapport préliminaire sur la campaigne 1949', *Annales du Service des Antiquités de l'Égypte*, 51, 59-110.

Derchain, P. (1965), *Le Papyrus Salt 825 (B.M. 10051)*, 2 vols. (Bruxelles: Palais des Académies).

De Meyer, M. (2011), 'The fifth dynasty royal decree of Ia-ib at Dayr Al-Barshā', *Revue d'égyptologie* 62, 57-64.

Dieleman, J. (2005), *Priests, Tongues, and Rites: The London-Leiden Magical Manuscripts and Translation in Egyptian Ritual* (Religions in the Ancient World; Leiden & Boston: E. J. Brill).

Dominicus, B. (1994), *Gesten und Gebärden in Darstellungen des Alten und Mittleren Reiches* (Studien zur Archäologie und Geschichte Altägyptens; Heidelberg: Heidelberger Orientverlag).

Donohue, V. A. (1978), '*"pr-nfr"*', *Journal of Egyptian Archaeology*, 64, 143-48.

Doxey, D. M. (2001), 'Priesthood', in D. Redford (ed.), *The Oxford Encyclopedia of Ancient Egypt*, 3 vols. (3; Oxford: Oxford University Press), 68-73.

Drioton, É. (1943), 'Description soumaines des chapelles funéraires de la VI dynasty', *Annales du Service des Antiquités de l'Égypte*, 43, 487-514.

--- (1948), *Le texte dramatique d'Edfou* (Le Caire: Imprimerie de l'Institut Français d'Archéologie Orientale).

Duell, P. (1938), *The Mastaba of Mereruka / by the Sakkarah Expedition*, 2 vols. (2; Chicago: University of Chicago Press).

Dümichen, J. (1877), *Baugeschichte des Denderatempels und Beschreibung der Einzelnen Theile des Bauwerkes* (Strassburg: K. J. Trübner).

Dunham, D. (1938), 'The biographical inscriptions of Nekhebu in Boston and Cairo', *Journal of Egyptian Archaeology*, 24 (1), 1-8.

Dunham, D. & Simpson, W. K. (1974), *Giza Mastabas Vol. 1: The Mastaba of Queen Meresankh III* (Boston: Museum of Fine Arts).

Eaton, K. J. (2007), 'Memorial temples in the sacred landscape of Nineteenth Dynasty Abydos: An overview of processional routes and equipment', in Z. Hawass & J. Richards (ed.), *The Archaeology and Art of Ancient Egypt. Essays in Honor of David B. O'Connor*, 2 vols. (1; Cairo: Service des Antiquités de l'Égypte), 231-50.

Eaton-Krauss, M. (1984), *The Representations of Statuary in Private Tombs of the Old Kingdom* (Ägyptologische Abhandlungen, Band 39; Wiesbaden: Otto Harrassowitz).

Edel, E. (1969), 'Beiträge zum ägyptischen Lexikon V', *Zeitschrift für Ägyptische Sprache und Altertumskunde*, 96, 4-14.

--- (1976), *Ägyptische Ärzte und ägyptische Medizin am hethitischen Königshof : neue Funde von Keilschriftbriefen Ramses' II aus Boğazköy* (Opladen: Westdeutscher Verlag).

Edgar, C. C. (1907), 'Middle Empire tombs in the Delta', in G. Maspero (ed.), *Le Musée Égyptien II* (Le Caire: L'Institut Français d'Archéologie Orientale du Caire), 109-18.

Egberts, A. (1995), *In Quest of Meaning: a Study of the Ancient Egyptian Rites of Consecrating the Meret-Chests and Driving the Calves*, 2 vols. (Egyptologische Uitgaven 8, 1; Leiden: Nederlands Instituut voor het Nabije Oosten).

Egyptian Monuments. http://www.egyptsites.wordpress/ Online. Accessed 15.07.2011.

Eichler, E. (1993), *'Untersuchungen zum Expeditionswesen des ägyptischen Alten Reiches'* (Göttinger Orientforschungen. IV. Reihe, Ägypten 26; Wiesbaden: Harrassowitz).

El-Amir, M. (1959), *A Family Archive from Thebes: Demotic Papyri in the Philadelphia and Cairo Museums from the Ptolemaic Period* (Cairo: General Organisation for Government Printing Offices).

El-Khouli, A. (1978), 'Excavations at the Pyramid of Userkhaf, 1976: Preliminary Report', *Journal of Egyptian Archaeology,* 64, 35-43.

--- (1980), 'Excavations at the Pyramid of Userkhaf, 1979: Preliminary Report', *Journal of Egyptian Archaeology,* 66, 46-8.

Englebach, R. (1923), *Harageh* (London: British School of Archaeology in Egypt).

Enmarch, R. T. (2011), 'Of spice and mine: The tale of the shipwrecked sailor and Middle Kingdom expedition inscriptions', in F. Hagen, J. Johnston, W. Monkhouse, K. Piquette, J. Tait & M. Worthington (ed.)' *Narratives of Egypt and the Ancient Near East: Literary and Linguistic Approaches.* (Orientalia Lovaniensia Analecta 189; Leuven: Peeters), 97-121.

Epigraphic Survey (1940), *Festival Scenes of Ramesses III: Medinet Habu IV* (Oriental Institute Publications 51; Chicago: University of Chicago Press).

--- (1980), *The Tomb of Kheruef, Theban Tomb 192* (Oriental Institute Publications 102; Chicago: The University of Chicago Press).

Erman, A. & Grapow, H. (ed.) (1926-63), *Worterbuch der äegyptischen Sprache,* 7 vols (Berlin & Leipzig: J.C. Hinrichs'sche Buchhandlung).

Erman, A. & Steindorff, G. (1902/1903), 'Besoldungsverhältnisse von Priestern im mittleren Reich', *Zeitschrift für Ägyptische Sprache und Altertumskunde,* 40, 113-17.

Espinel, A. D. (2005), 'A newly identified stela from Wadi el-Hudi (Cairo JE 86119)', *Journal of Egypian Archaeology,* 91, 55-70.

Étienne, M. (2000), *Heka: magie et envoûtement dans l'Égypt ancienne* (Paris: Réunion des Musées Nationaux).

Eyre, C. J. (1992), 'Yet again the wax crocodile: P. Westcar 3, 12ff', *Journal of Egyptian Archaeology,* 78, 280-1.

--- (2002), *The Cannibal Hymn: A Cultural and Literary Study* (Liverpool: Liverpool University Press).

Fairman, H. W. (1954-1955), 'Worship and festivals in an Egyptian temple', in The Librarian (ed.), *Bulletin of the John Rylands Library* (Manchester: Manchester University Press), 165-203.

--- (1958), 'The kingship rituals of Egypt', in S. H. Hooke (ed.), *Myth, Ritual and Kingship: Essays on the Theory and Practice of Kingship in the Ancient Near East and in Israel* (Oxford: Clarendon Press), 74-104.

--- (1974), *The Triumph of Horus* (London: B. T. Batsford Ltd.).

Fakhry, A. (1943), 'A note on the tomb of Kheruef at Thebes', *Annales du Service des Antiquitiés de L'Égypte,* 42, 449-508.

--- (1952), *The Inscriptions of the Amethyst Quarries at Wadi El Hudi* (Cairo: Government Press).

--- (1961), *The Monuments of Sneferu at Dahshur: Vol. 2, The Valley Temple: Part 2, the Finds* (Cairo: General Organization for Government Printing Offices).

Faulkner, R. O. (1936), 'The Bremner-Rhind Papyrus - I', *Journal of Egyptian Archaeology,* 23 (2), 121-40.

--- (1937a), 'The Bremner-Rhind Papyrus - II', *Journal of Egyptian Archaeology,* 23 (1), 10-16.

--- (1937b), 'The Bremner-Rhind Papyrus - III', *Journal of Egyptian Archaeology,* 23 (2), 166-85.

--- (1962), *A Concise Dictionary of Middle Egyptian* (Oxford: Griffith Institute).

--- (1969), *The Ancient Egyptian Pyramid Texts* (Oxford: Clarendon Press).

--- (1973), *The Ancient Egyptian Coffin Texts, Volume 1* (Warminster: Aris & Phillips).

--- (1977), *The Ancient Egyptian Coffin Texts, Volume 2* (Warminster: Aris & Phillips).

--- (1978), *The Ancient Egyptian Coffin Texts, Volume 3* (Warminster: Aris & Phillips).

--- (1985), *The Ancient Egyptian Book of the Dead* (London: British Museum Press).

Firth, C. M. & Gunn, B. (1926), *Teti Pyramid Cemeteries* (Le Caire: Imprimerie de l'Institut Français d'Archéologie Orientale).

Fischer, H. G. (1963), 'A Stela of the Heracleopolitan Period at Saqqara', *Zeitschrift für Ägyptische Sprache und Altertumskunde,* 90, 35-41.

--- (1966a), 'An Old Kingdom monogram', *Zeitschrift für Ägyptische Sprache und Altertumskunde,,* 93, 56-69.

--- (1966b), 'Egyptian turtles', *The Metropolitan Museum of Art Bulletin, New Series,* 24 (6), 193-200.

--- (1997), *Egyptian Titles of the Middle Kingdom; A Supplement to Wm. Ward's Index* (New York: Metropolitan Museum of Art).

Fischer-Elfert, H. -W. (1998), *Die Vision von der Statue im Stein* (Heidelberger Akademie Der Wissenschaften; Heidelberg: Universitätsverlag C. Winter).

Forman, W. & Quirke, S. (1996), *Hieroglyphs and the Afterlife* (London: British Museum).

Forshaw, R. J. (2009), 'The practice of dentistry in ancient Egypt', *British Dental Journal,* 206, 481-6.

--- (2014), 'Before Hippocrates: Healing practices in ancient Egypt', in E. Gemi-Iordanou, S. Gordon, R. Matthew, E. McInnes & R. Pettit (ed.), *Medicine, Healing and Performance* (Oxford & Philadelphia: Oxbow Books), 25-41.

Frankfort, H., de Buck, A. & Gunn, B. (1933), *The Cenotaph of Seti I at Abydos. Vol I: Texts* (Excavation Memoirs, The Egypt Exploration Society; London: Egypt Exploration Society).

--- (1933), *The Cenoptah of Seti I at Abydos. Vol II: Plates* (Excavation Memoirs, The Egypt Exploration Society; London: Egypt Exploration Society).

Frankfort, H. (1948), *Kingship and the Gods* (Chicago: University of Chicago Press).

Frankfurter, D. (1994), 'The magic of writing and the writing of magic: The power of the word in Egyptian and Greek traditions', *Helios,* 21 (2), 191-221.

--- (1995), 'Narrating power: the theory and practice of the magical *historiola* in ritual spells', in M. Meyer & P. Mirecki (ed.), *Ancient Magic and Ritual Power* (Leiden: E. J. Brill), 451-70.

Gaballa, G. A. & Kitchen, K. A. (1969), 'The Festival of Sokar', *Orientalia,* 38, 1-76.

Galán, J. M. (2000), 'The ancient Egyptian Sed-festival and the exemption from corvée', *Journal of Near Eastern Studies,* 59 (4), 255-64.

Gardiner, A. H. (1905), *The Inscription of Mes* (Untersuchungen zur Geschichte und Altertumskunde Aegyptens IV, 3; Leipzig: J. C. Hinriches).

--- (1906), 'Four papyri of the 18th Dynasty from Kahun', *Zeitschrift für Ägyptische Sprache und Altertumskunde,* 43, 27-47.

--- (1917), 'Professional magicians in ancient Egypt', *Proceedings of the Society of Biblical Archaeology,* 39, 31-44.

--- (1925), 'The autobiography of Rekhmire', *Zeitschrift für Ägyptische Sprache und Altertumskunde,* 60, 62-76.

--- (1931), *The Library of A. Chester Beatty: The Chester Beatty Papyri I* (London: Oxford University Press).

--- (1935), *Hieratic Papyri in the British Museum, Third Series Chester Beatty Gift*, 2 vols. (1; London: British Museum).

--- (1937), *Late Egyptian Miscellanies* (Bruxelles: Édition de la Fondation Égyptologique Reine Élisabeth).

--- (1938a), 'The House of Life', *Journal of Egyptian Archaeology,* 24, 157-79.

--- (1938b), 'The Mansion of Life and the Master of the King's Largess', *Journal of Egyptian Archaeology,* 24 (1), 83-91.

--- (1947), *Ancient Egyptian Onomastica*, 3 vols. (1; London: Oxford University Press).

--- (1950), 'The baptism of the Pharaoh', *Journal of Egyptian Archaeology,* 36, 3-12.

--- (1952), 'Tuthmosis III returns thanks to Amun', *Journal of Egyptian Archaeology,* 38, 6-23.

--- (1955a), 'A unique funerary liturgy', *Journal of Egyptian Archaeology,* 41, 9-17.

--- (1955b), *The Ramesseum Papyri* (Oxford: Oxford University Press for the Griffith Institute).

--- (1957), *Egyptian Grammar* (Oxford: Griffith Institute, Ashmolean Museum).

Gardiner, A. H. & Peet, T. E. (1917), *The Inscriptions of Sinai. Part I: Introduction and Plates* (London: Sold at the offices of the Egypt Exploration Fund).

Gardiner, A. H. & Weigall, A. E. P. (1913), *A Topographical Catalogue of the Private Tombs of Thebes* (London: Bernard Quaritch).

Gardiner, A. H., Peet, T. E. & Černý, J. (1955), *The Inscriptions of Sinai. Part II: Translations and Commentary*, 2 vols. (2; London: Egypt Exploration Society).

Garstang, J. (1913), 'Excavations at Abydos 1909. Preliminary description of the principal finds', *Liverpool Annals of Archaeology & Anthropology,* 5, 107-11.

Gauthier, H. (1922), 'À travers la Basse-Égypte', *Annales du Service des Antiquités de l'Égypte,* 22, 199-208.

Gayet, A. (1889), *Musée du Louvre: stèles de la XIIe dynastie* (Paris: E. Vieweg).

Gee, J. L. (1998), *The Requirements of Ritual Purity in Ancient Egypt* (New Haven: Yale University).

--- (2004), 'Prophets, initiation and the Egyptian temple', *Journal of the Society for the Study of Egyptian Antiquities,* 31, 97-107.

Ghalioungui, P. (1963), *Magic and Medical Science in Ancient Egypt* (London: Hodder and Stoughton).

--- (1983), *The Physicians of Pharaonic Egypt* (Cairo: Al-Ahram Center for Scientific Translations).

--- (1987), *The Ebers Papyrus* (Cairo: Academy of Scientific Research and Technology).

Gillam, R. (2009), *Performance and Drama in Ancient Egypt* (London: Duckworth).

Giorgini, M. S., Robichon, C. & Leclant, J. (1998), *Soleb V: Le Temple* (Le Caire: L'Institut français d'archéologie orientale du Caire).

Giveon, R. (1974), 'Investigations in the Egyptian mining centres in Sinai', *Tel Aviv,* 1, 100-08.

--- (1978), *The Stones of Sinai Speak* (Tokyo: Gakuseisha Publishing Co., Ltd.).

Godron, G. (1990), *Études sur l'Horus Den et quelques problèmes de l'Égypte archaïque* (Cahiers d'Orientalisme 19; Geneva: Patrick Cramer).

Goedicke, H. (1959), 'A new inscription from Hatnub', *Annales du Service des Antiquités de l'Égypte,* 56, 55-8.

--- (1963), ''Was magic used in the Harem Conspiracy against Ramesses III? (P. Rollin and P. Lee)", *Journal of Egyptian Archaeology,* 49, 71-92.

--- (1964), 'Some remarks on stone quarrying in the Egyptian Middle Kingdom (2060-1786 BC)', *Journal of the American Research Center in Egypt* 3, 43-50.

--- (1974), 'The Berlin Leather Roll (Papyrus Berlin 3029)', in W. Müller (ed.), *Festschrift zum 150 jährigen Bestehen des Berliner Ägyptischen Museums, Staatliche Museen zu Berlin* (Mitteilungen aus der Ägyptischen Sammlung, Band VII; Berlin: Akademie-Verlag), 87-104.

--- (1994), *Comments on the "Famine Stela"* (San Antonio, Texas: Van Siclen Books).

Goelet, O. (2001), 'Tomb Robbery Papyri', in D. B. Redford (ed.), *The Oxford Encyclopedia of Ancient Egypt* (3; Oxford: Oxford University Press), 417-8.

Goetze, A. (1947), 'A new letter from Ramesses to Hattusilis', *Journal of Cuneiform Studies,* 1 (3), 241-51.

Gohary, J. (1992), *Akhenaten's Sed-Festival at Karnak* (London and New York: Kegan Paul International).

--- (1913 (this edition 1993)), *Les transcriptions des papyrus hiératiques nos. 1116A (verso) et 1116B (verso) de l'Ermitage Impérial à St-Pétersbourg* (San Antonio, Texas: Van Siclen).

Golénischeff, V. S. (1927), *Papyrus Hiératiques* (Cairo: Catalogue général des antiquités égyptiennes du Musée du Caire 83).

Goyon, G. (1957), *Nouvelles inscriptions rupestres du Wadi Hammamat* (Paris: Imprimerie Nationale, Librarie d'Amérique et d'Orient Adrien-Masionneuve).

Goyon, J-C. (1972), *Rituels funéraires de l'ancienne Egypte (Le Rituel de l'Embaumement, le Rituel de* *l'Overture de la Bouche, les Livres des Respirations)* (Paris: Éditions du Cerf).

--- (1978), 'La fête de Sokaris à Edfou à la lumière d'un texte liturgique remontant au Nouvel Empire', *Bulletin de l'Institut Français d'Archéologie Orientale* 78, 415-38.

--- (1979), 'The decoration of the Edifice', in R. A. Parker, J. Leclant & J-C. Goyon (ed.), *The edifice of Taharqa by the sacred lake* (Brown Egyptological Studies; Providence: Brown University), 11-45.

Grajetzki, W. (2006), *The Middle Kingdom of Ancient Egypt* (London: Duckworth & Co. Ltd.).

--- (2009), *Court Officials of the Egyptian Middle Kingdom* (London: Duckworth & Co. Ltd.).

Grajetzki, W., Quirke, S. & Shiode, N. (2000), 'Digital Egypt for Universities', http://www.digitalegypt.ucla.ac.uk, University College London. Online. Accessed 06.02.2012.

Grandet, P. (1994), *Le Papyrus Harris 1 (BM 9999)*, 2 vols. (Bibliothèque d'Étude 109/1-2, 1; Le Caire: Imprimerie de l'Institut Français d'Archéologie Orientale du Caire).

Grapow, H. (1958), *Die Medizinischen Texte in Hieroglyphischer Umschreibung Autographiert*, 11 vols. (Grundriss der Medizin der Alten Ägypter, 5; Berlin: Akademie-Verlag).

Grdseloff, B. (1938), 'La lecture et le sens du mot *db3ḫ*', *Annales du Service des Antiquités de l'Égypte,* 38, 353-4.

--- (1941), *Das Ägyptische Reinigungszelt* (Le Caire: L'Institut Français d'Archéologie Orientale du Caire).

--- (1949), *Une Stèle scythopolitaine du roi Séthos ler* (Le Caire: Imprimerie Le Scribe Égyptien).

--- (1951), 'Nouvelles données concernant la tente de purification', *Annales du Service des Antiquités de L'Égypte,* 51, 129-40.

Green, L. (2001), 'Clothing and personal adornment', in D. B. Redford (ed.), *Oxford Encyclopedia of Ancient Egypt* (1; Oxford: Oxford University Press), 274-9.

Gregorian Egyptian Museum Collection Online. "22690" http://mv.vatican.va/, Gregorian Egyptian Museum, Vatican. Online. Acessed 14.07.2011.

Griffith, F. Ll. (1889), *The Inscriptions of Siût and Dêr Rîfeh* (London: Trübner and Co.).

--- (1898), *Hieratic Papyri from Kahun and Gurob* (London: Bernard Quaritch).

--- (1900), *Stories of the High Priests of Memphis*, 2 vols. (1; Oxford: Clarendon Press).

Grimal, N. (1992), *A History of Ancient Egypt* (Oxford: Blackwell Publishing).

Grunert, S. (1981), *Thebanische Kaufvertrage Des 3. Und 2. Jahrhunderts V. U. Z. (Demotische Papyri Aus Den Staatlichen Museen Zu Berlin)* (Berlin: Akademie-Verlag).

Gundlach, R. (2011), 'The Berlin Leather Roll (pBerlin 3029)', in R. Gundlach & K. Spence (ed.), *5th Symposium on Egyptian Royal Ideology: Palace and Temple* (Wiesbaden: Harrassowitz Verlag), 103-14.

Günther, R. (1913), *Äegyptische Inschriften aus den Königliche Museen zu Berlin* (Leipzig: J. C. Hinrichs).

Habachi, L. & Ghalioungui, P. (1971), 'The "House of Life" at Bubastis', *Chronique d'Égypte,* 91, 59-71.

Haeny, G. (1997), 'New Kingdom 'mortuary temples' and 'mansions of millions of years'', in B. E. Shafer (ed.), *Temples of Ancient Egypt* (Ithaca, New York: Cornell University Press), 86-126.

Haikal, F. M. H. (1970-1972), *Two Hieratic Funerary Papyri of Nesmin,* 2 vols. (Bibliotheca Aegyptiaca, 2; Bruxelles: Fondation Égyptologique Reine Elisabeth).

Haiying, Y. (1995), 'The Famine Stela: A source-critical approach and historical-comparative perspective', in C. Eyre (ed.), *Proceedings of the Seventh International Congress of Egyptologists* (Orientalia Lovaniensia Analecta; Leuven: Uitgeverij Peeters), 515-21.

Halioua, B. & Ziskind, B. (2005), *Medicine in the Days of the Pharaohs* (Cambridge, Massachusetts and London: Belknap Press of Harvard University).

Handleman, D. (1990), *Models and Mirrors: Towards an Anthropology of Public Events* (Cambridge: Cambridge University Press).

Haring, B. J. J. (1997), *Divine Households: Administrative and Economic Aspects of the New Kingdom Royal Memorial Temples in Western Thebes* (Egyptologische Uitgaven 12; Leiden: Nederlands Institut voor Het Nabije Oosten).

Harpur, Y. & Scremin, P. (2006), *The Chapel of Kagemni: Scene Details*, (Egypt in Miniature: Volume One; Oxford: Oxford Expedition to Egypt).

Harrell, J. A. (2002), 'Pharaonic stone quarries in the Egyptian deserts', in R. Friedman (ed.), *Egypt and Nubia: Gifts of the Desert* (London: British Museum Press), 232-43.

Hassan, S. (1932-1960), *Excavations at Giza*, 10 vols. (Cairo: Government Press, Bulâq).

--- (1938), 'Excavations at Saqqara (1937-1938)', *Annales du Service des Antiquités de l'Égypte,* (38), 503-21.

Hayes, W. C. (1953), *The Scepter of Egypt: A Background for the Study of the Egyptian Antiquities in the Metropolitan Museum of Art. Part I: From the Earliest Times to the End of the Middle KIngdom* (New York: Metropolitan Museum of Art).

--- (1955), *A Papyrus of the Late Middle Kingdom in the Brooklyn Museum* (New York: The Brooklyn Museum).

--- (1959), *The Sceptre of Egypt: A Background for the Study of the Egyptian Antiquities in the Metropolitan Museum of Art. Part II: The Hyksos Period and The New Kingdom (1675-1080 BC)* (New York: Metropolitan Museum of Art).

Hays, H. M. (2009a), 'Between identity and agency in ancient Egyptian ritual', in R. Nyord & A. Kyolby (ed.), *Being in Ancient Egypt: Thoughts on Agency, Materiality and Cognition* (Oxford: Archaeopress), 15-30.

--- (2009b), 'The Ritual Scenes in the Chapels of Amun', *Medinet Habu IX. The Eighteenth Dynasty Temple, Part I: The Inner Sanctuaries* (OIP 136; Chicago: The Oriental Institute of the University of Chicago), 1-14.

--- (2010), 'Funerary rituals (Pharaonic Period)', in J. Dieleman & W. Wendrich (ed.), *UCLA Encyclopedia of Egyptology* (Los Angeles: http://www.escholarship.org/uc/item/1r32g9zn).

Helck, W. (1954), *Untersuchungen zu den Beamtentiteln des Ägyptischen Alten Reiches* (Glückstadt, Hamburg & New York: Verlag J. J. Augustin).

--- (1958), *Zur Verwaltung des Mittleren und Neun Reiches, no. 3* (Probleme der Ägyptologie; Leiden: E. J. Brill).

--- (1963), 'Der Papyrus Berlin P 3047', *Journal of the American Research Center in Egypt,* 2, 65-73.

--- (1970), *Die Prophezeiung des Nfr-ty* (Wiesbaden: Otto Harassowitz).

--- (1977), 'Die "Weihinschriften" aus dem Taltempel des Sonnenheiligtums des Königs Neuserre bei Abu Gurob', *Studien zur Altägyptischen Kultur,* 5, 47-77.

--- (1984), "Schamane und Zauberer", *Mélanges Adolphe Gutbub* (Montpellier: Université Paul Valéry de Montpellier), 103-08.

--- (1988), *Die Lehre für König Merikare* (Wiesbaden: O. Harrassowitz).

Herbin, F. R. (1994), *Le Livre de Parcourir l'Éternité* (Orientalia Lovaniensia Analecta 58; Leuven: Peeters).

Hernández, R. A. Diaz (2014), 'Der Ramesseumpapyrus E in Ritualbuch für Bestattungun aus dem Mittleren Reich', *Göttinger Miszellen,* Beihefte Nr. 15.

Herodotus & de Sélincourt, A. (1996), *The Histories / Herodotus; Newly Translated and with an Introduction by Aubrey de Sélincourt* (Harmondsworth, Middlesex: Penguin Books).

Hill, J. (2010), http://wwwancientegyptonline.co.uk, 'Ancient Egypt Online'. Online. Accessed 15.7.2011.

Hikade, T. (2001), *Das Expeditionswesen im ägyptischen Neuen Reich: Ein Beitrag zu Rohstoffversorgung und Aussenhandel* (Studien zur Archäologie und Geschichte Altägyptens 21; Heidelberger: Heidelberger Orientverlag).

Hofmann, E. (1995), *Das Grab des Neferrenpet gen; Kenro (TT 178)* (Mainz am Rhein: von Zabern).

Hornung, E. & Staehelin, E. (1974), *Studien Zum Zedfest* (Aegyptiaca Helvetica I; Geneva: Édition de Belles-Lettres).

Hornung, E. (1982), *Der Ägyptische Mythos von der Himmelskuh. Eine Ätiologie des Unvollkommenen* (Orbis Biblicus et Orientalis, 46; Freiburg: Universitätsverlag).

--- (1999), *The Ancient Egyptian Books of the Afterlife (Translated from German by D. Lorton)* (New York: Cornell University Press).

Houlihan, P. F. (2001), 'Hedgehogs', in D. B. Redford (ed.), *Oxford Encyclopedia of Ancient Egypt,* 3 vols. (2; Oxford: Oxford University Press), 87-8.

Ikram, S. (2001), 'Diet', in D. B. Redford (ed.), *Oxford Encyclopedia of Ancient Egypt,* 3 vols. (1; Oxford: Oxford University Press), 390-5.

Jackson, R. & La Niece, S. (1986), 'A set of Roman medical instruments from Italy', *Britannia,* 17, 267-71.

Jacquet-Gordon, H. (2003), *The Graffiti on the Khonsu Temple Roof at Karnak: A Manifestation of Personal Piety vol. 3* (Oriental Institute Publications; Chicago 123: The Oriental Institute of the University of Chicago).

James, T. G. H. & Apted, M. R. (1953), *The Mastaba of Khentika called Ikhekhi* (London: Egypt Exploration Society).

Jéquier, G. (1938), *Fouilles à Saqqarah: Le monument funéraire de Pepi II,* 2 vols. (2; Le Caire: Imprimerie de l'Institut Français d'Archéologie Orientale).

Johnson, J. (1986), 'The role of the Egyptian priesthood in Ptolemaic Egypt', in L. H. Lesko (ed.), *Egyptological Studies in Honor of Richard A. Parker* (Hanover and London: University Press of New England), 70-84.

--- (2001), *The Demotic Dictionary of the Oriental Institute of the University of Chicago* (Chicago: The Oriental Institute of the University of Chicago).

Jonckheere, F. (1958), *Les Médecins de l'Égypte Pharaonique, essai des Prosopographie* (Brussels: Edition de la Fondation Égyptologique Reine Elizabeth).

Jones, D. (2000), *An Index of Ancient Egyptian Titles, Epithets and Phrases of the Old Kingdom,* 2 vols. (BAR International Series 866; Oxford: Archaeopress).

Junge, F. (2001), *Late Egyptian Grammar: An Introduction* (Oxford: Griffith Institute).

Junker, H. (1929-1955), *Gîza : Bericht über die von der Akademie der Wissenschaften in Wien auf gemeinsame Kosten mit Dr. Wilhelm Pelizaeus unternommenen Grabungen auf dem Friedhof des Alten Reiches bei den Pyramiden von Gîza* 12 vols. (Wien und Leipzig: Hölder-Pichler-Tempsky A. G.).

--- (1932), 'Die Grabungen der Akademie der Wissenschaften in Wien auf der Vorgeschichtlichen Siedlung Merimde-Benisalame', *Mitteilungen des Deutschen Archäologischen Instituts, Abteilung Kairo,* 3, 168-69.

Kaiser, W. (1971), 'Die kleine Hebseddarstellung im Sonnenheiligtum des Neuserre', in Geburtstag von Herbert Ricke. (ed.), *Beiträge zur ägyptischen Bauforschung und Altertumskunde* (12; Wiesbaden: Schweizerische Institut für Ägyptische Bauforschung und Altertumskunde in Kairo), 87-105.

Kamal, A, Bey (1912), 'Fouilles à Dara et à Qoçéir el-Amarna', *Annales du Service des Antiquités de l'Égypte,* 12, 128-42.

Kargacin, A. (2010), 'Archaeology and Literature: The Case of the Ramesseum Tomb Assemblage', MPhil unpublished (University of Cambridge).

Karkowski, J. (1979), 'Schriften zur Geschichte und Kultur des Alten Orients', in W. F. Reineke (ed.), *First International Congress of Egyptology, Cairo 1976* (Berlin: Akademie Verlag), 359-64.

--- (1992), 'Notes on the Beautiful Feast of the Valley as represented in Hatshepsut's temple at Deir el-Bahri', in S. Jakobielski & J. Karkowski. (ed.), *50 Years of Polish Excavations in Egypt and the Near East* (Warsaw University: Varsovie), 155-66.

Kees, H. (1914), 'Hierzu eine Abbildung', *Recueil de Travaux,* 36, 1-16.

--- (1926), *Totenglauben und Jenseitsvorstellungen der alten Ägypter: Grundlagen und Entwicklung bis zum Ende des Mittleren Reiches* (Leipzig: J. C. Hinrichs).

--- (1953-8), *Das Priestertum im ägyptischen Staat vom neuen Reich bis zur Spätzeit*, 2 vols. (Leiden: E. J. Brill).

--- (1956), *Der Götterglaube im alten Ägypten* (Berlin: Akademie Verlag).

--- (1962), 'Der sogenannte oberste Vorlespriester', *Zeitschrift für Ägyptische Sprache und Altertumskunde*, 87, 119-39.

Kemp, B. J. (1989), *Ancient Egypt: Anatomy of a Civilisation* (London and New York: Routledge).

Kemp, B. J. & Merrillees, R. (1980), *Minoan Pottery in Second Millennium Egypt* (Mainz Am Rhein: Verlag Philipp von Zabern).

Kitchen, K. A. (1969-1990), *Ramesside Inscriptions: Historical and Biographical*, 8 vols. (Oxford: B. H. Blackwell Ltd.).

--- (1982), *Pharaoh Triumphant: The Life and Times of Ramesses II* (Warmister: Aris & Phillips).

--- (1996), *The Third Intermediate Period* (Oxford: Aris & Phillips).

Köp-Junk, H. (2013), 'Travel', in E. Frood & W. Wendrich (ed.), *UCLA Encyclopedia of Egyptology*, Los Angeles. http://digital2.library.ucla.edu/viewItem.do?ark=21198/zz002gvznf

Kousoulis, P. I. M. (2003), 'The function of *ḥkꜣ* as a mobilized form in a theological environment: the apotropaic "Ritual of Overthrowing Apophis" ', in Z. Hawass (ed.), *Egyptology at the Dawn of the Twenty-first Century. Volume 2 History, Religion* (Cairo & New York: The American University in Cairo Press), 362-71.

Krauss, R. (1985), *Sothis- und Monddaten: Studien zur astronmischen und technischen Chronologie Altägyptens* (Hildesheim: Gerstenberg).

Kruchten, J-M. (2001), 'Law', in D. B. Redford (ed.), *Oxford Encyclopedia of Ancient Egypt*, 3 vols. (2; Oxford: Oxford University Press), 277-82.

Kucharek, A. (2005), '70 Tage - Trauerphasen und Trauerriten in Ägypten', in J. Assmann *et al.* (ed.), *Der Abschied von den Toten: Trauerrituale im Kulturvergleich* (Göttingen: Wallstein), 342-58.

Kurth, D. (2004), *The Temple of Edfu. A Guide by an Ancient Egyptian Priest* (Cairo: The American University in Cairo Press).

Kyffin, J. (2011), ''A true secret of the House of Life': Prosody, intertext and performance in magical texts', in J. Johnston, F. Hagen, W. Monkhouse, K. Piquette, J. Tait & M. Worthington (ed.), *Narratives of Egypt and the Ancient Near East* (Orientalia Lovaniensia Analecta, 189; Leuven: Peeters), 224-55.

Lacau, P. & Chevrier, H. (1977-79), *Une Chapelle d'Hatshepsout à Karnak*, 2 vols. (Le Caire: L'Institut Français d'Archéologie Orientale).

Lacau, P. & Lauer, J.-P. (1959-1961), *La Pyramide À Degrés. Tome IV Inscriptions Gravées sur les Vases*, 2 vols. (Fouilles À Saqqarah; Paris: Institut Français d'Archéologie Orientale).

Lange, E. (2009), 'The Sed-festival reliefs of Osorkon II at Bubastis: New investigations', in G. P. F. Broekman, R. J. Demarée & O. E. Kaper (ed.), *The Libyan Period in Egypt* (Leiden: Nederlands Instituut Het Nabije Oosten), 203-18.

Lange, H. O. (1927), *Der magische Papyrus Harris* (Copenhagen: Andr. Fred. Høst & Søn).

Lange, H. O. & Schäfer, H. (1902-1925), *Grab- und Denkstein des Mittleren Reiches*, 4 vols. (Catalogue Général des Antiquités Égyptiennes du Musée du Caire; Berlin: Reichsdruckerei).

Leach, B. (2006), 'A conservation history of the Ramesseum Papyri', *Journal of Egyptian Archaeology*, 92, 225-40.

Leahy, A. (1984), 'Death by fire in ancient Egypt', *Journal of the Economic and Social History of the Orient*, 27 (2), 199-206.

Leblanc, C. (2004), 'L'école du temple (ât-sebaït) et le per-ankh (maison de vie): À propos de récentes découvertes effectuées dans le contexte du Ramesseum.' *Memnonia*, 15, 93-101.

Lefebvre, G. (1929), *Histoire des grands prêtres d'Amon de Karnak* (Paris: Librairie Orientaliste Paul Geuthner).

Leiden, Rijksmuseum van Oudheden te (1905), *Beschreibung der Ägyptischen Sammlung des Niederländischen Reichsmuseums der Altertümer im Leiden*, 9 vols. (1; Haag: M. Nijhoff).

Leitz, C. (1999), *Magical and Medical Papyri of the New Kingdom* (Hieratic Papyri in the British Museum. Vol 7; London: British Museum).

Lichtheim, M. (1973), *Ancient Egyptian Literature Volume 1: The Old and Middle Kingdoms* (Berkeley, Los Angeles, London: Unversity of California Press).

--- (1976), *Ancient Egyptian Literature. Volume II: The New Kingdom* (Berkeley, California: University of California Press).

--- (1980), *Ancient Egyptian Literature. Volume III: The Late Period* (Berkeley, California: University of California Press).

--- (1988), *Ancient Egyptian Autobiographies Chiefly of the Middle Kingdom: A Study and an Anthology* (Orbis Biblicus et Orientalis; Freiburg: Universitätsverlag).

von Lievan, A. (2012), 'Book of the Dead, Book of the Living: BD Spells as temple texts', *Journal of Egyptian Archaeology*, 98, 249-67.

Lloyd, A. B. (1982), 'The inscription of Udjaḥorresnet: A collaborator's testament', *Journal of Egyptian Archaeology*, 68, 166-80.

--- (1983), 'The Late Period', in B. J. Kemp, B. G. Trigger, D. O'Connor & A. B. Lloyd (ed.), *Ancient Egypt a Social History* (Cambridge: Cambridge University Press), 279-348.

Lorand, D. (2009), *Le Papyrus Dramatique du Ramesseum* (Leuven: Peeters).

Lorton, D. (1977), 'The treatment of criminals in ancient Egypt: Through the New Kingdom', *Journal of the Economic and Social History of the Orient,* 20 (1, Special Issue on the Treatment of Criminals in the Ancient Near East), 2-64.

--- (1999), 'The theology of cult statues in ancient Egypt', in M. B. Dick (ed.), *Born in Heaven Made on Earth: the Making of a Cult Statue in the Ancient Near East* (Winowa Lake, Indiana: Eisenbrauns), 123-210.

Louvre Atlas Database of Exhibits. "A94" http://www.louvre.fr/, Louvre Museum. Online. Accessed 15.07.2011.

Malinine, M., Posener, G. & Vercoutter, J. (1968), *Catalogue des Stèles du Sérapéum de Memphis* (Paris: Éditions des musées nationaux).

Manniche, L. (1987), *Music and Musicians in Ancient Egypt* (London: Kegan Paul International).

Mariette, A. (1889 (this edition 2006)), *Les Mastabas de L'Ancien Empire* (Hildesheim: Georg Olms Verlag AG).

Martin, G. T. (1971), *Egyptian Administrative and Private-name Seals Principally of the Middle Kingdom and Second Intermediate Period* (Oxford: Griffith Institute).

--- (1974, 1989b), *The Royal Tombs of El-Amarna*, 2 vols. (Archaeological Survey of Egypt; London: Egypt Exploration Society).

--- (1989a), *The Memphite Tomb of Horemheb, Commander-in-Chief of Tutankhamun. 1. The Reliefs, Inscriptions, and Commentary* (Egypt Exploration Society Memoir, no. 52; London: Egypt Exploration Society).

Maspero, G. (1882), 'Rapport sur une mission en Italie (suite)', *Recueil de Travaux à la Philologie et à L'Archéologie Égyptiennes et Assyriennes,* 3, 103-28.

Mathieu, B. (1996), *La poésie amoureuse de l'Égypte ancienne: Recherches sur un genre littéraire au Nouvel Empire* (Bibliothèque d'Étude, 115; Le Caire: Institut Français d'Archéologie Orientale).

Matthey, P. (2002), 'Von «heiligen» Büchern und wissenschaftlichen Schriften: Bibliothekan im alten und hellenistischen Ägypten', in W. Hoepfner (ed.), *Antike Bibliothekan* (Mainz Am Rhein: Verlag Philipp von Zabern).

McDowell, A. G. (1990), *Jurisdiction in the Workmen's Community at Deir el-Medîna* (Leiden: Nederlands Instituut Voor Het Nabije Oosten).

--- (1999), *Village Life in Ancient Egypt: Laundry Lists and Love Songs* (Oxford: Oxford University Press).

Meeks, D. (1979), 'Pureté et purification en Égypte', *Dictionnaire de la Bible, Supplément IX* (Paris: Centre d'étude des Religions du Livre), 430-52.

--- (2001), 'Fantastic animals', in D. B. Redford (ed.), *Oxford Encyclopedia of Ancient Egypt,* 3 vols. (1; Oxford: Oxford University Press), 504-7.

Meulenaere, H. de (1982), 'La statue d'un vizier Thébain', *Journal of Egyptian Archaeology,* 68, 139-44.

Meyer-Dietrich, E. (2010), 'Recitation, speech acts, and declamation', in W. Wendrich (ed.), *UCLA Encyclopedia of Egyptology* (Los Angeles: http://digital2.library.ucla.edu/viewItem.do?ark=21198/zz000252xth).

Möller, G. (1913), *Die beiden totenpapyrus Rhind des Museums zu Edinburg* (Leipzig: J. C. Hinrichs).

Montet, P. (1928), 'Les tombeaux de Siout et du Deir Rifeh', *Kêmi,* 1, 53-68.

--- (1931), 'La stèle de l'an 400 retrouvée', *Kêmi,* 4, 191-215.

--- (1962), 'Le Rituel de Fondation des temples Égyptiens', *Kêmi,* 16, 74-100.

Morenz, L. D. (2003), 'Schamanismus in der Frühzeit Ägyptens?' *Archiv für Religionsgeschichte* (Arg 5; Munchen, Leipzig: Wissenschaftlicher Aufsetz), 212-26.

de Morgan, J. (1903), *Fouilles à Dahchour en 1894-1895/ par J. de Morgan; avec la collaboration de G. Legrain et G. Jéquier* (Vienne: Holzhausen).

--- (1903), *Fouilles à Dahchour, Vol. 2: 1894-1895* (Vienne: Holzhausen).

Morkot, R. (2003), 'Archaism and innovation at work', in J. Tait (ed.), *'Never Had the Like Occurred'; Egypt's view of its past* (Encounters with Ancient Egypt; London: UCL Press), 79-99.

Mueller, D. (1975), 'Some remarks on wage rates in the Middle Kingdom', *Journal of Near Eastern Studies,* 34 (4), 249-63.

Muhlestein, K. (2008), 'Execration ritual', in J. Dieleman & W. Wendrich (ed.), *UCLA Encyclopedia of Egyptology* (Los Angeles: http://digital2.library.ucla.edu/viewItem.do?ark=21198/zz000s3mqr).

Müller, H. W. E. (1940), *Die felsengräber der fürsten von elephantine Aus der zeit des mittleren reiches* (Glückstadt, Hamburg & New York: J. J. Augustin).

Murnane, W. J. (1980), *United with Eternity* (Chicago and Cairo: The Oriental Institute, University of Chicago and The American University in Cairo Press).

--- (1981), 'The *Sed*-Festival: A problem in historical method', *Mitteilungen des Deutschen Archäologischen Instituts Abteilung Kairo,* 37, 369-76.

Murray, M. (1905), *Saqqara Mastabas*, 2 vols. (1; London: Quaritch).

Naville, E. (1892), *The Festival-Hall of Osorkon II in the Great Temple of Bubastis* (The Egypt Exploration Fund, 10th Memoir; London: Kegan Paul, Trench, Trübner & Co., Ltd.).

--- (1895-1908), *The Temple at Deir el-Bahari*, 6 vols. (London: The Egypt Exploration Fund).

Nelson, H. H. (1981), *The Great Hypostyle Hall at Karnak, Volume 1, Part 1: The Wall Reliefs*, (ed.) W. J. Murnane (Oriental Institute Publications 106; Chicago: The Oriental Institute of the University of Chicago).

Nelson, H. N. (1949a), 'Certain reliefs at Karnak and Medinet Habu and the ritual of Amenophis I', *Journal of Near Eastern Studies,* 8 (3, 4), 211-32, 310-45.

--- (1949b), 'The rite of 'Bringing the Foot'', *Journal of Egyptian Archaeology,* 35, 82-6.

Newberry, P. E. (1893), *Beni Hasan: Part I* (London: K. Paul, Trench, Trübner & Co.).

--- (1895), *El Bersheh, Part I, The Tomb of Tehuti-Hetep*, (ed.) F. L. Griffith (Archaeological Survey of Egypt; London: Egypt Exploration Fund).

Newberry, P. (1912), 'The inscribed tombs of Ekhmim', *Annals of Archaeology and Anthropology,* 4, 99-120.

Nims, C. (1948), 'The Term Hp, "Law, Right" in Demotic', *Journal of Near Eastern Studies,* 7 (4), 243-60.

Nunn, J. (1996), *Ancient Egyptian Medicine* (London: British Museum Press).

O'Connor, D. B. & Silverman D. P. (1995), *Ancient Egyptian Kingship* (Leiden, New York: E. J. Brill).

Ogden, J. (2000), 'Metals', in P. T. Nicholson & I. Shaw (ed.), *Ancient Egyptian Materials and Technology* (Cambridge: Cambridge University Press), 148-76.

Ogdon, J. R. (1979), 'Observations on a ritual gesture, after some Old Kingdom reliefs', *Journal of the Society for the Study of Egyptian Antiquities,* 10, 71-73, pls. 2-4.

Osing, J. (1992), 'Zu zwei literarischen Werken des Mittleren Reiches', in J. Osing & A. K. Neilsen (ed.), *The Heritage of Ancient Egypt; Studies in Honour of Erik Iversen* (Copenhagen: Carsten Niebuhr Institute), 101-19.

Otto, E. (1950), 'An ancient Egyptian hunting ritual', *Journal of Near Eastern Studies,* 9 (3), 164-77.

--- (1954), *Die biographischen Inschriften der Ägyptischen Spätzeit: Ihre geistesgeschichtliche und literarische Bedeutung* (Leiden: E. J. Brill).

--- (1960), *Das Ägyptische Mundöffnungsritual*, 2 vols. (Ägyptologische Abhandlungen; Wiesbaden: Harrassowitz).

Parkinson, R. B. (1999), *The Tale of Sinuhe and other Ancient Egyptian Poems* (Oxford World's Classics; Oxford: Oxford University Press).

--- (2009), *Reading Ancient Egyptian Poetry* (Chichester: Wiley-Blackwell).

--- (2012), 'The Ramesseum Papyri', (British Museum Online Research Catalogue), http://www.british museum.org, Online. Accessed 10.01.2013.

Peden, A. J. (2001), *The Graffiti of Pharaonic Egypt* (Leiden: Brill).

Peet, T. E. (1930), *The Great Tomb Robberies of the Twentieth Egyptian Dynasty* (Oxford: Clarendon Press).

Pestman, P. W. (1963), 'Les documents juridiques des "Chanceliers du Dieu" de Memphis à lépoque Ptolémaïque', *Oudheidkundige Mededelingen uit het Rijksmuseum van Oudheden* (40; Leiden: Rijksmuseum van Oudheden), 8-23.

--- (1982), 'Who were the owners, in the "Community of Workmen", of the Chester Beatty Papyri', in R. J. Demarée & J. J. Janssen (ed.), *Gleanings from Deir el-Medîna* (Te Leiden: Nederlands Inst. Voor Het Nabije Oosten), 155-72.

Petrie, W. M. F. (1890), *Kahun, Gurob and Hawara* (London: Kegan Paul, Trench, Trübner & Co.).

--- (1894), *Tell el-Amarna* (London: Methuen & Co.).

--- (1906), *Researches in Sinai* (London: J. Murray).

--- (1925), *Tombs of the Courtiers and Oxyrhynkhos* (London: B. Quaritch).

Piankoff, A. (1968), *The Pyramid of Unas* (Bollingen Series; Princeton, New Jersey: Princeton University Press).

Picardo, N. S. (2010), '(Ad)dressing Washptah: Illness or Injury in the Vizer's Death, as Related in his Tomb Biography', in Z. Hawass & J. Houser (ed.), *Millions of Jubilees: Studies in Honor of David P. Silverman* 2 vols. (2; Cairo: Conseil Suprême des Antiquités), 93-104.

Piehl, K. (1894), 'La Statue A 93 du Musée du Louvre', *Zeitschrift für Ägyptische Sprache und Altertumskunde,* 32, 118-22.

Pierret, P. (1978), *Recueil d'Inscriptions Inédites du Musée Égyptien du Louvre* (Hildesheim, New York: Georg Olms Verlag).

Pinch, G. (1993), *Votive Offerings to Hathor* (Oxford: Griffith Institute, Ashmolean Museum).

--- (2006), *Magic in Ancient Egypt* (London: British Museum Press).

Polz, D. (1990), 'Die sna-Vorsteher des Neuen Reiches', *Zeitschrift für Ägyptische Sprache und Altertumskunde,* 117, 43-60.

Posener, G. (1936), *La première domination perse en Égypte: receuil d'inscriptions hiéroglyphiques* (Bibliothèque d'Étude, 11; Le Caire: Institut Français d'Archéologie Orientale).

--- (1956), *Littérature et politique dans l'Égypte de la XIIe dynastie* (Paris: Librarie Ancienne Honoré Champion).

--- (1968), 'Une stèle de Hatnoub', *Journal of Egyptian Archaeology,* 54, 67-71.

--- (1975), 'Ächtungstexte', in W. Helck & E. Otto (ed.), *Lexikon der Ägyptologie* (1; Wiesbaden: Harrassowitz), cols. 67-69.

--- (1976), 'Philogie et archéologie égyptiennes', *Annuaire du Collège de France,* 76, 435-42.

--- (1985), *Le Papyrus Vandier* (Bibliothèque Genérale, vol. 7; Le Caire: L'Institut Français d'Archéologie Orientale du Caire).

--- (1987), *Cinq Figurines d'Envoûtement* (Le Caire: Institut Français d'Archéologie Orientale).

Posener-Kriéger, P. (1976), *Les archives du temple funéraire de Néferirkarê-Kakaï (Les papyrus d'Abousir): traduction et commentaire*, 2 vols. (Bibliothèque d'étude, t. 65/1-2; Le Caire: Institut Français d'Archéologie Orientale).

Posener-Kriéger P. & de Cenival, J. (1968), *Hieratic Papyri in the British Museum: The Abusir Papyri, Fifth Series* (London: British Museum Press).

Price, C. (2008), 'Monuments in context: Experiences of the colossal in ancient Egypt', in K. Griffin (ed.), *Current Research in Egyptology 2007. Proceedings of the Eighth Annual Symposium, Swansea University 2007* (Oxford: Oxbow Books), 113-21.

Quack, J. F. (2002), 'Die Dienstanweisung des Oberlehers aus dem Buch vom Temple', in H. Beinlich (ed.), *5 Ägyptologische Tempeltagung: Würzburg, 23. -26. September 1999* (Wiesbaden: Harrassowitz), 159-71.

--- (2005), 'Ein prätext und sine Realisierungen: Facetten des ägyptischen Mundöffnungsrituals', in B. Dücker & H. Roeder (ed.), *Text und Ritual: Kulturwissenschaftliche Essays und Analysen von Sesostris bis Dada* (Heidelberg: Synchron), 165-85.

--- (2006a), 'Opfermahl und feindvernichtung im altägyptischen ritual', *Mitteilungen der Berliner Gessellschaft fürAnthropologie, Ethnologie und Urgeschichte,* 27, 67-80.

--- (2006b), 'Zur lesung und deutung des Dramatischen Ramesseum papyrus', *Zeitschrift für Ägyptische Sprache und Altertumskunde,* 133, 72-89.

Quaegebeur, J. (1985), 'On the Egyptian equivalent of biblical *Hartumim*', in S. Israelit-Groll (ed.), *The Bible and Christianity* (Jerusalem: Magnes), 162-72.

Quibell, J. E. (1902), 'Rapport de M. J. E. Quibell', *Annales du Service des Antiquités de l'Égypte,* 3, 254-8.

--- (1905-1914), *Excavations at Saqqara* 6 vols. (Le Caire: Imprimerie de l'Insitut Français d'Archéologie Orientale).

Quibell, J. E., Pirie, A. A., Spiegelberg, W., Paget, R. F. E. & Griffith, F. Ll. (1898), *The Ramesseum; and The Tomb of Ptah-hetep; copied by R. F. E. Paget and A. A. Pirie: With commets by F. Ll. Griffith* (London: B. Quaritch).

Quirke, S. (1990), *The Administration of Egypt in the Late Middle Kingdom* (New Maldon, Surrey: SIA Publishing).

--- (1992), *Ancient Egyptian Religion* (London: British Museum Press).

--- (1996), 'Archive', in A. Loprieno (ed.), *Ancient Egyptian Literature: History and Forms* (Leiden: E. J. Brill), 379-401.

--- (2004), *Egyptian Literature 1800 BC: Questions and Readings* (Golden House Publications, Egyptology 2; London: Golden House Publications).

--- (2005), *Lahun* (London: Golden House Publications).

Ranke, H. (1935-1977), *Die Ägyptischen Personennamen* 3 vols. (Glückstadt: J. J. Augustin).

Raven, M. (1983), 'Wax in Egyptian magic and symbolism', *Oudheidkundige Mededeelingen uit het Rijksmuseum van Oudheden te Leiden,* 64, 7-47.

Redford, D. B. (2001), 'Textual evidence', in D. B. Redford (ed.), *Oxford Encyclopedia of Ancient Egypt,* 3 vols. (2; Oxford: Oxford University Press), 104-8.

Redford, S. (2002), *The Harem Conspiracy* (Dekalb: Northern Illinois University Press).

Reeves, N. (2001), *Akhenaten: Egypt's False Prophet* (London: Thames & Hudson).

Reeves, N. & Taylor, J. (1992), *Howard Carter before Tutankhamun* (London: British Museum Press).

Reich, N. (1914), *Papyri juristischen Inhalts im hieratischer und demotischer Schrift aus dem British Museum 1* (Volume 55, Book 3 of Denkschriften der kaiserlichen Akademie der Wissenschafter in Wien; Wien: Hölder).

Reisner, G. (1913), 'A family of builders of the Sixth Dynasty, about 2600 B.C.' *Bulletin of the Museum of Fine Arts, Boston,* 11 (66), 53-66.

--- (1918), 'The tomb of Hepzefa, Nomarch of Siut', *Journal of Egyptian Archaeology,* 5 (2), 79-98.

Reymond, E. A. E. (1977), *From the Contents of the Libraries of the Suchos Temples in the Faiyum II. From Ancient Egyptian Hermetic Writings* (Mitteilungen aus der Papyrussammlung der Österreichischen Nationalbibliothek (Papyrus Erzherzog Rainer), 11; Vienna: Brüder Hollinek).

Ritner, R. K. (1993), *The Mechanics of Ancient Egyptian Magical Practice* (Studies in Ancient Oriental Civilisation, vol. 54; Chicago: The University of Chicago).

--- (2001a), 'Magic: Magic in medicine', in D. B. Redford (ed.), *Oxford Encyclopedia of Ancient Egypt* (2; Oxford: Oxford University Press), 326-9.

--- (2001b), 'Medicine', in D. B. Redford (ed.), *The Oxford Encyclopedia of Ancient Egypt* (2; Oxford: Oxford University Press), 353-6.

--- (2003a), 'The Bentresh Stela', in W. K. Simpson (ed.), *The Literature of Ancient Egypt* (New Haven & London: Yale University Press), 361-6.

--- (2003b), 'The Famine Stela', in W. K. Simpson (ed.), *The Literature of Ancient Egypt* (New Haven & London: Yale University Press), 386-91.

--- (2003c), 'The adventures of Setna and Si-Osire (Setna II)', *The Literature of Ancient Egypt* (New Haven & London: Yale University Press), 470-89.

--- (2006), ' "And Each Staff Transformed into a Snake": The serpent wand in ancient Egypt', in K. Szpakowska (ed.), *Through a Glass Darkly* (Swansea: The Classical Press of Wales), 205-25.

von Roeder, G. (1915), *Urkunden zur religion des alten Ägypten, übersetzt und eingeleitet von Günther Roeder* (Jena: Verlegt Bei Eugen Diederichs).

Roth, A. M. (1992), 'The *psš-kf* and the 'Opening of the Mouth' ceremony: A ritual of birth and rebirth', *Journal of Egyptian Archaeology,* 78, 113-47.

--- (1993), 'Fingers, stars, and the 'Opening of the Mouth': The nature and function of the *ntrwi*-Blades', *Journal of Egyptian Archaeology,* 79, 57-79.

--- (2001), 'Opening of the Mouth', in D. B. Redford (ed.), *The Oxford Encyclopedia of Ancient Egypyt* (2; Oxford: Oxford University Press), 605-9.

Rothe, R. D., Rapp, G. & Miller, W. K. (1996), 'New hieroglyphic evidence for Pharaonic activity in the Eastern Desert of Egypt', *Journal of the American Research Center in Egypt,* 33, 77-104.

Russman, E. R. (2001), 'Kneeling figure of Nekhthoreb', in E. R. Russman (ed.), *Eternal Egypt: Masterworks of Ancient Art from the British Museum* (London: British Museum Press), 239-41.

Sadek, A. I. (1980), *The Amethyst Mining Inscriptions* (Warminster: Aris & Phillips).

--- (1987), *Popular Religion in Egypt During the New Kingdom* (Hildesheimer Ägyptologische Beiträge 27; Hildesheim: Gerstenberg Verlag).

Sauneron, S. (1962), *Les Fêtes Religieuses d'Esna: aux derniers siècles du paganisme* (Le Caire: Imprimerie de l'Institut Français d'Archéologie Orientale).

--- (2000), *The Priests of Ancient Egypt* (Ithaca & London: Cornell University Press).

Sauneron, S. & Yoyotte, J. (1952), 'Le texte hiératique Rifaud', *Bulletin de L'Institut Français d'Archéologie Orientale,* 50, 107-17.

Schäfer, H. (1905), *Urkunden des ägyptischen Altertums, Abteilung 111: Urkunden der älteren Äthiopenkönige* (Heft 1; Leipzig: J. C. Hinrichs).

Schott, S. (1929), *Urkunden mythologischen Inhalts. Bücher und Sprache gegen den Gott Seth.* (Urkunden 6; Leipzig: J. C. Hindrichs).

--- (1934), 'The feasts of Thebes', in H. H. Nelson & U. Hölscher (ed.), *Work in Western Thebes 1931-33* (Chicago: University of Chicago Press), 63-90.

--- (1950), *Altägyptische Festdaten* (Abhandlungen der Geistes- und Sozialwissenschaftlichen Klasse 10; Wiesbaden: Verlag Akademie der Wissenschaften und der Literatur, Mainz; Wiesbaden, in Kommission bei F. Steiner).

--- (1952), *Das schöne Fest vom Wüstentale: Festbräuche einer Totenstadt* (Abhandlungen der Geistes- und Sozialwissenschaftlichen Klasse 11; Wiesbaden: Verlag Akademie der Wissenschaften und der Literatur, Mainz; Wiesbaden in Kommission bei F. Steiner).

Schulman, A. R. (1984), 'The iconographic theme: "Opening of the Mouth" on stelae', *Journal of the American Research Center in Egypt,* 21, 169-96.

Serrano, A. J. (2002), *Royal Festivals in the Late Predynastic Period and the First Dynasty* (BAR International Series 1076; Oxford: Archaeopress).

Sethe, K. (1898), 'Altes und neues zur Geschichte der thronstreitigkeiten unter den nachfolgern Tuthmosis' I', *Zeitschrift für Ägyptische Sprache und Altertumskunde,* 36, 14-81.

--- (1910), *Die Ältaegyptischen Pyramidentexte* (2; Leipzig: J. C. Hinrichs'sche Buchhandlung).

--- (1912), *Zur altägyptischen sage vom Sonnenauge das in der fremde war* (Untersuchungen zur Geschite und Altertumskunde Aegyptens 5,3; Leipzig: J. C. Hinrichs).

--- (1926), *Die Ächtung feindlicher Fürsten, Völker und Dinge auf altägyptischen Tongefäßscherben des Mittleren Reiches* (Berlin: Akademie der Wissenschaften).

--- (1928), *Dramatische Texte zu altägyptischen Mysterienspielen* (Untersuchungen zur Geschichte und Altertumskunde Ägyptens; Leipzig: J. C. Hinrichs'sche Buchhandlung).

--- (1933), *Urkunden des Alten Reiches* (2nd. Revised edn.; Leipzig: J. C. Hinrichs'sche Buchandlung).

Settgast, J. (1963), *Untersuchungen zu altägyptischen Bestattungsdarstellungen* (Abhandlungen des Deutschen Archäologischen Instituts Abteilung Kairo: Ägyptologische Reihe; Glückstadt: J. J. Augustin).

Seyfried, K. J. (1981), *Beiträge zu den Expeditionen des Mittleren Reiches in die Ost-Wüste* (Hildesheim: Gerstenberg Verlag).

Shafer, B. E. (1997), 'Temples, priests, and rituals: an overview', in B. E. Shafer (ed.), *Temples of Ancient Egypt* (Ithaca, New York: Cornell University Press), 1-30.

Shaw, I. (1986), 'A survey at Hatnub', in B. J. Kemp (ed.), *Amarna Reports III* (London: Egypt Exploration Society), 189-212.

--- (1987), 'The 1986 survey of Hatnub', in B. J. Kemp (ed.), *Amarna Reports IV* (London: Egypt Exploration Society), 160-7.

--- (1998), 'Exploiting the desert frontier: The logistics and politics of ancient Egyptian mining expeditions', in B. Knapp, V. Pigott & E. Herbert (ed.), *Social Approaches to an Industrial Past: The Archaeology and Anthropology of Mining* (London and New York: Routledge), 242-58.

--- (2001), 'Quarries and mines', in D. Redford (ed.), *The Oxford Encyclopedia of Ancient Egypt,* 3 vols. (3; Oxford: Oxford University Press), 99-104.

--- (2010), *Hatnub: Quarrying Travertine in Ancient Egypt* (London: Egypt Exploration Society).

Shaw, I. & Jameson, R. (1993), 'Amethyst mining in the Eastern Desert: A preliminary survey at Wadi el-Hudi', *Journal of Egyptian Archaeology,* 79, 81-97.

Shaw, I. & Nicholson, P. (1997), *British Museum Dictionary of Ancient Egypt* (London: British Museum Press).

Shore, A. F. & Smith, H. S. (1960), 'A Demotic Embalmers' Agreement (Pap. dem. P. M. 10561)', *Acta Orientalia,* 25, 277-94.

Sigerist, H. E. (1951), *A History of Medicine*, 2 vols. (2; New York: Oxford University Press).

Simpson, W. K. (1959), 'Historical and lexical notes on the New Series of Hammamat Inscriptions', *Journal of Near Eastern Studies,* 18 (1), 20-37.

--- (1974), *The Terrace of the Great God at Abydos: the Offering Chapels of Dynasties 12 and 13* (New Haven & Philadelphia: Peabody Museum of Natural History of Yale University).

--- (1976), *The Mastabas of Qar and Idu* (Boston, Massachusetts: Museum of Fine Arts).

--- (2003), 'King Cheops and the magicians', in W. K. Simpson (ed.), *The Literature of Ancient Egypt* (New Haven & London: Yale University Press), 13-24.

--- (2003), 'The satire of the trades', in W. K. Simpson (ed.), *The Literature of Ancient Egypt* (New Haven & London: Yale University Press), 431-7.

Smith, M. (1993), *The Liturgy of Opening the Mouth for Breathing* (Oxford: Griffith Institute, Ashmolean Museum).

Smith, R. W. & Redford, D. B. (1976), *The Akhenaten Temple Project. Volume 1: The Initial Discoveries*, 2 vols. (Warminster: Aris & Phillips Ltd.).

Smith, W. S. (1949), *A History of Egyptian Sculpture and Painting in the Old Kingdom* (Oxford: Oxford University Press).

Snape, S. (2011), *Ancient Egyptian Tombs: The Culture of Life and Death* (Chichester: Wiley-Blackwell).

Spalinger, A. J. (1985), 'A redistributive pattern at Assiut', *Journal of the American Oriental Society,* 105 (1), 7-20.

Stadelmann, R. (1982), 'Prozessionen', in W. Helck & W. Westendorf (ed.), *Lexikon der Ägyptologie* (4; Wiesbaden: Harrassowitz), columns 1160-64.

Stadler, M. (2008), 'Procession', in J. Dielman & W. Wendrich (ed.), *UCLA Encyclopedia of Egyptology* (Los Angeles: http://digital2.library.ucla.edu/viewItem.do?ark=21198/zz001nf7bz).

Staehelin, E. (1966), *Untersuchungen zur ägyptischen Tracht im Alten Reich* (Berlin: Hessling).

Steindorff, G. (1901), 'Ein grabstein des Mittleren Reiches im Museum von Stuttggart', *Zeitschrift für Ägyptische Sprache und Altertumskunde,* 39, 117-21.

--- (1946), 'The magical knives of ancient Egypt', *Journal of the Walters Art Gallery,* 9, 41-51, 106-7.

Stewart, H. M. (1979), *Egyptian Stelae, Reliefs and Paintings from the Petrie Collection. Part II: Archaic to Second Intermediate Period* (Warminster: Aris & Phillips).

Strouhal, E. (1997), *Life of the Ancient Egyptians* (Liverpool: Liverpool University Press).

Strudwick, N. C. (1985), *The Administration of Egypt in the Old Kingdom* (London: Kegan Paul International).

--- (2005), *Texts from the Pyramid Age,* (ed.), R. J. Leprohon (Writings from the Ancient World; Atlanta: Society of Biblical Literature).

--- (2006), *Masterpieces of Ancient Egypt* (London: British Museum Press).

Szpakowska, K. (2008), *Daily Life in Ancient Egypt* (Oxford: Blackwell Publishing).

Tabanelli, M. (1958), *Lo strumento chirurgico e la sua storia epoche greca e romana al secolo decimosesto* (Forli: Romagna medico).

Tacke, N. (2012), *Das Opferritual des ägyptischen Neuen Reiches* (Orientalia Lovaniensia Analecta 222; Leuven: Peeters).

Tallet, P. (2003), 'Notes sur la zone minière du Sud-Sinaï au Nouvel Empire', *Bulletin de l'Institut Français d'Archéologie Orientale,* 103, 459-86.

Tambiah, S. J. (1968), 'The magical power of words', *Man (New Series),* 3(2), 175-208.

--- (2002), 'Form and meaning of magical acts', in M. Lambeck (ed.), *A Reader in the Anthropology of Religion* (Oxford: Blackwell Publishers), 240-357.

Taylor, J. (2001), *Death and the Afterlife in Ancient Egypt* (London: British Museum Press).

--- (2010), *Journey through the Afterlife: Ancient Egyptian Book of the Dead* (London: British Museum Press).

Teeter, E. (2011), *Religion and Ritual in Ancient Egypt* (Cambridge: Cambridge University Press).

Théodoridès, A. (1971a), 'The concept of law in ancient Egypt', in J. R. Harris (ed.), *The Legacy of Egypt* (Oxford: Clarendon Press), 291-322.

--- (1971b), 'Les Contrats d'Hâpidjefa (XIIe dynastie, 20e s. av. J. C.)', *Revue Internationale des Droits de l'Antiquité,* 18, 108-251.

Thompson, H. (1934), *A Family Archive from Siut,* 2 vols. (Oxford: Oxford University Press).

Tobin, V. A. (2003a), 'The teaching for King Merikare', in W. K. Simpson (ed.), *The Literature of Ancient Egypt* (New Haven & London: Yale University Press), 152-65.

--- (2003b), 'The love songs and the song of the harper', in W. K. Simpson (ed.), *The Literature of Ancient Egypt* (New Haven & London: Yale University Press), 307-33.

--- (2003c), 'The Prophecies of Neferty', in W. K. Simpson (ed.), *The Literature of Ancient Egypt* (New Haven & London: Yale University Press), 214-20.

Traunecker, C., La Saout, F. & Masson, O. (1981), *La Chapelle d'Achôris à Karnak. II Text,* 2 vols. (Recherche sur les grands civilsations; Paris: Éditions ADPF).

Troy, L. (2006), 'Religion and cult during the time of Thutmose III', in E. H. Cline & D. O'Connor (ed.), *Thutmose III: A New Biography* (Ann Arbor: University of Michigan Press).

Uphill, E. (1963), 'The Sed-Festivals of Akhenaten', *Journal of Near Eastern Studies,* 22 (2), 123-7.

--- (1965), 'The Egyptian Sed-Festival Rites', *Journal of Near Eastern Studies,* 24 (2), 365-83.

Valbelle, D. & Bonnet, C. (1996), *Le sanctuaire d'Hathor, maîtresse de la turquoise. Sérabit el-Khadim au Moyen Empire* (Lille: Picard).

van de Walle, B. & Meulenaere, H. (1973), 'Compléments à la prosopographie médicale', *Revue d' Égyptologie,* 25, 58-83.

Vassilika, E. (1995), *Egyptian Art* (Cambridge: Fitzwilliam Museum).

Vermeersh, P. M., Gijselings, G. & Paulissen, E. (1984), 'Discovery of the Nazlet Khater Man, Upper Egypt', *Journal of Human Evolution,* 13, 281-6.

Vernus, P. (2003), *Affairs and Scandals in Ancient Egypt* (Ithaca & London: Cornell University Press).

VerSteeg, R. (2002), *Law in Ancient Egypt* (Durham, North Carolina: Carolina Academic Press).

Virey, P. (1900), 'La tombe des vignes Thèbes', *Recueil de Travaux relatifs à la philologie et à l'archéologie égyptiennes et assyriennes; pour server de bulletin à la Mission français du Caire,* (Paris: Champion), 22, 83-97.

Vleeming, S. P. (1995), 'The office of a choachyte in the Theban area', in S. P. Vleeming (ed.), *Hundred-Gated Thebes* (Leiden: E. J. Brill), 241-55.

Vogelsang-Eastwood, G. (1993), *Pharaonic Egyptian Clothing* (Leiden, New York & London: E. J. Brill).

von Deines, H., Grapow, H. & Westendorf, W. (1958), *Übersetzung der Medizinischen Texte,* 11 vols. (Grundriss der Medizin der Alten Ägypter, 4, 1; Berlin: Akademie-Verlag).

Walsem, van, R. (2008), *Mastabase: the Leiden Mastaba Project* (Leuven: Peeters/Leiden University).

Waraksa, E. A. (2008), 'Female figurines (Pharaonic Period)', in W. Wendrich (ed.), *UCLA Encyclopedia of Egyptology* (Los Angeles: http://digital2.library.ucla.edu/viewItem.do?ark=21198/zz000s3mm6).

Ward, W. A. (1982), *Index of Egyptian Administrative and Religious Titles of the Middle Kingdom: with a glossary of words and phrases used* (Beirut: American University of Beirut).

Weeks, K. R. (1980), 'Ancient Egyptian dentistry', in J. E. Harris & E. F. Wente (ed.), *An X-Ray Atlas of the Royal Mummies* (Chicago: University of Chicago Press), 99-121.

Wegner, J. W. (2001), 'Cenotaphs', in D. B. Redford (ed.), *Oxford Encyclopedia of Ancient Egypt,* 3 vols. (1; Oxford: Oxford University Press), 244-8.

Wente, E, F. (1990), *Letters from Ancient Egypt* (Atlanta Ga.: Scholars Press).

Wieczorek, A. & Rosendahl, W. (2013), *Mummies of the World* (Munich, Berlin, London, New York: Prestel).

Wilkinson, J. G. (1878), *The Manners and Customs of the Ancient Egyptians (A new edition revised and corrected by Samuel Birch)*, 3 vols. (2; London: John Murray, Albermarle Street).

Wilkinson, R. H. (1985), 'The coronational circuit of the walls, the circuit of the *ḥnw* barque and the Heb-Sed 'Race' in Egyptian kingship ideology', *Journal of the Society for the Study of Egyptian Antiquities,* 15 (1), 46-51.

--- (1992), *Reading Egyptian Art* (London: British Museum Press).

--- (1994), *Symbol and Magic in Egyptian Art* (London: Thames & Hudson Ltd.).

--- (2000), *The Complete Temples of Ancient Egypt* (London: Thames & Hudson).

--- (2003), *The Complete Gods and Goddesses of Ancient Egypt* (London: Thames & Hudson).

Wilson, J. A. (1936), 'Illuminating the thrones at the Egyptian Jubilee', *Journal of the American Oriental Society,* 56 (2), 293-6.

--- (1944), 'Funeral services of the Egyptian Old Kingdom', *Journal of Near Eastern Studies,* 3 (4), 201-18.

--- (1954), 'A group of Sixth Dynasty inscriptions', *Journal of Near Eastern Studies,* 13 (4), 243-64.

Winlock, H. E. (1947), *The Rise and Fall of the Middle Kingdom in Thebes* (New York: The Macmillan Company).

Worth Estes, J. (1993), *The Medical Skills of Ancient Egypt* (Canton, Massachusetts: Science History Publications).

Wreszinski, W. (1909), *Der grosse medizinische Papyrus des Berliner Museums (Pap. Berl. 3038): in Facsimile und Umschrift mit Übersetzung, Kommentar und Glossar* (Leipzig: J. C. Hinrichs).

--- (1912), *Der Londoner medizinische Papyrus (Brit. Museum Nr. 10059) und der Papyrus Hearst in Transkription, Übersetzung und Kommentar* (Leipzig: J. C. Hinrichs).

--- (1913), *Der Papyrus Ebers*, 2 vols. (1. Teil: Umschrift; Leipzig: J. C. Hinrichs).

Zandee, J. (1964), 'Das Schöpferwort im Alten Ägypten', in T. P. van Baaren (ed.), *Verbum: essays on some aspects of the religious function of words. Dedicated to Dr. H. W. Obbink* (Utrecht: Kemink), 33-66.

Zauzich, K. T. (1968), *Die ägyptische Schreibertradition in Aufbau. Sprache und Schrift der demotischen Kaufverträge aus ptolemäischer Zeit* (Ägyptologische Abhandlungen, Bd. 19; Wiesbaden: O. Harrassowitz).

Zinn, K. (2011), 'Temples, palaces and libraries', in R. Gundlach & K. Spence (ed.), *5th Symposium on Egyptian Royal Ideology: Palace and Temple* (Wiesbaden: Harrassowitz Verlag), 181-202.